Higher Education Literature: An Annotated Bibliography

Higher Education Literature: An Annotated Bibliography

Edited by Jane N. White and Collins W. Burnett

ORYX PRESS
1981

The rare Arabian Oryx is believed to have inspired the myth of the unicorn. This desert antelope became virtually extinct in the early 1960s. At that time several groups of international conservationists arranged to have 9 animals sent to the Phoenix Zoo to be the nucleus of a captive breeding herd. Today the Oryx population is nearing 300 and herds have been returned to reserves in Israel, Jordan, and Oman.

Copyright © 1981 by The Oryx Press
2214 North Central at Encanto
Phoenix, AZ 85004

Published simultaneously in Canada

Printed and Bound in the United States of America.

Library of Congress Cataloging in Publication Data

White, Jane N.
    Higher education literature.

    Includes indexes.
    1. Education, Higher—Bibliography. I. Burnett,
Collins W., 1914–   . II. Title.
Z5814.U7W53 [LB2322]   016.378   81-11206
    ISBN 0-912700-80-7   AACR2

CONTENTS

Higher Education as a Specialized Field of Study   137
Education as a Field of Study   139

Appendices   141

Author Index   161

Subject Index   169

ACKNOWLEDGEMENTS

Acknowledgement is given to our colleagues at the University of Kentucky. We are grateful for the support of Dr. James P. Chapman of the office of vice-president for academic affairs and Paul A. Willis, director of university libraries, in the preparation of the manuscript. The encouragement of the associate director of libraries, Mary Ruth Brown, was an important factor. The staff of the education library, Betty Sutton and Margaret Williams, helped in many ways and often assumed additional duties. The book would have been impossible without the services of our diligent graduate assistant, Sharman Jones. She deserves our special thanks for her helpfulness in searching and other detailed work involved in preparing this book. The typist, Vicki New, provided her skill and care to our work.

INTRODUCTION

The two editors of this bibliography have had the challenges and surprises that can result from utilizing the interdisciplinary approach of Library Science and Higher Education. Together, we developed an outline of major categories: Historical Backgrounds and Nature and Scope of Higher Education, Teaching-Learning Environment, Organization and Administration, Community and Junior Colleges, Comparative Systems of Higher Education, and Higher Education as a Specialized Field of Study. Items were classified only once, although some could have been alternately classified. An effort was made to examine each book listed. We relied on book reviews for the few that could not be located.

Our definition of higher education limits our study to programs and phenomena in 2- and 4-year accredited colleges and universities that offer degrees. Postsecondary vocational schools are not included in this framework. Our range of content is also limited by the fact that many concerns and new developments (for example, in funding as influenced by the economy, minority opportunities, alternative programs, academic freedom, faculty development and tenure) are currently examined in journal articles and have not, except generally, become the subjects of books. Our range then includes topics that were identified and of concern in the 1970s and will spill over into the quandaries of the 1980s. These problems include areas of finance; decreasing enrollments; legal conflicts; state and federal government controls; adjustments between administration and faculty, including accountability and collective bargaining; and adjustment among students, faculty, and administration, including curriculum changes and student governance.

We decided to begin with a few books on ancient and early medieval education in order to remind us all in American higher education of our roots in the past. The 9 Colonial colleges were modeled after Oxford and Cambridge and the concept of the research university was borrowed from Germany. The development of the land-grant college (with the Morrill Acts of 1862 and 1890) and the community college (with the first public junior college developed in 1902) are uniquely home-grown and American.

The terminology in American higher education is as diverse as its components. We refer our readers to Appendix 3 where we have attempted to clarify a few of these terms that have come into use and are modified in meaning as the decades pass—community education, lifelong learning, open university, and multiversity, to name a few.

We hope that we have provided a comprehensive background for the student and scholar launching into a study of the phenomena of higher education in the 1980s.

Note: Jane N. White is currently librarian, College of Education, and Collins W. Burnett is professor of Higher Education at the University of Kentucky, Lexington, KY.

Historical Backgrounds and Nature and Scope of American Higher Education

HISTORICAL BACKGROUNDS

ANCIENT

1. Beck, Robert Holmes. *A Social History of Education.* Englewood Cliffs, NJ: Prentice-Hall, 1965. 149 pp.

Very useful for an interpretation of education in ancient Greece and Rome and later education in Western Europe from 476 to 1700 A.D. This background serves as a lead into developments in American education.

2. Dongerkery, Sunderrao R. *University Education in India.* Bombay, India: Manaktalas, 1967. 360 pp.

Discusses the nature of learning centers and universities developed in ancient times in India, e.g., Taxila and Nalanda, seventh century B.C., and 450 A.D., respectively.

MEDIEVAL

3. Rashdall, Hastings. *The Universities of Europe in the Medieval Ages.* Vols. 1, 2, 3. Oxford: Clarendon Press, 1936.

The classic guide for the study of universities during the medieval period within the Renaissance of the twelfth century. In vol. 1, the universities of Salerno, Bologna, and Paris are discussed. Vol. 2 focuses on the universities in Italy, Spain, Portugal, France, Germany, Bohemia, the Low countries, Poland, Hungary, Denmark, Sweden, and Scotland. Vol. 3 emphasizes the English universities with an excellent discussion of Oxford and Cambridge, including relationships to the town, the Church, program of studies, and student life.

4. Wieruszowski, Helene. *The Medieval University Masters, Students, Learning.* New York: Van Nostrand Reinhold, 1966. 207 pp.

Excellent for higher education in the medieval period. Discusses student life, the cathedral schools, universities of Paris, Oxford, Bologna, and Salerno.

UNITED STATES

1636–1850

5. Beach, Mark, ed. *A Bibliographic Guide to American Colleges and Universities: From Colonial Times to the Present.* Westport, CT: Greenwood Press, 1975. 314 pp.

A bibliography which includes books, journal articles, and doctoral dissertations concerning higher education in the 50 states, Puerto Rico, and the District of Columbia. Some biographies of faculty and presidents are included. Arranged alphabetically by authors and states.

6. Brubacher, John S., and Rudy, Willis. *Higher Education in Transition: A History of American Colleges and Universities. 1636–1976.* 3d ed. New York: Harper and Row, 1971. 536 pp.

An excellent interpretation of the social forces that contributed to the change and development of philosophy, curriculum, organization, administration, student and faculty characteristics, professional education, and graduate school.

7. Miller, Howard. *The Revolutionary College: American Presbyterian Higher Education,1707–1837.* New York: New York University, 1976. 381 pp.

Uses research in original sources to portray debates and divisions of American Presbyterians and the development of colleges under the guidance of the church. The gradual accommodation of the Presbyterians to the political and denominational pressures is clearly shown.

8. Novak, Steven J. *The Rights of Youth: American Colleges and Student Revolt, 1798–1815.* Cambridge, MA: Harvard University Press, 1977. 218 pp.

Descriptions of revolts and activities at 7 colleges are included. William and Mary, Chapel Hill, Princeton, Dartmouth, Dickerson, University of Virginia, and Yale are the institutions in which there was student unrest, and each institution was unique in circumstances and issues, as well as reaction of administrators.

9. Sloan, Douglas. *Scottish Enlightenment and the American College Ideal.* New York: Teachers College Press, 1971. 298 pp.

The Scottish Enlightenment was centered in the universities and its leaders were university professors. By the middle of the eighteenth century, strong programs were developed in medicine and other scientific subjects. Influence of the Scottish schools was shown in the careers of John Witherspoon and Samuel S. Smith, presidents of Princeton, and Frances Alison and Benjamin Rush of the College of Philadelphia. Other influences upon American education are also noted.

1850–1950

10. Diner, Steven J. *A City and Its Universities: Public Policy in Chicago, 1892–1919.* Chapel Hill, NC: University of North Carolina Press, 1979. 264 pp.

University of Chicago, Johns Hopkins, Columbia, and other urban universities are discussed in relation to their social and historical influences. The main focus concerns the University of Chicago, the emergence of professional scholars, political and social power.

11. Kinnison, William A. *Building Sullivant's Pyramid: An Administrative History of the Ohio State University.* Columbus, OH: Ohio State University Press, 1970. 225 pp.

On a nationwide basis, the Land-Grant Act in 1862 meant a curriculum change to more kinds of learning for more kinds of people. On a statewide basis, it meant often that there was bickering and lack of agreement about how to best use the proceeds from the sale of land. The early administrative history from 1870–1907 is the carefully documented struggle of the emergence of the land-grant college in Ohio, the Ohio State University. Major topics discussed are: the Cannon Act, a preliminary consensus; freedom and tenure; students and the emergence of the university; the farmers' victory; and consensus through structure and process.

12. McKevitt, Gerald, S. J. *The University of Santa Clara: A History, 1851–1977*. Stanford, CA: Stanford University Press, 1979. 385 pp.

Founded to provide moral training as well as classical education, this Jesuit college was California's first institution of higher learning. After many years of academic and financial problems, rapid modernization occurred following World War II. Some factors which influenced the change included: increased enrollment, more acceptance of secular values, faculty change to more lay persons, and need for professional accreditation.

13. Oleson, Alexandra, and Voss, John, eds. *The Organization of Knowledge in Modern America, 1860–1920*. Baltimore, MD: Johns Hopkins University Press, 1979. 478 pp.

Describes the growth and development of learning in the United States in relation to institutions of higher learning and other organizations. Specialization of science and scholarship comprises one large section and the institutional context of learning is the next largest section.

14. Olson, Keith W. *The G.I. Bill, the Veterans, and the Colleges*. Lexington, KY: University Press of Kentucky, 1974. 139 pp.

A history of the G. I. Bill, which gave many World War II veterans the opportunity to attend colleges and universities. Although some educators were opposed to the bill, many veterans distinguished themselves by their educational achievements. The author mentions Korean and Vietnam was educational benefits but the main part of the book concerns World War II veterans.

15. Portman, David N., ed. *Early Reform in American Higher Education*. Chicago: Nelson-Hall, 1972. 221 pp.

Eleven articles reprinted from *Century* and other post-Civil War periodicals convey the thinking of educators of that period. A knowledge of the history of higher education gives perspective to current problems in higher education. Particularly interesting are the chapters on the state university, women, liberal education, and the influence of Chautauqua.

16. Reed, Germaine M. *David F. Boyd: Founder of Louisiana State University*. Baton Rouge, LA: Louisiana State University Press, 1977. 315 pp.

David Boyd was professor, superintendent, or president at L.S.U. for more than 25 years beginning in 1860 when it was called Louisiana State Seminary of Learning. He also served as head of military institutions in Kentucky, Ohio, and Michigan during a 10-year period. A revision of a dissertation; primary sources are consulted extensively.

1950–Present

17. Henry, David D. *Challenges Past, Challenges Present: An Analysis of American Higher Education since 1930*. San Francisco, CA: Jossey-Bass, 1975. 173 pp.

Records the history of higher education from the viewpoint of an educator who spent 7 years as president of Wayne State University; 3 as executive vice-chancellor of New York University; and 16 as president of the University of Illinois. References from literature of higher education are cited for further reading.

18. Otten, C. Michael. *University Authority and the Student: The Berkeley Experience*. Berkeley, CA: University of California Press, 1970. 222 pp.

Discusses university authority and the relationship of individual freedom of students. The author outlines the history of administrative control over students at Berkeley. The decline of paternalism and rise of bureaucracy led to the student unrest, demands, and finally violence and alienation. In the last chapter, the author makes some suggestions to remedy the problems of that time and predicts some future changes.

GENERAL

19. Clark, Thomas D. *Indiana University: Midwestern Pioneer. Years of Fulfillment*. Vol. 3. Bloomington, IN: Indiana University Press, 1977. 678 pp.

Recounts the years 1937 to 1962 when Herman B. Wells was president. His leadership was instrumental in development of the multiversity. Included in the book are chapters concerning faculty, curriculum, student life, World War II impact, financial history, and graduate education.

20. Duryea, Edwin D. *Prologue to the American System of Higher Education: Higher Learning in Western Culture*. Buffalo, NY: State University of New York, 1979. 81 pp.

Contains a history of the development of higher education with descriptions of university/society relations, reforms, and undergraduate curriculum.

21. Fortenbaugh, Samuel B. *In Order to Form a More Perfect Union: An Inquiry into the Origins of a College*. Syracuse, NY: Union College Press, 1978. 130 pp.

Delineates the history of Union College, which was one of the few American colleges founded before 1800. The political conditions of the time are described and the effect of Governor George Clinton's role upon the college is explained.

22. Frank, Charles E. *Pioneer's Progress; Illinois College, 1892–1979*. Carbondale, IL: Southern Illinois University Press, 1979. 409 pp.

Abridges a 1928 history, *Illinois College: A Centennial History*, by Charles H. Rammelkamp and brings it up-to-date by the addition of new material. The successes and failures of each administration of the college are presented.

23. Hackensmith, Charles William. *Higher Education in the Ohio Valley in the 19th Century*. Bureau of School Service Bulletin, Vol. 45, No. 3. Lexington, KY: University of Kentucky, 1973. 132 pp.

Discusses Transylvania University, denominational colleges in Kentucky, Miami University, Ohio University, and Indiana University. Emphasizes leadership ability, the college president, and how religious bickering adversely affected many early colleges.

24. Jencks, Christopher, and Riesman, David. *The Academic Revolution*. New York: Doubleday, 1968. 580 pp.

Important to the history of colleges and universities. Discusses the history of higher education in the United States within the context of social, political, and economic factors. Social stratification; nationalism vs. localism; class interests; Protestant, Catholic, and Black colleges; as well as professional and graduate schools, are discussed.

25. Morrison, Theodore. *Chautauqua: A Center for Education, Religion, and the Arts in America*. Chicago: University of Chicago Press, 1974. 351 pp.

Chautauqua, with its beginnings going back to 1874, had great influence on the cultural history of America. To many Americans, it gave meaning, culture, awareness, and appreciation for music and entertainment. Many prominent persons were associated with Chautauqua. William Rainey Harper was head of its College of Liberal Arts before becoming president of the University of Chicago.

26. Power, Edward J. *Catholic Higher Education: A History.* New York: Appleton-Century-Crofts, 1972. 493 pp.

The first 2 parts of the book consist of the history of Catholic colleges from 1786–1870 and the development to World War II. The third part of the book, 1940–72, discusses intellectual and quality research objectives when they conflict with the dominance of moral and character education. Governmental financial aid and the new power of boards of trustees are also analyzed.

27. Rainsford, George N. *Congress and Higher Education in the Nineteenth Century.* Knoxville, TN: University of Tennessee Press, 1972. 156 pp.

Discusses the ways that public land usage strengthened education, with an emphasis on the Morrill Acts of 1862 and 1890 and the subsequent development of the land-grant colleges.

28. Sammartino, Peter. *A History of Higher Education in New Jersey.* New York: Barnes & Noble, 1978. 196 pp.

Depicts the institutions of higher learning in their socioeconomic relationships. Some early colleges are treated individually but attention is also given to broad movements, such as state colleges and community colleges.

29. Smith, David Clayton. *The First Century: A History of the University of Maine, 1865–1965.* Orono, ME: University of Maine, 1979. 295 pp.

For many years the curriculum of this institution was controversial. The unresolved question was whether to restrict its work to agricul-ture and technology or to become a liberal arts institution with professional schools of law and pharmacy. The controversy was resolved in 1897 when Justin Morrill stated that his act was meant to provide instruction in all areas. Included is information about student life, extension services, World War II expansion, and accomplishments of faculty research in genetics and breeding, entomology, forestry, and potatoes.

30. Stone, Lawrence, ed. Vol. 1, *Oxford and Cambridge from the 14th to the Early 19th Century,* 351 pp. Vol. 2 *Europe, Scotland, and the United States from the 16th to the 20th Century,* 287 pp. The University in Society. Princeton, NJ: Princeton University Press, 1974.

Vol. 1 is limited to Oxford and Cambridge Universities. Descriptions are given of the student body, the academic profession, and the environment. Includes a computer-analysis of the Oxford student body from 1580 to 1909. Vol. 2 includes chapters on the student protest in Germany (1815–48) at a time when the German academic system was developing into an important one.

31. Thackrey, Russell I. *The Future of the State University.* Urbana, IL: University of Illinois Press, 1971. 138 pp.

Reviews the progress and growth of the state university, beginning with land grant institutions of the nineteenth century. Also noted are changes which have taken place from the 1950s to the time of the book's publication. Characteristics of land-grant universities at the time of the Morrill Act are described. Concern for the future and financing are expressed.

32. Whitehead, John S. *The Separation of College and State: Columbia, Dartmouth, Harvard, and Yale 1776–1876.* New Haven, CT: Yale University Press, 1973. 262 pp.

Examines public support of private colleges and the amount of control which may result from state or federal funding. Before the Civil War both private and public funding was commonplace.

NATURE AND SCOPE OF AMERICAN HIGHER EDUCATION

DIVERSITY

Private

33. American Association of Presidents of Independent Colleges and Universities. *Private Higher Education: Leadership or Liquidation?* Washington, DC: American Association of Presidents of Independent Colleges and Universities, 1971.

Reports on the conference of 1970 and suggests ways to deal with problems. Some solutions discussed are: refusal of public tax support, use of law to control student protestors, and control of drug use.

34. Askew, Thomas A. *The Small College: A Bibliographic Handbook.* AAHE/ERIC Higher Education. Washington, DC: American Association for Higher Education, 1973. ED 082 699. 136 pp.

Entries relating to or applicable to the small college are contained in this annotated bibliography. Among the 12 categories included are: general studies in the small college, teaching and learning, faculty, students, governance, finance, budgeting, and long-range planning.

35. Astin, Alexander W., and Lee, Calvin B. T. *The Invisible Colleges: A Profile of Small, Private Colleges with Limited Resources.* Carnegie Commisssion on Higher Education. New York: McGraw-Hill, 1972. 146 pp.

Surveys the mission, role, and strengths of the small, private, often church-affiliated colleges. These colleges have enrollments under 2,500, generally open-admissions policies, and constitute one-third of 4-year colleges in the United States. They add diversity to the higher education system.

36. Bender, Richard N., ed. *The Church-Related College Today: An Anachronism or Opportunity?* Nashville, TN: General Board of Education, United Methodist Church, 1971.

A declining student body and financial problems plague most institutions. Several contributions can be made by church-related colleges to American society: encouragement of innovation and creativity, openness to divine/human contributions to life's problems, values-related teaching, and a good teaching/learning environment.

37. Benezet, Louis T. *Private Higher Education and Public Funding.* ERIC/Higher Education Research Report No. 5. Washington, DC: American Association for Higher Education, 1976. ED 130 552. 62 pp.

Private higher education has been a strong complement of public higher education since the early nineteenth century. Private higher education is in trouble: reasons for needing help from state and federal sources are given, and arguments are made for the private college.

38. Bowen, Howard, and Minter, John. *Private Higher Education: First Annual Report on Financial and Educational Trends in the Private Sector of American Higher Education.* 3d edition. Washington, DC: American Association of Colleges, 1975. ED 119 570. 123 pp.

Information for this report was gathered from private colleges and universities. The base year used was 1969–70; financial trends are noted from that date through 1976–77 for some data. The financial and academic relationship is emphasized and statistics support the conclusions.

39. Breneman, David W., and Finn, C. Hester E., eds. *Public Policy and Private Higher Education.* Washington, DC: The Brookings Institution, 1978. 468 pp.

Financial problems confronting private higher education are studied at length. Discussion is philosophical, as well as practical. Trends in tuition, political problems, enrollment patterns, and demographic trends are examined. Suggestions and varied solutions are given.

40. Carnegie Council on Policy Studies in Higher Education. *The States and Private Higher Education: Problems and Policies in a New Era.* San Francisco, CA: Jossey-Bass, 1977. 206 pp.

State policies can help maintain the dual system of private and public institutions of higher education. State policies in relation to many aspects of private education are indicated. Enrollments, finances, autonomy, and academic freedom are areas of interest.

41. Duberman, Martin. *Black Mountain: An Exploration in Community.* New York: E. P. Dutton, 1972. 527 pp.

A definitive treatment of the story of Black Mountain College (1933–1956), where a radical college education may have had the best chance of surviving. The college was organized in the belief that mutual learning and creation without bureaucratic harassment could merge life and classroom. The first 18 years were dedicated to teaching in a relatively conventional way but the last 5 years were more radical in art and life-style.

42. Education Commission of the States. *Final Report and Recommendations: Task Force on State Policy and Independent Higher Education.* Denver, CO: Education Commission of the States, 1977. ED 144 464. 52 pp.

Constitutional and legal issues are discussed in relation to each state. Recommendations are made that each state develop a policy concerning the conditions and role of independent colleges and universities. Statistics are given as documentation.

43. Heath, Roy. *Princeton Retrospectives: Twenty-Fifth-Year Reflections on a College Education.* Princeton, NJ: Darwin Press, 1979. 298 pp.

In his first book, *The Reasonable Adventurer,* Heath traced the development of 36 undergraduates through 4 years at Princeton. Twenty-five years later he visited 32 of these advisees and 32 of their classmates. Aids in understanding how a liberal education can influence the lives of students.

44. Holmes, Robert Merrill. *The Academic Mysteryhouse: The Man, The Campus, and Their New Search for Meaning.* Nashville, TN: Abingdon Press, 1970. 197 pp.

The responsibility of "transmitting, transforming, and reflecting culture" is traditionally charged to the university. There is an identity crisis at the present time at the institutional level, as well as personal level. This is compared to the "tragedy of our religious life." Church-related colleges could play a leadership role at the present time.

45. Jonsen, Richard W. *Small Liberal Arts Colleges: Diversity at the Crossroads?* AAHE-ERIC/Higher Education Research Report No. 4. Washington, DC: American Association for Higher Education, 1978. ED 154 680. 54 pp.

Although this report is not overly optimistic about the survival of colleges in this category, the review is helpful. Major focus is on historical background, the fiscal crisis, role and contributions, and recommendations.

46. Keeton, Morris T. *Models and Mavericks: A Profile of Private Liberal Arts Colleges.* Carnegie Commission on Higher Education. New York: McGraw-Hill, 1971. 191 pp.

Several reasons are provided to show the need for private colleges. Qualitative achievement is defined to include: freedom to guide student life and provide a curriculum which recognizes a particular religious or philosophical viewpoint, unique instructional achievement, and freedom for innovative practices.

47. Koch, Raymond, and Koch, Charlotte. *Educational Commune: The Story of Commonwealth College.* New York: Schocken Books, 1972. 211 pp.

Commonwealth College was founded in 1923 and survived for 17 years (1923–40). The school did not grant degrees nor seek accreditation. Teachers served without salary and worked with students as the students did farm, kitchen, and laundry chores. The first president was William E. Zeuch (1923–31), who believed that disadvantaged young people should have opportunities for cultural improvement. The students were highly motivated and were a challenge to the teachers. Approximately 1,000 students attended Commonwealth at one time or another and many of them became labor leaders of various kinds.

48. McFarlane, William H.; Howard, A.E.D.; and Chronister, Jay. *State Financial Measures Involving the Private Sector of Higher Education*. Washington, DC: Association of American Colleges, 1974. 105 pp.

The rationale for state aid to private education is examined. Taken into consideration are histories, legal programs, and policy bases.

49. McGill, Samuel H. *The Contribution of the Church Related College to the Public's Good*. Washington, DC: Association of American Colleges, 1970. 113 pp.

Discusses contributions to American society by church colleges. Moral and ethical values and regard for the individual are some of the diverse needs met by these colleges.

50. Miller, Ann F., ed. *College in Dispersion: Women at Bryn Mawr, 1968–1975*. Boulder, CO: Westview, 1976. 315 pp.

A study conducted to collect information and opinions from alumnae and to inform them concerning current conditions at the college. The majority of the information was collected by telephone calls. Part of the report is in narrative form but statistics compose the major section.

51. Minter, John W., and Bowen, Howard R. *Private Higher Education. Third Annual Report on Financial and Educational Trends in Private Sector of American Higher Education*. Washington, DC: Association of American Colleges, 1977. ED 145 793. 107 pp.

Outlines financial trends from 1969–70 through 1976–77 and describes financial and academic relationships in private colleges and universities. One hundred accredited 4-year institutions are the basis for the study. Topics of interest are: admissions, enrollment, faculty, curriculum, financial and economic aspects, and analysis of individual institutions.

52. Moots, Philip R., and Gaffney, Edward M., Jr. *Church and Campus: Legal Issues in Religiously Affiliated Higher Education*. Notre Dame, IN: University of Notre Dame Press, 1979. 207 pp.

The first study report from the University of Notre Dame Law School Center for Constitutional Studies. Administrators and other leaders in religious affiliated higher education will find many topics interesting. Questions dealt with include: liability, public financial assistance, admissions, academic freedom, and government regulations.

53. Moran, Gerald P. *Private Colleges: The Federal Tax System and Its Impact*. Toledo, OH: Center for the Study of Higher Education, University of Toledo, 1977. 88 pp.

The philosophy and historical precedents of the tax exemption for donations to private colleges and universities are examined. Charitable deduction is a motivation for providing much financial support to the private sector of higher education.

54. National Commission on United Methodist Higher Education. *Endangered Service: Independent Colleges, Public Policy and the First Amendment*. Nashville, TN: National Commission on United Methodist Higher Education, 1976. 144 pp.

Constitutional questions are the subject of issues related to institution-state and church-state relationships. Tax exemptions, freedom of choice of students regarding higher education, diversity, autonomy, excessive regulation, and reporting requirements are also given attention.

55. Nosow, Sigmund, and Clark, Frederick R. *Goals/Aims/Objectives—Duquesne University: A Case Study*. Atlantic Highlands, NJ: Humanities Press, 1976. 243 pp.

Looks at the goals of the university as they are perceived by the members of the board, administration, faculty, alumni, graduate, and undergraduate students. A systems approach is used to assist in the analysis.

56. Pace, C. Robert. *Education and Evangelism: A Profile of Protestant Colleges*. Carnegie Commission on Higher Education. New York: McGraw-Hill, 1972. 120 pp.

Diversity in higher education is illustrated from data gathered from 88 institutions. Three major types of institutions are included: those with Protestant roots but no longer legally Protestant; those which retain a connection with the establishing church; and those associated with evangelical, fundamentalist, and interdenominational Christian churches.

57. Parsonage, Robert R., ed. *Church Related Higher Education: Perceptions and Perspectives*. Valley Forge, PA: Judson Press, 1978. 344 pp.

In addition to general problems and issues in higher education, church-related colleges have a special role and contribution to make in higher education. They contribute to the quality of life and churches of the United States. Fourteen institutions and the values and religious activities which they promote are studied.

58. Reinert, Paul C. *To Turn the Tide*. Englewood Cliffs, NJ: Prentice-Hall, 1972. 111 pp.

The financial crisis in private higher education is explored. Various solutions are offered, such as improvement in internal management of institutions, state and federal aid, and better leadership.

59. Sloan Study Consortium. *Paying for College: Financing Education at Nine Private Institutions*. Hanover, NH: University Press of New England, 1974. 137 pp.

Studies financial stress, options for expansion of financial aid, and possible solutions. A well-organized loan program is important.

60. Task Force of the National Council of Independent Colleges and Universities. *A National Policy for Private Higher Education*. Washington, DC: Association of American Colleges, 1974. 80 pp.

The financing of private higher education is the subject of this book. The many contributions to society and students are discussed: problems which beset private education are examined, and tuition differences are explored.

61. Thompson, Daniel C. *Private Black Colleges at the Crossroads*. Westport, CT: Greenwood Press, 1973. 308 pp.

Details the unique contribution the private Black colleges have made to the education of Black Americans and indirectly to all of American society. The author lists the problems facing these colleges today and makes suggestions for improving the quality of education offered and for obtaining financial support.

62. Trivett, David A. *Proprietary Schools and Postsecondary Education*. ERIC/Higher Education Research Report No. 2. Washington, DC: American Association for Higher Education, 1974. ED 090 889. 64 pp.

These postsecondary institutions are privately owned, profit-oriented, and train students for job entry. Some of the major topics are: past and future images; number and types of such institutions; distinctive operating features; students, faculty, and instruction; social value; and accreditation and regulation.

63. Wilson, Charles H., Jr. *Tilton v. Richardson: The Search for Sectarianism in Education.* Washington, DC: Association of American Colleges, 1971. 53 pp.

The decision made by the U.S. Supreme Court, June 28, 1971, stated that church-related colleges may receive federal grants to construct academic and other buildings under the Higher Education Facilities Act of 1965 with the restriction that such buildings may never be used for religious instruction or worship.

64. Wynn, Daniel W. *The Protestant Church-Related College.* New York: Philosophical Library, 1975. 108 pp.

Provides facts and opinions about college administration and governance for trustees, college presidents, and administrators of the small church-related college.

Public

65. Altbach, Phillip, et al., eds. *Academic Supermarkets: A Critical Case Study of a Multiversity.* San Francisco, CA: Jossey-Bass, 1971. 369 pp.

Events of 1967–70 are examined by 18 authors from the University of Wisconsin. The authors deal with the power structure, the faculty, teaching assistants, and students as they were affected by the upheaval of those years.

66. Commission on External Degree Programs. *The 1,000 Mile Campus: The California State University and Colleges.* Los Angeles, CA: Commission on External Degree Programs, 1972. 87 pp.

Explains the concept of external degree programs which are available for every student. This innovative educational opportunity for students of all ages makes it possible to earn a degree without physical presence on campus.

67. Elmendorf, John. *Transmiting Information about Experiments in Higher Education.* New York: Interbook, Inc., 1975. 49 pp.

Outlines the history of New College in Sarasota, Florida and discusses developments since 1960 beginning in 1960. Also examines other innovative colleges in relation to New College. Suggests ways to transmitt information about experiments in higher education.

68. Hightower, Jim. *Hard Tomatoes, Hard Times.* Task Force on the Land Grant College Complex, Agribusiness Accountability Project. Cambridge, MA: Schenkman, 1978. 332 pp.

Examines the land grant college-agricultural complex and concentrates on colleges of agriculture, agriculture experiment stations, and state extension services. Alleges that these tax-supported services are used by public corporate interests for their profit and that small farmers are forced out of farming by industrial agribusiness interests.

69. Kendall, Elaine. *Peculiar Institutions: An Informal History of the Seven Sister Colleges.* New York: G. P. Putnam's, 1976. 275 pp.

A history of the 7 sister colleges, Bryn Mawr, Smith, Wellesley, Barnard, Holyoke, Radcliffe, and Vassar. These colleges are now either coeducational or considering the change. An interesting, readable study of pioneer institutions devoted to the education of women.

70. Knoll, Robert E., and Brown, Robert D. *Experiment at Nebraska: The First Two Years of a Cluster College.* University of Nebraska Studies Series No. 44. Lincoln, NE: University of Nebraska, 1972. 127 pp.

A description of an innovative, lower-division, undergraduate program at the University of Nebraska which lasted 2½ years. This attempt to alter and improve undergraduate education included a residential hall for 125 freshman, 40 upperclassmen, several fellows, and some faculty. Many problems surfaced when traditional course structures and class meetings were changed. Lack of personal responsibility and goals, as well as disagreement within the leadership caused some confusion.

71. National Association of State Universities and Land-Grant Universities. "The State and Land-Grant Universities." In *Handbook on Contemporary Education,* edited by S. E. Goodman. New York: Bowker, 1976, pp. 44–48.

One of the few references which lists the 70 land-grant universities alphabetically by state. Major topics discussed are: the public university concept, the Morrill landmark, the 1890 colleges, curriculum reform, professional training, and areas of controversy.

72. National Advisory Committee on Black Higher Education. *Black Colleges and Universities: An Essential Component of a Diverse System of Higher Education.* Washington, DC: National Advisory Committee on Black Higher Education and Black Colleges and Universities, 1979. ED 183 066 103 pp.

Diversity in American education is examined, especially as it relates to Black students. The historical development of diversity, the role of diversity, and the role of Black colleges in meeting the needs of Black students are topics discussed in this book.

73. Perry, Walter. *The Open University.* San Francisco, CA: Jossey-Bass, 1977. 298 pp.

Perry is vice-chancellor of the innovative British Open University, where radio and television are used extensively. Some topics discussed are: historical and political background, curriculum development, administration of the university, and future prospects.

74. Riesman, David; Gusfield, Joseph H.; and Gamson, Zelda. *Academic Values and Mass Education: The Early Years of Oakland and Monteith.* Garden City, NY: Doubleday, 1970. 332 pp.

Beginning with the early seventies, reforms were generally concerned with: accountability and economy, systems theory, faculty evaluation, and curricula and governance innovations. Two new and innovative colleges were Monteith (Wayne State University) and Oakland (Michigan State University). In time Oakland became larger, diversified, and conventional, Monteith stayed smaller, and the experiment was stabilized.

GOALS AND PURPOSES

75. Ballotti, Geno A., and Graubard, Stephen R., eds. *The Embattled University.* New York: Braziller, 1970. 451 pp.

Contemporary university problems are discussed by well-known educators. Challenges to the university were issued by dissatisfied students, by faculty, and by political powers who wished to have control of the university during the late 60s and early 70s.

76. Bell, R. E., and Youngson, A. J., eds. *Present and Future in Higher Education*. London: Tavistock, 1973. 202 pp.

Presents papers from a seminar which considered the current state of higher education and recommended future policies. Some questions of interest are: the role of new universities; the junior college; colleges of education; finance; excellence in universities; control; and planning for the future.

77. Bloland, Harland G., and Bloland, Sue M. *American Learned Societies in Transition: The Impact of Dissent and Recession*. Carnegie Commission on Higher Education. New York: McGraw-Hill, 1974. 142 pp.

Describes the effect upon academic disciplines when their national learned societies are influenced by large numbers of radical faculty members. Three case studies are used to show the changes in direction of learned societies in recent years.

78. Carnegie Commission on Higher Education. *The Purposes and the Performance of Higher Education in the United States: Approaching the Year 2000*. Report and Recommendations by the Carnegie Commission on Higher Education. New York: McGraw-Hill, 1973. 107 pp.

Five main purposes of higher education are enumerated and rated by the Commission. Several ways are suggested to improve performance, such as concern about quality of educational environment, more federal research funding, and recruiting minority and low-income groups.

79. Dietze, Gottfried. *Youth, University and Democracy*. Baltimore, MD: Johns Hopkins, 1970. 117 pp.

The pursuit of truth anc clarity should be the main concerns of the university. Considers recent disturbances and violence on campus unfortunate.

80. Foshay, Arthur W., ed. *The Professional as Educator*. New York: Teachers College Press, 1970. 120 pp.

Questions the current role of American universities. Discusses the ideas of the university as the center for social action and change and as the seat of scholarship and research.

81. Godwin, Winfred L., and Mann, Peter B., eds. *Higher Education Myths, Realities, and Possibilities*. Atlanta, GA: Southern Regional Education Board, 1972. 184 pp.

Presents articles which were collected from a meeting of the Southern Regional Education Board, May–July 1972. Some specific topics are: financing higher education, improving productivity, time-shortening experiments, and nontraditional learning programs. Some of the contributors include: Lyman Glenny, Howard Bowen, Samuel Gould, and Allan Cartter.

82. Grant, Gerald, and Riesman, David. *The Perpetual Dream: Reform and Experiment in the American College*. Chicago: University of Chicago Press, 1978. 474 pp.

Provides an overview of the diversity of undergraduate education in America and the reforms which have taken place in recent years. Some institutions described include: St. John's; New York City's College for Human Resources; New College of Sarasota; Cluster Colleges at Santa Cruz; Stockton and Ramapo State College of New Jersey.

83. Mood, Alexander. *The Future of Higher Education*. Carnegie Commission on Higher Education. New York: McGraw-Hill, 1973. 166 pp.

Begins with a description of the present condition of higher education and the forces involved in it. Several radical suggestions are made, such as one year of residential college for everyone. Education would then continue on a part-time basis. The use of videotapes would be promoted, decreasing the need for more faculty. Other drastic changes are also advocated.

84. Parsons, Talcott, and Platt, Gerald. *The American University*. Cambridge, MA: Harvard University Press, 1973. 463 pp.

The primary function of the university is as a guardian of cognitive culture and the interests which support it. Graduate faculties and scholarly research are essential to the academic system. Tenure and academic freedom are of the utmost importance.

85. Tuckman, Howard P., and Ford, W. Scott. *The Demand for Higher Education: A Florida Case Study*. Lexington, MA: Heath, 1972. 125 pp.

Studies the demand for higher education by students and analyzes the factors which influence the choice of institution. Some factors which have influence are: tuition and income, self-concept, college major, and minority group access.

86. Urban, George. *Hazards of Learning: A Symposium on the Crisis of the University*. La Salle, IL: Open Court, 1976. 294 pp.

Considers the university in the late sixties and early seventies and discusses goals and purposes related to society and individual education. A symposium with an international viewpoint.

87. Wagner, Geoffrey. *The End of Education: The Experience of the City University of New York with Open Enrollment and the Threat to Higher Education in America*. Cranbury, NJ: Barnes & Noble, 1976. 252 pp.

A professor who teaches basic writing to poorly prepared undergraduates unfavorably compares CUNY with a "real university," such as Oxford of the 1930s which was devoted to developing the cultured gentleman. Deplores CUNY with its open access, remediation, affirmative action, community colleges, urban higher education, and student activists.

PHILOSOPHY

88. Ashworth, Kenneth H. *American Higher Education in Decline*. College Station, TX: Texas A&M University Press, 1979. 105 pp.

Higher education is overmanaged by all branches of government. Quality can be improved with regained independence and autonomy for the institutions of higher education. Reduction in admission standards and competition for students, as well as acceptance of federal funds, have contributed to the decline. Some suggestions for improvement include rotating assignments for university personnel and people in federal agencies concerned with higher education.

89. Ben-David, Joseph. *Trends in American Higher Education*. Chicago: University of Chicago Press, 1974. 137 pp.

Recommended for new faculty in higher education. Gives a historical background for higher education and discusses the forces which will influence the future. Institutions discussed are research universities and other postsecondary schools.

90. Bragg, Ann K. *The Socialization Process in Higher Education*. ERIC/Higher Education Research Report No. 7. Washington, DC: American Association for Higher Education, 1976. ED 132 909. 45 pp.

Since Sputnik, there has been an undue emphasis on cognitive learning and learning in many colleges lacks integration. Emphasizes that it is the socialization process that unites the affective and cognitive domains. Suggests implications for reform to facilitate the socialization process.

91. Brann, Eva T. H. *Paradoxes of Education in a Republic*. Chicago: University of Chicago, 1979. 172 pp.

Asserts that reflection on the purpose of education is important. Planning and projections follow. Utility of education, tradition, and rationality are 3 concepts which are in conflict with American society.

92. Brubacher, John S. On *the Philosophy of Higher Education*. San Francisco, CA: Jossey-Bass, 1977. 143 pp.

Gives an introduction to American institutions of higher learning and a general survey of problems relating to higher education. Some subjects treated are: autonomy, academic freedom, and the confrontation of liberal and vocational education.

93. Cangemi, Joseph P. *Higher Education and the Development of Self-Actualizing Personalities*. New York: Philosophical Library, 1977. 96 pp.

Outlines self-actualization from an historical viewpoint and reports research showing concern in the academic world. Supports the ideal of liberal education.

94. Casso, Henry J., and Roman, Gilbert D., eds. *Chicanos in Higher Education: Proceedings of a National Institute on Access to Higher Education for the Mexican American*. Albuquerque, NM: University of New Mexico Press, 1976. 177 pp.

Access to postsecondary education for Chicanos is discussed. Several authors consider various aspects of the problem.

95. Cappa, Judith. *Improving Equity in Postsecondary Education: New Directions for Leadership*. Washington, DC: National Institute of Education, 1977. 50 pp.

Report of a conference concerned with equity in postsecondary education. Participants at the conference represented groups which were underserved at the time by postsecondary education.

96. Goldberg, Maxwell H. *Design in Liberal Learning*. San Francisco, CA: Jossey-Bass, 1971. 188 pp.

A scholar devoted to humanistic values and content in higher education takes a forceful, reasoned stand in behalf of liberal arts studies. Research is needed to produce evidence that there is a difference in the quality of life of an educated and uneducated person.

97. Harcleroad, Fred F., ed. *Issues of the Seventies: The Future of Higher Education*. San Francisco, CA: Jossey-Bass, 1970. 192 pp.

Surveys the issues of the seventies with suggestions for improvement. Three concerns are: the needs of society, student problems and needs, and the response by institutions. Access for each person

is important for society and the curriculum should allow some flexibility for students. Administrators could be improved by using better management practices and information systems.

98. Henderson, Algo D. *The Innovative Spirit*. San Francisco, CA: Jossey-Bass, 1970. 308 pp.

Delineates the university of 1970 and comments on several aspects. Expresses the wish for a serious look at the university as an institution. Opposes large complex state organizations and believes universities function best with a single board and much independence. Descriptions of innovations of the late sixties are included.

99. Hesburgy, Theodore. *The Hesburgh Papers: Higher Values in Higher Education*. Mission, KS: Andrews and McMeel, 1979. 206 pp.

Believes Catholic universities should lead students to see the importance of human dignity and rights. Discusses Christian higher education and problems in higher education. Values should occupy a very important place in the education of an individual.

100. Hodgkinson, Harold L., and Bloy, Myron B., Jr., eds. *Identity Crisis in Higher Education*. San Francisco, CA: Jossey-Bass, 1971. 212 pp.

Assumes that all students and some faculty wish to change universities to conform to new social order. Culture and traditions of universities are looked upon as repressive influences. Colleges and universities reflect the maturity of faculty and administrators of their institutions.

101. Lenning, Oscar T. *The "Benefits Crisis" in Higher Education?* ERIC/Higher Education Research Report No. 1. Washington, DC: American Association for Higher Education, 1974. ED 090 888. 69 pp.

Among the issues concerning the benefits of higher education that are reviewed are: student benefits, private postgraduate benefits, and social benefits. A benefits program model is prepared for ordering priorities in higher education.

102. Leslie, Larry L. *Higher Education Opportunity: A Decade of Progress*. ERIC/Higher Education Research Report No. 3. Washington, DC: American Association for Higher Education, 1977. ED 142 125. 57 pp.

Intends to assess the degree of progress made since 1967 in meeting the goals of student aid programs which include: the promotion of equal access, promotion of equal institutional choice, and the advancement of equal retention and completion. Numerous tables and figures document the content.

103. Newman, John Henry. *The Idea of a University*. Edited by I. T. Kerr. New York: Oxford University Press, 1976. 684 pp.

An annotated critical edition of the essays and lectures of John Henry Newman. Newman's reputation as the basis for all modern thinking on university education is questioned by some authorities.

104. Solmon, Lewis C., and Taubman, Paul J. *Does College Matter?* New York: Academic Press, 1973. 415 pp.

Impacts of higher education on individuals and society are examined by economists, educators, sociologists, and psychologists. More research is needed in this area.

105. Wilson, Logan. *Shaping American Higher Education*. Washington, DC: American Council on Education, 1972. 301 pp.

Wilson has experience as faculty member, administrator, and professional leader in higher education. Stresses the planning needed for change. Emphasizes the concern for quality and the intellectual and cultural character of higher education institutions.

PROBLEMS IN 1970s

106. American Assembly of Columbia University. *Disorders in Higher Education*. Englewood Cliffs, NJ: Prentice-Hall, 1979. 212 pp.

Leaders in higher education trace the development of various problems in higher education today and offer recommendations toward their solution.

107. Atelsek, Frank J., and Gomberg, Irene L. *Young Doctorate Faculty in Selected Science and Engineering Departments, 1975–1980*. Washington, DC: American Council on Education, 1976. 31 pp.

Based on a 1976 survey. The problem of smaller proportions of young faculty will continue to grow in the 80s. Early retirement, increased funding, sabbaticals, changing tenure systems, and hiring only young faculty are some of the suggestions offered.

108. Bowen, Frank M., and Glenny, Lyman A. *State Budgeting for Higher Education: State Fiscal Stringency and Public Higher Education*. Berkeley, CA: Center for Research and Development in Higher Education, University of California, 1976. 268 pp.

How do public universities and colleges respond to retrenchment? Budget cuts cause universities and colleges to examine their needs and priorities. Projections of 5 or 10 years may need revision. The 1970s and 1980s will be times of stringency in fiscal affairs.

109. Brown, Charles I., and Sanford, Timothy R. *IR: A Look towards the 1980s and Institutional Research and Student Aid*. Chapel Hill, NC: University of North Carolina, 1979. 58 pp.

Details information gained from 2 conferences; one studies the effects of federal and state financial aid to students and the other considers institutional research in the 1980s.

110. Brubacher, John S. *The University—Its Identity Crisis*. New Britain, CT: Central Connecticut State College, 1972. 77 pp.

By a respected educational theorist and the first person to occupy the Herbert D. Welte Chair at Central Connecticut State College, this is a critical examination of the problems and issues in contemporary higher education in the United States.

111. Carnegie Commission on Higher Education. *A Digest of Reports of the Carnegie Commission on Higher Education*. New York: McGraw-Hill Co., 1974. 399 pp.

Twenty-one reports were issued by the Commission from 1968 through 1973. The digests contain general trends and conclusions which are drawn from the reports.

112. ———. *New Students and New Places, Policies for the Future Growth and Development of American Higher Education*. New York: McGraw-Hill, 1971. 158 pp.

An attempt to project enrollment for American higher education to the year 2000 and to define the number of additional institutions needed to meet those projections. Two types of institutions were

recommended as needed: community colleges and comprehensive colleges located in metropolitan areas. Diversity, high quality, innovations, and better management were recommended for further study.

113. ———. *Priorities for Action: Final Report of the Carnegie Commission on Higher Education*. New York: McGraw-Hill, 1973. 243 pp.

This final report considers hundreds of suggestions and recommendations which are contained in the various commissioned research reports. Selection has been made of key priorities which should be recognized by institutions. Specifc recommendations are included.

114. Carnegie Corporation of New York. *Research Univesities and the National Interest: A Report from Fifteen University Presidents*. New York: Ford Foundation, 1977. 140 pp.

University presidents involved in this report believe that the federal government will need to increase financial support to research universities, that all institutions of higher learning share common concerns, and that the welfare of all higher education and the national interest should be considered. The partnership of the federal government and research universities is explored and the priorities for graduate education in the 1980s are discussed. Major research libraries' roles and support are another topic considered.

115. Carnegie Council on Policy Studies in Higher Education. *Fair Practices in Higher Education*. San Francisco, CA: Jossey-Bass, 1979. 91 pp.

The decline in number of students is expected to cause great competition among institutions of higher learning. Further deterioration of ethical standards in academic life is warned against. Indications of this decline are listed as: increased cheating by students; grade inflation; marginal off-campus and out-of-state degree programs; theft of library books and journals; theft of many kinds and vandalism; misuse of public financial aid; and inflated, misleading advertising by institutions.

116. ———. *Giving Youth a Better Chance: Options for Education, Work and Service*. San Francisco, CA: Jossey-Bass, 1979. 41 pp.

Explores new approaches to youth problems to ensure that all young people may have a better chance. Secondary schools need major changes in order to prepare students for higher education, business, or public service. Vocational and career education in community colleges should be improved and the transition from school to work could be facilitated.

117. ———. *Next Steps for the 1980s in Student Financial Aid*. San Francisco, CA: Jossey-Bass, 1979. 255 pp.

Divided into 3 main sections: (1) conclusions and recommendations of the Council, (2) present policies and practices in problem areas, and (3) relationships of various student aid programs and needs for recommendations of the Council.

118. ———. *Three Thousand Futures: The Next Twenty Years for Higher Education*. Final Report of the Carnegie Council on Policy Studies in Higher Education. San Francisco, CA: Jossey-Bass, 1980. 155 pp.

Published in 1980, this is the last in the prestigious series of Carnegie Council reports on higher education. Major topics are: base point, 1980; judgment about prospective enrollments; anticipating the next 2 decades; courses of action; and higher education and the world of the future. The appendix includes a brief glossary and a list of Carnegie Council Surveys, including response rates from public and private institutions.

119. Carnegie Foundation for the Advancement of Teaching. *More than Survival: Prospects for Higher Education in a Period of Uncertainty: A Commentary with Recommendations.* San Francisco, CA: Jossey-Bass, 1975. 166 pp.

Recommendations for the next 25 years in American higher education are contained in this report. Three major suggestions for public policy are made: (1) financial provisions to allow universal access, (2) steady support at adequate levels for research and research training, and (3) support for the private sector of higher education.

120. Chambers, Merritt Madison. *Keeping Higher Education Moving.* Danville, IL: Interstate, 1976. 342 pp.

Surveys with optimism the prospects for the future of higher education. More people in more countries will be able to obtain more and better education. Facts concerning openness, students, teachers, and finance are presented to support this favorable outlook.

121. Christoffell, Pamela H. *Vocational Education: Alternatives for New Federal Legislation.* Policy Study from the Washington Office of the College Entrance Examination Board. New York: College Entrance Examination Board, 1975. 57 pp.

Many problems caused in part by the 1976 amendments to the Vocational Education Act of 1963 remain to be solved in the 1980s. State and federal planning for secondary vocational and postsecondary technical education will continue into the 1980s.

122. College Entrance Examination Board. *A Role for Marketing in College Admissions.* New York: College Entrance Examination Board, 1976. 113 pp.

Administrators concerned about survival in the 1980s will find suggestions for future planning in this publication. The principles of marketing theory and practice should be applied to college admissions. Consumer needs should be assessed and prospective students need to be informed about the institution and what it has to offer. Programs may need modification and new programs ought to be developed in order to meet consumer needs.

123. Committee of Presidents of Universities of Ontario. *Towards 2000: The Future of Post-Secondary Education in Ontario.* Toronto: McClelland and Stewart, 1971. 176 pp.

Considers the future of postsecondary education in Canada. Expansion of higher education has brought problems with Ph.D. programs. The writers believe in 3 tracks for Ph.D.s: for researchers, teachers, and those in applied fields.

124. DeWitt, Laurence, and Tussing, A. Dale. *The Supply and Demand for Graduates of Higher Education: 1970–1980.* Syracuse, NY: Educational Policy Research Center, 1971. 51 pp.

Predicts the overproduction of Ph.D.s and the surplus of elementary and secondary school teachers in the 1970s. Suggests adjustments ought to be made by schools of education and state governments. Human resources planning should be adopted and could start with a national inventory of the teacher force.

125. Feingold, S. Norman. *Counseling for Careers in the 1980s.* Garrett Park, MD: Garrett Park Press, 1979. 186 pp.

Outlines responsibilities of counselors on issues which involve matching occupations and assignments of work with individual capabilities. Other current problems which counselors must face are discussed. Lifelong learning, as well as career development, is covered, with a good section on retirement. Special needs of the handicapped and other minorities are noted, and projections for opportunities in occupations, 1980–2000, are listed.

126. Furniss, W. Todd, and Gardner, David P., eds. *Higher Education and Government: An Uneasy Alliance.* Washington, DC: American Council on Higher Education, 1979. 145 pp.

Outlines the thoughts of 22 educators on government control and accountability from higher education institutions and how the autonomy of the institutions may be affected. Topics discussed include: change, faculty appointments, curriculum, admissions, research, and finance.

127. Ginzberg, Eli. *Good Jobs, Bad Jobs, No Jobs.* Cambridge, MA: Harvard University Press, 1979. 219 pp.

Job prospects for college graduates are not always the ones for which they planned. Overqualified people may become common in the near future and attitudes of employees for whom promotion opportunities are limited may cause problems for employers.

128. Glazer, Nathan, ed. *The Third Century: Twenty-Six Prominent Americans Speculate on the Educational Future.* New Rochelle, NY: Change, 1977. 196 pp.

The 26 contributors to this book, who were nominated in a national poll as among the most influential Americans in higher education, comment on the future of higher education. Included are: Clark Kerr, Lewis Mayhew, John Silber, Theodore M. Hesburgh, and Nathan Glazer. Some predictions for the future include: growth of lifelong learning, increasing equalitarianism, and the growing influence of the federal government.

129. Gordon, Margaret S., and Trow, Martin. *Youth Education and Unemployment Problems: An International Perspective.* Berkeley, CA: Carnegie Council on Policy Studies in Higher Education, 1979. 170 pp.

Summarizes manpower and educational policies in Western industrial countries and compares experiences in Poland, Japan, Mexico, and South Asia. A chapter on aspects of youth unemployment in the United States, which are different from in Western Europe, contains information on inner-city illicit employment and on groups such as the disadvantaged, alienated, and deprived.

130. Grupe, Fritz H. *Managing Interinstitutional Change: Consortia in Higher Education.* Potsdam, NY: Associated Colleges of the St. Lawrence Valley in cooperation with Council for Interinstitutional Leadership. 1975. 111 pp.

Describes the management of a consortium of higher education institutions and also the problems which may appear. Both organizational and interorganizational change is required for success. Each member's goals can be better achieved if there is voluntary cooperation. Systematic planning is necessary to achieve cooperation and to establish objectives which can be achieved and evaluated.

131. Harcleroad, Fred F., ed. *Financing Postsecondary Education in the 1980's.* Tucson, AZ: Center for the Study of Higher Education, University of Arizona, 1979. 126 pp.

Financial problems loom ahead of others for the coming years. Higher education administrators and faculty need to consider the impact of several topics such as: budgeting, financial management, tuition, and student financial aid.

132. Harcleroad, Fred F.; Molen, Theodore, Jr.; and Van Ort, Suzanne. *The Regional State Colleges and Universities in the Middle 1970's.* Tucson, AZ: Center for the Study of Higher Education, University of Arizona, 1976. 103 pp.

Regional state colleges and universities are generally former teachers colleges and urban universities. During the 1980s there are already indications that the mission, program offerings, and enrollment size will need to be examined.

133. Harmon, Lindsey R. *A Century of Doctorates: Data Analysis of Growth and Change.* Washington, DC: National Academy of Sciences, 1978. 173 pp.

Outlines the growth of the Ph.D. degree from 1861 to 1974. Americans believe more years of schooling will result in a higher paying job and higher social status. This report endeavors to show how great the oversupply of Ph.D.s has grown. Data is given to support this growth but no solutions are suggested.

134. Harrington, Fred H. *The Future of Adult Education.* San Francisco, CA: Jossey-Bass, 1977. 238 pp.

The decline in enrollment by 18- to 20-year-old students has made administrators and faculty more willing to welcome adult students. This study offers practical advice and experience to institutions of higher education. Some adjustments will need to be made in programs; the needs and characteristics of adults will need to be assessed; and reexamination in such areas as admissions, prior credit for experience, financial assistance, housing, and transportation, will be necessary.

135. Kemerer, Frank R., and Satryb, Ronald P., eds. *Facing Financial Exigency: Strategies for Educational Administrators.* Lexington, MA: Heath, 1977. 137 pp.

Financial problems are expected to increase in the 1980s and 1990s. The editors offer some management strategies which may help institutions of higher learning adjust to financial realities. One believes that campus administrators should become involved in politics; another advises senior administrators with ''power bases'' to become ''change catalysts.'' Faculty unions may make financial demands which cannot be met because of financial problems.

136. Landini, Richard, and Douglas, Patricia, eds. *Quality in Higher Education in Times of Financial Stress: Proceedings of the Pacific Northwest Conference on Higher Education.* Corvallis, OR: Oregon State University Press, 1976. 80 pp.

Discusses the prospects of less financial support and the survival techniques necessary. Attended by 18 presidents, deans, and professors.

137. McMurren, Sterling M., ed. *On the Meaning of the University.* Salt Lake City, UT: University of Utah Press, 1976. 123 pp.

Essays by 5 well-known educators who comment on contemporary education and make predictions for future consideration. Contributors are Eric Ashby, Brand Blanshard, John Gardner, T. R. McConnell, Mina Rees, and the editor. Some issues which must be faced in the eighties are: greater access, drop in funding, more government involvement, more part-time students, and technological developments.

138. Marien, Michael. *Beyond the Carnegie Commission: A Policy Study Guide to Space/Time/Credit Preference for Higher Education.* Syracuse, NY: Educational Policy Research Center, 1972. 177 pp.

Explores new forms and patterns of education as they are related to the future. Recommendations for futher study include: preparation for more adult students, informal or credit-free learning, external degree programs, open university, and extended campus.

139. Mayhew, Lewis B. *Legacy of the Seventies.* San Francisco, CA: Jossey-Bass, 1977. 366 pp.

Considers the recent past and looks toward trends for the future in higher education. Some topics discussed are nontraditional higher education, educational technology, curriculum, finances, and governance.

140. Meyer, Peter. *Awarding College Credit for Non-College Learning.* San Francisco, CA: Jossey-Bass, 1975. 195 pp.

Presents the process of awarding undergraduate credit for experience and/or learning which occurs before beginning college and which cannot be measured in an exemption examination. Prior learning is already in force in 100 or more colleges in the United States. With the influx of adults into higher education this indicates a problem for future consideration.

141. Millett, John D. *Allocation Decisions in Higher Education.* Washington, DC: Academy for Educational Development, 1975. ED 116 573. 57 pp.

Contends that the allocation of resources in higher education is a major problem. Describes 3 models which may be used: market-price (the resources are given to programs that enroll the greatest numbers of students), planning mechanism (some departments may not have enough students to pay the costs of operating the department), and mixed-economy mechanism (a combination of the other 2 models).

142. ———. *Managing Turbulence and Change.* New Directions for Higher Education, No. 19. San Francisco, CA: Jossey-Bass, 1977. 100 pp.

Seven contributors describe present matters of concern to those in higher education and predict problems which will continue into the 1980s. Management, governance, and leadership are some topics which are examined.

143. Mortimer, Kenneth P., and Tierney, Michael L. *The Three ''R's'' of the Eighties: Reduction, Reallocation, and Retrenchment.* AAHE-ERIC/Higher Education Research Report No. 4. Washington, DC: American Association for Higher Education, 1979. 84 pp.

Only a few institutions in the 1980s will escape the effects of lowered enrollments and fewer resources. Among the major changes will be: a decrease of 15 percent to 20 percent in the number of 18-year-olds between 1980 and 1990, institutional costs will rise faster than revenues, and a shift to career-oriented programs. Tables and an excellent appendix are valuable.

144. National Board on Graduate Education. *Outlook and Opportunities for Graduate Education.* Final Report with Recommendations, No. 6. Washington, DC: National Research Council, 1975. 73 pp.

Many problems now confronting higher education will be intensified in the 1980s. Among these problems are: reduction in financial support, less federal money for research, reduced demand for Ph.Ds, and state government concern with graduate education planning.

145. National Center for Higher Education Management Systems. *Planning, Managing, and Financing in the 1980's: Achieving Excellence, Diversity, and Access in the Context of Stable Resources and Demands for Increased Productivity.* Boulder, CO: N.C.H.E.M.S., 1978. 140 pp.

In these proceedings of the center's 1977 national assembly, predictions concerning future problems in the 1980s are discussed.

146. National Science Foundation. *Projections of Science and Engineering Doctorate Supply and Utilization 1980 and 1985.* Washington, DC: U.S. Government Printing Office, 1975. 39 pp.

New Data and new methodology were used to project science and engineering doctorate supply and utilization beyond 1980 to 1985.

147. Nielsen, Waldemar A. *The Endangered Sector.* New York: Columbia Press, 1979. 277 pp.

The "third sector" of the United States is composed of private nonprofit institutions. These institutions face serious financial problems and greater government influence. The federal government has increased its financing for student aid, research, and other facilities and also the amount of pressure on the institutions. The economic problems now projected for the coming years may cause liquidation of many private colleges and universities and higher education will suffer a great loss.

148. Sanford, Nevitt, and Axelrod, Joseph, eds. *College and Character.* Berkeley, CA: Montaigne, 1979. 278 pp.

Prominent educators give their views on subjects of current interest in higher education. Topics include: students as consumers, personal development of students, campus environments, teaching and learning, and the future of higher education.

149. Schoenfeld, Clay. *The Outreach University: A Case History in the Public Relationships of Higher Education. University of Wisconsin Extension 1885–1975.* Madison, WI: University of Wisconsin—Madison, Office of Inter-College Programs, 1977. 226 pp.

The university extension program in Wisconsin depends on several factors: good public relations which gain public support and good relations within the university to gain teaching and research cooperation from academic colleagues. The concept of service to the whole state is also important. These ideas have been successful in Wisconsin and should be of interest as more universities realize that continuing education is important for survival.

150. Shulman, Carol H. *Enrollment Trends in Higher Education.* ERIC/Higher Education Research Report No. 6. Washington, DC: American Association of Higher Education, 1976. ED 129 197. 45 pp.

Although enrollments are declining and the 18- to 22-year-old group may no longer continue as the major enrollment base, perhaps the needs of older people for postsecondary education will become the new support group. Topics such as the following are discussed: historical perspective and current conditions, future developments in enrollment patterns, and current adjustment to downward enrollment trends.

151. ———. *Private Colleges: Present Conditions and Future Prospects.* ERIC/Higher Education Research Report No. 9. Washington, DC: American Association for Higher Education, 1974. ED 098 888. 54 pp.

Private higher education, which has been such an important part of the uniqueness of American higher education, faces decreasing enrollments and reduced budgets. Major topics discussed are: historical perspective, current problems in defining goals, government relations with private institutions, and financing problems in the private sector.

152. Southern Regional Education Board. *Higher Education Perspectives '78.* Atlanta, GA: Southern Regional Education Board, 1978. 47 pp.

The SREB Legislative Advisory Council met to discuss future problems on legislative agendas. Of particular interest was the description by Lyman Glenny of "Financing Higher Education in the 1980s: Fewer Students More Dollars?" Other educators discussed private higher education, health manpower, the *Bakke* decision, and state and federal influence in higher education.

153. ———. *Priorities for Postsecondary Education in the South.* Atlanta, GA: Southern Regional Education Board, 1976. 36 pp.

Gives 9 priorities for higher education in the South in a position statement. The board, which is composed of educators, legislators, and governors of 14 southern states, advises that financial problems may make it imperative that adjustments be made in many existing programs.

154. Spence, David S. *A Profile of Higher Education in the South in 1985.* Atlanta, GA: Southern Regional Education Board, 1977. 34 pp.

Projection of enrollment is the central topic in this publication. Projections are made for 1980 and 1985 and include: kinds of students, kinds of participation, faculty, and implications of enrollment changes.

155. Spies, Richard R. *The Effect of Rising Costs on College Choice.* New York: College Entrance Examination Board, 1978. 69 pp.

This study uses a group of 30 selective, expensive, private institutions and the top 18 percent scorers on SAT from 2,500 high school students, examines the possibility of these students applying to the 30 institutions. Some of the conclusions reached include the facts that high scorers are most likely to apply to private institutions with a fine academic reputation.

156. Task Force on Graduate Education. *The States and Graduate Education.* Denver, CO: Education Commission of the States, 1975. 29 pp.

Suggests that graduate education is necessary to the welfare of the nation and that an effective coalition of institutions, state and federal governments is of great importance. Many questions remain to be answered about graduate education: the kinds of graduate education the state should support, enrollment and geographical distribution of graduate programs, and institutions designated to grant Ph.D.s.

157. Texas College and University System. *Texas Higher Education in Transition.* Austin, TX: Coordinating Board, Texas College and University System, 1978. 168 pp.

Suggests ways of dealing with expected problems for 1978 and 1980 in Texas institutions of higher learning. Topics are: enrollments, student costs, finances, and other matters of concern to public and private 2- and 4-year colleges and universities.

158. U.S. Department of Labor (Bureau of Labor Statistics.) *Occupational Outlook for College Graduates 1976–77.* Bulletin 1878. Washington, DC: Government Printing Office, 1977. 266 pp.

Delineates an attempt to analyze the supply and demand for college graduates, in appropriate positions, through the 1980s. Information is given for each career, such as nature of the work, education and training needed, employment outlook, approximate salary, and working conditions.

159. ⸻. *Ph.D. Manpower: Employment Demand and Supply.* Bulletin 1860. Washington, DC: U.S. Government Printing Office, 1975. 21 pp.

Human resources data for Ph.D.s is one of the major concerns for those faculty and administrators who make policy and guide vocational choices. Professional degrees such as M.D. and D.D.S. are not included in the data. Projections are made through 1985 by using data collected from past years.

160. Wagschal, Peter H., and Kahn, Robert D., eds. *R. Buckminister Fuller on Education.* Amherst, MA: University of Massachusetts Press, 1979. 192 pp.

Views which were given 17 years ago by the inventor of the geodesic dome on higher education. He believed that faculty would have lectures televised so that they would be available at any time; information would be available over 2-way television; home study except for graduate work; and more compact, smaller campuses which would be covered with a geodesic dome.

161. Wilke, Arthur S., ed. *The Hidden Professoriate: Credentialism, Professionalism and the Tenure Crisis.* Westport, CT: Greenwood, 1979. 290 pp.

Charges that the job squeeze in the past 10 years has resulted in a "hidden professoriate" composed of graduate students and non-tenured faculty. Short-term appointments, few fringe benefits, and dismissals are sometimes the results of power politics. Nine personal case studies are used to describe campus situations.

RELATIONSHIP TO LARGER SOCIETY

162. Anderson, C. Lester, ed. *Land Grant Universities and Their Continuing Challenge.* East Lansing, MI: Michigan State University Press, 1976. 351 pp.

Discusses the history and purposes of land-grant institutions. Authorities in various subject areas comment on such fields as engineering, home economics, liberal arts, social and behavioral sciences, and others. Notabale deficiencies in these colleges are treatment of Blacks, women, other minorities, and problems of urban communities.

163. Ashby, Eric. *Adapting Universities to a Technological Society.* San Francisco, CA: Jossey-Bass, 1974. 158 pp.

Presents the belief of a noted British educator that universities should use technological advances to benefit society and also to improve the learning process.

164. Ashworth, Kenneth H. *Scholars and Statesmen.* San Francisco, CA: Jossey-Bass, 1972. 160 pp.

Examines the relationships between the federal government and institutions of higher education and warns of different goals of each, especially as they are related to institutional autonomy and diversity. The public should understand the need for academic freedom.

165. Bennis, Warren. *The Unconscious Conspiracy: Why Leaders Can't Lead.* New York: AMACOM, a division of American Management Associations, 1976. 180 pp.

The varied aspects of administration, management, and leadership are addressed in this publication. As conditions change in society, there must be leaders who are able to look into the future and plan ahead even while feeling the current pressures of the daily work. Leaders need to create an atmosphere in which people are able to work happily and creatively.

166. Berube, Maurice R. *The Urban University in America.* Westport, CT: Greenwood Press, 1978. 149 pp.

Advocates a national policy of urban-grant universities supported by the federal government with a goal of universal access to higher education. This would be a system similar to land-grant universities which do not meet the needs of urban populations. The present urban universities are frequently hostile to the minorities living near them.

167. Bledstein, Burton J. *The Culture of Professionalism: The Middle Class and the Development of Higher Education in America.* New York: Norton, 1976. 354 pp.

Analyzes middle-class way of life during the nineteenth century and describes the contributions of the American university to the growth of professionalism. Careers of 9 prominent university presidents who came to their positions in the 1860s and 1870s are discussed. A description of the colleges of that time with emphasis on students, courses offered, outside activities, and institutional activities is given. The author attempts to show the relationship among the American society and university and related changes.

168. Blocker, Clyde E.; Bender, Louis W.; and Martorana, S. V. *The Political Terrain of American Postsecondary Education.* Fort Lauderdale, FL: Nova University, 1975. 223 pp.

Tries to identify and present a better understanding of the politics of postsecondary education. There are 5 primary levels: institutional, community, state, federal, and nongovernmental organizations.

169. Bowles, Frank, and De Costa, Frank A. *Between Two Worlds: A Profile of Negro Higher Education.* Study for the Carnegie Commission on Higher Education. New York: McGraw-Hill, 1971. 326 pp.

Before the 1960s the role of the historically Black college was unique and its mission was clear. The future mission of the predominately Black college is now more complex and no answers to the problems are yet available.

170. Brown, Frank, and Stent, Madelon D. *Minorities in U.S. Institutions of Higher Education.* New York: Praeger, 1977. 178 pp.

Data from several sources is used by the authors to determine social and psychological benefits gained by minorities and personal characteristics of students involved. Graduate as well as undergraduate programs are investigated. Minorities examined are American Indians, Blacks, Asian Americans, and Hispanic Americans.

171. Bushnell, David S., ed. *Help Wanted: Articulating Occupational Education at the Postsecondary Level.* Columbus, OH: Center for Vocational Education, Ohio State University, 1977. 49 pp.

The use of community resources is one phase to be considered by academic and occupational education administrators. Institutions should be more sensitive to the needs of students and community needs. Joint ventures of state and local planners with the academic community have been successful.

172. Campbell, Alexander. *The Trouble with Americans.* New York: Praeger, 1971. 215 pp.

Reflections and criticisms of a British citizen about many aspects of American culture and higher education.

173. Carnegie Commission on Higher Education. *The Campus and the City, Maximizing Assets and Reducing Liabilities.* New York: McGraw-Hill, 1972. 205 pp.

Outlines roles of various institutions in higher education and suggests ways in which they might contribute to urban areas needs. Missions and responsibilities of 2-year community colleges, comprehensive colleges, and universities are discussed. Problems of importance which these institutions may face are: number of spaces, equal access, remedial work, curriculum innovations, urban studies, impact on city life, and research.

174. Cross, K. Patricia; Valley, John R.; et al. *Planning Non-Traditional Programs.* San Francisco, CA: Jossey-Bass, 1974. 263 pp.

Presents findings from several research projects which challenge traditional practices and programs in higher education. Suggestions are made to planners in colleges and universities so that programs may be adapted to changing needs.

175. Dore, Ronald P. *The Diploma Disease: Education, Qualification and Development.* Berkeley, CA: University of California Press, 1976. 214 pp.

Examinations were devised originally to weed out the best qualified for a job. They have evolved into tickets for a job. In Europe, especially, diplomas began to be required for many jobs. Money and power were the ultimate aims for a degree rather than learning in order to do a job well or just simply to enjoy learning.

176. Dressel, Paul L., and Faricy, William H. *Return to Responsibility: Constraints on Autonomy in Higher Education.* San Francisco, CA: Jossey-Bass, 1972. 232 pp.

Describes growth of constraints on the autonomy of the modern university. Growth of institutions of higher learning has necessitated the allocation of more public resources to higher education. Power struggles of groups within the university threaten the freedom of the whole university.

177. Driver, Christopher P. *The Exploding University.* Indianapolis, IN: Bobbs-Merrill, 1972. 377 pp.

Describes several universities in different countries and periods in relation to the existing society. Some universities examined are: Balliol College at Oxford; universities at Manchester and Lancaster; Berkeley; Chicago; universities of Bologna, Vincennes, and Tokyo. The second half of the book deals with access, governance, and function of the university.

178. Gould, Samuel B. *Today's Academic Condition.* New York: McGraw-Hill, 1970. 101 pp.

Describes the academic situation of 1970. Gould, former chancellor of the State University of New York, mentions various pressures of the time, and evaluates them as he tries to understand them. Believes that the university will meet the challenge of a changing society now and in the future.

179. Handlin, Oscar, and Handlin, Mary F. *The American College and American Culture.* New York: McGraw-Hill, 1970. 104 pp.

The historical evaluation of the role of socialization is considered in this description of development in the United States. Religion is a prominent factor in the establishment of many institutions of higher learning. Students consider higher education as a means for social mobility.

180. Hawkins, Hugh. *Between Harvard and America: The Educational Leadership of Charles W. Eliot.* New York: Oxford University Press, 1972. 416 pp.

Traces the relationships of the institution's history and Eliot and their interaction with American society. During his years as president of Harvard, Eliot made many internal administrative changes, as well as academic reforms. The elective system, professsional schools, written classroom examinations, and other innovations helped to upgrade Harvard and eventually were accepted in other institutions. College preparation and admission requirements resulted in changes in high school curriculum.

181. Hobbs, Nicholas, ed. *The Prospects for Higher Education.* Atlanta, GA: Southern Newspaper Publishers Association Foundation, 1971. 95 pp.

Discusses 3 issues of importance in higher education as they were presented at a seminar: the relationship of the college or university to contemporary society; the doctrine of equal access to opportunity and influence of radical tradition in higher education; and two elements in American society, "participatory democracy" and "Black identity" or "personal awareness." Participants included newspapermen, educators, and publishers.

182. Hodgkinson, Harold L. *Institutions in Transition: A Profile of Change in Higher Education.* Carnegie Commission on Higher Education. New York: McGraw-Hill, 1971. 295 pp.

Uses data from the 1950s and 1960s to identify changes in higher education and predict trends for the 1970s. Two changes of note are greater diversity in students and a decrease in institutional diversity. Faculty interest in research is more pronounced and there is less reward for teaching.

183. Jencks, Christopher, et al. *Inequality: A Reassessment of the Effect of Family and Schooling in America.* New York: Basic Books, 1972. 399 pp.

Assumptions in the early sixties among educators included that adult inequalities could be eliminated by equalizing inputs which children brought with them into the schools. (Headstart is an example of programs designed to accomplish this .) Considers that family background rather than quality of education is most important and that schools should improve the quality of life. Adult inequality should be changed in other ways.

184. Kriegel, Leonard. *Working Through: A Teacher's Journey in the Urban University.* New York: Saturday Review, 1972. 210 pp.

An autobiographical description of experiences as student and English professor at Columbia, N.Y.U., C.C.N.Y., and Long Island University.

185. Kruytbosch, Carlos E., and Messinger, Sheldon L., eds. *The State of the University.* Beverly Hills, CA: Sage, 1970. 379 pp.

Describes authority in higher education: those who use it, changes in authority, and prospects for the future. Also comments on changes in the relationship of the university and society. Questions concern use of authority and freedom within the university.

186. Laub, Julian Martin. *College and Community Development: A Socioeconomic Analysis for Urban and Regional Growth.* New York: Praeger, 1972. 304 pp.
Describes the social and economic impacts of colleges in rural and urban areas and also predicts changes which may occur. Educational, city, county, and regional planners will find this book helpful.

187. Lipset, Seymour, ed. *The Third Century: America as a Post-Industrial Society.* Stanford, CA: Hoover Institution Press, 1979. 468 pp.
Sixteen scholars have contributed to this publication which concerns the social and political problems facing postindustrial America. Solutions for the future issues are suggested in such topics as: mass media, the presidency, political parties, the university, minorities, labor, national values, and futurology.

188. Lipset, Seymour M., and Riesman, David. *Education and Politics at Harvard.* Carnegie Commission on Higher Education. New York: McGraw-Hill, 1975. 440 pp.
Describes the university and its relationship to society in 2 sections: "Political Controversies at Harvard, 1963–1974" and "Educational Reform at Harvard College: Meritocracy and Its Adversaries."

189. Lowi, Theodore J. *The Politics of Disorder.* New York: Basic Books, 1971. 193 pp.
Attempts to show how universities should respond to social interests represented by the campus disorders of the late sixties and early seventies. Radical changes in society normally precede reconstruction in higher education.

190. Mills, Olive, and Wilson, Logan, eds. *Universal Higher Education: Costs, Benefits, Options.* Washington, DC: American Council on Education, 1972. 342 pp.
Differing views of educators, concerning open access to education, are apparent in this report of the fifty-fourth annual meeting of the American Council on Higher Education. Studies were presented concerning open admissions at CUNY, the access system in California, and Britain's Open University. The financial costs and benefits to society were considered.

191. Mitchell, Howard, and Adelson, Daniel, eds. *The University and the Urban Crisis.* Vol. 2. New York: Behavioral Publications, 1974. 212 pp.
Sets out ways in which American higher education should respond to the problems of the larger community. Any venture in this field should be carefully planned and have clearly stated goals, objectives, and programs.

192. Morris, Lorenzo. *Elusive Equality: The Status of Black Americans in Higher Education.* Institute for the Study of Educational Policy. Washington, DC: Harvard University Press, 1979. 369 pp.
Investigates equal opportunity for Black Americans in higher education, especially during the years 1975 through 1977. Specific topics are: access, equalitarian motives, inequality measurement, Black institutions, and graduate and professional education.

193. Murphy, Thomas P., ed. *Universities in the Urban Crisis.* New York: Dunellen, 1975. 418 pp.

Divided into 4 areas: universities and government, universities and the community, universities and students, and the internal dynamics and the future of urban higher education. Contributors from government, higher education, and research centers have written chapters on different aspects of higher education in urban areas.

194. Nagai, Michio. *An Owl before Dusk?* Carnegie Commission on Higher Education. New York: McGraw-Hill, 1975. 49 pp.
Defines the role of higher education as contributing to a balanced industrial society which has been redesigned to cope with problems of national, international, and global importance. Proposals are made for achieving these goals in the future.

195. Nash, George, et al. *The University and the City.* Carnegie Commission on Higher Education. New York: McGraw-Hill, 1973. 151 pp.
Presents case studies of 8 institutions and their involvement with the urban areas in which they are located; University of Chicago, Southern Illinois, University of California at Los Angeles, Our Lady of the Lake, Morgan State, Northeastern, Columbus, and Wayne State. The role of educational institutions is the instruction, growth, and development of students. Each one must determine its service to the community.

196. Newman, Frank, et al. *Report on Higher Education.* U.S. Department of H.E.W., Office of Education. Washington, DC: U.S. Government Printing Office, 1971. 130 pp.
The first Newman report found that there were many dropouts in education, there was too rigid a structure, financial problems were increasing, minority access was still a problem, and alternative ways of obtaining credentials should be found.

197. Norris, Donald M.; Lasher, W. F.; and Brandt, Floyd S. *Manpower Studies in Postsecondary Education.* ERIC/Higher Education Research Report No. 10. Washington, DC: American Association of Higher Education, 1977. ED 149 661. 53 pp.
Due to the fact that American society is changing rapidly, a 2- to 3-year projection in manpower studies seems to be the maximum for accuracy. Recommends, instead of fixed coefficient models, new market-responsive models which incorporate the market plan interaction between the supply of educated people and the demand for them.

198. Pace, Charles Robert. *Measuring Outcomes of College: Fifty Years of Findings and Recommendations for the Future.* San Francisco, CA: Jossey-Bass, 1979. 188 pp.
The benefits of higher education to the individual and to the larger society are examined in this book. Achievement tests reveal attainment of students in knowledge, understanding, and intellectual skills. Participation of college graduates in business, civic, and cultural affairs is explored. Lists ideas for the future, such as: new kinds of achievement measures, more useful surveys of alumni, and models for more effective institutional studies.

199. Parker, Gail Thain. *The Writing on the Wall: Inside Higher Education in America.* New York: Simon and Schuster, 1979. 208 pp.
Criticizes many aspects of higher education, such as: college degrees no longer guarantee financial success; curricula is not relevant to the job market; recruitment policies are not always ethical in their promises; power plays are time-consuming; and decisions are made slowly. Suggests eliminating tenure and the bachelor's degree and

making clear distinction between liberal arts, vocational, and professional training.

200. Perkins, James A. *Is the University an Agent for Social Reform?* New York: Interbook, 1973. 30 pp.

The university is an agent for social reform in the sense that graduates will be educated to analyze situations and be precise in evaluations. The university is a corporate institution but it is also an academic community. The influence of educated persons can bring about changes in society.

201. Pifer, Alan. *Foundations and Public Policy Formation.* Carnegie Corporation of New York. New York: McGraw-Hill, 1974. 14 pp.

Considers the controversial question of tax-exempt foundations and their participation in public policy formation. Since higher education institutions are frequently the recipients of financial assistance from foundations, this report from the Carnegie Corporation will be of interest.

202. Spitzberg, Irving J., Jr., ed. *Universities and the International Order.* 4 vol. Council on International Studies. Amherst, NY: State University of New York at Buffalo, 1979.

This 4-vol. set is concerned with the relationship of universities and the New International Order. Each vol. contains discussions concerning transfer of knowledge between the developed and the developing worlds and planning for educational change in Third World and postindustrial countries.

203. Stephens, Michael D., and Roderick, Gordon W., eds. *Higher Education Alternatives.* New York: Longman, 1978. 176 pp.

Discusses higher education and how it should be made available to the majority of citizens. Alternatives to traditional education are suggested. Access, developing countries, industry's involvement, mass media, the open university, and other aspects of higher education are described. Trends and future policies are predicted in the final chapter.

204. Task Force to the Secretary of Health, Education, and Welfare. *The Second Newman Report; National Policy and Higher Education.* Cambridge, MA: MIT Press, 1973. 227 pp.

The report discusses the need for better training for more citizens. Greater access to more diverse institutions by a growing number of students may require a need for more government assistance.

205. Touraine, Alain, ed. *The Academic System in American Society.* Carnegie Commission on Higher Education. New York: McGraw-Hill, 1974. 319 pp.

By a French neo-Marxist, this study views higher education as a part of society rather than an autonomous institution and uses the theme that American higher education has become an arm of the ruling class and a part of economic, military, and political institutions.

206. Ulam, Adam. *Fall of the American University.* La Salle, IL: Library Press, 1972. 217 pp.

A critical commentary on political and social movements in higher education in recent years.

207. Walberg, Herbert J., and Kopan, Andrew T., eds. *Rethinking Urban Education.* San Francisco, CA: Jossey-Bass, 1972. 334 pp.

Outlines contemporary issues in urban education under 6 perspectives and lists questions to be answered. The perspectives are: psychological, evaluation, sociological, systems, historical, and philosophical.

208. Walizer, Michael H., and Herriott, Robert E. *The Impact of College on Students' Competence to Function in a Learning Society.* Iowa City, IA: American College Testing Program, 1971. 43 pp.

Discusses personal characteristics of college graduates and noncollege graduates. College graduates assume leadership roles more frequently in society and are more independent, autonomous, flexible, and socially involved. The research shows that student change is related to student characteristics upon entrance to college and also to the social structure of the college attended.

209. Westerhoff, John H., ed. *Church Ministry in Higher Education: Papers and Responses Presented to a Conference at Duke Divinity School, January 27–28, 1978.* New York: United Ministries in Higher Education, 1978. 294 pp.

Includes papers from a conference for campus ministers in the South. Questions which were discussed included: academic study of religion, role of the church in secular higher education, and more involvement of women and minorities in campus religious groups. The problems of the Black church-related college were presented by the president of Dillard University, Samuel Dubois Cook.

210. Wolfle, Dael. *The Home of Science: The Role of the University.* Profile prepared for the Carnegie Commission on Higher Education. New York: McGraw-Hill, 1972. 202 pp.

Intellectual and economic influences have been instrumental in the evolution of the American university as the principal institution of science and research activities. The involvement of the federal government in the growth of university science is shown by monetary support given.

SIZE OF THE ESTABLISHMENT

211. National Center for Education Statistics. *Higher Education General Information Survey HEGIS.* Washington, DC: U.S. Department of Health, Education, and Welfare.

Each fall all 2- and 4-year public and nonpublic institutions of higher learning contribute statistics of many kinds to HEW for the HEGIS report. These data are probably the most complete of any statistical information available.

TERMINOLOGY

212. Carnegie Council on Policy Studies in Higher Education. *A Classification of Institutions of Higher Education.* Report of the Carnegie Council on Policy Studies in Higher Education. Berkeley, CA: CCPSHE, 1976. 126 pp.

This classification scheme groups institutions by mission: doctoral-granting universities, comprehensive universities, liberal arts colleges, 2-year institutions, and specialized or professional institutions. There are subgroupings within each category and a division between public and private governance.

213. Cloud, Sherrill, comp. *A Glossary of Standard Terminology for Postsecondary Education. 1978–79.* Boulder, CO: National Center for Higher Education Management Systems, 1979. 109 pp.

A standarized terminology is necessary in reporting data dealing with institutions, governmental agencies, and educational associations. The glossary reflects the compiler's experience at NCHEMS in monitoring national and state data-collection efforts. The arrangement is alphabetical, with an emphasis on terms used in budgeting and finance, systems, exporting data, and state and federal government operations. The appendix groups the terms under 6 categories: academic-related, facilities-related, financial-related, general, personnel-related and employer characteristics, and student-related and student characteristics.

214. Collier, Douglas J. *Program Classification Structure: Second Edition*. Technical Report 101. Boulder, CO: National Center for Higher Education Management Systems, 1977. 65 pp.
The accomplishment of an institution's objectives and its operations to meet those objectives may be examined more effectively if the categories and definitions are standardized. The Program Classification Structure (PCS) is used by state-level agencies, federal education planning agencies, and institutions of higher education as a help in standardizing terminology.

215. Lange, Carl J. "Higher and Postsecondary Education: An Over-View." In *Handbook on Contemporary Education*, edited by S. E. Goodman. New York: Bowker, 1976, pp. 35–38
While higher education is limited to the 2,600 4-year colleges and universities and community and junior colleges, postsecondary education includes this area plus all other agents of education beyond the high school, such as proprietary schools, business colleges, technical institutes, and correspondence courses. The goal of extending access to more students has been illustrated in a major way by the community colleges. Collective bargaining, management techniques, faculty development, and faculty evaluation are current areas of interest.

216. Sell, G. Roger. *Adult/Continuing Education: A Handbook of Standard Terminology for Describing the Learning Activities of Adults*. National Center for Education Statistics. Boulder, CO: National Center for Higher Education Management Systems, 1978. 248 pp.
This handbook supplies precise terms and definitions which may be used to describe the learning activities of adults. Use of these terms by those institutions which serve adult learners can be helpful as they communicate with each other.

UNIQUE CHARACTERISTICS

217. Adkins, Douglas L. *The Great American Degree Machine: An Economic Analysis of the Human Resource Output of Higher Education*. Carnegie Commission on Higher Education. New York: McGraw-Hill, 1975. 663 pp.
Studies the total number of holders of bachelor's and advanced degrees from 1930 to 1971 and gives annual estimates of degree holders in 44 fields. Describes 4 models that might account for the number of degrees awarded. Concludes that the "sociogenic" model is the one of most value since it shows the desire for upward social mobility.

218. Ashby, Eric. *Any Person, Any Study: An Essay on Higher Education in the United States*. New York: McGraw-Hill, 1971. 110 pp.
Describes both strengths and weaknesses of American higher education. One weakness is high attrition rate, which is partially the

result of admission standards and lack of financial support for students. Some strengths are land-grant colleges, the quality of research done in the universities, lack of state entrance examinations resulting in a diversity of programs, and the effective graduate and professional schools.

219. Bailey, Frederick George. *Morality and Expediency: The Folklore of Academic Politics*. Chicago: Aldine, 1977. 230 pp.
Explores the politics of academia from the standpoint of an anthropologist. Finds that many faculty believe they live in an orderly and rational world and are still able to rationalize as they compromise their principles to solve problems in the real world.

220. Ben-David, Joseph. *American Higher Education: Directions Old and New*. New York: McGraw-Hill, 1972. 137 pp.
Observes major trends in American higher education and comments on many specific characteristics, such as institutional autonomy, operation, administrative problems, teaching and research, general education, and egalitarianism.

221. Butler, Addie Louise Joyner. *The Distinctive Black College: Talladega, Tuskegee and Morehouse*. Metuchen, NJ: Scarecrow, 1977. 169 pp.
Gives short historical sketches of 3 interesting and important Black institutions: Talladega, Tuskegee, and Morehouse. Good background information for a study of significant Black colleges.

222. Carnegie Commission on Higher Education. *Sponsored Research of the Carnegie Commission on Higher Education*. New York: McGraw-Hill, 1975. 397 pp.
During the 6 years of the Commission's existence comprehensive studies have been made of colleges and universities. This book contains the abstracts of those studies.

223. Collier, Gerald; Tomlinson, Peter; and Wilson, John, eds. *Values and Moral Development in Higher Education*. New York: Wiley, 1974. 225 pp.
The study is based on a basic definition of moral development: A morally developed person is one who is able to use freedom in a responsible way and does not accept an imposed ideology. Contributions to moral development may be made by academic study of philosophy, literature, drama, theology, history, and science.

224. Furniss, W. Todd, ed. *Higher Education for Everybody*. Washington, DC: American Council on Education, 1971. 284 pp.
Discusses universal education with attention to desirability, feasibility, and support by society. Some circumstances which may affect feasibility are: admissions policies, quality, fundamentals of reform, alternatives to traditional college instruction, adult students, and backgrounds of students.

225. Helsabeck, Robert E. *The Compound System: A Conceptual Framework for Effective Decisionmaking in Colleges*. Center for Research and Development in Higher Education. Berkeley, CA: University of California, 1973. 144 pp.
There are 2 main levels of decision making in colleges. One concerns goal setting; the faculty are involved in many of these decisions. The other level entails the decisions involved in running the college or university. Administrators generally make decisions at

this second level. The author uses charts to show the relationship between the decision-making section and organizational effectiveness.

226. Ladd, Dwight R. *Change in Educational Policy: Self Studies in Selected Colleges and Universities.* New York: McGraw-Hill, 1970. 222 pp.

Explains how change was undertaken at 11 institutions. The process of change in an academic atmosphere is accomplished gradually. It is possible to improve the quality of teaching, improve the curriculum, and achieve better results from advising procedures.

227. MacDonald, Gary B., ed. *Five Experimental Colleges: Bensalem, Antioch-Putney, Franconia, Old Westbury, Fairhaven.* New York: Harper and Row, 1973. 257 pp.

Educational change and innovation come about in many ways in higher education. Case studies of 5 experimental colleges, leaders in reform movements, are related by faculty, students, and administrators.

228. Mayhew, Lewis B. *The Carnegie Commission on Higher Education: A Critical Analysis of the Reports and Recommendations.* San Francisco, CA: Jossey-Bass, 1974. 441 pp.

Comments on attempts by the Carnegie Commission to make a comprehensive survey of higher education, to analyze its parts, and to make recommendations for the future. Each report is critically reviewed in the second chapter.

229. Miller, Jerry W., and Mills, Olive. *Credentialing Educational Accomplishments.* Task Force on Educational Credit and Credentials. Washington, DC: American Council on Education, 1978. 175 pp.

Modification of the system for awarding credit and credentials is needed in order to serve more adequately educational and social needs. Many aspects of educational credit and credentials are examined in this publication. Social uses of credentials relate to qualification for employment and ability to communicate meaning of credentials.

230. Montefiore, Alan, ed. *Neutrality and Impartiality: The University and Political Commitment.* New York: Cambridge University Press, 1975. 292 pp.

Records how some educators in higher education faced and reacted to the attacks against academic neutrality and impartiality in the late sixties and early seventies. The first part of the book attempts to define the terms used: neutrality, impartiality, disinterestedness, and independence as they are related to the academic context.

231. Niblett, W. Roy. *Universities between Two Worlds.* London: University of London press, 1974. 179 pp.

Universities are under attack from many directions and the pressures are of great intensity. There is danger of becoming too narrowly utilitarian. There should be scholarship and action on campus. The university should be a bridge from the past into the future and also meet the personal education needs of the students.

232. Smith, Bardwell L., et al. *The Tenure Debate.* San Francisco, CA: Jossey-Bass, 1973. 254 pp.

Advocates further inquiry into the tenure question because not enough studies have been done. The book is divided into 3 major sections: "Dilemmas of Tenure," proposed reforms for tenure, and problems of tenure as they are related to faculty unions.

233. Tubbs, Walter E., Jr., ed. *Toward A Community of Seekers: A Report on Experimental Higher Education.* Lincoln, NE: University of Nebraska, 1972. 299 pp.

A report on the National Symposium on Experimental Higher Education. An effort is made to list experimental programs in operation, enumerate the problems encountered, and evaluate the benefits of the innovative programs. The 3 appendices give further information on admissions, external degrees and role of the federal government in accreditation. A list of experimental colleges is included.

234. Walton, Clarence C., and Bolman, Frederick, de W., eds. *Disorders in Higher Education.* Englewood Cliffs, NJ: Prentice-Hall, 1979. 212 pp.

A collection of papers on the issues and opportunities which will confront higher education in the future. Current problems are discussed. The responsibility of all members of the college or university to the advancement of learning is the main theme. Recommendations are made which should help restore public confidence in higher education and improve the service rendered to society by higher education.

235. Williams, Thomas T., ed. *The Unique Resources of the 1890 Land Grant Institutions and Implications for International Development.* Revised edition. Southern University Unemployment-Underemployment Institute. Baton Rouge, LA: Louisiana State University, 1979. 50 pp.

Outlines the role of the 1890 land-grant institutions as agents for change and development in the United States. These institutions are able to help developing nations of the world to meet educational, economic, and social needs because of previous experiences in the United States.

236. Willie, Charles V., and Edmonds, Ronald R., eds. *Black Colleges in America: Challenge, Development, Survival.* New York: Teachers College Press, 1978. 292 pp.

Sixteen Black administrators and faculty members at Black institutions provide information on the history and purpose of Black colleges, teaching and learning, administration financing, and governance. They show that a great deal has been accomplished by Black colleges, even under difficult conditions.

Teaching-Learning Environment

CONTINUING EDUCATION (LIFELONG LEARNING)

237. Advisory Panel on Research Needs in Lifelong Learning during Adulthood. *Lifelong Learning during Adulthood.* New York: College Entrance Examination Board, 1978. 59 pp.

A summary of current research in lifelong learning is listed and the need for further research is recommended. Priority areas for needed research are: adult learners; providers of learning opportunities, society; and the interactions of learners, providers, and society.

238. Apps, Jerold W. *Problems in Continuing Education.* New York: McGraw-Hill, 1979. 204 pp.

Describes the characteristics of adult learners. Curricula and procedures may need to be adapted to meet the needs of these students. More research is needed.

239. ———. *Study Skills for Those Adults Returning to School.* New York: McGraw-Hill, 1978. 237 pp.

Anticipates the difficulties faced by returning students. Gives advice on: obtaining financial aids, using the library, reading a book, writing a research paper, and many other problems. Written in a simple style so that any returning student may use it.

240. Carnegie Commisssion on Higher Education. *Toward A Learning Society: Alternative Channels to Life, Work and Service.* New York: McGraw-Hill, 1973. 122 pp.

Concerns the adult or nontraditional student in higher education. Colleges and universities should make more effort to attract these students and to provide courses of interest for them.

241. Cross, K. Patricia. *The Missing Link: Connecting Adult Learners to Learning Resources.* Princeton, NJ: College Board, 1978. 79 pp.

Describes current trends in adult learning. Educators need to supply the ''missing link'' which can connect learning resources to the millions of people interested in continuing their education. Three areas need attention: easier access for those who wish to learn, information to adult learners about available resources, and counseling in order to match learners to resources.

242. Eldred, Marilou D., and Marineau, Catherine. *Adult Baccalaureate Programs.* AAHE-ERIC/Higher Education Research Report No 9, Washington, DC: American Association for Higher Education, 1979. ED 180 328. 65 pp.

The awareness of the trend for lifelong learning and the bolstering of enrollments with adult learners beyond the traditional 18- to 22-year-old groups are 2 reasons for colleges' becoming interested in adult learners. Clientele, access to degree programs, institutional contexts of adult degree programs, and academic components are major topics discussed.

243. Ellwood, Caroline. *Adult Learning Today: A New Role for the Universities?* Beverly Hills, CA: Sage, 1977. 265 pp.

Describes and analyzes adult education in British universities. The British university has offered liberal studies of a university standard and nonvocational nature but has recently become interested in vocational programs for adults. The American universities began with county extension work and recently have become interested in technical, vocational, and adult education. Both countries are now developing programs to meet lifelong learning needs.

244. Gaylord Professional Publicators. *Continuing Education: A Guide to Career Development Programs.* Syracuse, NY: Gaylord Professional Publications, 1977. 696 pp.

Describes continuing education programs (arranged by state) of 2,000 schools, colleges, and other institutions. The second section offers an arrangement by 200 subject and career areas. Organizations in continuing education are also listed.

245. Gilder, Jamison, ed. *Policies for Lifelong Education.* Washington, DC: American Association of Community and Junior Colleges, 1979. 128 pp.

A 3-year study is underway with the objective of development of new policies on lifelong education. Recommendations for a more effective approach are listed.

246. Gross, Ronald. *Diversity in Higher Education: Reform in the Colleges.* Bloomington, IN: Phi Delta Kappa, 1976. 28 pp.

Discusses innovations and reforms in higher education and outlines concepts, such as individualized learning, planning portfolio, access, the learning contract and the teaching/learning relationship. Lifelong education will cause many changes in teaching styles.

247. Hesburgh, Theodore M.; Miller, Paul A.; and Wharton, Clifton R., Jr. *Patterns for Lifelong Learning.* San Francisco, CA: Jossey-Bass, 1973. 135 pp.

Delineates the nature of a learning society and makes recommendations which will be helpful in achieving this ideal. Michigan State University is used to illustrate what a large land-grant university has accomplished toward its commitment to lifelong learning.

248. Houle, Cyril O. *The Design of Education.* San Francisco, CA: Jossey-Bass, 1972. 323 pp.

A historical account of adult education written by a leader in this field. Current practices may be improved by considering the history of this movement.

249. ———. *Residential Continuing Education.* Syracuse, NY: Syracuse University Publications in Continuing Education, 1971. 86 pp.

Describes the historical background for continuing education, using Chautauqua agricultural short courses and teacher institutes as illustrations.

250. Jacobson, Myrtle S. *Night and Day: The Interaction between an Academic Institution and Its Evening College.* Metuchen, NJ: Scarecrow, 1970. 358 pp.

Investigates the problems which arise between the evening division of Brooklyn College, the School of General Studies, and the parent organization. The evening division is considered a second-class section by many because it has different standards of admission, lower faculty pay, and a different clientele from the main part of the college. The evening classes are generally made up of people with full-time jobs who wish to continue their education.

251. Kersh, Bert Y., et al. *Faculty Development for Inservice Education in the Schools.* Washington, DC: American Association of Colleges for Teacher Education, 1978. 62 pp.

Intends to contribute to the awareness of college and university faculty in education of the current issues and problems in continuing education of public school teachers. There is also information concerning different approaches used by colleges and universities as they try to upgrade staff development services to schools.

252. Knowles, Malcolm. *The Adult Learner: A Neglected Species*. Building Blocks of Human Potential Series. Houston, TX: Gulf Publishing, 1973. 244 pp.

Based on research conducted since 1973. Theories on adult development and the adult learning process are discussed.

253. ———. *The Modern Practice of Adult Education: Andragogy versus Pedagogy*. New York: Association Press, 1970. 384 pp.

Discusses differences in planning teaching/learning experiences for adults. Purposes and objectives used in developing a program and evaluation processes are described in a handbook for those interested in adult learning, both teachers and learners.

254. Knox, Alan B. *Adult Development and Learning*. San Francisco, CA: Jossey-Bass, 1977. 679 pp.

A handbook for those people interested in adult learning and/or continuing education. There is information on internal and external factors which inhibit or facilitate learning. The book is comprehensive and informative on the ways in which adults adapt, learn, and grow.

255. LeBreton, Preston P., et al., eds. *The Evaluation of Continuing Education for Professionals: A Systems View*. Seattle, WA: University of Washington, 1979. 416 pp.

Evaluation of continuing education programs for professionals and reports of implemented evaluation systems are contained within this book. Models developed by persons in continuing education are described for professions such as those in allied health, business and management, librarianship, public affairs, and law.

256. Lengrand, Paul. *An Introduction to Lifelong Education*. Paris: UNESCO Press, 1975. ED 118 024. 156 pp.

Describes lifelong education as a series of events and achievements from birth until death. The needs of the learner should determine the education offered.

257. Lowe, John. *The Education of Adults: A World Perspective*. Paris: UNESCO Press, 1975. 229 pp.

Provides a good beginning for understanding adult education as an international undertaking. The national interest is the motivating force for providing adult education in many of the developing countries of the world.

258. O'Keefe, Michael. *The Adult, Education, and Public Policy*. Palo Alto, CA: Aspen Institute for Humanistic Studies, 1977. 63 pp.

O'Keefe predicts less support by government for adult education in future years and recognizes that women, minorities, and other under-educated people may need help in order to reach their potential.

259. Portman, David N. *The Universities and the Public: A History of Higher Adult Education in the United States*. Chicago: Nelson-Hall, 1978. 214 pp.

General extension services, community services, and evening college classes are discussed in this book. Initially, a peak was reached with Chautauqua and experiments with extension work in the 1890s. In 1907 the extension division of the University of Wisconsin began a new wave of interest with a commitment to higher adult education. The development of adult education is traced giving characteristics of each period and people of importance. problems encountered currently in adult education are also included.

260. Shay, Thomas M., and Engdahl, Lilla E. *Extended Degree Programs in the West*. Boulder, CO: Western Interstate Commission for Higher Education, 1976. 88 pp.

Nontraditional degree-oriented programs are surveyed in this report and recommendations are made. Also included are the survey instrument, lists of institutions with programs offered, and results of survey questionnaire.

261. Shulman, Carol H. *Premises and Programs for a Learning Society*. ERIC/Higher Education Research Report No. 8. Washington, DC: American Association for Higher Education, 1975. ED 118 024. 48 pp.

A timely and well-documented alert to the concepts of a lifelong learning society that accommodates to changing social and personal goals. Postsecondary education is reexamined, the adult population is defined as special new learners, and developments toward a learning society are major topics.

262. Thomson, Frances C., ed. *The New York Times Guide to Continuing Education in America*. New York: Quadrangle, 1972. 811 pp.

Lists courses available to adults who wish to continue to learn. The first 79 pages constitute an overview of adult education in relation to present society and explain terms used in higher education. The remaining pages list alphabetically, by state, institutions of higher learning, with descriptions, and correspondence schools.

263. Troutt, Roy. *Special Degree Programs for Adults*. Iowa City, IA: American College Testing Program, 1971. 69 pp.

Explores nontraditional programs in higher education. American colleges have been guilty of discrimination against adult students but are now recognizing their needs. Special programs are in process of development.

264. UNESCO and the International Association of Universities. *Lifelong Education and University Resources*. Paris: UNESCO, 1978. 193 pp.

Studies the effects of lifelong learning on the use of university resources. Discussed in the study are: Sweden, Quebec, Canada, Geneva, Zambia, Venezuela, Poland, Ghana, and France. Situations vary greatly in these countries but trends are noted by the authors.

265. Weinstock, Ruth. *The Graying of the Campus*. New York: Educational Facilities Laboratory, 1978. 160 pp.

Challenges university administrators to meet the educational needs of those students over 55 who are enrolling in large numbers. Over 2 million have enrolled within the past 10 years. Some adjustments will be necessary to accommodate the potential enrollment of this group. Curriculum, financing, physical barriers, and political problems are among the problems for the future.

266. Williams, Gareth L. *Towards Lifelong Education: A New Role for Higher Education Institutions*. Paris: UNESCO, 1978. 188 pp.

The issues involved in lifelong education and a review of the literature are contained in this volume. The opening chapter gives a rationale for lifelong education and the closing chapter relates principles which may mold the future. ·

CURRICULUM (LEARNING EXPERIENCES; TREATMENT PROCESS)

267. Allen, Edward L. "Three-Year Baccalaureate Programs." In *Handbook on Contemporary Education,* edited by S.E. Goodman. New York: Bowker, 1976, pp. 590–95.

These 3-year programs are carefully designed baccalaureate curricula which stress achievement and mastery of educational content. In 1973 there were 34 institutions offering 3-year baccalaureate programs. Major topics are: rationale, models, applied models, and pros and cons.

268. Axelrod, Joseph. *The University Teacher as Artist: Toward an Aesthetics of Teaching with Emphasis on the Humanities.* San Francisco, CA: Jossey-Bass, 1973. 246 pp.

On the issues involved in instructional reform in higher education. Observations of univesity classrooms and professors in the day-to-day activity of teaching and interaction with students, with interviews and tape recordings to show various teaching styles.

269. Barley, Stephen K. *Academic Quality Control: The Case of College Programs on Military Bases.* Washington, DC: American Association for Higher Education, 1979. 66 pp.

Examines the quality of off-campus courses, using those offered on military bases as case histories. The kinds of credits and courses offered, the sponsoring institution and the military base where the program is given, and competition are described. Guidelines are suggested for measuring quality. Admission policies, libraries, and other learning facilities should be examined carefully.

270. Beard, Ruth Mary; Healy, Frank G.; and Holloway, P. J. *Objectives in Higher Education.* 2d edition. London: Society for Research into Higher Education, 1974. 147 pp.

This publication is the second edition of the first vol. of a series concerning teaching/learning. Vol. 2 is titled *Aims and Techniques of Group Teaching* by M. L. J. Abercrombie and Vol. 3 is *Technical Aids to Teaching in Higher Education* by Colin Flood Page. These publications contain theories and experimental research, as well as specific examples of various learning experiences.

271. Bengelsdorf, Winnie. "Ethnic Studies in Higher Education," In *Handbook on Contemporary Education.* edited by S. E. Goodman. New York: Bowker, 1976, pp. 506–10.

Major programs in ethnic studies are identified at approximately 358 colleges and minor programs at about 186 institutions. Courses in Black studies rank first. Major topics discussed are: review of recent literature and developments, specific programs, and current controversies.

272. Bonham, George W., ed. *Great Core Curriculum Debate: Education as a Mirror of Culture.* New Rochelle, NY: Change Magazine, 1979. 102 pp.

Includes the 1978 "Harvard Report on the Core Curriculum," designed for the improvement of Harvard undergraduate education. Educators in higher education comment on issues and problems involved. The book concludes with "An Alternative: Yale's Dahl Report."

273. Boyer, Ernest L., and Kaplan, Martin. *Educating for Survival.* New Rochelle, NY: Change Magazine, 1977. 79 pp.

The U. S. Commissioner of Education and his executive assistant give their views on a core curriculum in higher education which is concerned with universal questions past, present, and future and look at the past 300 years in education as a basis for their conclusions.

274. Burnett, Collins W., and Badger, Frank W., eds. *The Learning Climate in the Liberal Arts College: An Annotated Bibliography.* Charleston, WV: Morris Harvey College, 1970. 87 pp.

This review of the literature for the 1950s and the 1960s is organized into the liberal arts approach curriculum, teaching methods and media, and the teaching-learning process.

275. Burns, Richard W., and Brooks, Gary D., eds. *Curriculum Design in a Changing Society.* Englewood Cliffs, NJ: Educational Technology, 1970. 353 pp.

Covers most major new developments in curriculum development in American education. Topics discussed are behavioral objectives, accountability, humanistic education, mass media effectiveness, and other pertinent developments.

276. Campbell, Dale T., and Korim, Andrews S. *Occupational Programs in Four-Year Colleges: Trends and Issues.* AAHE-ERIC/Higher Education Research Report No. 5. Washington, DC: American Association for Higher Education, 1979. ED 176 645. 35 pp.

Aware of the shift to occupational programs in community colleges, 4-year institutions have developed associate degree programs in order to compete for enrollment. Major topics are: status of occupational programs in 4-year colleges, shift in mission, and persistent issues and regulation in articulation.

277. Carnegie Foundation for the Advancement of Teaching. *Missions of the College Curriculum: A Contemporary Review with Suggestions.* San Francisco, CA: Jossey-Bass, 1977. 322 pp.

Considers the needs of the college to provide systematic approaches to curriculum planning in order to meet current and future problems. Suggestions are made regarding improvements in the curriculum. Some topics are: diversity, curriculum, mission of undergraduate education, general education, majors, electives, work experiences, and basic skills.

278. Collins, Stewart B. "Cooperative Education and Internships—College." In *Handbook on Contemporary Education,* edited by S. E. Goodman. New York: Bowker, 1976, pp. 585–90.

Cooperative education, which began at the University of Cincinnati in 1906, has had a slow growth; but in 1975 there were 600–700 institutions with this type of program. Major topics are: educational advantages to the student, advantages to the cooperating organization, types of programs, levels of education, conduct of programs, academic credit, administrative requirements, new and innovative programs, and the future.

279. Conrad, Clifton F. *The Undergraduate Curriculum: A Guide to Innovation and Reform.* Boulder, CO: Westview Press, 1978. 213 pp.

Changes in curriculum are generally compromises in the academic world. Designing the curriculum, getting it accepted, and making it work involve more than intellectual assent. Political and personal biases are frequently obstructive. Discusses variations in the curriculum and gives examples.

280. Cross, K. Patricia. *The Integration of Learning and Earning: Cooperative Education and Nontraditional Study.* AAHE-ERIC/Higher Education Research Report No. 4. Washington, DC: American Association for Higher Education, 1973. ED 080 100. 70 pp.

Both cooperative education and nontraditional study are perceived as ways of removing higher education from its historical isolation. The first relates students into the world of work, while the second area brings into the classroom adults who completed their college work in previous years.

281. Davies, Ivor Kevin. *The Management of Learning.* New York: McGraw-Hill, 1971. 256 pp.

Systematic instructional design is extremely important in the teaching/learning process. The introduction explains the background necessary; the 4 sections which follow are: planning, organizing, leading, and controlling. Each chapter begins with a list of learning objectives, cognitive and affective.

282. Dressel, Paul L. *College and University Curriculum.* 2d Edition. Berkeley, CA: McCutchan, 1971. 325 pp.

Surveys recent tendencies and issues in curriculum in the United States in higher education. Stresses evaluation and change.

283. Eisner, Elliott W., and Vallance, Elizabeth, eds. *Conflicting Conceptions of Curriculum.* Berkeley, CA: McCutchan, 1974. 200 pp.

Controversy occurs frequently among educators concerning the form and content of curriculum and the extended goals. Identifies and examines 5 common conceptions concerning the curriculum: development of cognitive processes, technology, self-actualization, social reconstruction, and academic rationalism, which concerns access to Western cultural tradition.

284. Epstein, Herman T. *A Strategy for Education.* New York: Oxford Univesity Press, 1970. 122 pp.

The research studies method is introduced in this study as a new and stimulating method which encourages curiosity and motivation in students.

285. Ferguson, John. *The Open University from Within.* New York: New York University Press, 1976. 165 pp.

The dean and director of Studies in Arts presents a fascinating account of the development of the British Open University. Selecting the site for headquarters about 50 miles from London, developing the staff, selecting the curiculum, and relating to the students are all a part of this development. The important role of the British Broadcasting System is acknowledged.

286. Finch, Curtis R., and Crunkilton, John R. *Curriculum Development in Vocational and Technical Education: Plan-*

ning, Content, and Implementation. Boston: Allyn and Bacon, 1978. 306 pp.

This publication will be of interest to faculty members, administrators, and educational directors in industry. The emphasis concerns the need to design the curriculum to meet the needs of industry. Plans to implement and evaluate a work-related curriculum are included.

287. Fleming, Malcolm, and Levie, W. Howard. *Instructional Message Design: Principles from the Behavioral Science.* Englewood Cliffs, NJ: Educational Technology, 1978.

Uses relevant research expressed in nontechnical language to assist professionals who design instructional materials.

288. Givens, Paul R. *Student Designed Curricula.* AAHE-ERIC/Higher Education Report. Washington, DC: American Association for Higher Education, 1972. ED 061 917. 4 pp.

Student-initiated academic planning is the theme of this report which describes curricula designed by students at 30 colleges and universities.

289. Gordon, Edmund W. *Opportunity Programs for the Disadvantaged in Higher Education.* ERIC/Higher Education Research Report No. 6. Washington, DC: American Association for Higher Education, 1975. ED 114 028. 28 pp.

The movement toward universal higher education and egalitarianism has created the need to develop programs which will help new students develop the necessary skills for academic survival. Total effort includes financial aid, tutorial support, adjusted curriculum, and behavior modification.

290. Gould, Samuel B., and Cross, K. Patricia, eds. *Explorations in Non-Traditional Study.* San Francisco, CA: Jossey-Bass, 1972. 137 pp.

Gives information about the pros and cons of nontraditional study. Some topics discussed include: lifelong learning; flexibility of curriculum; cooperation with industry, business, and governmental agencies; other local concerns; and individualized learning.

291. Grant, Gerald, et al. *On Competence: A Critical Analysis of Competence-Based Reforms in Higher Education.* San Francisco, CA: Jossey-Bass, 1979. 592 pp.

Discusses the competence approach to learning in higher education and how it affects teaching, the curriculum, and academic standards. Includes 4 years of research from competence-based institutions. The origins, accomplishments, problems, and future predictions for competence-based reforms in higher education are outlined.

292. Harrington, Elbert. *Janus on the Campus: Status of the Liberal Arts.* Vermillion, SD: Dakota Press, 1972. 90 pp.

Attempts to answer the questions concerning the status of the liberal arts. The author believes there will be a combination of past programs and changes in the future but the liberal arts will endure.

293. Hook, Sidney. *Education and the Taming of Power.* La Salle, IL: Open Court, 1973. 310 pp.

Maintains that "consumerism," the practice of allowing students to choose what they wish to study, is of little value because they are not educated enough to make intelligent decisions. Contends that John Dewey's philosophy has been misinterpreted by many educators in the university system.

294. Kaysen, Carl, ed. *Content and Context: Essays on College Education*. Carnegie Commission on Higher Education. New York: McGraw, 1973. 565 pp.

Describes the history of undergraduate curriculum. Six essays concern the content of the curriculum and 4 relate to the institutional, social, and intellectual climate of the academic environment.

295. Kockelmans, Joseph J., ed. *Interdisciplinarity and Higher Education*. University Park, PA: Pennsylvania State University Press, 1979. 372 pp.

Outlines the issues, aims, and problems which characterize the movement in higher education curriculum. The historical and philosophical background from Plato's Academy to present times is discussed. Current problems and case studies in several countries are described.

296. Kolka, James W. "Innovation." In *Handbook on Contemporary Education*, edited by S. E. Goodman. New York: Bowker, 1976, pp. 20–25.

Innovation refers to a program that introduces a significant new dimension to the academic program of the institution. Major topics are: historical antecedents, contemporary efforts at innovation, and conclusions.

297. Kreplin, Hannah S. "Credit by Examination: A Review and Analysis of the Literature." In *Handbook on Contemporary Education*, edited by S. E. Goodman. New York: Bowker, 1976, pp. 574–78.

Programs of credit by examination which provide the student with the opportunity to complete course requirements by examination have existed since the early 1920s but have become more popular since the early 1970s. Six major types of credit by examination programs are discussed.

298. Levi, Albert William. *The Humanities Today*. Bloomington, IN: Indiana University Press, 1970. 96 pp.

Defines the humanities, generally called the liberal arts, and discusses the differences and similarities to the natural and social sciences. Although there are problems in humanistic teaching and research, the humanities are important and still relevant.

299. Levine, Arthur. *Handbook on Undergraduate Curriculum*. San Francisco, CA: Jossey-Bass, 1978. 662 pp.

Describes curricular development in recent times and contains examples and illustrations. The first section of the book contains a chapter on: general education; the major; skills, tests, and grades; education for work; advising; credits and degrees; instructional methods; and the academic calendar. The second section relates the curricular views of 7 educational philosophers from John Henry Newman to Clark Kerr.

300. Levine, Arthur E., and Weingart, John R. *Reform of Undergraduate Education*. San Francisco, CA: Jossey-Bass, 1973. 160 pp.

Devotes a chapter to each of the following subjects: advisement, general education, comprehensive examinations and the senior year, majors, alternatives to departments, student-centered curricula, and grading. Two recent college graduates traveled to 26 campuses to examine their programs and to see what improvements might be made to reform the curriculum.

301. McKeachie, Wilbert J. *Teaching Tips: A Guidebook for the Beginning College Teacher*. Lexington, MA: D. C. Heath and Company, 1978. 338 pp.

Intended primarily for the beginning college teacher, gives teaching tips and notes theory and research concerning various teaching methods. A practical guide for all teachers who may need to reassess the teaching/learning process.

302. Mayhew, Lewis B. *Higher Education for Occupations*. Atlanta, GA: Southern Regional Education Board, 1974. 140 pp.

Examines the response of 2-year and 4-year institutions as the demand for occupational curricula grows. The author finds little change in traditional practice but much discussion of theory and suggestions for counseling, testing, and guidance. The most innovative developments are in engineering, community experiences in nursing, and simulated games in business.

303. Mayhew, Lewis B., and Ford, Patrick J. *Changing the Curriculum*. San Francisco, CA: Jossey-Bass, 1971. 188 pp.

Contends that the curriculum does need to be changed and that the characteristics and needs of the learner ought to be considered. One chapter describes changes which some colleges and universities have made. Another chapter includes stories of great teachers and the response of their students.

304. Mayville, William V. *Interdisciplinarity: The Mutable Paradigm*. AAHE-ERIC/Higher Education Research Report No. 9. Washington, DC: American Association for Higher Education, 1978. ED 167 043. 72 pp.

The integration of 2 or more diciplines (including concepts, methodology, and procedures) may receive more favorable attention in the 1980s than in the past due to increased complexity of modern knowledge and because of the need for academic disciplines to survive. Major topics include meaning of interdisciplinarity, educational models, and interdisciplinary programs.

305. Meinert, Charles W. *Time Shortened Degrees*. ERIC/Higher Education Research Report No. 8. Washington, DC: American Association for Higher Education, 1974. Ed 098 857. 76 pp.

The concept of the time-shortened degree is one example of accommodation that the college can make for the benefit of selected students. Major topics are: historical background, benefits of the time-shortened degree, criticisms, approaches to time shortening, and analysis.

306. Olson, Paul A. *Concepts of Career and General Education*. ERIC/Higher Education Research Report No. 8. Washington, DC: American Association for Higher Education, 1977. ED 145 761. 41 pp.

A comprehensive treatment with historical and philosophical considerations of an old-new problem of how to help students combine vocational preparation with learning experiences that help them understand a changing world and adapt to new conditions. Career education needs to be considered as a part of an education that causes the individual to be critical, to search for answers, and to live beyond the restrictions of the job.

307. Powers, Thomas F. *Educating for Careers: Policy Issues in a Time of Change*. University Park, PA: Pennsylvania State University Press, 1978. 224 pp.

Explores the issues of the current debate which concerns the proponents of a liberal arts education and those who advocate vocational or work-related education. Describes the historical, social, and vocational views of 18 people who are interested in higher education.

308. Ramsey, Paul, and Wilson, John F., eds. *The Study of Religion in Colleges and Universities*. Princeton, NJ: Princeton University Press, 1970. 353 pp.

A discussion on the place of religious study in higher education, consisting of papers from a conference at Princeton in 1968 that attempted to make a distinction between courses taught in seminaries, the liberal arts college, or graduate school. Some consideration should be given to the place and importance of religious discipline in the university.

309. Robinson, Lora H. *Renovating the Freshman Year*. AAHE-ERIC/Higher Education Report. Washington, DC: American Association for Higher Education, 1972. ED 068 075. 4 pp.

For many college freshmen, the first year is a tragedy due to large classes, poor teaching, lack of interest in the individual student, and rather boring classes. Some institutions are beginning to personalize the first year with peer-tutor programs and interdisciplinary courses with close student-faculty contact.

310. Rowntree, Derek. *Educational Technology in Curriculum Development*. New York: Harper and Row, 1974. 197 pp.

Concerns the design and evaluation of curricula and learning experiences and also how to implement and renew them. The introductory chapter is concerned with instructional objectives. There is a bibliography for further information.

311. Rudolph, Frederick. *Curriculum: A History of the American Undergraduate Course of Study since 1636*. San Francisco, CA: Jossey-Bass, 1977. 362 pp.

Begins with the curriculum set up by Henry Dunster at Harvard College in 1642 and shows its development through the years. Increasing pressure of social forces has helped to clutter the curriculum with electives, commercial subjects, and vocational courses.

312. Runkel, P.; Harrison, R.; and Runkel, M., eds. *The Changing College Classroom*. San Francisco, CA: Jossey-Bass, 1972. 359 pp.

Pictures situations in college classrooms as they existed in the early 1970s. Case studies are used to present the innovations and experiments in colleges and universities in the United States.

313. Sexton, Robert F., and Ungerer, Richard A. *Rationales for Experimental Education*. ERIC/Higher Education Research Report No. 3. Washington, DC: American Association for Higher Education, 1975. ED 111 319. 49 pp.

Learning activities outside the normal classroom environment are the basis for discussing experimental education. Major topics include the individual as learner, worker, and citizen.

314. Sherman, Lawrence W. *The Quality of Police Education: A Critical Review with Recommendations for Improving Programs in Higher Education*. National Advisory Commission on Higher Education for Police Officers. San Francisco, CA: Jossey-Bass, 1978. 278 pp.

Recommends changes in the college curriculum for police officers. More than 1,000 colleges and universities offer police career degree programs. Since the quality of many programs is poor, the commission was formed to investigate and make recommendations to improve the curriculum.

315. Shoenfeld, Janet D. *Student Initiated Changes in the Academic Curriculum*. AAHE-ERIC/Higher Education Report. Washington, DC: American Association for Higher Education, 1972. ED 065 105. 47 pp.

This survey summarized student-initiated changes in the curriculum in more than 230 different kinds of higher education institutions. Much of this student participation has come about from the student protests of the 1960s and early 1970s.

316. Shulman, Carol H. *A Look at External Degree Structures*. ERIC Clearinghouse on Higher Education. Washington, DC: American Association for Higher Education, 1972. ED 068 070. 4 pp.

Discusses different types of external degree programs such as nontraditional forms of learning and more flexible curricula. Among the unique factors of these programs are: geographically accessible learning centers, few or no residency requirements, student-designed curricula, independent study, and work-experience programs. Three factors to ensure quality in these programs are: motivated students, adequate resources, and proper guidance and rigorous assessment of the student.

317. ———. *Open Admissions in Higher Education*. ERIC Clearinghouse in Higher Education, Review 6. Washington, DC: George Washington University, 1971. ED 051 440. 17 pp.

Presents an examination of issues in an annotated bibliography of 43 items published during the last 3 years. As higher education has expanded from a universal to a mass basis, the emphasis is on open admissions and nontraditional programs.

318. Snyder, Benson R. *The Hidden Curriculum*. Cambridge, MA: MIT Press, 1971. 200 pp.

Describes the "hidden curriculum" as the academic game in which the student learns the patterns of behavior which are appropriate to the institution and which will result in a high grade with the least effort. Quotations from interviews at MIT are used. Faculty should recognize and solve this problem.

319. Steinaker, Norman W., and Bell, M. Robert. *The Experimental Taxonomy: A New Approach to Teaching and Learning*. New York: Academic Press, 1979. 198 pp.

Traces the development of a taxonomy of experience and shows its usefulness and relation to learning principles. Examples of experiential taxonomy-based curricula and teaching strategies are listed. Other practical aids for teachers include a chart of sequenced teaching strategies, the nature and sequence of lessons, and evaluation processes.

320. Trivett, David A. *Academic Credit for Prior Off-Campus Learning*. ERIC/Higher Education Research Report No. 2. Washington, DC: American Association for Higher Education, 1975. ED 105 796. 72 pp.

As one form of nontraditional education, prior off-campus learning, e.g., CLEP, seems to be growing in popularity. Major topics discussed are: rationale and definitions in academic credit for off-campus learning, college level examination program, academic credit for prior learning in noncollegiate organizations, academic credit for prior learning for life and work experience, and academic credit for prior learning in special degree programs.

321. ———. *Competency Programs in Higher Education*. ERIC/Higher Education Research Report No. 7. Washington, DC: American Association for Higher Education, 1975. ED 118 023. 68 pp.

By the very nature of competency programs, an emphasis is placed on behavioral objectives, mastery learning, and testing for competencies related to the objectives. The major headings are basis concepts, origins of competency programs, institutional implementation, sample competency programs, and conclusions.

322. Tuckman, Bruce Wayne. *Evaluating Instructional Programs*. Boston: Allyn and Bacon, 1979. 309 pp.

Contains a digest of knowledge concerning evaluation of educational programs and processes. Case studies and pertinent instruments are included, as well as a glossary, appendices, and a reference section.

323. Union for Experimenting Colleges and Universities. *The University without Walls: A First Report*. Yellow Springs, OH: Union for Experimenting Colleges and Universities, 1971. 48 pp.

Twenty colleges and universities enrolled 3,000 students, ages 16 to 73, in a nontraditional program designed for the needs of the individual student. The adviser (learner-facilitator) and the student use many learning experiences to complete work for a degree and the time span for graduation varies.

324. Wedemeyer, Charles A. "Independent Study." In *Handbook on Contemporary Education*, edited by S. E. Goodman. New York: Bowker, 1976, pp. 579–85.

Discusses independent study in the United States in two contexts: the early honors program and the extension movement influenced early by the correspondence concept developed at the University of Chicago. Later this term was changed at the University of Wisconsin to independent study. Major topics are: internal learners, external learners, scope, review of the literature, programs and applications, and current issues.

325. Wegener, Charles. *Liberal Education and the Modern University*. Chicago: University of Chicago Press, 1978. 163 pp.

Describes the history of liberal education in the United States. The author recommends new programs which should drastically change the present undergraduate curricula and make it more rewarding for students.

326. Wey, Herbert W. *Alternatives in Higher Education: Innovations and Changing Practices in Selected Post-Secondary Institutions around the World*. Boone, NC: Appalachian State University, 1976. 244 pp.

Identifies and summarizes 617 innovative programs as the culmination of a 6-month travel-study grant. The programs are listed under chapters which consist of broad subject areas such as learning, curriculum, lifelong learning, students, administration, and faculty. The final chapter is a summary of trends.

327. Wood, Lynn, and David, Barbara G. *Designing and Evaluating Higher Education Curricula*. AAHE-ERIC/Higher Education Research Report No. 8. Washington, DC: American Association for Higher Education, 1978. ED 165 669. 65 pp.

Tight budgets and accountability have caused college administrators and faculty to review the curriculum. Emphasizing the interacting relationship between design and evaluation, the major topics are: higher education and curricula today; design and evaluation; concepts and linkages; evaluation as needs assessment, curriculum design, implementation, and evaluation.

328. Zauderer, Donald G. *Urban Internships in Higher Education*. AAHE/ERIC-Higher Education Report No. 9. Washington, DC: American Association for Higher Education, 1973. ED 085 039. 44 pp.

The concept of organized and planned internships in higher education is rather new, particularly in an urban center, and is another example of nontraditional education. Major topics are: goals and opportunities of internship training, role allocation, further issues, and conclusions.

FACULTY

329. Adams, Hazard. *The Academic Tribes: A Wry View of the American University—With a Dash of Bitters*. New York: Liveright, 1976. 144 pp.

Describes various situations and personalities in a humorous way from his own experiences in higher education. Enjoyable reading but not a serious assessment of needs.

330. Aiken, Henry David. *Predicament of the University*. Bloomington, IN: Indiana University Press, 1971. 404 pp.

Criticizes higher education and the ideas of many educators such as Clark Kerr, Daniel Bell, and Sidney Hook. Shows sympathy with young dissenters' confrontations with faculty.

331. Astin, Alexander W. *Academic Gamesmanship: Student Oriented Change in Higher Education*. New York: Praeger, 1976. 209 pp.

Student-oriented data was provided to 19 universities on the characteristics of each institution's students during the period 1966–70. Each institution formed an ad hoc committee to produce a report which would recommend specific innovations.

332. Bayer, Alan E. *Teaching Faculty in Academe: 1972–73*. Washington, DC: American Council on Education, 1973. 68 pp.

Presents and analyzes data from a survey of more than 100,000 college and university faculty and staff. Major findings are in the following areas: demographic background, educational background, work history, current position, and faculty opinions and attitudes.

333. Bergquist, William H., and Phillips, Steven R. *Handbook for Faculty Development.* Council for the Advancement of Small Colleges. Berkeley, CA: Pacific Soundings Press. Vol. 1, 306 pp. Vol. 2, 313 pp.

Examines faculty development as it is related to goals and values, teaching methods, relationships to students, and other aspects of professional life. The first vol. contains chapters on instructional, organizational, and personal development. The second vol. offers more theory.

334. Bornheimer, Deane G.; Burns, Gerald P.; and Dumke, Glenn S. *The Faculty in Higher Education.* Danville, IL: Interstate Printers and Publishers, 1973. 213 pp.

Informative overview of faculty in higher education. The book is divided into 3 sections: functions of the faculty; building the faculty, and problems of faculty. The quality of teaching is often poor and more innovative teaching should take place on campuses.

335. Butts, C. P. "College Faculty as Change Agents." In *Handbook on Contemporary Education,* edited by S. E. Goodman. New York: Bowker, 1976, pp. 17–20.

College faculty are regarded as a major resource in initiating change in public schools, in other colleges, and on their own campuses. Discusses 2 illustrations of this kind of change and the issues.

336. Buxton, Thomas H., and Prichard, Keith W., eds. *Excellence in University Teaching: New Essays.* Columbia, SC: University of South Carolina Press, 1975. 291 pp.

A survey of 25 teachers from various universities found many with similar characteristics. These people were recognized as excellent teachers. All were enthusiastic about teaching; they were concerned about students; and they had knowledge in the subject area in which they were teaching.

337. Carnegie Commission on Higher Education. *Reform on Campus: Changing Students, Changing Academic Programs.* New York: McGraw-Hill, 1972. 137 pp.

Based on an opinion poll conducted in 1969-70 (the peak years of student unrest) involving 70,000 undergraduates, 30,000 graduate students, and 60,000 faculty members, the findings from the study recommended that colleges and universities should move toward reform. The changes needed should be undertaken for the sake of students and society to broaden the opportunities for students to find an academic environment and curriculum which improve the quality of their lives. The survey showed that students and faculty agreed that good teaching rather than voluminous research should be the primary criterion for faculty promotions, that courses should be more relevant to contemporary life, and that more attention should be paid to the emotional growth of the students. Students and faculty disagreed on 2 proposed changes: 59 percent of the students favored but only 33 percent of faculty agreed on abolishing all grades; 51 percent of the students supported making all courses elective, but only 19 percent of the faculty agreed.

338. Centra, John A. *Faculty Development Practices in U.S. Colleges and Universities.* Princeton, NJ: Educational Testing Service, 1976. 88 pp.

Institutions use many activities to assist faculty in their various roles and activities. Some ways in which faculty may renew or gain interests include workshops, seminars, sabbatical leaves, course development, use of technology, teaching awards, and assessment procedures.

339. ———. *Strategies for Improving College Teaching.* ERIC Clearinghouse on Higher Education. Washington, DC: American Association for Higher Education, 1972. ED 071 616. 51 pp.

This report combined with a consideration of strategies for improving student learning would be ideal. It is excellent in presenting a teaching-learning model, research implications for teaching and learning, self-analysis for improving teaching, student ratings, institutional programs, and the technological impact on teaching improvement.

340. Cole, Charles C. *To Improve Instruction.* ERIC/Higher Education Research Report No. 2. Washington, DC: American Association of Higher Education, 1978. ED 153 538. 80 pp.

There are 2 major points of emphasis, a summary of innovative programs to improve instruction between 1971 and 1976, and a review of the literature concerning instructional improvement during these 5 years. Some of the major topics are: rationale for instructional improvement, improving instructors, types of programs to improve faculty, examples of innovative instructional methods, and research on improving instruction.

341. Commission on Academic Tenure in Higher Education. *Faculty Tenure.* San Francisco, CA: Jossey-Bass, 1973. 276 pp.

The most complete reference on faculty tenure available at this time. It is a report of findings of the Commission and also gives recommendations for the future. Tight budgets, enrollment declines, and new retirement policies make this information of current interest.

342. Davis, Robert H.; Abedor, Allan J.; and Witt, Paul W. F. *Commitment to Excellence: A Case Study of Educational Innovation.* East Lansing, MI: Educational Development Program, Michigan State University, 1976. 189 pp.

Describes the Michigan State University educational development program which has encouraged good instruction by the faculty. Current trends and future predictions are included, as well as 8 appendices and a bibliography.

343. Eble, Kenneth E. *The Craft of Teaching: A Guide to Mastering the Professor's Art.* San Francisco, CA: Jossey-Bass, 1976. 179 pp.

Believes teaching and learning can be a pleasurable experience. Discusses lectures, discussion, seminars, texts, assignments, and grades. "Publish or perish" is not imposed from outside but from inside the institution. Faculty members feel the respect of their peers comes from publishing and not from excellence in teaching.

344. ———. *Professors as Teachers.* San Francisco, CA: Jossey-Bass, 1972. 202 pp.

Discusses 2 years of visiting 70 schools in the United States. Describes classroom teaching and attitudes of professors, student needs, faculty development, rewards of teaching, and other aspects of teaching. Makes some suggestions to improve teaching and raises questions concerning graduate education.

345. ———. *The Recognition and Evaluation of Teaching.* Project to Improve College Training. Salt Lake City, UT:

American Association of University Professors, 1970. 111 pp.

Material for a student evaluation of faculty was gathered from a literature search, information from students, faculty and administrators, campus visits, and a conference in 1970. Instruments and procedures used are given and evaluations made by students are assessed. Reports of some visits are in the appendices.

346. Eckert, Ruth Elizabeth, and Williams, Howard Y. *College Faculty View Themselves and Their Jobs.* Minneapolis, MN: University of Minnesota, 1972. 62 pp.

Comparison of a 1968 faculty member study with a similar study in 1956 of Minnesota's 43 institutions of higher learning. Included in the data is personal information concerning career choice, preparation, present position, and career appraisal. Some conclusions of the study are: desirability of dissimilar backgrounds of faculty; need for more scholarships, financial aid, and research assistance; clarification of faculty duties, and reassessment of committee and administrative duties.

347. Entwistle, Noel, and Hounsell, Dai, eds. *How Students Learn.* Lancaster, England: University of Lancaster, 1975. 199 pp.

Suggests ways in which students learn from teachers and scholars and also from teacher-scholars. Contributions include Skinner, McKeachie, Bruner, and Rogers.

348. Erickson, Stanford C., and Cook, John A. *Support for Teaching at Major Universities.* Ann Arbor, MI: Center for Research on Learning and Teaching, 1979. ED 180 312. 114 pp.

Shows how universities can support and improve instruction. Maintains that quality instruction should be equal in importance to research and other scholarly activities. Some recommendations designate the need for efficiency and cost-effectiveness. The 10 chapters are written by the Committee on Institutional Cooperation (CIC).

349. Fournoy, Don M., et al. *The New Teachers.* San Francisco, CA: Jossey-Bass, 1972. 206 pp.

Concerns the opinions and experiences of "new" teachers who wish to undermine the traditional teaching and teaching methods and who believe contact with students is improtant but disregard substantial course context or structure.

350. Gaff, Sally S., et al. *Professional Development: A Guide to Resources.* New Rochelle, NY: Change Magazine, 1978. 110 pp.

A guide prepared for faculty who wish to keep informed on developments in higher education. The book is divided into 11 sections; each section consists of a brief overview, an annotated bibliography, and a general bibliography. Topics include: faculty and teaching, students and learning, course development, advising, and institutional change.

351. Graybeal, William S. *Salaries Scheduled for Faculty in Higher Education, 1978-79.* Washington, DC: National Education Association, 1979. 15 pp.

Statistics on salaries in higher education from 2-year and 4-year institutions are listed in this NEA research project. Tables list salaries according to rank, education, and institution.

352. Grites, Thomas J. *Academic Advising: Getting Us through the Eighties.* AAHE-ERIC/Higher Education Research Report No. 7. Washington, DC: American Association for Higher Education, 1979. ED 178 023. 67 pp.

Academic effectiveness or fit of the student with the curriculum is a major test of the relationship between the 2. Advising includes helping the student identify goals, relating to resources, and making appropriate changes.

353. Group for Human Development. *Faculty Development in a Time of Retrenchment.* New Rochelle, NY: Change Magazine, 1974. 90 pp.

Discusses many aspects of the teaching/learning process. The need for faculty development and challenge in teaching is discussed. Several suggestions to improve academic teaching are given: mid-career transitions, intellectual mobility, faculty exchanges among institutions, evaluation of graduate student's teaching, campus programs for teaching improvement, involvement of professors in a program to improve teaching, and recognition of good teaching.

354. Higham, Robin D. S. *The Complete Academic: An Informal Guide to the Ivory Tower.* New York: St. Martin's, 1974. 371 pp.

A descriptive guide on how to succeed in the academic world by a successful professor. Much of the detailed information is of interest to a professor who is seeking promotion but relevant material is hard to locate.

355. Hildebrand, Milton. *Evaluating University Teaching.* Berkeley, CA: Center for Research and Development in Higher Education, 1971. 57 pp.

Defines and describes effective teaching in order that teachers and graduate students can improve. Three questionnaires were used with students, faculty, and staff to elicit their comments on effective teaching and teachers. Effective teachers make many contributions to students and a personal relationship seems to be valuable.

356. Hislop, Codman. *Eliphalet Nott.* Middletown, CT: Wesleyan University Press, 1971. 680 pp.

A biography of an educational reformer who was prominent in the generation before Horace Mann. He was president of Nott College for 66 years, encouraged scientific studies, believed in optional courses, and invented a coal burning stove. He was active in politics and in New York State's first education lottery.

357. Kohler, Emmett T. "Faculty Evaluation." In *Handbook on Contemporary Education,* edited by S. E. Goodman. New York: Bowker, 1976, pp 224–29.

Student evaluation of faculty in spite of limitations is widely used to measure faculty competence to bring about learning on the part of students. Among the topics discussed are: gaining the cooperation of faculty, defining purposes and goals, arriving at means and procedures, making crucial policy and decisions, and financing a continuing program.

358. Kolstoe, Olive P. *College Professoring: Or, Through Academia with Gun and Camera.* Carbondale, IL: Southern Illinois University Press, 1975. 150 pp.

Depicts the academic world with humor and with cartoons although it is based on knowledge and facts. Discusses academic freedom, research, advancement of knowledge, and teaching with wit and understanding.

359. Kramer, Howard C., and Gardner, Robert E. *Advising by Faculty.* Washington, DC: National Education Association, 1977. 55 pp.

Many practical suggestions are offered to interested faculty who are willing to improve their services to the students.

360. Ladd, Everett Carll, Jr., and Lipset, Seymour Martin. *The Divided Academy: Professors and Politics.* Carnegie Commission on Higher Education. New York: McGraw-Hill, 1975. 407 pp.

Separated into 3 sections. Part 1 describes faculty members as a distinct group with more liberal views on political and social questions than most of American society. Part 2 discusses the "Divided Academy" as the diversity within the group. Part 3 looks at specific issues such as 1960 campus protests, effects of unionism on faculty, and other points of conflict.

361. Lewis, Darrell R., and Becker, William E., eds. *Academic Rewards in Higher Education.* Cambridge, MA: Ballinger Publishers, 1979. 339 pp.

This study, based on economics and economic theory, covers the subject of how faculty are motivated and rewarded in American higher education. The major areas are: theoretical views of faculty behavior in academic labor markets, a conceptual understanding of academic labor markets in higher education, conceptual problems in measuring both individual and institutional outcomes, and empirical aspects of current reward structures in higher education.

362. Light, D. W., Jr., et al. *The Impact of the Academic Revolution on Faculty Careers.* AAHE-ERIC/Higher Education Report Washington, DC: American Association for Higher Education, 1973. ED 072 758. 79 pp.

The 3-strand model for faculty development which is the focus of this report includes the disciplinary, the institutional, and the external career. Some of the topics covered are faculty power, influence, prestige, recruitment and promotion, academic markets, the socialization of faculty toward their discipline, and teaching role.

363. Livesey, Herbert B. *The Professors: Who They Are, What They Do, What They Really Want and What They Need.* New York: Charter House, 1975. 343 pp.

Uses conversations with professors, writings, classroom speeches, and lectures to report the thoughts of professors on a variety of topics. Professors from large, small, public, and private colleges and universities discuss tenure, politics, salary, research, teaching problems, goals, and rewards.

364. Mandell, Richard D. *The Professor Game.* New York: Doubleday, 1977. 274 pp.

Pictures the American academic in the 1970s and offers some suggestions for reform. Topics discussed are: publication, recruiting, cheating, plagiarism, library theft, sex with students, office size and status, and reward systems. The author believes that most faculty are lazy and underworked and also that many students do not belong in college. He proposes more specific job assignment, changing the hiring and reward system, and replacing tenure with 5- to 7-year contracts.

365. Miller, Richard I. *Developing Programs for Faculty Evaluation: A Sourcebook for Higher Education.* San Francisco, CA: Jossey-Bass, 1974. 248 pp.

Examines reasons for new interest in evaluations. Discusses strategies which may be used for purposes of evaluation, student ratings of teachers, and evaluations of administrators. Examples of evaluation forms and an annotated bibliography are also included.

366. ———. *Evaluating Faculty Performance.* San Francisco, CA: Jossey-Bass, 1972. 145 pp.

Proposes 9 categories for evaluating faculty performance rather than the usual teaching, research, and service. The 9 categories are: classroom teaching, advising, faculty service, management, performing arts, professional services, publications, public service, and research. Promotes student evaluations; otherwise the chairperson of department is responsible.

367. Patton, Carl V. *Academia in Transition: Mid-Career Change or Early Retirement.* Cambridge, MA: Abt Books, 1979. 212 pp.

An important book for those faculty during the 1980s who are interested in career options, including early retirement. The faculty age projection charts are valuable. Major topics include rationale for career options, career options in industry, government, and academia, experiences in incentive, early retirees, fiscal implications of early retirement, career options, and legal questions concerning early retirement.

368. Pezzullo, Thomas R., and Brittingham, Barbara E., eds. *Salary Equity: Detecting Sex Bias in Salaries among College and University Professors.* Lexington, MA: D. C. Heath, 1979. 162 pp.

Outlines research on salary differences using multiple regression. Case studies are presented and, also, differing viewpoints using multiple regression and statistical analysis. Includes a bibliography at the end of each chapter.

369. Pincoffs, Edmund L., ed. *The Concept of Academic Freedom.* Austin, TX: University of Texas Press, 1975. 272 pp.

Discusses various aspects of academic freedom. Some topics are: the limitations of academic freedom, academic tenure, disruption of meetings and speakers on campus, and freedom of research.

370. Risenhoover, Morris, and Blackburn, Robert T. *Artists as Professors: Conversations with Musicians, Painters, Sculptors.* Urbana, IL: University of Illinois Press, 1976. 217 pp.

Concerns interviews with artists who hold regular full-time faculty appointments: painters, composers, musicians, and sculptors. The responses of these artists are interesting. The questions asked concern motivation to teach, experiences in the university community, and attitudes toward instruction.

371. Shaw, B. N. *Academic Tenure in American Higher Education.* Chicago: Adams, 1971. 116 pp.

Outlines the policies for acquiring academic tenure and the procedures for implementation of policies in land-grant colleges and state universities. The official publications of the colleges and universities are used as a basis for a comparative analysis of tenure policies and procedures. A questionnaire is used to procure information about the number of tenured teachers and cases of tenure termination.

372. Sheffield, Edward F., ed. *Teaching in the Universities: No One Way.* Quebec: McGill-Queen's University Press, 1974. 252 pp.

A survey of excellent teachers in Canadian universities brought out some interesting observations. The teachers' most important job is to stimulate students ot be active learners; the best teachers like students and respect them; teachers enjoy teaching; and teachers work hard to prepare for teaching.

373. Shulman, Carol H. *Old Expectations, New Realities: The Academic Profession Revisited.* AAHE-ERIC/ Higher Education Research Report No. 2. Washington, DC: American Association for Higher Education, 1979. ED 169 874. 51 pp.

The former academic model which enabled faculty to make several gains is changing due to such forces as declining enrollments, lack of professor mobility, and collective bargaining. Major topics include the academic model, faculty job-mobility, the academic reward system, and faculty autonomy.

374. Smith, Albert B. *Faculty Development and Evaluation* in *Higher Education.* ERIC/Higher Education Research Report No. 8. Washington, DC: American Association of Higher Education, 1976. ED 132 891. 76 pp.

Both faculty development and faculty evaluation are so closely related that they are considered together. Research literature in both areas is considered. Four faculty development programs are discussed, as well as 3 faculty evaluation programs.

375. Smith, Goldwin, ed. *The Professor and the Public: The Role of the Scholar in the Modern World.* Detroit, MI: Wayne State University Press, 1972. 124 pp.

Comments on the role of the scholar in society. The emphasis is on the historian's responsibility to provide continuity for the general public. The author believes that scholarship and responsibility carry the obligation to write history with as little bias as possible. Scholars should not venture into fields beyond their own knowledge.

376. Stoddard, George D. *The Outlook for American Education.* Carbondale, IL: Southern Illinois University Press, 1974. 276 pp.

Describes the experiences and observations of an educator. The first part deals with elementary and secondary education; the second part with higher education. High school seniors should begin to specialize with higher education in mind. Topics include the nature of liberal arts, education of women, consumer education, curricular changes, open university methods, open admission, and egalitarianism.

377. Trow, Martin, ed. *Teachers and Students: Aspects of American Higher Education.* New York: McGraw-Hill, 1975. 419 pp.

Student and faculty attitudes in colleges and universities are the basis for 8 reports. Some topics considered are: research vs teaching, Black students, women in academia, educational goals, and professional advancement.

378. Truckman, Howard P. *Publication, Teaching, and the Academic Reward Structure.* Lexington, MA: Lexington Books, 1976. 122 pp.

Examines the academic reward structure that exists in higher education. Some of the rewards are: merit raise, personal satisfaction and peer recognition, promotion, administrative position, research activities, and consulting. These rewards and their implications are discussed with some supporting statistics.

379. Wilson, Logan. *American Academics: Then and Now.* New York: Oxford University Press, 1979. 309 pp.

Describes the current status of the American academic profession based on a survey of the literature. Many issues and problems of 40 years ago are topics today: length of Ph.D. programs, evaluation procedures, "publish or perish," bargaining power of academic employees, and inadequate support of higher education. Other topics include the academic job market of the 70s, administrators, role of graduate students, admission policies, and hiring practices.

380. Wilson, Robert C., et al. *College Professors and Their Impact on Students.* New York: John Wiley, 1975. 220 pp.

Delineates the ways in which college faculty influence different kinds of students. Based on 2 surveys: one covers faculty views of teaching; the other reports on undergraduates and some faculty. Fourteen institutions were involved. Examines how faculty who are considered good teachers act with students, as well as what they believe and teach. Learning experiences and outcomes are considered.

381. Yuker, Harold E. *Faculty Workload: Facts, Myths and Commentary.* Research Report No. 6. Washington, DC: American Association for Higher Education. 1974. ED 095 756. 62 pp.

Methods by which faculty workload studies can be performed are examined. Considers definitions and activities used in workload assessment, such as instructional time, institutional and public service, research, and creative efforts. The report stresses the need for research in this area in order to avoid using factors that may not apply to a specific institution.

GENERAL

382. American Association for Higher Education. *Current Documents in Higher Education: A Bibliography.* Washington, DC: ERIC Clearinghouse on Higher Education, 1970. ED 047 660. 161 pp.

A list of the papers and reports on higher education that appeared in the issues of *Research in Education* from July 1969 through June 1970. Major topics are: alumni, curriculum and innovations, disadvantaged, faculty, finance, foreign students and international education, governance, graduate and professional education, and institutional structure.

383. Change Magazine. *The Yellow Pages of Undergraduate Innovations.* New Rochelle, New York: Change Magazine, 1974. 243 pp.

A listing (not evaluative) of innovations in 4-year colleges and universities. There are 3 major sections: instructional innovations (9 categories), curricular innovations (7 categories), and institutional innovations (7 categories). There is a guilde for use and a subject index.

384. Entwistle, N. J. and Wilson, J. *Degrees of Excellence: The Academic Achievement Game*. London: Hodder and Stoughton, 1977. 226 pp.

Explores methodological innovations in an attempt to predict academic performance in higher education. Two studies are used to predict student success or failure. The findings of the 2 studies may be used for planning by administrators.

385. Goodman, Steven E., ed. *Handbook on Contemporary Education*. New York: Bowker, 1976. 622 pp.

For 118 separate subject topics, presents overview, reviews the important literature, identifies issues, and gives a selected bibliography. Approximately 40 papers concern higher education directly and are grouped in 8 categories such as educational change and planning, administration and management of education, teacher/faculty issues, students and parents, teaching and learning strategies, and alternatives and opinions in education.

386. Heller, Louis G. *The Death of the American University: With Special Reference to the Collapse of City College of New York*. New Rochelle, NY: Arlington House, 1973. 215 pp.

Tries to clarify issues involved in campus insurrections. Issues include problems of inequities, lack of civility among faculty with differing beliefs, procedural guarantees for faculty misconduct charges, faculty cowardice, and open enrollment.

387. Hodgkinson, Harold L. *How Much Change for a Dollar? A Look at Title III*. ERIC/Higher Education Research Report No. 3. Washington, DC: American Association for Higher Education, 1974. ED 090 905. 61 pp.

A summary of programs provided in the Developing Institutions Program (Title III of the 1965 Higher Education Act) and based on Title III data and institutional characteristics from 1965–66 to 1970–71 for 325 institutions receiving Title III funds. Case studies are included of 41 colleges and 4 agencies detailing their use of Title

III funds during 1972. A model of institutional development is presented and applied to the case studies of Title III institutions.

388. Knowles, Asa S., et al. *Handbook of Cooperative Education*. San Francisco, CA: Jossey-Bass, 1971. 386 pp.

Gives the history, values, and objectives of cooperative education. Cooperative education involves a combination of academic study and planned off-campus experience under the guidance and supervision of the college. There are also descriptions of programs in Canada and England, including their problems of administration, programs for women and minorities, placement policies, and new programs.

389. Lindquist, Jack. *Strategies for Change*. Berkeley, CA: Pacific Soundings Press, 1978. 268 pp.

Covers both the theory and practice in planning to bring about change. The emphasis of the research is change in teaching, curriculum, and evaluation in the American college. Six liberal arts colleges and 2 universities which participated in this action-research project during 1971–75 provide the case histories of planned change.

390. Pilon, Daniel H., and Berquist, William H. *Consultation in Higher Education. A Handbook for Practitioners and Clients*. Washington, DC: Council for the Advancement of Small Colleges. 1979. 152 pp.

A practical approach to the expanding area of consultation intended for both consultants and clients. Although oriented toward the private college, it is generally helpful in both public and private sectors. Although the consulting function relates to all areas of the institution, this reference seems to fit best in the teaching-learning environment. Some of the major topics are: role and functions of a consultant, the consulting process, 3 models of consultation, using the consultant's expertise, and values and ethical considerations.

391. Willingham, Warren W. *The No. 2 Access Problem: Transfer to the Upper Division*. Prepared by the ERIC Clearinghouse on Higher Education. Washington, DC: American Association for Higher Education, 1972. ED 066 140. 60 pp.

Concerns the articulation problems between 2- and 4-year institutions. Four national projects are identified and 10 transfer problems are discussed.

GOALS AND PURPOSES

392. Abercrombie, Nicholas, et al. *The University in an Urban Environment*. Beverly Hills, CA: Sage Publications, 1973. 246 pp.

The location of a university in an urban location does not mean that there will be strong involvement with the urban environment. Faculty members need to become involved in needs and resources within the urban setting.

393. Anderson, Scarvia B., et al. *Encyclopedia of Educational Evaluation: Concepts and Techniques for Evaluating Education and Training Programs*. San Francisco, CA: Jossey-Bass, 1975. 515 pp.

Arranged like an encyclopedia, this study treats 11 areas. Included are: evaluation models, functions and targets of evaluation, program objectives and standards, social context of evaluation, planning and design, systems technologies, variables, measurement approaches and types, technical measurement considerations, reactive concerns, and analysis and interpretation. Some topics are more informative than others and some are weak.

394. Averill, Lloyd J., and Jellema, William W., eds. *Colleges and Commitments*. Philadelphia, PA: Westminster, 1971. 236 pp.

Discusses values in higher education with a hope that in the future liberal arts colleges will accept a greater commitment to development a whole human being. Educational models and attitudes should be given great consideration by teachers.

395. Carnegie Commission on Higher Education. *Less Time, More Options. Education beyond the High School.* Special Report and Recommendations by the Carnegie Commission on Higher Education. New York: McGraw-Hill, 1971. 45 pp.

The cooperation of many groups is necessary if major changes are made and more flexibility is used in higher education. Some topics considered are: lifelong education, adult learning, new patterns in work and education, and access for women and minorities.

396. Gould, Samuel B., Chairman. *Diversity by Design*. Commission on Non-Traditional Study. San Francisco, CA: Jossey-Bass, 1973. 178 pp.

This is the final report of a 2-year study which recommends that the needs of the student be considered first and the institution second. Recommendations are made concerning emphasis in higher education on degree granting, changing faculty understandings and attitudes, use of educational technology, evaluation tools, and better cooperation among all agencies concerned.

397. Harris, Norman C., and Grede, John F. *Career Education in Colleges: A Guide for Planning Two-and-Four-Year Occupational Programs for Successful Employment.* San Francisco, CA: Jossey-Bass, 1977. 419 pp.

Describes the career education movement in colleges in recent years as opposed to the views of academic humanities. There are 3 general sections: the first gives the history and background of career education; the second discusses programs and categories of 5 different areas; the third concerns planning, finances, and governance. Mid-level career programs include allied-health, public and human service, business, liberal arts, and science and technology.

398. Harrison, Shelley A., and Stolurow, Lawrence M., eds. *Improving Instructional Productivity in Higher Educa-*

tion. State University of New York at Stony Brook. Englewood Cliffs, NJ: Educational Technology Publications, 1975. 272 pp.

Problems faced in many institutions include less financial support, a diverse student body, and need for individualization of instruction for students. In the context of goals, higher education should look at quality, as well as quantity of productivity.

399. Jevons, F. R., and Turner, H. D., eds. *What Kinds of Graduates Do We Need?* London: Oxford University Press, 1972. 120 pp.

Discusses viewpoints of academics and business people concerning the educational needs of professional people. There is a need to declare objectives in behavioral terms and to agree about the failure of teaching and assessment to meet the goals and objectives of employers. Changes in curriculum are necessary for people to learn how to live and work.

400. Lenning, Oscar T.; Cooper, Edward M.; and Passmore, J. Robert. *Identifying and Assessing Needs in Postsecondary Education: A Review and Synthesis of the Literature.* Boulder, CO: National Center for Higher Education Management Systems, 1977. 126 pp.

Institutions of higher learning must identify the needs of the communities and students which they serve. This book tries to organize and summarize needed information for needs assessment for postsecondary institutions.

401. Miller, Harry L. *Choosing a College Major: Education*. New York: David McKay, 1979. 181 pp.

Evaluation of personality, aptitudes, and goals by a prospective teacher will aid in making an informed decision. This book gives accurate, up-to-date information about a career in education. Information is given on undergraduate programs, specific required courses, student teaching, needed teaching skills, salary trends, the outlook for teaching jobs, and teacher license requirements for each state.

402. Romney, Leonard C. *Measures of Institutional Goal Achievement*. Boulder, CO: National Center for Higher Education Management Systems, 1978. 57 pp.

It is difficult to link institutional statements of goals to specific measures of outcomes. Fourteen types of information have been set up which would indicate progress towards the 7 goal areas rated most important by institutions surveyed.

GRADUATE EDUCATION

403. Allen, George R. *The Graduate Students' Guide to Theses and Dissertations: A Practical Manual for Writing and Research.* San Francisco, CA: Jossey-Bass, 1973. 108 pp.

Should assist a beginning graduate student but some chapters are too short to be helpful to a student who is actually engaged in writing his

dissertation. The 7 chapters deal with academic research: research topics, research committee, research proposal, data collection, writing the research report, and dissertation defenses.

404. Breneman, David W., and Bush, Sharon C. "Graduate Education in Transition." In *Handbook on Contempo-*

rary Education, edited by S. E. Goodman. New York: Bowker, 1976, pp. 38–43.

When Yale awarded 3 Ph.D. degrees in 1861 and, later, when Johns Hopkins University, modeled after the German research university, was founded in 1876, graduation education was fact in the United States. Major topics are: the labor market for Ph.D.s, costs and financing of graduate institutions, teaching, quality of graduate education, the master's degree, and nontraditional graduate education.

405. Breneman, David W. *Graduate School Adjustments to the "New Depression" in Higher Education.* Washington, DC: National Board on Graduate Education, 1975. 96 pp.

Trends in graduate enrollment, financial support, and job placements of new Ph.D.s were studied over a 6-year period, 1968–73. The findings were reported and recommendations for the future were discussed.

406. Brown, Sanborn C., and Schwartz, Bryan B. *Scientific Manpower: A Dilemma for Graduate Education.* Cambridge, MA: M.I.T. Press, 1971. 180 pp.

Implications for graduate education in future years are discussed at a conference on manpower needs. Scientific manpower will be needed in the future and there may even be a shortage of scientists and engineers.

407. Calvert, Jack G.; Pitts, James N.; and Dorion, George H. *Graduate School in the Sciences: Entrance, Survival and Careers.* New York: Wiley-Interscience, 1972. 304 pp.

A resource book which would be helpful for making educational choices. Included are discussions on: choice of graduate school; requirements of schools and departments; research and dissertations; and employment.

408. Clark, Mary J.; Hartnett, Rodney T; and Baird, Leonard L. *Assessing Dimensions of Quality in Doctoral Education.* Princeton, NJ: Educational Testing Service, 1976. 131 pp.

To develop and field test measures in order to understand doctoral program educational quality, questionnaires were sent to faculty, students, and recent alumni. Departmental records were used. Programs in chemistry, psychology, and history were considered. Appendices with figures and tables are included.

409. Clark, Richard J., Jr., et al. *Perspectives on Graduate Programs in Education.* Washington, DC: American Association of Colleges for Teacher Education and ERIC Clearinghouse on Teacher Education, 1979. 116 pp.

Examines present and future graduate teacher education. Discusses the problem of who will provide inservice education for teachers.

410. Dolan, W. Patrick. *The Ranking Game: The Power of the Academic Elite.* Lincoln, NE: Study Commission on Undergraduate Education and the Education of Teachers, 1976. 108 pp.

A critical look at the American Council on Education's ranking of graduate programs in the United States. Claims are made that the evaluative processes are based on narrow assumptions and elitist structures which predominate in higher education. Accreditation, testing (entrance criteria), and certification of specific skills are discussed.

411. Dresch, Stephen P. *An Economic Perspective on the Evolution of Graduate Education.* Technical Report No. 1.

Washington, DC: National Board on Graduate Education, 1974. 76 pp.

Assesses the rapid growth of graduate education during the 1950s and 1960s and the gradual decline in the 1970s. Fundamental changes in the environment will continue through and beyond the 1970s. The future of graduate education is closely related to public policy and financial support.

412. Dressel, Paul, and Thompson, Mary M. *A Degree for College Teachers: The Doctor of Arts.* Berkeley, CA: Carnegie Council on Policy Studies in Higher Education, 1977. 71 pp.

Describes the Doctor of Arts (D.A.) degree. This degree is designed to prepare students for college teaching and is an alternative to the Ph.D. and Ed.D. History of the degree is presented and a list of institutions offering the degree is included.

413. Educational Testing Service. *Scholarship for Society.* Report of a panel sponsored by the Graduate Record Examination Board of the Council of Graduate Schools in the United States. Princeton, NJ: Educational Testing Service, 1973. 60 pp.

There are many complaints about graduate schools and some demands are conflicting in nature. Standards of performance are frequently criticized as too low or too inflexible or unrealistic. However, the report does acknowledge that there may be differences in missions of graduate schools and that graduate schools need to be evaluated.

414. Francis, J. Bruce; Bork, Christopher E.; and Carstens, Steven P. *The Proposal Cookbook: A Step by Step Guide to Dissertation and Thesis Proposal Writing.* 3d edition. Buffalo, NY: Action Research Associates, 1979. 113 pp.

A practical guide to the research process which must be undertaken by graduate students who are engaged in research and reporting this research for a thesis or dissertation. Discusses proposals, topics, designing the study, and writing.

415. Fairfield, Roy P. *Person-Centered Graduate Education.* Buffalo, NY: Prometheus Books, 1977. 269 pp.

Describes an innovative nontraditional graduate program based on student needs, backgrounds, and interests at Union Graduate School. High standards are maintained and the graduates are comparable with others who reach the doctoral degree by traditional routes.

416. Grant, Mary K., and Hoeber, Daniel R. *Basic Skill Programs: Are They Working?* AAHE-ERIC/Higher Education Research Report No. 1. Washington, DC: American Association for Higher Education, 1978. ED 150 918. 51 pp.

As enrollment decline threatens, colleges and universities have become alert to providing a treatment process to help students succeed and thereby reduce attrition. Historical perspectives, program development, evaluation, and recommendations are the major topics.

417. Harvey, James. *The Student in Graduate School.* ERIC Clearinghouse on Higher Education. Washington, DC: American Association for Higher Education, January 1972. ED 057 258. 74 pp.

An effort to clarify the role and position of the student in doctoral programs. Topics relate to the following: ambiguity of the student position, length of doctoral study, components of Ph.D. programs, and financial status of graduate students.

418. Heiss, Ann M. *Challenges to Graduate Schools: The Ph.D. Program in Ten Universities.* San Francisco, CA: Jossey-Bass, 1970. 328 pp.

Describes reactions of faculty and graduate students to problems involved in doctoral studies. Two-thirds of 2,308 faculty members and 4,806 doctoral students in 10 departments answered the questionnaires. Department chairperson and deans of graduate schools believe there is need for reform. Most faculty seemed satisfied with current conditions, and students are negative in their reactions by a 2-to-1 ratio. The author proposes some needed reforms.

419. Katz, J., and Hartnett, R. T., eds. *Scholars in the Making: The Development of Graduate and Professional Students.* Cambridge, MA: Ballinger, 1976. 287 pp.

Studies the graduate student and the problems which are common to most graduate students. Two studies are reported: one at Wright Institute at Berkeley, and another at the Educational Testing Service at Princeton. A brief history of graduate education is given, including characteristics of students and family background, relationships of graduate students with teachers, development of the student, and women and minority students.

420. Kent, Leonard J., and Springer, George P., eds. *Graduate Education Today and Tomorrow.* Albuquerque, NM: University of New Mexico Press, 1972. 217 pp.

Contains essays by scholars on contemporary and future problems of graduate schools. Graduate deans will face such problems as needs for professors who are concerned about the student; problems caused by reduction in the close personal contact of professors and students; need for good teachers, as well as research specialists; and cooperation of related departments.

421. Mayhew, Lewis B. *Graduate and Professional Education, 1980.* The Carnegie Commission on Higher Education. New York: McGraw-Hill, 1970. 38 pp.

Reports on plans for graduate and professional education from many universities across the United States. Conclusions are: an oversupply of Ph.D.s; lower quality graduate education; increased tensions between new and old faculty, as well as between developing universities and state agencies; and lack of financial support.

422. ———. *Reform in Graduate Education.* Atlanta, GA: Southern Regional Education Board, 1972. 182 pp.

Analyzes graduate education and recommends changes in curriculum, instruction, administration, and other areas.

423. Mayhew, Lewis B., and Ford, Patrick J. *Reform in Graduate and Professional Education.* San Francisco, CA: Jossey-Bass, 1974. 254 pp.

Describes curricular reform and experimental methods in use in professional schools. Systematic evaluation of these reforms is needed. Graduate education changes very slowly in spite of widespread criticism. Recommends changes in curriculum, instruction, and administration in graduate schools. These questions will continue to be important in the 1980s.

424. Mayville, William V. *A Matter of Degree: The Setting for Contemporary Master's Programs.* Research Report No. 9. Washington, DC: American Association for Higher Education, 1973. 51 pp.

The value of the master's degree is controversial. This report reviews the history and development of the degree and standards and significance in several disciplines, including psychology, science, engineering, international relations, law, and public health. The degree is assessed for teaching in the community and 4-year colleges.

425. National Academy of Science. *Mobility of Ph.D.'s before and after the Doctorate.* Career Patterns Report No. 3, National Academy of Sciences. Chicago: The Academy, 1971. 200 pp.

Contains comparative state data concerning the mobility of Ph.D.s, proportion of high school and college graduates who complete Ph.D.s, and state production of doctorates.

426. National Board on Graduate Education. *Graduate Education: Purposes, Problems and Potential.* Washington, DC: National Board on Graduate Education, 1972. 37 pp.

Reviews the purposes and practices of graduate education and analyzes its future relationship to American society. Some topics of concern include: costs and financing of graduate education, access and recruitment of minorities and women, number of Ph.D.s, relationship of graduate and undergraduate education, new graduate degrees, and graduate programs in Black colleges.

427. ———. *Minority Group Participation in Graduate Education.* Washington, DC: National Academy of Sciences, 1976. 272 pp.

Intends to assist program planning that would reduce barriers now facing minorities who are in graduate schools and those who wish to apply for admission. Agencies and institutions involved who wish to increase minority enrollment and success will be interested.

428. National Science Foundation. *Scientific and Technical Manpower Projections: Report of the Ad Hoc Committee on Manpower.* Washington, DC: U.S. Government Printing Office, 1974. 69 pp.

Accuracy of past projection, methodologies, assumptions, and limitations of projections are assessed in this report. The doctoral level degree is considered in relation to supply and demand.

429. Roose, Kenneth D., and Andersen, Charles J. *A Rating of Graduate Programs.* Washington, DC: American Council on Education, 1970. 115 pp.

Implications and data are given of a study of graduate programs at 130 institutions and in 36 disciplines.

430. Sacks, Herbert S., et al. *Hurdles: The Admissions Dilemma in American Higher Education.* New York: Atheneum, 1978. 364 pp.

Thirteen contributors depict life in higher education from the standpoint of the student. The psychological effects which occur because of interviewing, testing, family expectations, and career choices are discussed. Chapters which are particularly interesting cover admission to law school at Yale, problems involved in admission to medical school, and struggles of women to be acepted as serious scholars.

431. Snelling, W. Rodman, and Boruch, Robert F. *Science in Liberal Arts Colleges: A Longitudinal Study of 49 Selective Colleges.* New York: Columbia University Press, 1972. 285 pp.

Study of science majors at 49 liberal arts colleges from 1958 to 1967 involving 20,833 graduates who returned 16,395 questionnaires. Three major areas were studied: backgrounds and preparation of students, undergraduate grades and economic aspects, and postgraduate work. The findings indicated that the graduates go on to successful careers. The students liked smaller classes and accessible faculty, as well as the liberal arts education provided.

432. Spurr, Stephen H. *Academic Degree Structures: Innovative Approaches.* The Carnegie Commission on Higher Education. New York: McGraw-Hill, 1970. 213 pp.

The president of the University of Texas at Austin outlines a system for fewer and broadly defined degrees. There is too much complexity and duplication in the degree structure and students are discouraged by the problems which arise.

433. Storr, Richard J. The *Beginning of the Future: A Historical Approach to Graduate Education in the Arts and Sciences.* New York: McGraw-Hill, 1973. 99 pp.

Reviews the history of graduate study in the United States and mentions specific institutions such as Yale, University of Virginia, Harvard, and Johns Hopkins. Early educators and their influence are also traced. Concludes with 5 propositions to improve the quality of graduate study.

434. Sugden, Virginia M. *The Graduate Thesis: The Complete Guide to Planning and Preparation.* New York: Pitman Publishing, 1973. 157 pp.

Helpful for graduate students who are engaged in writing a dissertation or thesis and for professors who advise students as they strive to write scholarly papers.

435. Trivett, David A. *Graduate Education in the 1970's.* ERIC/Higher Education Research Report No. 7. Washington, DC: American Association for Higher Education, 1977. ED 145 763. 56 pp.

This analysis of the changing forces that affect graduate education and concerns covers such topics as complex enterprise, major problems and conditions, changing clientele and colleagues, quality assessment, new purposes, and new role for the states in graduate study.

436. Vetter, Betty M. *Supply and Demand for Scientists and Engineers: A Review of Selected Studies.* Washington, DC: Scientific Manpower Commission, 1977. 54 pp.

The supply for each field is listed and compared with the demand for new graduates, as well as for those with experience. Women are included in this survey. Supply and demand for the next 10 years is projected.

437. Welsh, J. M. *The First Year of Postgraduate Research Study.* Research into Higher Education Monographs. Society for Research into Higher Education. London: University of Surrey, 1979. 62 pp.

The main focus of the book concerns the way students approach research and the problems they confront. Work attitudes and supervision are also investigated.

438. Whaley, W. Gordon. *In These Times: A Look at Graduate Education with Proposals for the Future.* Austin, TX: University of Texas, 1971. 259 pp.

A collection of 23 essays on graduate education. Some conclusions reached are: Ph.D. training does not fit career needs of graduates or needs of society; more Ph.D.s should be trained as teachers rather than researchers; much Ph.D. research is trivial and useless; quality standards have been lowered. Financial pressure, as well as federal and state pressure, may force reforms in higher education.

439. Worthen, Blaine R., and Roaden, Arliss L. *The Research Assistantship: Recommendations for Colleges and Universities.* Bloomington, IN: Phi Delta Kappa, 1975. 116 pp.

Concerns the expectations, actions, and relationships in the research assistantship. Research assistants should be used so that both faculty supervisor and graduate assistant benefit. Concludes with 7 recommendations which are based on research and approved by faculty and administrators.

INSTRUCTIONAL TECHNOLOGY

440. AECT Task Force on Definition and Terminology. *Educational Technology: Definition and Glossary of Terms.* Vol. 1. AECT Task Force on Definition and Terminology. Washington, DC: Association for Educational Communications and Technology, 1977. 365 pp.

Instructional and educational definitions are given in this book. Theoretical, professional, and historical standpoints are defined. A good reference book for planners and administrators, as well as for teachers.

441. Bass, R. K., and Lumsden, D. B. *Instructional Development: The State of the Art.* Institute for Aging Studies and Programs. Columbus, OH: Collegiate, 1978. 258 pp.

Describes instructional development in the United States. The area is defined; different organizations are listed; and strategies and successful ventures are evaluated. Predictions for the future, planning models, and evaluation instruments are included.

442. Brong, Gerald R., ed. *Media in Higher Education: The Critical Issues—Ideas, Analysis, Confrontation.* Pullman, WA: Information Futures, 1976. 111 pp.

A collection of papers from a conference on issues of importance to the media field in higher education includes such topics as merger of media and library resources, budget, and improving teaching and learning through use of media.

443. Brown, James W., ed. *Educational Media Yearbook.* New York: Bowker, Annual. 500 pp.

An annual review which should be helpful to planners in higher education. Present practices, as well as trends and projections, many reference tools, periodicals, media reviews, databases, etc. are listed.

444. Brown, James W., and Thornton, James W. *College Teaching: A Systematic Approach.* New York: McGraw-Hill, 1971. 217 pp.

Comments on frequently used methods of instruction including lecture and discussion. Illustrates the use of instructional technology in colleges and evaluates the role of the teacher in terms of new facilities and student needs.

445. Carnegie Commission on Higher Education. *The Fourth Revolution: Instructional Technology in Higher Education.* A Report and Recommendations by the Carnegie Commission on Higher Education. New York: McGraw-Hill, 1972. 106 pp.

A study of the use of new technology in higher education and predictions of greater use in coming years. Many specific predictions concern sharing resources by institutions of higher learning, use of computers, and learning kits for independent study.

446. DeLand, Edward C., ed. *Information Technology in Health Science Education.* New York: Plenum Press, 1978. 608 pp.

Computer assisted instruction in biology, medicine, and health professions is discussed in this publication. Specific systems and programs are described, as well as specific subject areas. Instruction on writing CAI lessons are included. A CAI system must meet 3 requirements in order to be accepted: user acceptance, reasonable cost, and ability to meet expected goals.

447. Dyer, Charles A. *Preparing for Computer Assisted Instruction.* Englewood Cliffs, NJ: Educational Technology, 1972. 187 pp.

Introduces the uses of computers in education. Explains how a computer works, how to program, and how to write CAI lessons. Also gives information on how to organize a file about computer use in education and where most information can be found.

448. Eisele, James E., et al. *Computer Assisted Planning of Curriculum and Instruction.* Englewood Cliffs, NJ: Educational Technology, 1971. 130 pp.

List ways in which computers are currently of benefit to educators, in planning curriculum and instruction. Individualized instruction is useful because of computer based resource units.

449. Emery, James C., ed. *Closing the Gap between Technology and Application.* EDUCOM Series in Computing and Telecommunications in Higher Education. Boulder, CO: Westview Press, 1978. 215 pp.

Proceedings of a 1977 EDUCOM conference which analyzes computing technology in higher education. Viewpoints of the technician, the administrator, and the user are given. This is vol. 1 of a series; each vol. has a distinctive title such as *The Reality of National Computer Networking for Higher Education* (vol. 3).

450. Heinich, Robert. *Technology and the Management of Instruction.* Washington, DC: Association for Educational Communications and Technology, 1970. 198 pp.

Advocates more attention to media in relation to teachers and their methods of instruction. Instructional technology has a definite role to play in the teaching/learning process.

451. Hoye, Robert E., and Wang, Anastasia C., eds. *Index to Computer Based Learning.* Englewood Cliffs, NJ: Educational Technology, 1973. 700 pp.

A comprehensive guide to available computer based courses and course modules, covering 98 subject matter fields at all educational levels. More that 1,750 specific subject matter programs are fully described; the programs are indexed 5 different ways for easy reference. An indispensable guide for all instructional developers.

452. Langdon, Danny G., ed. *The Instructional Design Library.* Englewood Cliffs, NJ: Educational Technology, 1978. 20 vols. About 70 pp. each vol.

Each vol. of this set is devoted to one teaching/learning strategy. Some topics are: audiotutorial, adjunct study, audiovisual training modules, backward chaining, simulation games, programed instruction, student contracts, group programs, and the teaching/learning unit.

453. Levien, Roger E., ed. *The Emerging Technology: Instructional Uses of the Computer in Higher Education.* Carnegie Commission on Higher Education. New York: McGraw-Hill, 1972. 585 pp.

Describes how computers work, how much they are used, their instructional use, and their cost. Uses nontechnical language to guide the layman to a better understanding and use of the computer.

454. Lipsitz, Lawrence, ed. *Technology and Education.* Englewood Cliffs, NJ: Educational Technology, 1971. 179 pp.

Basic information concerning educational technology is included in this book. As the use of technology gains importance in teaching, more persons involved in the teaching/learning process will find this information important.

455. McKeachie, Wilbert J. "Instructional Psychology." In *Annual Review of Psychology,* edited by Mark R. Rosenzweig and Lyman B. Porter. Vol. 25. Palo Alto, CA: Annual Reviews, 1974, pp. 166–93.

A nationally known psychologist presents a review and analysis of the literature dealing with research on effective college teaching. Major topics are the learner, the teacher, teaching methods, technology, and characteristics of the class, objectives, content testing, and feedback, information processing strategies, and principles of learning and instruction. Literature cited contains 174 items.

456. Morgan, Robert P. "Communications Satellites in Education." In *Handbook on Contemporary Education,* edited by S.E. Goodman. New York: Bowker, 1976, pp. 61–66.

Communications satellites are one of the modern developments in projecting educational programs to large numbers of people and institutions. Some of the major topics are: communication satellites, educational uses, experiments, emerging U.S. domestic satellite systems, and current issues.

457. Olmstead, Joseph A. "Small Group Methods of Instruction." In *Handbook on Contemporary Education,* edited by S.E. Goodman. New York: Bowker, 1976, pp. 367–70.

Small-group instruction refers to methods that can be used with small groups—not merely reducing the size of the group to no more than 200. Major topics are: rationale for small-group methods, common methods, research, potential uses, and cautions.

458. O'Shea, Tim. *Self-Improving Teaching Systems: An Application of Artificial Intelligence to Computer Assisted Instruction.* Basel: Birkhaueuser, 1979. 183 pp.
Investigates the feasibility of constructing teaching programs which can improve their own performance. The cycle of operations is to select an educational objective, experiment with teaching strategy, evaluate the performance, and update the set of production rules and set of assertions.

459. Perrott, Elizabeth. *Microteaching in Higher Education: Research, Development, and Practice.* Guilford, CT: Society for Research into Higher Education, 1977. 107 pp.
Examines and defines microteaching. Improvement in teaching performance results from microteaching and costs are low, as the research shows. A bibliography is included for further information.

460. Postlethwait, S. N.; Novak, J.; and Murray, H. T., Jr. *The Audio-Tutorial Approach to Learning through Independent Study and Integrated Experiences.* Minneapolis, MN: Burgess Publishing, 1972. 184 pp.
A handbook which describes the needed physical facilities, details of program operation by personnel, and preparation of tapes, films, and printed materials. The program was developed at Purdue University for botany classes.

461. Rockart, John Fralick, and Morton, Michael S. Scott. *Computers and the Learning Process in Higher Education.* Carnegie Commission on Higher Education. New York: McGraw-Hill, 1975. 356 pp.
There will be an increase in the use of computer technology brought about by decreased costs of equipment, software and development of the mini-computer. Television has increased the teaching/learning possibilities because of the 2-way feedback development.

462. Rushby, Nicholas John. *Computers in the Teaching Process.* New York: Wiley and Sons, 1979. 74 pp.
Presents the essentials of using the computer in the teaching-learning situation in a sophisticated but very readable style. Discusses computer assisted learning (CAL) and its use, computer managed learning, informatics and education, and technological aspects. Bibliography and glossary are included.

463. ———. *An Introduction to Educational Computing, New Patterns of Learning.* London: Croom Helm, 1979. 123 pp.
Stresses use of computers in computer assisted and computer managed learning. Examples and diagrams permit interested persons to consider the potential of computer use. A glossary and bibliography aid in educating newcomers.

464. Ruskin, Robert S. *The Personalized System of Instruction: An Educational Alternative.* ERIC/Higher Education Research Report No. 5. Washington, DC: American Association for Higher Education, 1974. ED 093 256. 50 pp.
Concerns the personalized system of instruction (PSI), which is one of the recent efforts which emphasizes mastery and self-pacing for the student. Major topics discussed are: history and basic principles of PSI, management of a personalized course, current research findings, and the future of PSI.

465. Seibert, Ivan N. *Educational Technology: A Handbook of Standard Terminology and a Guide for Recording and Reporting Information about Educational Technology: Handbook X.* Washington, DC: U.S. Department of Health, Education, and Welfare, Office of Education, 1975. 276 pp.
Attempts to identify and standardize terminology and definitions which are used in the field of educational/instructional technology.

466. Shore, Bruce M. "Microteaching." In *Handbook on Contemporary Education,* edited by S.E. Goodman. New York: Bowker, 1976, pp. 371–74.
Microteaching, which is actual teaching but reduced in time, number of students, and range of activities, was introduced at Stanford University in 1963. Major topics are: versatility and adaptability of microteaching, guidelines based on research, an example in use, advantages in teacher training, and controversies.

467. Thiagarajan, Sivasaelam. "Programmed Instruction." In *Handbook on Contemporary Education,* edited by S.E. Goodman. New York: Bowker, 1976. pp. 463–67.
Although no longer a live concept, programed instruction (PI) has contributed a number of spin-off ideas, e.g., educational technology has replaced the old audiovisual field. Major topics are: recent developments, specific applications, and research and controversies.

468. Tickton, Sidney G., ed. *To Improve Learning: An Evaluation of Instructional Technology.* Vol. 1: Part 1: "A Report by the Commission on Instructional Technology"; Part 2: "Instructional Technology: Selected Working Papers on the State of the Art." Vol. 2: Part 3: "Instructional Technology—Theories and General Application"; Part 4: "Instructional Technology—Practical Considerations"; Part 5: "Instructional Technology—Implications for Business and Industry"; Part 6: "Instructional Technology—Economy Evaluations." New York: Bowker, 1970. Vol. 1, 441 pp. Vol. 2, 1096 pp.
These two vols. review instructional technology in use in 1970. After identification of present status there are predictions for the future. Six recommendations are made to advance the effectiveness of instruction using instructional technology.

469. Tuma, David T., ed. *Innovation and Productivity in Higher Education.* San Francisco, CA: San Francisco Press, 1977. 171 pp.
Innovation and productivity in higher education are discussed in the context of application of hardware and equipment, software, evaluations, and future directions.

470. UNESCO. *The Economics of New Educational Media: Present Status of Research and Trends.* Educational Methods and Techniques. Paris: UNESCO, 1977. 200 pp.
The findings from 200 studies are used to show processes currently used to determine the costs and to evaluate results of using various technological tools in education.

471. Venables, Peter. *Higher Education Developments: The Technological Universities, 1956-1976.* Salem, NH: Faber and Faber, 1978. 406 pp.
Describes the development, philosophy, and performances of technological higher education in Britain. This aspect of higher education has grown rapidly and that growth is discussed, as well as the academic profession, students, programs and philosophy, and recent drop in growth.

472. Weinstock, Ruth, ed. *Communications Technologies in Higher Education: 22 Profiles.* Educational Facilities Laboratories. Washington, DC: Communications Press, 1977. 155 pp.
Descriptions of innovative applications of instructional technology in college teaching from 22 institutions are given and analyzed. The use of television, computers, telephone, and other equipment is shown in detailed presentations.

LEARNING

473. Armstrong, R. H. R., and Taylor, John L., eds. *Instructional Simulation Systems in Higher Education*. Cambridge, England: Cambridge Institute of Education, 1970. 216 pp.

Describes instructional simulation systems in higher education and presents some case descriptions of techniques used in some subject areas. Each chapter is written by a specialist in a particular area and includes a bibliography. Primarily concerns the United Kingdom experiences.

474. Association for Educational Communications and Technology. *College Learning Resources Programs*. Washington, DC: Association for Educational Communications and Technology, 1977. 80 pp.

Planners in colleges and universities who are interested in learning resources, services, and functions will find these recommendations helpful.

475. Beard, Ruth M. *Teaching and Learning in Higher Education*. 2d edition. Hamondsworth, England: Penguin, 1972. 253 pp.

Provides a description of skills needed to improve college teaching for both beginning and experienced teachers. It is important to define one's objectives and to teach with these objectives in mind.

476. Berte, Neal R., ed. *Individualizing Education through Contract Learning*. Tuscaloosa, AL: University of Alabama Press, 1975. 192 pp.

Describes in detail the meaning of contract learning and gives a rationale for its use. The student determines his learning needs and a faculty member or committee determines the credit (or reward) which the student will receive for his accomplishments. Case studies of learning contracts are cited and problems are noted. Programs of nontraditional study and continuing education might find contracts a way to individualize learning for many students.

477. Blaze, Wayne, et al. *Guide to Alternative Colleges and Univesities: A Comprehensive Listing of over 250 Innovative Programs*. Boston: Beacon Press, 1974. 141 pp.

Describes programs in 5 categories: campus based B.A., 2-year A.A., external degree, special, and free universities. Uses various methods to get information and indicates by symbols the method used. Methods include visiting schools, phoning schools, reading literature, corresponding with schools, and using word-of-mouth.

478. Bowen, Howard R., and Douglass, Gordon K. *Efficiency in Liberal Education*. New York: McGraw-Hill, 1971. 151 pp.

The conventional approach to instruction should be carefully studied to see if it can be improved upon in quality and with lower costs. The costs of 6 different modes of instruction are compared in this study.

479. Bramley, Wyn. *Group Tutoring: Concepts and Case Studies*. London: Kogan Page, 1979. 221 pp.

Discusses several effective methods of group tutoring, for large and small groups. Case studies are used to show the nature of small groups within large groups and how they might help to improve staff relations, curriculum development, and students' learning.

480. Brown, George. *Lecturing and Explaining*. London: Methuen, 1978. 134 pp.

A guide to effective lecturing and explaining which covers the structure of explanations and lectures. Outlines how to design and evaluate lectures and reviews research on the subject. Effective communication is essential and some special skills are involved if students are to learn.

481. Claxton, Charles S., and Ralston, Yvonne. *Learning Styles. Their Impact on Teaching and Administration*. AAHE-ERIC/Higher Education Research Report No. 10. Washington, DC: American Association for Higher Education, 1978. ED 167 065. 68 pp.

The subject of how a person learns has been neglected in preference to a past emphasis on research dealing with the effect of different teaching techniques on the individual. Learning styles, including cognitive styles and cognitive mapping, and implementation plans are major topics.

482. Cockburn, Barbara, and Ross, Alec. *Teaching in Higher Education Series*. 9 booklets. Lancaster, England: University of Lancaster, School of Education, 1977.

Covers 3 main areas of teaching: lecture method, group management and discussion, and evaluation. Each booklet has specific suggestions for the particular teaching/learning method and contains a recommended, annotated bibliography.

483. Collier, K. G., ed. *Innovation in Higher Education*. New York: Humanities Press, 1974. 146 pp.

Reports innovations of a group of teachers whose work was sponsored by the Society for Research into Higher Education. Describes the Enfield experiment, education of architects, Goldsmith's College curriculum laboratory, and other innovations.

484. Cross, Kathryn Patricia. *Accent on Learning: Improving Instruction and Reshaping the Curriculum*. San Francisco, CA: Jossey-Bass, 1976. 291 pp.

Concerned with the obligation of higher education to provide educational opportunity to those students in the lower third of their high school class. Changes in instruction and curriculum through individualization, mastery learning, computer assisted instruction, audiotutorial and other methods are suggested to accomplish these goals.

485. Davis, James R. *Teaching Strategies for the College Classroom*. Boulder, CO: Westview Press, 1976. 136 pp.

Covers teaching strategies related to learning theory and research. Examples are used from many academic disciplines. Includes a bibliography on college teaching.

486. Diamond, Robert M., et al. *Instructional Development for Individualized Learning in Higher Education*. Englewood Cliffs, NJ: Educational Technology Publications, 1975. 189 pp.

Helpful for faculty interested in academic innovations for individualization. Many practical suggestions are made. The appendix includes helpful sections on copyrights, equipment, and types of independent learning facilities.

487. Dressel, Paul L., ed. *The New Colleges: Toward An Appraisal.* Iowa City, IA: American College Testing program, 1971. 320 pp.

Describes programs and evaluative procedures in new colleges with innovative and experimental programs. These colleges are begun because of the rigidity and disdain of institutions of higher learning but frequently the new colleges become just as unyielding as the older institutions. Imagination and evaluation are necessary in order to be responsive to the needs of the students.

488. Dressel, Paul L., and Thompson, Mary M. *Independent Study.* San Francisco, CA: Jossey-Bass, 1973. 162 pp.

Defines independent study as self-directed, self-determined academic pursuits in which each student proceeds at his/her own pace to accomplish certain goals. Honors work, close faculty supervision, and high costs per student are generally asociated with independent study but the authors assert that research shows these assumptions are not based on real assessment.

489. Ericksen, Stanford C. *Motivation for Learning.* Ann Arbor, MI: University of Michigan Press, 1974. 259 pp.

Explores the conditions for learning and is based on findings and principles from research and theory on motivation. Discusses the student as an individual; theory of the learner; instructional objectives; transfer of learning; self-esteem, attitudes and values; reinforcement; teaching students to think; technology instruction; grading and evaluation.

490. Gagne, Robert M., and Briggs, Leslie J. *Principles of Instructional Design.* New York: Holt, Rinehart, and Winston, 1974. 270 pp.

Systematic curriculum design and necessary procedures to accomplish this purpose are contained in this book of theoretical principles. Principles of human learning are the basis for suggestions to improve the teaching/learning process.

491. Heywood, John. *Assessment in Higher Education.* New York: Wiley, 1977. 289 pp.

The process of teaching and learning in universities is examined. Evaluation is considered a part of the teaching activity. The goals of the institution, as well as objectives for the course, should be of concern to the teacher. Differences and similarities in American and British educational systems and grading are clarified.

492. Hiestand, Dale L. *Changing Careers after Thirty-Five: New Horizons through Professional and Graduate Study.* New York: Columbia University press, 1971. 170 pp.

Studies people over 35 (''middle age'') who decided to change their occupation through formal study and who were enrolled full-time in colleges and universities in 4 cities. Generally, older students have received little encouragement and frequently opposition from universities. They have to overcome some difficulties not common to younger students but also they have some advantages. Fifteen case studies are given.

493. Hills, Phillip. *Teaching and Learning as a Communication Process.* New York: John Wiley, 1979. 128 pp.

Outlines practical guidelines for better communication between teacher and student. Various kinds of teaching/learning processes are described; learning theories are listed and defined; verbal and nonverbal communication, as well as audiovisual communication, are discussed; and group communication and mass communication are also examined.

494. Houle, Cyril O. *The External Degree.* San Francisco, CA: Jossey-Bass, 1973. 214 pp.

Describes nontraditional learning as a new form of lifelong learning with a utilization of many teaching/learning procedures. Students find some difficulty in adjusting to the responsibility for their own learning and teachers find it equally hard to help self-directed learners.

495. Johnston, James M., ed. *Behavior Research and Technology in Higher Education.* Springfield, IL: Charles C Thomas, 1975. 517 pp.

Provides a description of the personalized system of instruction (PSI) which has been effective in college teaching. The papers in the report concern one or more of the features associated with PSI: frequent evaluation and testing, self-pacing, student proctors, certain objectives, few formal lectures but more written materials, and high mastery requirements.

496. Keeton, Morris T., et al. *Experimental Learning: Rationale, Characteristics and Assessment.* San Francisco, CA: Jossey-Bass, 1976. 265 pp.

Describes experiences of students prior to enrollment in institutions of higher learning. The 3 sections deal with rationales, characteristics, and assessment. Another kind of experience for students includes practicums and internships but these are not the experimental learning experiences described in this book.

497. Keller, Fred S., and Sherman, J. Gilmour. *The Keller Plan Handbook: Essays on a Personalized System of Instruction.* Reading, MA: W. A. Benjamin, 1974. 99 pp.

These papers are intended as an explanation of the ''personalized'' system of instruction (PSI) which is also known as the Keller Plan. In higher education teaching this plan has been in use for about 15 years.

498. Kemp, Jerrold. *Instructional Design: A Plan for Unit and Course Development.* 2d edition. Belmont, CA: Fearon, 1977. 162 pp.

Instructional design applied to courses in higher education institutions is emphasized in this book. Components of instructional design are listed: goals and topics, learner characteristics, learning objectives, subject content, preassessment of learner, teaching/learning activities, support services, and evaluation. Planning is given great importance.

499. Kirk, Russell. *Decadence and Renewal in the Higher Learning: An Episodic History of American University and College Since 1953.* South Bend, IN: Gateway Editions, 1978. 354 pp.

Discusses the decline of higher education since 1953 when administrators began to push for increased enrollments even though academic standards began to drop. Many students enter college unprepared for academic work. Suggestions to improve conditions are: decrease centralization of colleges and universities; admit the multiversity was not feasible; support the external degree and off-campus classes; and have an honors college for those interested students.

500. Kozma, Robert B.; Belle, Lawrence W.; and Williams, George W. *Instructional Techniques in Higher Education.* Englewood Cliffs, NJ: Educational Technology, 1978. 419 pp.

Explores teaching methods for college and university faculty members. Techniques of teaching are grouped in 3 sections: one-way (books and television), 2-way (discussion and simulation or role playing), and self-instruction (computers, PSI, independent study).

501. LaFauci, Horatio M., and Richter, Paton E. *Team Teaching at the College Level.* New York: Pergamon, 1971. 157 pp.

Describes team teaching in a general education program of several courses in the College of Basic Studies at Boston University.

502. Lancaster, Otis E. *Effective Teaching and Learning.* New York: Gordon and Breach, 1974. 358 pp.

Intended for use in conferences, workshops, and institutes by engineering faculty. The principles involved may be readily adapted to other subject areas. Emphasizes the theme that teachers must actively engage students in the learning process. Discusses the importance of objectives, improvement of speaking and listening, uses of lecture and discussion, cases, and guided design.

503. Lenning, Oscar T., ed. *Improving Educational Outcomes, New Directions for Higher Education.* No. 16. San Francisco, CA: Jossey-Bass, 1976. 105 pp.

A major work on how to improve higher education learning outcomes. It covers a broad range of approaches of ways to promote student learning.

504. Lessinger, Leon M. *Every Kid a Winner: Accountability in Education.* New York: Simon and Schuster, 1970. 239 pp.

Recommends precise learning objectives and ways and means to achieve those objectives. Accountability in educational achievement should be considered of prime importance. Some ways of achieving objectives are suggested: performance contracting, use of learning technology, and independent educational outcome audit.

505. McKeefery, William J. *Parameters of Learning: Perspective in Higher Education Today.* Carbondale, IL: Southern Illinois University Press, 1970. 169 pp.

Divides the learning experience into 7 sections: people, space, instructional method, time, materials, student interaction, and gain in knowledge. There has not been much change in education practice for many years but technology has provided the means for innovative ways to encourage learning.

506. MacKenzie, Norman, et al. *Teaching and Learning: An Introduction to New Methods and Resources in Higher Education.* New York: UNESCO, 1970. 209 pp.

Inquires into new methods and resources in the teaching/learning process. There are 4 parts to the book: expansion and innovation, media, systematic approaches to teaching and learning, and management of resources.

507. Mann, Richard D., et al. *The College Classroom: Conflict, Change, and Learning.* New York: Wiley, 1971. 389 pp.

Describes what happens in the college classroom and finds a pattern using factor analysis.

508. Maxwell, Martha. *Improving Student Learning Skills: A Comprehensive Guide to Successful Practices and Programs for Increasing the Performance of Underprepared Students.* San Francisco, CA: Jossey-Bass, 1979. 518 pp.

Poorly prepared high school students need remedial help at the college level. Explains ways to identify learning difficulties of students, diagnose the problems, and help rectify the difficulties. Suggestions include: workshops, small classes, mastery learning, and flexible schedules so that students have more time to prepare.

509. Mayo, Douglas G., and Gilliland, Burl E., eds. *Learning and Instructional Improvement Digests.* J. W. Brister Library Monograph Series 8. Memphis, TN: Memphis State University Press, 1979. 120 pp.

Intended for teachers in higher education who wish to improve instruction. Contains condensed information concerning learning, instruction, and measurement.

510. Messick, Samuel, et al. *Individuality in Learning: Implications of Cognitive Styles and Creativity for Human Development.* San Francisco, CA: Jossey-Bass, 1976. 382 pp.

There is no one best approach to learning in higher education; some students learn better one way and others in a different way. This book discusses the differences in students and the implications for programs. Differences in sex, cultural background, cognitive style, and creativity affect learning.

511. Merrill, Irving R., and Drob, Harold A. *Criteria for Planning the University Learning Resources Center.* Washington, DC: Association for Educational Communications and Technology, 1977. 96 pp.

This study at the University of California discusses all aspects concerned in developing a learning resource center in an institution of higher learning. Such areas as staff, space requirements, budget, faculty involvement, and evaluation are discussed.

512. Milton, Ohmer. *Alternatives to the Traditional: How Professors Teach and How Students Learn.* San Francisco, CA: Jossey-Bass, 1972. 156 pp.

Discusses several new projects which concern learning: university without walls, cluster colleges, interdisciplinary strategies, and others. Many innovations which have been proposed and tried have not been successful.

513. Milton, Ohmer, et al. *On College Teaching: A Guide to Contemporary Practices.* San Francisco, CA: Jossey-Bass, 1978. 404 pp.

Covers traditional teaching methods, such as lecture and discussion and using description and criticism. Objectives, feedback, and testing are listed. Newer methods given include: simulation, contract learning, computer assisted instruction, case studies, and field teaching. The special needs of mature students and evaluation of teachers are treated also.

514. Morris, William H., ed. *Effective College Teaching: The Quest for Relevance*. Washington, DC: American Council on Education, 1970. 162 pp.

College students today do not want useless knowledge which has been taught in the past. They wish to have course work which will be of value now and enrich their lives later. They also wish to have teachers with real feeling for and interest in students.

515. Olmstead, Joseph A. *Small Group Instruction: Theory and Practice*. Alexandria, VA: Human Resources Research Organization, 1974. 129 pp.

Describes the instructional methods suitable for use in small groups. The author makes clear the need to tie instructional methods to specific course objectives. Nine methods are discussed in part 1.

516. Peterson, Richard E., et al. *Lifelong Learning in America: An Overview of Current Practices, Available Resources, and Future Prospects*. San Francisco, CA: Jossey-Bass, 1979. 532 pp.

A survey of current concepts and resources available for adult learning in the United States. Projections for the future are included. All those concerned with continuing and adult education will find this book helpful.

517. Rives, Stanley G., et al. *Academic Innovation: Faculty and Instructional Development at Illinois State University*. Normal, IL: Illinois State University, 1979. 179 pp.

Advises faculty how to improve teaching skills and discusses faculty development. Five faculty give profiles of university programs.

518. Roueche, John E., and Pitman, John C. *A Modest Proposal: Students Can Learn*. San Francisco, CA: Jossey-Bass, 1972. 142 pp.

Describes philosophy, theory, and practical instruction methods in order to provide education for all. Programed instruction units permit students to work at their own speed. Each student should be motivated individually as needed. Students in the program stay in school longer, achieve better, and like the system.

519. Russell, James D. *Modular Instruction: A Guide to the Design, Selection, Utilization, and Evaluation of Modular Materials*. Minneapolis, MN: Burgess Publishing, 1974. 142 pp.

This method of teaching uses "modules" (small units of learning) as an approach to individualized instruction, thus recognizing the different learning abilities of students.

520. Suczek, Robert F. *The Best Laid Plans*. San Francisco, CA: Jossey-Bass, 1972. 177 pp.

Outlines the Experimental College Program (ECP) which began in fall, 1965 at University of California, Berkeley. This experimental program was a failure and many mistakes are recounted. The program, involving the first 2 years of college, was self-contained with its own administration, faculty, teaching assistants, a house for learning and recreation, and a special curriculum. Students were concerned that they were not prepared for further study involving their careers and faculty sometimes were unwilling to be out of the mainstream of campus life.

521. Tunstall, Jeremy, ed. *The Open University Opens*. Amherst, MA: University of Massachusetts Press, 1974. 191 pp.

Describes the Open University in Britain, in contrast to adult education, and its implications for open independent learning for adults. The open university relies on media technology and correspondence, residential or campus universities. Courses are designed by faculty teams working with BBC experts, education technologists, and consultants.

522. Udolf, Roy. *The College Instructor's Guide to Teaching and Academia*. Chicago, IL: Nelson Hall, 1976. 155 pp.

A teacher with experience in engineering, management, and criminal law describes how to: lecture, lead discussion, manage a laboratory, teach inductively, and conduct a case study.

523. Valley, John R. "External Degree Programs." In *Handbook on Contemporary Education*, edited by S. E. Goodman. New York: Bowker, 1976, pp. 599–605.

LIke other kinds of nontraditional programs which developed in the early 1970s, external degree programs have brought flexibility to the standard college program and added to the concept of lifelong learning. Other names for this type of program are open universities, universities without walls, and extended universities. Some of the major topics discussed are: the extension of degree-granting authority, geographic extension of institutional operations, use of the community as an educational resource, and current issues.

524. ———. *Increasing the Options: Recent Developments in College and University Degree Programs*. New York: College Entrance Examination Board, 1972. 56 pp.

Supplies information on innovative developments which relate to college degree programs. Activities still in the planning stage and supporting services for programs are also described.

525. Voeks, Virginia. *On Becoming an Educated Person: An Orientation to College and Life*. 4th edition. Philadelphia, PA: Saunders, 1979. 249 pp.

Suggests ways in which each person can benefit from an education. Some general recommendations are to identify goals; and to develop skill in reading, listening and reasoning. Time management, examinations, and concentrations are discussed.

526. Weisgerber, Robert A. "Individualized Learning." In *Handbook on Contemporary Education*, edited by S. E. Goodman. New York: Bowker, 1976, pp. 397–402.

Since learning is done on an individual basis, the concept of individualized learning, which means that the learner perceives that the instructional system is responsive to his/her own needs, seems like a normal emphasis. Major topics are: definition, scope, specific programs, impact, and current controversies.

LIBRARY

527. Allen, Kenneth W. *Use of Community College Libraries: A Study*. Hamden, CT: Linnet Books, 1971. 159 pp.

Studies library use in 3 community colleges in Illinois and attitudes of students and faculty towards the library. The questionnaire used in the study and tabulated results are included. More research should be done in this area.

528. Anders, Mary Edna. *Libraries and Library Science in the Southeast: A Report of the Southeastern States Cooperative Library Survey, 1972–74*. Tuscaloosa, AL: University of Alabama Press, 1976. 263 pp.

Describes library services and libraries in the southeastern region of the United States. Recommendations are made to improve collections and services.

529. Avram, Henriette D., and Maruyama, Lenore S., eds. *Towards a National Library and Information Service Network: The Library Bibliographic Component*. Library of Congress, Network Advisory Group. Washington, DC: Library of Congress, 1977. 66 pp.

Describes networks in the United States. National services at the Library of Congress such as National Union Catalog, Conversion of Serials, and MARC database are also described.

530. Baumol, William J., and Marcus, Matityahu. *Economics of Academic Libraries*. Washington, DC: American Council on Education, 1973. 98 pp.

Examines economic data on college and university libraries with the intention of providing help for projection and long-range planning. Some aspects considered are growth rates, library costs, trends, and long-range plans. Statistics have been assembled and used to support the text of the book.

531. Breivik, Patricia S. *Open Admissions and the Academic Library*. Chicago: American Library Association, 1977. 131 pp.

The impact of open admissions on the library should be of great concern to librarians. This book is based on research from an experiment at Brooklyn College in 1972. Librarians should be actively involved in campus affairs and this includes developing remedial support for disadvantaged students. Library instruction must be flexible and there should be research and evaluation.

532. Budington, William S. *The Independent Research Library*. National Commission on Libraries and Information Science. Washington, DC: NCLIS, 1974. 31 pp.

Independent research libraries are a national information resource but they will need support if they are made available to the general public.

533. Burlingame, Dwight F., et al. *The College Learning Resource Center*. Littleton, CO: Libraries Unlimited, 1978. 176 pp.

Explains how to organize, establish, and administer libraries and/or learning resource centers in 4-year institutions of higher learning.

534. California State College. *Report on the Development of the California State College Libraries: A Study of Book, Staffing, and Budgeting Problems*. Sacramento, CA: California State Colleges, Office of the Chancellor, Division of Academic Planning, 1970. 116 pp.

Discusses budget formulas for library growth and staffing. State plans seldom give much consideration to academic library cooperation.

535. Chen, Ching-chih, ed. *Quantitative Measurement and Dynamic Library Service*. Phoenix, AZ: Oryx Press, 1978. 290 pp.

Divided into 2 parts: part 1 describes different aspects of the quantitative evaluation of library services; part 2 outlines types of practical library statistical studies which can be used by a variety of libraries. A statistical background is not necessary to make use of tools and techniques described in this publication.

536. Cowley, John, ed. *Libraries in Higher Education: The User Approach to Service*. Hamden, CT: Shoe String, 1975. 163 pp.

The development and organization of polytechnics and their libraries in Great Britain is discussed in this book. Practice in British and American university libraries is discussed in relation to polytechnics. Some ways to promote library use are explored: reader services, public relations, nonprint media, and library instruction. Subject specialists also present their own problems and solutions.

537. Cuadra, Carlos A., and Bates, Marcia J. *Library and Information Service Needs of the Nation, Proceedings of a Conference on the Needs of Occupational, Ethnic and Other Groups in the United States*. Washington, DC: U.S. Government Printing Office, 1974. 314 pp.

In order to plan for improvement or change in academic library structure, it is necessary to assess client needs, information needs and consider future trends in desired library services.

538. Dahnke, Harold L., et al. Higher Education Facilities Planning and Management Manuals. Vol. 4: *Academic Support Facilities*. Boulder, CO: Western Interstate Commission for Higher Education, 1971. 72 pp.

One vol. of a 7-vol. set which uses the library as a model. It is a good example of measurement and evaluation of facility needs as applied to academic libraries.

539. Futas, Elizabeth, ed. *Library Acquisition Policies and Procedures*. Phoenix, AZ: Oryx Press, 1977. 448 pp.

Current selection and acquisition policies of public and academic libraries for print and nonprint materials are presented. A cross section of policies from 12 public and 14 academic libraries selected from over 300 policies contains helpful information. Selected sections from other libraries are also used. Subjects covered include: philosophy and goals, objectives, selection responsibilities, problem areas, special formats, and weeding.

540. Gates, Jean Key. *Guide to the Use of Books and Libraries*. 4th edition. New York: McGraw-Hill, 1979. 292 pp.

A brief history of libraries is given in the first chapter and chapter 2 deals with arrangement and organization of library materials. General information sources and specific sources in various subjects compose the rest of the publication. The emphasis is on academic libraries and how they may be used effectively. Reference librarians and those librarians who provide library instruction will find the basic information helpful.

541. Hamburg, Morris, et al. *Library Planning and Decision-Making Systems*. Cambridge, MA: MIT Press, 1974. 374 pp.

All libraries must take into consideration cooperative arrangements with other libraries to meet present and future needs of clients. In the federal government there are 3 important centers for decision making: the national libraries, Congress, and the Department of Education. State library agencies are also of growing importance.

542. Hayes, Robert M. *The National Library Network, Its Economic Rationale and Funding*. Washington, DC: NCLIS, 1974. 49 pp.

National planning for libraries is the focus for this paper. Attempts to assign financial responsibility to various levels of government and segments of society for various types of libraries.

543. Honke, Arthur. *Academic Libraries: Into the Eighties*. Chicago: Association of College and Research Libraries, 1977. 10 pp.

As enrollments of colleges and universities decrease in the 1980s, the per student cost of higher education will become greater and will increase the financial problems of academic libraries. Solutions to library problems will be partially solved by more cooperative programs, networks, computer applications, use of microforms, centralized storage, interlibrary loans, and improved management.

544. Jones, Dennis, et al. *Library Statistical Data Base Formats and Definitions* and *Commentary to Library Statistical Data Base*. Boulder, CO: National Center for Higher Education Management Systems, 1977. 349 pp. 23 pp.

The manual and commentary evaluate a library statistical database for management information needs of public and academic libraries.

545. Josey, E. J., ed. *New Dimensions for Academic Library Service*. Metuchen, NJ: Scarecrow Press, 1975. 349 pp.

A collection of 25 essays which describe new ways for libraries to meet new demands even with reduced funding. Some innovations include new organizational patterns, new technologies, and cooperative library networks.

546. Kennedy, James R., Jr. *Library Research Guide to Education: Illustrated Search Strategy and Sources*. Library Research Guide Series, No. 3. Ann Arbor, MI: Pierian Press, 1979. 80 pp.

Explains techniques which are useful and effective in library searching, especially for the student who is not well-versed in library research. Sections include: choosing a topic, narrowing a topic, card catalog, evaluating books, U.S. government documents, guides to the literature, tests for library knowledge, and an extensive bibliography which is arranged by subject.

547. Kent, Allen, ed. *Resource Sharing in Libraries: Why/How/When/Next, Action Steps*. New York: Marcel Dekker, 1974. 393 pp.

Based on 1973 conference "Resource Sharing in Libraries" which was aimed at presidents and librarians of institutions of higher learning. Cooperation and sharing of resources are principal topics discussed.

548. Kent, Allen, and Galvin, Thomas J., eds. *The On Line Revolution in Libraries*. Proceedings at the 1977 Conference in Pittsburg, PA. New York: Marcel Dekker, 1978. 303 pp.

Libraries now furnish online access to bibliographic databases as an ordinary service. This conference met to seek additional and creative ways to use online services. The librarians discussed the potential, impact, and training related to online services. Also considered were costs, quality control, evaluation, and training problems.

549. Ladd, Boyd. *National Inventory of Library Needs, 1975*. National Commission on Libraries and Information Science. Washington, DC: NCLIS, 1977. 277 pp.

This document gives current data measuring library collections, staffs, acquisitions, space, hours, and operating expenditures. All the data has implications for institutions but not for client needs.

550. Lubans, John Jr., ed. *Progress in Educating the Library User*. New York: Bowker, 1978. 230 pp.

Describes current library instruction at all levels. Of special interest is the study of 302 junior and community college library-user education programs. Most of these programs are library orientation rather than instruction. There is also a survey of 220 undergraduate libraries and instructional efforts.

551. Lyle, Guy Redvers. *The Administration of the College Library*. 4th edition. New York: Wilson, 1974. 320 pp.

Discusses the college library and defines various kinds of 2-year and 4-year institutions. There are chapters concerning every aspect of library work from governance through library buildings and equipment. The final chapter concerns library evaluation.

552. Lynch, Beverly P. *National Programs of Library and Information Services of NCLIS: Implication for College and Community College Libraries*. National Commission on Libraries and Information Science. Washington, DC: NCLIS, 1974. 28 pp.

Planners at the state, multistate, and national level should be planning for college and community college libraries. As educational costs rise and financial support declines, it will be more important than ever before for college and community college libraries to join in a national plan to share library resources and information networks.

553. MacDonald, John P. *National Planning and Academic Libraries*. Washington, DC: Association of Research Libraries, 1974. 21 pp.

Reviews the efforts of university libraries to develop multilibrary planning on the state, regional, and national level. Cites several examples of library cooperation in current use in the United States, such as the Center for Research Libraries and the Ohio College Library Center, and concludes that more cooperative planning is essential.

554. McInnis, Raymond G. *New Perspectives for Reference Service in Academic Libraries*. Westport, CT: Greenwood Press, 1978. 351 pp.

The reference librarian and faculty need to work together in order to assist students to be effective in research. Integrating classroom instruction and library research is the focus of this book. Research guides are important in reaching the desired goals.

555. Martin, Susan K. *Library Networks, 1976–77*. White Plains, NY: Knowledge Industry Publications, 1976. 131 pp.

Describes library networks as they pertain to library operations. Computer applications to interlibrary cooperation become more important each year.

556. Massman, Virgil F. *Faculty Status for Librarians*. Metuchen, NJ: Scarecrow, 1972. 229 pp.

Reviews the history of faculty status for librarians and relates arguments which support that goal. Differences and similarities of faculty and librarians are cited. Part 1 is a survey of the literature and part 2 contains the results of a survey.

557. National Commission on Libraries and Information Science. *Effective Access to the Periodical Literature: A National Program*. Task Force on a National Periodicals System. Washington, DC: U.S. Government Printing Office, 1977. 92 pp.

Contains the recommendations of a program which would coordinate existing local, state, and regional library system services and collections with major national research libraries. The Library of Congress has developed a comprehensive periodicals collection.

558. ———. *Toward a National Program for Library and Information Services: Goals for Action*. Washington, DC: U.S. Government Printing Office, 1975. 106 pp.

Concerned with national planning for academic and all other libraries and information centers for the 1970s and 1980s. Major research libraries would constitute the bibliographic foundation for a nationwide information network.

559. Palmour, Vernon E.; Bellassai, Marcia C.; and Roderer, Nancy. *Resources and Bibliographic Support for a Nationwide Library Program: Final Report to the National Commission for Libraries and Information Science*. National Commission on Libraries and Information Science. Washington, DC: U.S. Government Printing Office, 1974. 282 pp.

A report which recommends establishment of a national library network, operated at the regional level with the support of the Library of Congress.

560. Penland, Patrick R., and Mathai, Aleyamma. *The Library as a Learning Center*. New York: Marcel Dekker, 1978. 237 pp.

Encourages librarians to take a more active role in their professional work. A learning consultant should identify the needs of the patron and work with the person to provide relevant materials to meet those needs. The librarian will need background knowledge in human learning psychology and behavioral patterns. The librarian would become the catalyst between the user needs and the information available.

561. Peterson, Gary. *The Learning Center: A Sphere for Nontraditional Approaches to Education*. Hamden, CT: Shoe String Press, 1975. 146 pp.

Useful to college and university administrators and faculty as they plan and implement a learning center. A multimedia library, with

services of various kinds, innovative assistance, and leadership, is recommended.

562. Poole, Herbert, ed. *Academic Libraries by the Year 2000: Essays Honoring Jerrold Orne*. New York: Bowker, 1977. 205 pp.

A review of academic librarianship in the past 15 years. National networks and library standardizations are among the topics discussed.

563. Rogers, Rutherford D., and Weber, David C. *University Library Administration*. New York: H. W. Wilson, 1971. 454 pp.

Important current issues are discussed from the viewpoint of the director of libraries. University libraries are complex organizations and this publication endeavors to present the whole picture.

564. Smith, Jessie Carney. *Black Academic Libraries and Research Collections: An Historical Survey*. Westport, CT: Greenwood Press, 1977. 303 pp.

Analyzes the role and development of Black academic libraries and research collections. History of these libraries is presented and trends of the 1970s with recent innovations is included. Eighty-nine libraries were studied with attention given to the collections and the people who worked in the libraries. Special collections of materials related to Black history and culture are listed. Concludes with recommendations to improve services, programs, and facilities.

566. Stevens, Robert D.; Swank, Raymond C.; and Welch, Theodore E., eds. *Japanese and U.S. Research Libraries at the Turning Point*. Proceedings from Third Japan–U.S. Conference on Libraries and Information Science in Higher Education. Metuchen, NJ: Scarecrow Press, 1977. 240 pp.

The turning point reached by Japanese and American libraries concerns the management of resources in view of the need for more services. Sharing resources seems to be a necessity. Japanese and American librarians discuss library networks, cooperation, change, and meeting information needs.

567. Stone, C. Walter, comp. *Academic Change and the Library Function*. Pittsburgh, PA: Library Association, 1970. 53 pp.

Implications of current and future developments in higher education and various developments in technology which will affect academic libraries are presented. Ralph W. Tyler discusses "Changing Responsibilities of Higher Education"; James W. Brown reviews for librarians the systems approach to college and university programs; and Allen Kent suggests regional data banks which can respond quickly to inquiries for information.

568. Stueart, Robert C., and Johnson, Richard D., eds. *New Horizons for Academic Libraries*. New York: Saur, 1979. 584 pp.

Consists of short papers presented in Boston at the 40th anniversary of ACRL in 1978. These papers can serve as a handbook for academic librarians. Some current topics are budget formulas, undergraduate libraries, faculty status, and collections management.

569. Veit, Fritz. *The Community College Library*. Westport, CT: Greenwood, 1975. 221 pp.

Institutional objectives in the community college have changed the concept of the library or learning resource center. A description of the community college is given. Each aspect is discussed, begin-

Note: Item 565 has been withdrawn.

ning with personnel and ending with planning the building and a look at future development.

570. Weibel, Kathleen, and Heim, Kathleen M. *The Role of Women in Librarianship 1876–1976: The Entry, Advancement and Struggle for Equalization in One Profession.* Phoenix, AZ: Oryx Press, 1979. 510 pp.

Details the contributions made by women in the field of librarianship ina period of 100 years. Arranged in chronological order. Contains articles covering many phases of women's role in

librarianship. An annotated bibliography of over 1,000 items is included for further information. United States and Great Britain are covered.

571. Young, Harold Chester. *Planning, Programming, Budgeting Systems in Academic Libraries.* Detroit, MI: Gale Research, 1976. 227 pp.

Defines PPBs, reports on a literature search, and gives the historical development of college and university libraries. Case studies are given to show how PPBS works. Recommendations for further research are listed.

PHILOSOPHY

572. Belknap, Robert L., and Kuhns, Richard. *Tradition and Innovation: General Education and the Reintegration of the University.* New York: Columbia University Press, 1977. 130 pp.

Outlines general education at Columbia since World War II. General education included 2 years of contemporary civilization and humanities, freshman English, physical education, 2 years of natural science or mathematics and 3 years of language. Some of these courses were discarded but the curriculum is being rebuilt.

573. Cahn, Steven M. *Education and the Democratic Ideal.* Chicago: Nelson-Hall, 1979. 111 pp.

Discusses the aims of a liberal arts education. Higher education today fails to provide education for students which will enable them to understand and deal with the complex world of today. Institutions should prepare students to read, write, and speak effectively and to understand public issues. Traditional knowledge of mathematics, science, literature, art, and music is necessary for an educated person.

574. Hare, William. *Open-Mindedness and Education.* Buffalo, NY: McGill-Queen's, 1979. 166 pp.

Discusses open-mindedness and its application to educational theory and practice. Alternative views are discussed. Concludes that open-mindedness is a condition of being educated.

575. Hook, Sidney, et al., eds. *The Philosophy of the Curriculum: The Need for General Education.* Buffalo, NY: Prometheus, 1975. 281 pp.

Divides the curriculum into 3 parts: humanities; physical and biological sciences; and the social sciences. The first part of the study shows the need for the general education curriculum. The divisions of the curriculum are discussed, analyzed, and recommendations are made.

576. Kukleck, Bruce. *The Rise of American Philosophy: Cambridge, MA, 1860–1930.* New Haven, CT: Yale University Press, 1977. 674 pp.

The 70 years between the Civil War and the Depression are significant in American philosophy. Uses the relation of philosophers to Harvard University to show the growth of the intellectual community and the effects on higher education. These men helped to establish graduate training programs and the doctoral apprenticeship system. The men involved included Charles Peirce, William James, Josiah Royce, George Santayana, Alfred North Whitehead, and C. I. Lewis.

PROFESSIONAL EDUCATION

577. Anderson, G. Lester. *Trends in Education for the Professions.* ERIC/Higher Education Research Report No. 7. Washington, DC: American Association for Higher Education, 1974. ED 096 889. 51 pp.

How people become educated in the professions has not received much attention. This report presents a review of similar studies and considers common concerns and practices among professional schools. Major topics discussed are: definitions and criteria, comparative aspects and concerns of professional education processes, professions and institutions, accreditation and professional education, social responsibility and professionalization, and human resources for professional services.

578. Argyris, Chris, and Sckon, Donald A. *Theory in Practice: Increasing Professional Effectiveness.* San Francisco, CA: Jossey-Bass, 1974, 224 pp.

The reform of professional education is the subject of this book. There is also great attention given to human organizations, and their interdependence with the social structure of the profession.

579. Boley, Bruno A. *Crossfire in Professional Education: Students, the Professions, and Society.* Elmsford, NY: Pergamon, 1977. 108 pp.

Report of a conference in which representatives of several professions examined the pressures, problems, and conflicts, which are common to professional education. Professions represented include dentistry, law, medicine, engineering, and management.

580. Boyer, Calvin J. *The Doctoral Dissertation as an Information Source: A Study of Scientific Information Flow.* Metuchen, NJ: Scarecrow, 1973. 129 pp.

Studies the extent of the use of dissertations as an information source. Four subject areas were investigated: botany, chemical engineering, chemistry, and psychology. Nearly one-third of all dissertations studied were not used to provide published materials. Concludes that little use was made of the research completed for the dissertation.

581. Carnegie Commission on Higher Education. *Higher Education and the Nation's Health: Policies for Medical and Dental Education.* New York: McGraw, 1970. 128 pp.

Examines programs which provide the education of professional health personnel and makes recommendations to expand and improve the programs. Some suggestions, which refer to doctors, dentists, and allied health personnel education, include: shortened time to educate a medical doctor, national health service corps that would permit a physician to use a period of duty in a medically deprived area to take the place of armed service duty, and more federal and state aid to medical and dental schools.

582. Carnegie Council on Policy Studies in Higher Education. *Progress and Problems in Medical and Dental Education: Federal Support versus Federal Control.* San Francisco, CA: Jossey-Bass, 1976. 178 pp.

The Council voices its concern about proposed new legislation concerning medical and dental education. There are 3 warnings given: There is danger in too many new medical schools; incentives should be used rather than new controls in regard to geographic distribution and excessive specialization; foreign medical graduates have been relied upon for too long.

583. Cheit, Earl Frank. *The Useful Arts and the Liberal Tradition.* New York: McGraw-Hill, 1975. 166 pp.

Considers the newer professional fields in higher education, agriculture, engineering, business administration, and forestry. Uses 4 case studies and makes some general comments. There is also a plea for more cooperation between the liberal arts and professional schools.

584. Cullen, John B. *Structure of Professionalism: A Quantitative Examination.* New York: Petrocelli, 1978. 290 pp.

Contains research on professionalism with a comparative/quantitative approach. Some occupational groups are able to acquire power,

prestige, autonomy, and money because of the designation of profession. Points out the need for more research.

585. Freeman, James, and Byrne, P. S. *Assessment of Postgraduate Training in General Practice.* London: Society for Research into Higher Education, 1973. 153 pp.

A research project to develop methods of assessment for postgraduates in general practice. Behavioral objectives, instruments of assessment, samples, and administration procedures are related with results. The appendix contains objective tests.

586. Gifford, James F., Jr., ed. *Undergraduate Medical Education and the Elective System: Experience with the Duke Curriculum, 1966–75.* Durham, NC: Duke, 1975. 243 pp.

Describes an innovative curriculum at Duke University School of Medicine. Each chapter is written by a faculty member in a special subject. Other schools have used this system in recent years because of the success of Duke University. Some schools have combined their traditional structured system with newer ideas.

587. Harvey, James. *Minorities and Advanced Degrees.* AAHE-ERIC/Higher Education Report. Washington, DC: American Association for Higher Education, 1972. ED 062 957. 4 pp.

During the 1960s the effort for minorities was an increased emphasis on recruitment and admission at the college freshmen level. In recent times, the emphasis has moved to the graduate and professional schools. Some of the efforts to increase enrollments of minority students in medical, legal, and graduate programs are examined.

588. Hughes, Everett C., et al., eds. *Education for the Professions of Medicine, Law, Theology, and Social Welfare.* Carnegie Commission on Higher Education. New York: McGraw-Hill, 1973. 273 pp.

Reports the theory and practical skills to be taught and learned in professional schools. History, status, current problems, curricula, and future outlook for each profession are discussed.

589. Nyre, Glenn F., and Reilly, Kathryn C. *Professional Education in the Eighties: Challenges and Responses.* AAHE-ERIC/Higher Education Research Report No. 8. Washington, DC: American Association for Higher Education, 1979. ED 179 187. 51 pp.

Major changes that occurred in the 1970s will continue into the 1980s without dramatic, new developments in curriculum or experimentation. Two major themes are emphasized: integration of theory and practice, and a growing effort toward integration of professional schools, professions, private, and government agencies.

590. Packer, Herbert L., and Ehrlich, Thomas. *New Directions in Legal Education.* Carnegie Commission on Higher Education. New York: McGraw-Hill, 1972. 384 pp.

Maintains that there is a great need for diversity in legal education. There should be more emphasis on the humanities and the social sciences as they relate to the law.

591. Sammartino, Peter. *Demanage Higher Education!* East Rutherford, NJ: Crispen Co., 1978. 188 pp.

Maintains that colleges and universities have forgotten the primary purpose of education—"to help the student grow." In order to accomplish this purpose good teaching must be reemphasized. Today there are too many administrators, too much paper work, too many services, and too much concern for expensive facilities. Students should come first and faculty second in an institution which is devoted to excellence.

592. Schein, Edgar, ed. *Professional Education: Some New Directions*. Carnegie Commission on Higher Education. New York: McGraw-Hill, 1972. 163 pp.

Shows the changing work patterns of professionals as they shift from self-employed individuals to employees of large bureaucracies. It is no longer possible for many professionals to have a one-to-one relationship with clients. In fact, it is sometimes difficult to decide on the identity of the client. Modules of instruction which allow students to proceed at their own rate of learning is one suggestion for the future.

593. Turner, John D., and Rushton, James, eds. *Education for the Professions*. Manchester, England: Manchester University Press, 1976. 119 pp.

Professionals in several professions discuss the education of students in their own professions from several viewpoints. The relationship between theoretical studies and practice continues to be a controversial issue and involves length of training, practical experiences, and inservice or continuing education. Other problems are paraprofessionals and the professional/client relationship.

RESEARCH AND EVALUATION

594. Anderson, Scarvia B., and Ball, Samuel. *The Profession and Practice of Program Evaluation*. San Francisco, CA: Jossey-Bass, 1978. 252 pp.

Describes many aspects of the evaluation process in a basic way. Purposes of evaluation are discussed, as well as methods and alternatives. Values and ethical responsibilities are covered in part 2 and include stories which illustrate various points. New trends in evaluation methods are outlined in the final chapter.

595. Ary, Donald; Jacobs, Lucy Cheser; and Razavieh, Asghar. *Introduction to Research in Education*. New York: Holt, Rinehart and Winston, 1972. 378 pp.

Useful for the beginning researcher. The topics covered are: scientific approach, research problem, related literature, hypotheses, statistical analysis, tools of research, research methods, research proposals, and interpreting and reporting results.

596. Borg, Walter R., and Gall, Meredith D. *Educational Research: An Introduction*. 3d edition. New York: Longman, 1979. 753 pp.

For graduate students interested in research for a project or dissertation but also of value to students who wish to understand the results of research. Research concepts and techniques are discussed in clear language and illustrations are used in order to show how to apply techniques.

597. Centra, John A. *Determining Faculty Effectiveness: Assessing, Teaching, Research and Service for Personnel Decisions and Improvement*. San Francisco, CA: Jossey-Bass, 1979. 204 pp.

The importance of faculty evaluations will continue to grow as enrollments decline and costs rise. Describes faculty evaluation, student ratings, self-assessment procedures, and colleague evaluations as they relate to classroom teaching. Assessments of student learning, research, advising, and public service are also included, with a concluding chapter concerned with assembling data and making decisions. The appendix contains descriptions of student-rating instruments.

598. Dressel, Paul Leroy. *Handbook of Academic Evaluation*. San Francisco, CA: Jossey-Bass, 1976. 518 pp.

Portrays evaluation as it exists at every level in higher education from students to administrators. Topics include: broad concept of evaluation in basic considerations; aspects in the university where there is constant evaluation; student experiences; and programs, faculty, trustees, administration, and statewide boards.

599. Glass, Gene V., and Stanley, Julian C. *Statistical Methods in Education and Psychology*. Englewood Cliffs, NJ: Prentice Hall, 1970. 596 pp.

An important book for graduate students preparing to do research in education. Concerned with introductory and intermediate statistical methods useful in educational and behavioral research. It is especially strong in the collection of examples, exercises, and statistical tables.

600. Huck, Schuyler W.; Cormier, William H.; and Bounds, William G., Jr. *Readings in Statistics and Research*. New York: Harper & Row, 1974. 387 pp.

Intended to assist undergraduate and graduate students to understand the results of research which has been done by others and also to help them evaluate journal articles. It is difficult to read research articles without some knowledge of statistical and research procedures and many students are deficient in research methods.

601. Knapper, Christopher K., et al., eds. *If Teaching Is Important*. . . . Canadian Association of University Teachers. Ottawa: Clarke, Irwin, 1977. 230 pp.

Describes many aspects of the teaching/learning process and discusses evaluation procedures in university and college settings. Academic freedom and its relationship to evaluation is an important chapter. Also teaching is examined in connection with university goals.

602. Krathwohl, David R. *How to Prepare a Research Proposal*. 2d edition. New York: Syracuse University, 1977. 112 pp.

Researchers in social or behavioral sciences will find this valuable as they prepare proposals of various kinds. Four sections contain: technical and practical help in designing a study, comments on general aspects, detailed information of proposal preparation, and other helpful aids.

603. Lenning, Oscar T. *Previous Attempts to Structure Educational Outcomes and Outcome-Related Concepts: A Compilation and Review of the Literature.* Boulder, CO: National Center for Higher Education Management Systems, 1977. 231 pp.

A summary of 2 extensive literature reviews undertaken by NCHEMS in 1974. One review was intended to define the concept educational outcome. The second search planned to develop an outcomes classification structure.

604. Mason, Emanuel J., and Denton, David E. *A Question for Graduate Training in Education: What Is Educational Research?* Lexington, KY: Center for Professional Development, 1979. 118 pp.

Reviews the history of educational research training as a basis for a view of the current condition of training researchers in education. The final chapter includes recommendations for preparing educational researchers.

605. Micek, Sidney S.; Service, Allan; and Lee, Yong S. *Outcomes Measures and Procedures Manual.* Technical Report 70. Boulder, CO: National Center for Higher Education Management Systems, 1975. 335 pp.

Suggests procedures for collecting data useful in measuring outcomes of programs in postsecondary education institutions. There are 3 categories: student growth and development, new knowledge and art forms, and community impact.

606. Miller, C. M. L., and Parlett, M. *Up to the Mark: A Study of the Examination Game.* London: Society for Research into Higher Education, 1974. 128 pp.

Explores the whole system of university assessment as it affects faculty and students. Looks at the teaching/learning process as it occurs in the college or university educational setting.

607. O'Connell, William R. Jr., and Meeth, L. Richard. *Evaluating Teaching Improvement Programs.* New Rochelle, NY: Change Magazine Press, 1978. 47 pp.

Concerns teaching improvement and evaluation. The relationship of teaching and learning is one which is in great need of research. Gives some suggestions on evaluating teaching improvement.

608. Parlett, Malcolm, and Dearden, Garry, eds. *Introduction to Illuminative Evaluation: Studies in Higher Education.* Berkeley, CA: Pacific Soundings Press, 1977. 155 pp.

Illuminative evaluation is concerned primarily with description and interpretation of program activities. Defines the purpose and methods used; contains 7 studies of college and university programs; and discusses the reasons for the use of illuminative evaluation in the study of teaching, learning, and motivation.

609. Popham, W. James, ed. *Evaluation in Education: Current Applications.* Berkeley, CA: McCutchan, 1974. 585 pp.

Contains 9 chapters written by recognized scholars in a theoretical or technical field. Each chapter deals with some aspect of educa-

tional evaluation. Some chapters include specified objectives with practice exercises so the reader may actually accomplish those objectives. The first chapter is titled "Evaluation Perspectives and Procedures" and the final chapter is "Formative Evaluation of Instruction."

610. Seldin, Peter. *How Colleges Evaluate Professors.* New York: Blythe-Pennington, 1975. 90 pp.

Describes a study concerned with the evaluation of full-time faculty who teach in an accredited liberal arts college. Academic deans are asked for information about policies and practices used in evaluation of teaching performance. Conclusions of the study and recommendations compose the final chapter. An appendix contains a sample questionnaire used in the study.

611. Smith, Virginia B., and Bernstein, Alison R. *The Impersonal Campus; Options for Reorganizing Colleges to Increase Student Involvement, Learning and Development.* San Francisco, CA: Jossey-Bass, 1979. 137 pp.

Relationship of an institution's size to its educational effectiveness has been the subject of some discussion. There is not a simple relationship between size and quality. Options are: cooperative agreements between institutions, small cluster colleges, weekend colleges, free universities, and counseling centers. More research needs to be done on this subject.

612. Thorndike, Robert L., ed. *Educational Measurement.* 2d edition. Washington, DC: American Council on Education, 1971. 768 pp.

Discusses the effectiveness and usefulness of testing instruments. The first edition was published in 1951 and some chapters in this edition are revised while others are completely rewritten.

613. Tuckman, Bruce W. *Conducting Educational Research.* 2d edition. New York: Harcourt Brace Jovanovich, 1978. 479 pp.

Describes the concepts and techniques needed to understand and apply educational research. Defines research and the role of research. Discusses selecting a problem, constructing a hypothesis, and reviewing the literature. Other steps are listed with full explanations. The final chapter concerns evaluation studies.

614. Wallhaus, Robert, ed. *Measuring and Increasing Academic Productivity.* New Directions for Institutional Research, No. 8. San Francisco, CA: Jossey-Bass, 1975. 133 pp.

In postsecondary education there is a need for research in productivity of programs and efficiency. Institutions should endeavor to expand benefits at the lowest possible costs. Several items mentioned for consideration include: class size, instructional techniques, phasing out and closing down, time-shortened degrees, faculty-initiated curricular reform, budget shifts, and reductions.

615. Wiles, David K. *Changing Perspectives in Educational Research.* Worthington, OR: Charles A. Jones, 1972. 183 pp.

The first part of this study is a description of "directed thinking." This is a process that may be used to gather, evaluate, and apply information concerning a specific problem. The second part is concerned with scientific inquiry and includes the language of research, constructing a problem, design, collecting and analyzing information, and interpretation.

RETENTION

616. Astin, Alexander W. *Preventing Students from Dropping Out.* San Francisco, CA: Jossey-Bass, 1975. 204 pp.
Astin's book is based on a follow-up study of 100,000 students who were freshmen in 1968. His questionnaire, which only 40 percent of the students completed, had very few questions concerning personality and motivation of students.

617. Carey, Phillip; Singh, Baldave; and Smith, Shirlee Stone. *The Summer of Seventy-Eight: A Creative Response to Minority Higher Education.* Office for Minority and Special Student Affairs. Minneapolis, MN: University of Minnesota, 1979. 34 pp.
Reports a pilot program which undertook to improve the academic success rate of a group of minority students at the University of Minnesota.

618. Cross, K. Patricia. *Beyond the Open Door: New Students to Higher Education.* San Francisco, CA: Jossey-Bass, 1971. 200 pp.
Implications for admitting the "new students" suggest that college faculty and administrators need to change attitudes and approaches. Simply admitting the nonconventional student is only the first step.

619. Diggs, Richard N. *Keeping Students from Dropping out of Post-Secondary Occupational Education.* Oshkosh, WI: Work Force Publications, 1979. 203 pp.

Suggests methods of retention to administrators who consider retention practices and wish to reduce student attrition in their institution.

620. Kowalski, Cash. *The Impact of College on Persisting and Nonpersisting Students.* New York: Philosophical Library, 1977. 106 pp.
Reports research on college dropouts. Expresses concern about those students who drop out.

621. Miller, Gordon W. *Success, Failure and Wastage in Higher Education: An Overview of the Problem Derived from Research and Theory.* London: Harrap, 1970. 264 pp.
Explores the reasons why students leave institutions before completing requirements for a degree. The investigation concerns mainly British students. Several aspects explored are: student characteristics, selection policies, and institutional factors.

622. Roueche, John E., and Snow, Jerry J. *Overcoming Learning Problems: A Guide to Developmental Education in College.* San Francisco, CA: Jossey-Bass, 1977. 188 pp.
The challenge of underprepared students is a common one with planners constantly trying to overcome this deficiency. Remedial or developmental education is one answer to this problem.

STUDENTS

623. Altbach, Philip G., and Kelly, David H. *American Students: A Selected Bibliography on Student Activism and Related Topics.* Lexington, MA: Heath, 1973. 537 pp.
Bibliography (not annotated) lists materials on student activism in American higher education. There are also other subjects covered such as, student attitudes, educational reform, minority students, women students, etc.

624. Astin, Alexander W. *Four Critical Years: Effects of College on Beliefs, Attitudes and Knowledge.* San Francisco, CA: Jossey-Bass, 1977. 293 pp.
This study concerns the effect of current trends in higher education on student development. Measurement is developed to examine effects of college experience on attitudes, values, aspirations, persistence, achievement, behavior patterns, and career development and satisfaction. Community colleges, open admissions, expansion of public institutions, increase in size, fewer single sex institutions, and less emphasis on residential responsibilities indicate these changes are detrimental to student development.

625. ———. *Predicting Academic Performance in College.* New York: Free Press, 1971. 299 pp.
The academic success of college freshmen can be predicted by looking at their academic and personal characteristics as high school seniors. The characteristics of the institution chosen are the next most important item in student survival and academic success.

626. Astin, Alexander W., et al. *The Power of Protest: A National Study of Student and Faculty Disruptions with Implications for the Future.* San Francisco, CA: Jossey-Bass, 1975. 208 pp.
A 3-year study by the American Council on Education which concerns student activism and attitudes during the late sixties and early seventies is summarized. These student protests did have wide-ranging effects on colleges and universities.

627. Astin, Helen S., and Hersch, Werner Z., eds. *The Higher Education of Women: Essays in Honor of Rosemary Park.* New York: Praeger, 1978. 182 pp.

Concerns higher education for women: development; intellectual abilities of women, scholarly achievements, and policy recommendations. Includes an interview with Rosemary Park.

628. Baird, Leonard L.; Clark Mary Jo; and Hartnett, Rodney T. *The Graduates: A Report on the Characteristics and Plans of College Seniors.* Princeton, NJ: Educational Testing Service, 1973. 210 pp.

A comprehensive picture of the college seniors of 1971 emerges from this report as the researchers inquire about the development of career choices and future plans. Overall, the data did not indicate major changes in students.

629. Bayer, Alan E. *The Black College Freshman: Characteristics and Recent Trends.* Washington, DC: American Council on Education, 1972. 98 pp.

Reports data from a comparison of surveys in 1968 and in 1971. Blacks attending White colleges tend to have a better academic record than Blacks attending all-Black institutions. Blacks and Whites in White institutions have many career aspirations in common.

630. Bergman, Brian A., and Siegel, Arthur I. "Training Evaluation and Student Achievement Measurement." In *Handbook on Contemporary Education,* edited by S. E. Goodman. New York: Bowker, 1976, pp. 266–71.

Using the concept that training is a learning process to bring about planned changes in behavior, there must be a quality control stage represented by training evaluation and student measurement. Major factors are current trends and new developments.

631. Bird, Caroline. *The Case against College.* New York: David McKay Co., 1975. 308 pp.

Counselors, parents, and young people will find some help in this book as they make decisions about higher education. Some young people may decide against college; others will want to consider costs, payoffs, and alternatives.

632. Blumhagen, Kathleen O'Connor, and Johnson, Walter D. *Women's Studies: An Interdisciplinary Collection.* Westport, CT: Greenwood Press, 1978. 142 pp.

Suggests that women's studies should be part of traditional departments and that faculty would carry on research within the department. As women's studies develop, there will be innovative changes in the future.

633. Boyd, William M. *Desegregating America's Colleges: A Nationwide Survey of Black Students 1972–73.* New York: Praeger, 1974. 110 pp.

A survey of 785 Black students and 194 Black or White faculty members at 40 predominantly White institutions was made to find attitudes and reactions of those involved. One finding which emerged was that students are generally better satisfied than was believed by faculty.

634. Brown, William F., and Holtzman, Wayne H. *A Guide to College Survival.* Englewood Cliffs, NJ: Prentice-Hall, 1972. 110 pp.

Intended for college freshmen as they attempt to adjust to academic life. The section on better study habits is based on consultation with students over a 6-year period. Good sections on motivation, organization, and techniques and discussions on note taking, test taking, and theme writing.

635. Carbone, Robert F. "Nonresident Students in Public Colleges." In *Handbook on Contemporary Education,* edited by S. E. Goodman. New York: Bowker, 1976, pp. 291–94.

Approximately half a million students attend public colleges located in states other than their home states. These out-of-state students represent a cluster of educational, legal, and fiscal problems. Major topics are: scope of the problem, rules and regulations, student migration, legal issues, and voting rights.

636. Chambers, Frederick. *Black Higher Education in the United States: A Selected Bibliography on Negro Higher Education and Historically Black Colleges and Universities.* Westport, CT: Greenwood Press, 1978. 268 pp.

A bibliography divided into sections which include doctoral dissertations, institutional histories, periodical literature, masters' theses, selected books, and general references and miscellaneous.

637. Cohen, Robert D., and Jody, Ruth. *Freshman Seminar: A New Orientation.* Boulder, CO: Westview Press, 1978. 142 pp.

A guide for those administrators, counselors, and faculty who are interested in preparing student to meet the academic challenges in higher education. Advocates a required seminar course for all freshmen so they will be able to take notes, to study effectively, and to obtain guidance from faculty.

638. Clark, Burton R., et al. *Students and Colleges: Interaction and Change.* Berkeley, CA: University of California Center for Research and Development in Higher Education, 1972. 327 pp.

The influence which a college or university exerts upon students is the subject of this study. Supports Feldman and Newcomb's dissertation of college impact upon students. Uses student input characteristics and college environment characteristics and finds that there is definitely a change in attitudes, values, and dispositions.

639. Cope, Robert, and Hannah, William. *Revolving College Doors: The Causes and Consequences of Dropping Out, Stopping Out, and Transferring.* New York: John Wiley, 1975. 190 pp.

Bases conclusions on extensive interviews with students. Finds that personal commitment to a goal is the best predictor of persistence in college. Student personalities, values, and needs and the way in which they are met by colleges are important determinants in their persistence. Student satisfaction comes when hopes and talents result in maturity.

640. Davidovicz, H. M. "Pass-Fail Grading Systems." In *Handbook on Contemporary Education,* edited by S. E. Goodman. New York: Bowker, 1976, pp. 176–80.

During the 1960s and 1970s this type of grading system has gained in popularity. Although this system is not popular with some faculty, it seems to be a viable option when used in a limited way. Major areas which are discussed are: problems in research, characteristics of pass-fail students, achievement under pass-fail grading, attitudes in pass-fail grading, problems, and solutions.

641. Davis, James R. *Going to College: The Study of Students and the Student Experience.* Boulder, CO: Westview Press, 1977. 248 pp.

Student development should be of the greatest importance to colleges and universities. Following a review of research literature on studies of student, there is a narrative account of a student preparing to go to college and a description of his 4 years there. The conclusion discusses the experiences of the student.

642. Doyle, Kenneth O., Jr. *Student Evaluation of Instruction*. Lexington, MA: Heath, 1975. 176 pp.

Discusses problems in using student evaluation. Gives criteria to be used in questionnaires, how to collect and analyze data, and how to guard against error. Included are sample rating forms, tables summarizing research, and a bibliography.

643. Fashing, Joseph, and Deutsch, Steven E. *Academics in Retreat: The Politics of Educational Innovation*. Albuquerque: University of New Mexico Press, 1971. 325 pp.

Describes innovative, student-activated programs at Berkeley, UCLA, San Francisco State, Western Washington, Oregon, and Stanford. Examples given are Black studies, ethnic studies, and Third World college programs. Also describes some related events, riots, assaults, various reactions of faculty, students, and legislatures.

644. Fay, Margaret A., and Weintraub, Jeff A. *Political Ideologies of Graduate Students: Crystallization, Consistency, and Contextual Effects*. Carnegie Commission on Higher Education. New York: McGraw-Hill, 1973. 140 pp.

Examines the relation between the student's self-concept and attitudes as shown by questionnaires. The first part consists mainly of analysis of data and results; the second part is more theoretical and points out the need for further research.

645. Feldman, Kenneth A., and Newcomb, Theodore M. *The Impact of Colleges on Students*. San Francisco, CA: Jossey-Bass, 1970. Vol. 1, 474 pp. Vol. 2, 171 pp.

In the final report of the Carnegie Foundation for the Advancement of Teaching, vol. 1 is the text and vol. 2 contains tables. Some topics considered are: change and stability during the college years, diversity in colleges and major fields, student residence, student culture, background, personality and college impacts.

646. Fenske, Robert H., and Scott, Craig S. *The Changing Profile of College Students*. Research Report No. 10. Washington, DC: American Association for Higher Education, 1973. 84 pp.

Enrollment trends and a recently completed comprehensive survey of student characteristics are presented. Although enrollment is declining, diversity among students seems to be increasing. One use of this study is that of a benchmark for evaluating future studies of enrollment trends.

647. Goode, Kenneth S. "Student Dissent: Always Was and Always Will Be." In *Handbook on Contemporary Education,* edited by S. E. Goodman. New York: Bowker, 1976, pp. 276–79.

Since medieval times universities and the students have been critics of society and have protested against various developments in various ways. Major topics are: student dissent, dissenters and their reasons, violent vs. nonviolent dissent, disintegration of the movement, and the future.

648. Gurin, Patricia, and Epps, Edgar. *Black Consciousness, Identity, and Achievement: A Study of Students in Historically Black Colleges*. New York: John Wiley, 1975. 545 pp.

Covers an 8-year period of research on Black college students in predominantly Black institutions. Some topics included are: emergence of Black consciousness among students, family backgrounds, achievement in the academic world, and civil rights movements.

649. Harrington, Thomas F. "Commuter Students in Urban Colleges." In *Handbook on Contemporary Education,* edited by S. E. Goodman. New York: Bowker, 1976, pp. 295–98.

Because about two-thirds of all full-time students commute to college, it is important to know about this group. Major topics are: development, lifestyle, and personal qualities; reasons for attending an urban college; and the environmental climate.

650. Henderson, William T. *A Handbook for College Success: A Psychological and Practical Approach*. Los Angeles, CA: Crescent Publications, 1978. 87 pp.

Designed to assist college students develop effective study techniques and habits. Suggestions and approaches are given to meet the needs of college students as they prepare for classwork and examinations.

651. Hyman, Herbert H.; Wright, Charles R.; and Reed, John S. *The Enduring Effects of Education*. Chicago: University of Chicago Press, 1975. 313 pp.

The results show that education does have enduring effects on the knowledge and receptivity to knowledge of adults.

652. Kesselman, Judi R. *Stopping Out*. Philadelphia, PA: Lippincott, 1976. 219 pp.

Offers advice to students who are thinking of leaving college for a period. Many colleges and universities recognize "stopping out" and give help to students who wish to leave school and return at a later date. More than 2 of every 3 who "stop out" do return to finish their degrees with more maturity and self-direction toward goals. Has valuable information not covered in other books but is not well-written and has some confusing references.

653. Klineberg, Otto. *At a Foreign University: An International Study of Adaptation and Coping*. New York: Praeger, 1979. 211 pp.

A study of postsecondary foreign students and how they are able to adapt and cope with a different environment as they seek a degree. Case studies and statistical data are included. Students react to many influences as they strive to reach desired goals.

654. Kohout, Karen, and Kleinfeld, Judith. *Alaska Natives in Higher Education*. Institute of Social, Economic, and Government Research. Fairbanks, AK: University of Alaska, 1974. 49 pp.

The progress made by Alaska colleges toward increasing the college success of native students is examined in this study. The time period is 1963 to 1972, with 3 institutions involved. Poor academic preparation and poor social adjustments are found to be the most frequent problems faced by native Alaskans.

655. Komarovsky, Mirra. *Women in the Modern World: Their Education and Their Dilemmas*. New York: Irvington, 1971. 319 pp.

Historical viewpoint of educating women is given along with testing, role, homemaker problems, place of education, and a philosophy of women's education. There is an index and a guide to case materials listed by the chapter in which they appear.

656. Lamont, Lansing. *Campus Shock: A Firsthand Report on College Life Today*. New York: E. P. Dutton, 1979. 144 pp.

Presents a picture of students and current conditions on campus, from interviews with students, parents, teachers, and administrators of the campuses of a dozen prominent universities in the United States. Depicts the academic and social pressures which affect students who are presently enrolled in higher education.

657. McClain, J. Dudley, Jr. *Political Profiles of College Students in Southern Appalachia: Socio-Political Attitudes, Preferences, Personality and Characteristics*. Atlanta, GA: Resurgens Publications, 1978. 315 pp.

Presents information about the political attitudes and preferences of 2,120 students who were interviewed in 4 groups at 8 colleges and universities in southern Appalachia. A wide range of topics is used in order to obtain a picture of these new potential voters.

658. ———. *Political Profiles of Female College Students in the South: Socio-Political Attitudes, Preferences, Personality and Characteristics*. Atlanta, GA: Resurgens Publications, 1978. 499 pp.

Presents information about the political attitudes and preferences of 4,577 female students interviewed at 50 public colleges and universities in 11 southern states. The data was collected in spring 1972 through fall 1973. A wide range of topics is covered in the study.

659. Millsap, Mary Ann; Bagenstos, Naida Tushnet; and Talburtt, Margaret. *Women's Studies: Evaluation Handbook*. U.S. Department of Health, Education and Welfare. Washington, DC: National Institute of Education, 1979. 70 pp.

Describes the problems of women's studies evaluation. Examples are given concerning the uses of evaluation, measurement of goals and objectives, research and instrument design, data analysis, and reports.

660. Orr, Lea. *A Year between School and University*. Atlantic Highlands, NJ: Humanities, 1974. 59 pp.

Examines the advantages and disadvantages of a year between the end of secondary schooling and the beginning of study at an institution of higher education. The main effects studied were the effect of this break upon performance at the university and students' views on delayed entry.

661. Pace, C. Robert. *The Demise of Diversity: A Comparative Profile of Eight Types of Institutions*. New York: McGraw-Hill, 1974. 131 pp.

Data was collected in 1969 from alumni of 1950 and current college juniors at 8 types of institutions of higher learning. The conclusions indicate that fewer students now have a rich and full campus experience. More benefits which should be expected are "personal and social development, liberal interests and attitudes, and involvement in civic and cultural affairs."

662. Parker, Betty J., and Parker, Franklin, eds. *Women's Education—A World View: Annotated Bibliography of Doctoral Dissertations*. Westport, CT: Greenwood Press, 1979. 470 pp.

A 2-vol. set which includes historical and contemporary research on studies of women's education. Vol. 1 is an annotated bibliography of doctoral dissertations. Vol. 2 is a listing of English language publications.

663. Peltason, J. W., and Massengale, M. V., eds. *Students and Their Institutions: A Changing Relationship*. Washington, DC: American Council on Education, 1978. 201 pp.

Probes the lives of students and their attitudes towards higher education. Students are likely to be more serious and career-minded and to regard themselves as customers rather than clients. States their concerns for present-day students in the following areas: more need for career counseling and placement services, need for a national center for student complaints, no compromise as far as graduation standards are concerned, ways to finance education, declining enrollment, and lifelong learning.

664. Redden, Martha Ross; Davis, Cheryl Arlene; and Brown, Janet Welsh. *Science for Handicapped Students in Higher Education*. Office of Opportunities in Science. Washington, DC: American Association for the Advancement of Science, 1978. 74 pp.

Reports discussion from a conference on the barriers which prevent handicapped students from attending classes in the sciences at the college level. Suggestions for solutions of these problems are given.

665. Robinson, Lora H. *College Student Morale*. AAHE-ERIC/Higher Education Report. Washington, DC: American Association for Higher Education, 1972. ED 061 918. 4 pp.

Deals with discussion and data which represent the attitudes of 372 students at 2 liberal arts colleges concerning the college impact on students. The student peer group was the source of the most frequent positive experiences.

666. ———. *The Emergence of Women's Courses in Higher Education*. AAHE-ERIC/Higher Education Report. Washington, DC: American Association for Higher Education, 1972. ED 066 139. 4 pp.

Women's courses which are defined to be those which explore the nature of women through various approaches, e.g., historical and psychological, are intended to help restore women's self-esteem and instill a sense of motivation and personal identity.

667. ———. *Women's Studies: Courses and Programs for Higher Education*. Research Report No. 1. Washington, DC: American Association for Higher Education, 1973. 54 pp.

The concern about women's studies developed from the Women's Liberation Movement. Women should be represented fairly in traditional subject matter in the disciplines. Major topics are: background of women's studies, development of these studies, courses, program operation, and the future.

668. Rowntree, Derek. *Assessing Students: How Shall We Know Them?* London: Harper & Row, 1977. 269 pp.

Questions the purposes of assessment and what qualities it should identify. Discusses learning goals and objectives and divides them into 3 areas: life-skill objectives, methodical objectives, and content objectives. He believes that most teachers do not encourage or assess uniqueness and differences among students.

669. Sandeen, Arthur. *Undergraduate Education Conflict and Change*. Lexington, MA: Lexington Books, 1976. 143 pp.

Describes current problems faced by students in institutions of higher learning. Some of the conditions which are of interest are rigid curricula which seem to be unrelated to student needs, decline of general education, emphasis on graduate programs, and publish or perish threat. Institutions should be more perceptive regarding student needs.

670. Schlossberg, Nancy K., and Berk, Janice M., eds. *Freeing Sex Roles for New Careers*. Washington, DC: American Council on Education, 1977. 142 pp.

College career counselors need to be aware of the effects of sex stereotyping and should develop strategies to overcome those effects so they may expand the career options of college students. Contributors discuss the sociocultural norms that influence vocational choices and recommend ways in which human beings may develop to their fullest extent.

671. Sharp, Laure M. *Education and Employment: The Early Careers of College Graduates*. Baltimore, MD: Johns Hopkins, 1970. 162 pp.

Based upon available data, a major finding is the importance of the undergraduate major. In 4 areas, engineering, health, teaching, and business, more students begin graduate degrees than in the other subject areas.

672. Spaulding, Seth, and Flack, Michael J. *The World's Students in the United States: A Review and Evaluation of Research on Foreign Students*. New York: Praeger, 1976. 520 pp.

A review of evaluation studies conducted on foreign students since 1967. The first chapter is an essay about the subject as portrayed in the literature. The following chapters consist of annotated bibliographies divided into empirical or nonempirical studies.

673. Tillery, Dale, and Kildegaard, Theodore C. *Educational Goals, Attitudes and Behavior*. Cambridge, MA: Ballinger Publishing Company, 1973. 251 pp.

Using a 4-state sample of 2,560 cases of high school seniors, investigates the educational aspirations of these students in relation to background and ability. The aspirations of students toward an educational goal begin as early as eighth or ninth grade and influence attitudes and behaviors.

674. Welsh, W. Bruce. *Theories of Person-Environment Interaction: Implications for the College Student*. Iowa City, IA: American College Testing Programs, 1973. 218 pp.

Presents and reviews some theories of person-environment interaction. Five viewpoints are included: Barker's theory of behavior settings, Holland's theory of personality types, Stern's need express-culture theory, Pervin's transactional approach, and the subcultural approach. Concludes that more research is needed.

675. Warnath, Charles F. et al. *New Directions for College Counselors: A Handbook for Redesigning Professional Roles*. San Francisco, CA: Jossey-Bass, 1973. 330 pp.

Explores current college counseling and proposes program alternatives to traditional methods. Counseling programs are frequently inadequate in meeting needs of students. Three sections deal with historical and current practices, alternative approaches, and counseling Blacks and women.

676. Waren, Jonathan R. "College Grading Systems." In *Handbook on Contemporary Education*, edited by S. E. Goodman. New York: Bowker, 1976, pp. 169–75.

Grading systems which are intended to measure, report, and record student performance are a long-term controversy because grades are peripheral to the educational process. Moreover, grades are used mostly by people who had no part in the instruction where the grades occurred. Major topics are purposes of grading systems and forms of grading systems.

677. Williams, Ora. *American Black Women in the Arts and Social Sciences: A Bibliographic Survey*. Metuchen, NJ: Scarecrow Press, 1978. 197 pp.

A revised edition which lists over 1,200 entries of contributions made by Black women in America. The bibliography includes Phyllis Wheatley, Shirley Graham Du Bais, and Nikke Giovanni.

678. Wright, Nathan, Jr., ed. *What Black Educators Are Saying*. New York: Hawthorne Books, 1970. 286 pp.

Recognizes that some special approaches are necessary to educate Black students. Proposes an Afro-American University completely under the control and operation of Afro-Americans supported by the White community, with no control by that community.

679. Zysking, Harold, and Sternfeld, Robert. *The Voiceless University: An Argument for Intellectual Autonomy*. San Francisco, CA: Jossey-Bass, 1973. 193 pp.

Disciplined inquiry and wide perspectives are necessary for students to mature during the years on campus. Stresses the need for the teaching-learning relationship on the part of college professors.

Organization and Administration

ORGANIZATION

EFFECTS OF ADMINISTRATIVE STYLES

680. Anderson, Richard E., and Haar, Jerry N. *Strategic Policy Changes at Private Colleges: Educational and Fiscal Implications*. New York: Teachers College Press, 1977. 97 pp.

Attempts to answer some questions regarding the ability of private liberal arts colleges to attract more students and to improve their financial status. Studies 40 private colleges that were either religiously oriented or single-sex in the 1960s. Immediate advantages may result from an expanded mission, such as change from female to coeducational institution, but sometimes there are disadvantages. In many cases the colleges lose their distinctive characteristics which had brought some students to them.

681. Bennis, Warren G. *The Leaning Ivory Tower*. San Francisco, CA: Jossey-Bass, 1973. 154 pp.

Reveals the inner manipulations of an American university during the years 1967–70 at the State University of New York at Buffalo. A "show and tell" account of an organization with its dilemmas and problem-solving attempts.

682. Clark, Burton R. *The Distinctive College: Antioch, Reed, and Swarthmore*. Chicago: Aldine Publishing Company, 1970. 280 pp.

Describes the factors which contribute to a distinctive college known for academic excellence. Each college is portrayed historically with emphasis on its mission. Special teaching styles and curricula, as well as a stable faculty, are also important. Finally the organizational structure contributes to an enduring legend which concerns the unique value of being a student of that institution.

683. Dressel, Paul L., et al. *The Confidence Crisis: An Analysis of University Departments*. San Francisco, CA: Jossey-Bass, 1970. 268 pp.

Analyzes departmental operations and how faculty members interact within departments. It offers a guide for departmental review and self-study, ways to control curriculum development, and uses for management information systems. Finds very little difference between scientists' and humanists' behavior.

684. Gaff, Jerry G., et al. *The Cluster College*. San Francisco, CA: Jossey-Bass, 1970. 249 pp.

Describes and analyzes the mission of the cluster colleges and their practices. Special kinds of students attend these colleges. The Claremont group is used as an example of successful cooperation.

685. Gallagher, Phillip J., and Demos, George D., eds. *The Counseling Center in Higher Education*. Springfield, IL: Charles C Thomas, 1970. 399 pp.

Attempts to offer some solutions to the problems caused by rapid growth of institutions of higher education and the effects felt by students, faculty, and administration. The increased used of technology has also contributed to the impersonality seen in large universities and colleges. Counseling centers' efforts to respond to various situations on California campuses are interesting.

686. Gerth, Donald R., et al. *An Invisible Giant: The California State Colleges*. San Francisco, CA: Jossey-Bass, 1971. 239 pp.

Describes the growth and development of the California State College system. Included are historical growth, functions of the board of trustees, activities of the chancellor's office, academic senates, financial management, minority group problems, faculty unionism, and issues in coordination and governance.

687. Gross, Edward, and Grambsch, Paul. *Change in University Organization: 1964–1971*. Carnegie Commission on Higher Education. New York: McGraw-Hill, 1974. 257 pp.

Using a study in 1964 as a basis for comparison, presents data collected from 11,700 respondents to study changes in 80 universities. Finds little change in goals or values but notes other changes which were improvements over the 1964 survey. Areas considered were power structure, faculty-administration relationships, and the shape of social change.

688. Perry, Richard R., and Hull, W. Frank, IV, eds. *The Organized Organization: The American University and Its Administration*. Toledo, OH: University of Toledo, 1971. 135 pp.

Considers the organization of the university and the administrators who try to provide education for the students. One chapter deals with organization and administration from a philosophical viewpoint and others consider the individual, as well as restructuring the university.

MODELS

689. Baldridge, J. Victor. *Power and Conflict in the University: Research in the Sociology of Complex Organizations*. New York: Wiley, 1971. 238 pp.

Outlines recent changes in New York University. Describes a model which is drawn from conflict theory, community power, and interest groups, and is used to show stages in decision making. Believes that political power underlies decision making in universities.

690. Blau, Peter M. *The Organization of Academic Work*. New York: Wiley, 1973. 310 pp.

Emphasizes the structure of the American system of colleges and universities, an analysis of the interrelationships of institutional characteristics. Some elements explained are: recruitment of faculty and students; faculty inclinations toward teaching and research, as well as loyalty to the institution; drop-out reduction; and graduates who continue to earn postgraduate degrees and publish. Also discussed are salaries which attract faculty, institution size and status, and number of departments.

691. Cameron, J. M. *On the Idea of a University*. Toronto: University of Toronto Press, 1978. 92 pp.

Criticizes the trends for more vocational education and more decision making by outside agencies in higher education. Suggested remedies include other approaches to the teaching/learning process, administrative governance, and improvements in the religious or church college. State support without state control is a strong point.

692. Correa, Hector, ed. *Analytical Models in Educational Planning and Administration*. New York: David McKay, 1975. 277 pp.

Attempts to show a wide audience the relevance of formal mathematical models to actual decision making in government or educational institutions. One paper of particular interest provides a model of decision-making issues in college admissions which deals with student quality, timing of applications, and enrollments.

693. Finch, Rogers B. *Campus Planning in an Urban Area*. New York: Praeger, 1971. 99 pp.

Plans for Rensselaer Polytechnic Institute which were done by an outside corporation show a good approach to planning. A broad regional plan is developed followed by one for areas which are close together.

694. McHenry, Dean E., et al. *Academic Departments: Problems, Variations, and Alternatives*. Jossey-Bass Series in Higher Education. San Francisco, CA: Jossey-Bass, 1977. 240 pp.

Presents the organization of 4 new American institutions of the 1960s based on interdisciplinary academic structures. Discusses problems of academic structure and governance; describes the 4 institutions; and addresses leadership concerns. The 4 institutions are: University of Wisconsin—Green Bay, University of California at Santa Cruz, Hampshire, and Evergreen State.

695. Martin, Warren B., "Cluster Colleges." In *Handbook in Contemporary Education,* edited by S. E. Goodman. New York: Bowker, 1976, pp. 595–99.

Cluster colleges which developed about 1960 are a group of related or federated colleges which are in close proximity to each other but separate from an organizational standpoint. The University of California at Santa Cruz and at San Diego are examples of cluster colleges. Major topics are: definition, variations, disadvantages, and prospects.

696. Patterson, Franklin E. *Colleges in Consort*. San Francisco, CA: Jossey-Bass, 1974. 182 pp.

Provides a look at the cooperative movement, descriptions of consortia, lists of problems, and questions. Suggestions are made to improve cooperation, to establish national and state commissions interested in cooperation, to organize a funding agency, and to begin a 5-year study.

697. Wolff, Robert Paul. *The Ideal of the University*. Boston: Beacon Press, 1970. 161 pp.

Describes 4 models for the university, an idealistic conception in many ways. Some of the problems are grading, admissions, and efficiency of the institution.

THEORY

698. Baldridge, J. Victor, et al. *Policy Making and Effective Leadership: A National Study of Academic Management*. San Francisco, CA: Jossey-Bass, 1978. 290 pp.

Studies the organizational characteristics of colleges and universities and reports findings based on the analysis of information gathered from a large number of faculty members and administra-

tors. Discusses influence of unions, outside agencies, government administrators, students, and courts.

699. Cameron, Kim S. *Organizational Effectiveness: Its Measurement and Prediction in Higher Education*. Washington, DC: National Technical Information Service, 1978. 385 pp.

This study intends to "define, measure, and predict organizational effectiveness as applied to undergraduate higher education." The appendices contained questionnaires used and instruments of various kinds. Includes an extensive bibliography.

700. Goodlad, Sinclair, ed. *Education and Social Action: Community Service and the Curriculum in Higher Education*. New York: Barnes & Noble, 1975. 203 pp.

Written from a British perspective but the philosophical, pedagogical, and idealogical issues apply to American education. Fosters the idea that the whole person should benefit through community education and also that higher education concentrates too much on intellectual development. Two recommendations are a voucher system for financing and independent accrediting agencies.

701. Louis, Karen Seashore, and Sieber, Sam Dixon. *Bureaucracy and the Dispensed Organization: The Educational Extension Agent Experiment*. Norwood, NJ: Ablex Publishers, 1979. 249 pp.

A study of an application of organizational theory to the educational extension program. In this program members are located in the field and also in central headquarters. Management and field problems are the reverse of those generally found in organizational theory.

702. March, James G., and Olsen, Johan P. *Ambiguity and Choice in Organizations*. 2d ed. Bergen, Norway: Universitetsforlaget, 1979. 408 pp.

A valuable theoretical presentation for planners and administrators in higher education. Complicated concepts are appropriate for decision makers in institutions of higher learning in Norway, Denmark, and the United States.

703. Martorana, S. V., and Kuhns, Eileen. *Managing Academic Change*. San Francisco, CA: Jossey-Bass, 1975. 218 pp.

Case studies of diverse types of institutions in which changes have recently occurred are tested to formulate a theory of managing change. Trustees, administrators and faculty can become aware of various forces within the institution which influence change by using information contained in this study.

704. Palola, Ernest G., and Padgett, William. *Planning for Self-Renewal: A New Approach to Planned Organizational Change*. Berkeley, CA: Center for Research and Development in Higher Education, 1971. 126 pp.

Outlines long-range institutional planning and promotes the use of talent which may be found within the university. Lists and discusses 3 major kinds of planning: substantive, expedient, and mixed.

705. Perkins, James A., ed. *The University as an Organization*. Carnegie Commission on Higher Education. New York: McGraw-Hill, 1973. 273 pp.

A good description of the organizational structure of the university and its unique characteristics. Among the topics discussed are: functions, evaluations, communinity concept, comparisons with other social organizations, and boards of trustees.

706. Pfeffer, Jeffrey. "A Case Study: The Organizational Design of a University." In *Organizational Design*. Arlington Heights, IL: AHM Publishing, 1978, pp. 195–221.
This case study of the University of California at Berkeley is presented within a theoretical consideration of organization. Major topics discussed are: basis of influence, effect of environment in governance, interdependence of information systems, controling behavior through reporting requirements, and structure.

707. Rice, A. K. *The Modern University*. London: Tavistock, 1970. 118 pp.
Uses organizational theory to analyze the university and to improve it. Suggests that several officers take the place of the university president. The university should hire the majority of the faculty from its own graduates.

708. Riley, Gary L., and Baldridge, J. Victor, eds. *Governing Academic Organizations: New Problems, New Perspectives*. Berkeley, CA: McCutchan, 1977. 347 pp.

Academic organizations possess unique organizational characteristics and there is a difference in belief about whether these differences are disappearing. The effect on innovations which may come from restricted funds and the impact of governmental controls are also discussed. Roles of faculty and administrators are evaluated.

ADMINISTRATION

ACADEMIC

709. Adams, Walter. *The Test*. New York: MacMillan, 1971. 240 pp.
Reports the problems encountered in 9 months as acting president of Michigan State University. Dealt with students in a personal way during the height of the student protest and feels that a change in administrative principles is often necessary.

710. Beann, James, and Emmet, Thomas A., eds. *Academic Department or Division Chairman: A Complex Role*. Detroit, MI: Balamp, 1972. 299 pp.
Describes many aspects of the topic such as departmental development, curriculum innovation, and rewards for new ideas. Those persons who are presently departmental or divisional chairpersons and doctoral students will find this most helpful.

711. Baldridge, J. Victor, ed. *Academic Governance*. Berkeley, CA: McCutchan, 1971. 579 pp.
Twenty-five papers contained in this book are arranged in 6 groups: organizational features, administrative process, faculty and the governance process, effect of student revolution, external environment, and conflict and policymaking.

712. Bloustein, Edward J. *The University and the Counter Culture*. New Brunswick, NJ: Rutgers University, 1972. 117 pp.
The president of Rutgers discusses contemporary theory and issues of higher education in the United States.

713. Budig, Gene A., ed. *Perceptions in Public Higher Education*. Lincoln, NE: University of Nebraska Press, 1970. 163 pp.
Presents a case study of a major university. Ten papers on academic administration are contributed by administrators and faculty members. Philosophical questions are raised and an effort is made to increase public understanding and trust in higher education.

714. Carnegie Foundation for the Advancement of Teaching. *Neutrality or Partisanship: A Dilemma of Academic Institutions*. New York: Carnegie Foundation for the Advancement of Teaching, 1971. 82 pp.
Discusses some of the critical questions which cause disagreement between professors, including disagreement of students with students, administrators with administrators, and trustees with other trustees. The report also gives some idea of the differing views of institutions.

715. Cartter, Allan M. *Ph.D.'s and the Academic Labor Market*. New York: McGraw-Hill, 1976. 260 pp.
The oversupply of Ph.D.s and implications for the future of the demand for teachers in higher education are the concerns of this discussion. Other factors involved are student-faculty ratios and retirements.

716. Cottle, Thomas J. *College: Reward and Betrayal*. Chicago: University of Chicago Press, 1977. 190 pp.
Describes 2 institutions, Earlham in Indiana and Columbia College in Chicago, and the lives of 5 individuals. Addresses educational achievement and the conflicts which result as institutions and individuals strive to accept or reject learning and achievement.

717. Creager, John A. *Goals and Accomplishments of the ACE Internship Program in Academic Administration*. Washington, DC: American Council on Education, 1971. 51 pp.
The Academic Administration Internship Program was designed to improve the quality of persons in administration and to encourage more qualified persons to consider academic administration as a career choice. Research on nomination, evaluation, and selection was cited and the results of the Career Status Follow-up Study were listed.

718. Folger, John K.; Astin, Helen S.; and Bayer, Alan E. *Human Resources and Higher Education*. New York: Russell Sage Foundation, 1970. 475 pp.

An attempt to deal with the supply, demand, and need for educated work force. More vocational counseling will be needed at several levels in order to guide educated persons into fields where there is a short supply.

719. Freeman, Richard B., and Breneman, David W. *Forecasting the Ph.D. Labor Market: Pitfalls for Policy*. Technical Report No. 2. National Board of Graduate Education. Washington, DC: National Academy of Sciences, 1974. 50 pp.

Presents a new methodology for forecasting the supply and demand for Ph.D.s. This information is needed by administrators for making decisions and policies.

720. Furniss, W. Todd. *Steady State Staffing in Tenure Granting Institutions, and Related Papers*. Washington, DC: American Council on Education, 1973. 33 pp.

Long-term planning is extremely important for faculty and administrators, especially in a time of little growth in students or faculty populations. Suggestions to ease problems related to tenure-granting institutions are offered.

721. Gruber, Carol S. *Mars and Minerva: World War I and the Uses of the Higher Education Learning in America*. Baton Rouge, LA: Louisiana State University, 1975. 293 pp.

Studies the impact of World War I on higher education. Two relationships are of interest in this regard: the university and the state, and the scholar and patriotic citizen. The loss of academic freedom, militarization of the campus, and objective research with regard to propaganda are discussed.

722. Hefferlin, J. B. Lon, and Phillips, Ellis L., Jr. *Information Services for Academic Administration*. San Francisco, CA: Jossey-Bass, 1971. 160 pp.

A handbook for administrators of institutions of higher education which can be consulted for information needed for quick decisions. Topics covered include ways to improve internal communication, major periodicals, sharing ideas and information, consulting services, information centers which answer questions about higher education, and agencies and organizations.

723. Heiss, Ann M. *An Inventory of Academic Innovation and Reform*. Berkeley, CA: Carnegie Commission on Higher Education, 1973. 123 pp.

Innovations or changes in accredited institutions which have been adopted in the past 5 or 6 years and have been critically reviewed are listed in this publication. Under academic calendar changes several developments, such as intersession and modular course plans, are listed and explained. Admissions innovations are another major division and under that topic are listed open admissions and advanced placement.

724. Heyns, Roger W., ed. *Leadership for Higher Education: The Campus View*. Washington, DC: American Council on Education, 1977. 206 pp.

Campus leaders in all aspects of the academic world give their experiences and observations concerning the leadership exerted in institutions of higher learning.

725. Hook, Sidney. *Academic Freedom and Academic Anarchy*. New York: Cowles Book Company, 1970. 269 pp.

Believes faculty apathy and lack of use of power have contributed to student unrest. The theme of the analysis is academic constitutionalism.

726. Knowles, Asa S., ed. *Handbook of College and University Administration: Academic*. New York: McGraw-Hill, 1970. 1,553 pp.

One hundred sixty contributors have written 200 chapters covering all aspects of academic administration. Topics covered include legal aspects, admissions, learning resources, adult education, athletics, health programs, and religion on campus. Chapters range from ''Curriculum Construction and Planning'' to ''Faculty Clubs.''

727. Lewis, Lionel Stanley. *Scaling the Ivory Tower: Merit and Its Limits in Academic Careers*. Baltimore, MD: Johns Hopkins University Press, 1975. 238 pp.

Considers publication records, letters of recommendation for faculty appointment and fellowship candidates, some academic freedom cases, and studies done by others. Concludes that merit is only one factor taken into account and it is difficult to measure teaching and research. Other qualities which contribute to advancement are hard work, ability to get along with colleagues, and not making waves.

728. Medsker, Leland L., and Edelstein, Steward L. *Policymaking Guidelines for Extended Degree Programs: A Revision*. Washington, DC: American Council on Education, 1977. 124 pp.

A report of research and a policy seminar which concerns degree credits earned by unconventional or nontraditional means. Planners in higher education need to consider the suggestions contained in this publication.

729. Morrison, Jack. *The Rise of the Arts on the American Campus*. Carnegie Commission on Higher Education. New York: McGraw-Hill, 1973. 223 pp.

Studies revealed a great diversity in conditions of the arts at 17 colleges and universities. The attitudes and support of administrators and faculty varied as much as the programs. Recommendations are made for improvement.

730. National Center for Education Statistics. *Earned Degrees Conferred 1975–1976, Summary Data*. Washington, DC: U.S. Government Printing Office, 1978. 50 pp.

Statistics in this annual report can be valuable to the researcher reviewing supply and demand factors in higher education as these relate to hiring, tenure, and retirement of faculty.

731. Nicholas, David C., ed. *Perspectives on Campus Tension*. Washington, DC: American Council on Education, 1970. 232 pp.

Deals with discontents of students, faculty, trustees, and administrators. Presents 20 papers which discuss such topics as campus crises and how to reduce tensions.

732. O'Neil, Robert M., et al. *No Heroes, No Villains*. San Francisco, CA: Jossey-Bass, 1972. 173 pp.

Studies the historical events which led to the tragic confrontations in 1970 at Jackson State College and Kent State University. These events are used as background for dealing with future problems that may occur at other universities. Recommendations are made for self-governance, communication, and community relations.

733. Quann, C. James, et al. *Admissions, Academic Records, and Registrar Services: A Handbook of Policies and Procedures*. San Francisco, CA: Jossey-Bass, 1979. 481 pp.

A comprehensive guide to policies and procedures for admissions directors and registrars. Topics include preadmission counseling, admissions, enrollment, registration, grade reporting, and graduation.

734. Robertson, D. B., ed. *Power and Empowerment in Higher Education: Studies in Honor of Louis Smith*. Lexington, KY: University Press of Kentucky, 1978. 150 pp.

Discusses power in higher education as it relates to various groups in the academic community striving to achieve their goals. Faculty members and administrators present their views in essays which concern politics on campus.

735. Salmen, Stanley. *Duties of Administrators in Higher Education*. New York: Free Press, 1971. 280 pp.

Describes the jobs of 50 different higher education administrators, including presidents and vice-presidents. Deans, safety officers, and other administrators are also portrayed. Those persons outside the academic campus but connected with it need to understand the complex nature of a large university and those who direct the affairs of the organization.

736. Shotland, R. Lance. *University Communication Networks: The Small World Method*. New York: John Wiley, 1976. 179 pp.

Begins with a history of the student protest movement of the 1960s, details students' perceptions of the university, and treats faculty-administrator-student relationships. Finds that students believe they have no part in decision making in their schools. Studies the communication channels between faculty, administrators, and students in a large university.

737. Speck, David G. "The Ombudsman in American Higher Education." In *Handbook on Contemporary Education*, edited by S. E. Goodman. New York: Bowker, 1976, pp. 299–303.

The office of ombudsman has been developed at colleges and universities in the United States since 1966. This position was created to reduce some of the frustrations for students which developed from size and impersonality of institutions. Responsibilities at various campuses are listed and discussed.

738. Tonsor, Stephen J. *Tradition and Reform in Education*. La Salle, IN: Open Court, 1974. 250 pp.

Discusses educational crisis in the United States. Believes the individual student can have more control over his/her destiny without strong authoritarian control by college administrators. Also presents a case for universal and continuing education that meets the needs of society.

ACCREDITATION

739. Casey, Robert J., and Harris, John W. *Accountability in Higher Education: Forces, Counterforces, and the Role of Institutional Accreditation*. Washington, DC: Council on Post-Secondary Accreditation, 1979. 27 pp.

Accountability assumes greater importance in higher education today as pressure is exerted from many sources. The responses of institutions to this pressure and the implications of those responses for accrediting agencies is discussed in this publication.

740. Dickey, Frank G., and Miller, Jerry W. *A Current Perspective on Accreditation*. ERIC Clearinghouse on Higher Education. Washington, DC: American Association for Higher Education, 1972. ED 068 071. 68 pp.

Since there is no national ministry of education, accreditation agencies in this country serve as monitoring systems with both educational and legal implications. Major areas discussed are the historical context, social change and social values in relation to accreditation, the professions, the courts, federal involvement, and the future of accreditation.

741. Harcleroad, Fred F., and Dickey, Frank G. *Educational Auditing and Voluntary Institutional Accrediting*. ERIC/ Higher Education Research Report No. 1. Washington, DC: American Association for Higher Education, 1975. ED 102 919. 35 pp.

An educational audit should be made of each institution to determine to what extent the college is effective in implementing goals and purposes. Appropriate standards need to be developed to strengthen the relationship between educational auditing and accreditation.

742. Harris, Sherry S., ed. *Accredited Institutions of Postsecondary Education, 1979–1980: A Directory of Accredited Institutions, Professionally Accredited Programs, and Candidates for Accreditation*. Washington, DC: American Council on Education, 1979. 382 pp.

Only complete brief directory of the 4,177 accredited postsecondary institutions and programs. The most up-to-date, accurate list of institutional names, addresses, names of chief executive officers, enrollments, degrees offered, type of academic calendar, and telephone numbers. Reports accreditations of junior and senior colleges, universities, and professional and specialized schools by 9 regional and 4 national institutional accrediting agencies, as well as specialized accreditations by 39 professional agencies for 56 programs.

743. Kirkwood, Robert. "Accreditation and Higher Education." *In Handbook on Contemporary Education*, edited by S. E. Goodman. New York: Bowker, 1976, pp. 33–35.

Accreditation is a process of recognizing colleges and universities whose performance and integrity have earned confidence and respectability. Major topics discussed are: specialized program accreditation, government and accreditation, new pressures, and FRACHE.

744. Koerner, James D. *The Parsons Collge Bubble: A Tale of Higher Education in America*. New York: Basic Books, 1970. 236 pp.

Concerns an innovative, exciting experiment in higher education which became mired in an obsession with profit. Accrediting problems, faculty problems, and many unhappy people are discussed in this account of a struggling private college.

745. Orlans, Harold. *Private Accreditation and Public Eligibility*. Lexington, MA: Heath, 1975. 261 pp.

A study to determine how accreditation of higher learning institutions is related to eligibility for federal funding. Covers a 3-year period and was funded by an Office of Education grant. Concludes that the present system should be improved.

746. Trivett, David A. *Accreditation and Institutional Eligibility*. ERIC/Higher Education Research Report No. 9. Washington, DC: American Association of Higher Education, 1976. ED 132 919. 96 pp.

Accreditation becomes the equivalent of eligibility when the federal government considers funding for colleges. The major topics considered are: development of the need for eligibility determination, eligibility issues, nongovernmental accreditation, rights and roles of the states, solutions, and eligibility models.

ADMINISTRATORS

747. Academy for Educational Development. *The Idea Handbook for Colleges and Universities*. Washington, DC: Academy for Educational Development, 1979. 158 pp.

Gives brief suggestions concerning solutions to various problems in higher education. Subjects covered include management recruitment, admissions, minority students, new courses, and technology. The last section of the study provides innovative ideas from various institutions.

748. Astin, Alexander W., and Scherrei, Rita A. *Maximizing Leadership Effectiveness: Impact of Administrative Style on Faculty and Students*. San Francisco, CA: Jossey-Bass, 1980. 238 pp.

Explores the premise that presidential leadership and institutional management have an impact on student and faculty performance. A section on classifying administrative styles identifies 4 types of college presidents: the Bureaucrat, the Intellectual, the Egalitarian, and the Counselor. Other major sections deal with administrators' effects on faculty and students and enhancing administrative leadership.

749. Birenbaum, William M. *Something for Everybody Is Not Enough*. New York: Random House, 1971. 293 pp.

The personal recollections of the president of Staten Island Community College of the City University of New York. Birenbaum attended the University of Chicago after World War II, received a doctorate in law, and has since served in many capacities in higher education.

750. Brown, David G. *Leadership Vitality: A Workbook for Academic Administrators*. Washington, DC: American Council on Education, 1979. 108 pp.

Intends to advise and guide college and university administrators on how they can improve their skills in leadership and decision making. Interviews with administrators are used to compile ideas, recommendations, and helpful hints. Exercises at the end of each chapter and a questionnaire are included.

751. Cohen, Michael D., and March, James G. *Leadership and Ambiguity*. Carnegie Commission on Higher Education. New York: McGraw-Hill, 1974. 270 pp.

Reports the results of a survey of college presidents and other personnel from 42 institutions of higher learning. The information shows a picture of the president, the presidency, and the institution.

752. Corbally, Marguerite Walker. *The Partners: Sharing the Life of a College President*. Danville, IL: Interstate, 1977. 164 pp.

A guidance resource in which more than 500 college presidents' wives were surveyed on many aspects of their roles. Questions ranged from personal role perception to items concerning budget, entertainment, and travel.

753. Eble, Kenneth E. *The Art of Administration*. San Francisco, CA: Jossey-Bass, 1978. 160 pp.

Focuses attention on the department chairperson, but also shows how all academic administrators can be effective leaders in the college community. Simple, as well as complex, tasks are discussed with recommendations for solutions. Management of daily workload, time budgeting, short-range and long-range planning, and decision making are considered, and guidance is offered by an administrator with 25 years' experience.

754. Farlow, Helen. *Publicizing and Promoting Programs*. New York: McGraw-Hill, 1979. 277 pp.

A manual for those engaged in publicizing continuing education programs in business, education or other institutions. Examples of various types of publicity for different purposes are described. An annotated bibliography and glossary are included.

755. Farmer, Charles H. *Administrator Evaluation: Concepts, Methods, Cases in Higher Education*. Richmond, VA: Higher Education Leadership and Management Society, 1979. 217 pp.

The increased emphasis on accountability has increased the need for evaluation methods for faculty and administrators in higher education. Four section are devoted to defining the issues, techniques and procedures in evaluation, case studies, and recommendations concerning evaluation and planning for evaluating.

756. Galloway, Sylvia, and Fisher, Charles, eds. *A Guide to Professional Development Opportunities for College and University Administrators*. Washington, DC: American Council on Education, 1978. Paging varies.

This annual publication of the American Council on Education gives information about opportunities for professional development. Lists seminars and workshops in career planning, administration, organization and personnel management, planning, budgeting, and decision making.

757. Metzler, Ken. *Confrontation: The Destruction of a College President*. Los Angeles: Nash, 1973. 337 pp.

The life and death of Charles E. Johnson, acting president of the University of Oregon, 1968–69. Problems within and without the university resulted in tremendous stress for the administrator of a college during a tumultuous period.

758. National Association of College and University Business Officers. *Student Records Manual*. Washington, DC: National Association of College and University Business Officers, 1970. 253 pp.

Describes the responsibilities of registrars, financial aid, and admissions officers. Arranged under 3 headings: admissions system, financial aid system, and registrar system. Recommends procedures manuals and systems manuals.

759. Nordvall, Robert C. *Evaluation and Development of Administrators*. ERIC/Higher Education Research Report No. 6. Washington, DC: American Association for Higher Education, 1979. ED 176 711. 60 pp.

Focuses on a topic which has not received enough emphasis, especially in an era of accountability. Reasons for administrative evaluation and development, types of evaluation programs, selecting and implementing an evaluation program, administrative development programs, and evaluation and development of college presidents are aspects considered.

760. Rainey, Homer R. *Tower and the Dome: A Free University versus Political Control.* Boulder, C0: Pruett, 1971.

Describes problems encountered by Rainey, president of the University of Texas, 1939–44. Academic freedom and institutional governance against political interests who wish to dominate the university are defended. Provides an interesting commentary, since he was removed from the presidency.

761. Ritchie, M. A. F. *The College Presidency: Initiation into the Order of the Turtle.* New York: Philosophical Library, 1970. 179 pp.

Delineates the experiences of 16 years of college presidency: 6 years at Hartwick College in Oneonta, New York, and 10 years at Pacific University at Forest Grove, Oregon. Discusses campus violence, fraternities, Black-White relations, the church college, and fund raising.

762. Scott, Robert A. *Lords, Squires, and Yeomen: Collegiate Middle Managers and Their Organizations.* ERIC/ Higher Education Research Report No. 7. Washington, DC: American Association of Higher Education, 1978. ED 165 641. 75 pp.

The focus is on the important group of middle managers such as registrar and chief planning officer who function below the level of president and vice-president. The organizational setting, women and minorities, effort for increased competence, training, role conflicts, and role of national professional associations are discussed.

763. Shtogren, John A., ed. *Administrative Development in Higher Education: The State of the Art.* Vol. 1. Richmond, VA: Higher Education Leadership and Management Society, 1978. 205 pp.

A collection of 16 articles emphasizing the practical, operational approach rather than the theoretical. Administrative development is stressed as institutional development. Some of the topics are: evaluation and development of college administrators, organizational diagnosis as an administrative skill, management development, the chairperson as a key facilitator, and a synthesis of administrative development.

764. Sims. O. Suthern Jr., ed. *New Directions in Campus Law Enforcement.* Athens, GA: University Center for Continuing Education, 1971. 79 pp.

Presents the views of campus public safety officers on responsibilities assigned to them. Believes that the head of campus police unit should report directly to the president, that regulations and processes should be clear, and that campus police be improved by requiring more education and professional experience.

765. Smart, John C., and Montgomery, James R., eds. *Examining Departmental Management.* New Directions for Institutional Research Series. San Francisco, CA: Jossey-Bass, 1976. 124 pp.

Academic departments are the fundamental organizational unit of colleges and universities. Outlines the roles of chairpersons, functions of departments, diversity of departments, and responses to issues.

766. Vaccaro, Louis C. *Notes from a College President.* Boston: Beacon Hill Press, 1975. 122 pp.

Concerns the role of the college president as administrator and social leader. Discusses issues with confronted Vaccaro as college president during the years 1966 through 1975.

767. Wainwright, Abbott, ed. *College and University Business Administration.* Washington, DC: National Association of College and University Business Officers, 1974. 267 pp.

During the sixties and early seventies new offices and officers were added to existing administrative offices in higher education. Some new officers were affirmative action directors, ombudsmen, and judicial administrators. Some topics include business administration, administrative management, purchasing, physical management, and financial accounting.

768. Walker, Donald E. *The Effective Administrator: A Practical Approach to Problem Solving, Decision Making, and Campus Leadership.* San Francisco, CA: Jossey-Bass, 1979. 208 pp.

University president Donald Walker draws on 20 years of experience to assist administrators to understand the political nature of the academic community. Problem solving and administrative teams should be used to aid in campus administration. Lists 27 axioms for effective administration.

769. Wingfield, Clyde J., ed. *The American University: A Public Administration Perspective.* Dallas, TX: Southern Methodist University Press, 1970. 101 pp.

Concludes that the university needs better management from the president and other administrators. Presidents are especially vulnerable to political pressure from within and without the university. The increasing importance of the university seems to also increase pressure.

ADMISSIONS

770. Academy for Educational Development. *Admissions/ Recruitment: A Study of Costs and Practices in Independent Higher Education Institutions.* Washington, DC: Academy for Educational Development, Management Division, 1978. 145 pp.

Discusses a 4-month study of the costs of recruitment and admissions at 21 liberal arts institutions of higher learning.

771. Aleamoni, Lawrence M. *Methods of Implementing College Placement and Exemption Programs.* New York: College Entrance Examination Board, 1979. 59 pp.

Intended as a guide to use in developing placement and exemption programs. Lists 8 steps to follow in placement and exemption activities and gives examples of various models. Models used were taken from the placement programs at the University of Illinois at Urbana-Champaign.

772. Anderson, C. Arnold, et al. *Where Colleges Are and Who Attends: Effect of Accessibility on College Attendance.* Carnegie Commission on Higher Education. New York: McGraw-Hill, 1972. 303 pp.

Presents a study which analyzes the relationship between geographic accessibility to a college and the proportion of high school graduates who attend. Generally, college enrollment does increase when a 2-year or 4-year public institution is located in a specific area.

773. Astin, Helen S., et al. *Higher Education and the Disadvantaged Student.* Washington, DC: Human Services Press, 1972. 359 pp.

Especially helpful to institutions with programs for the disadvantaged because of information on student characteristics and the response of institutions. Based on case studies and questionnaires, completed by students.

774. Bailey, Robert, and Hafner, Anne L. *Minority Admissions*. Lexington, MA: Lexington Books, 1978. 213 pp.

Explores issues involved when colleges and universities make efforts to increase minority enrollments. Discusses general admission practices, transfer admissions, special admission programs, testing and minority students, and constitutional issues using *Brown, DeFunis, Alvey, Washington,* and *Bakke* as examples.

775. Breland, Hunter M. *Population Validity and College Entrance Measures*. New York: College Entrance Examination Board, 1979. 86 pp.

Reviews and summarizes research measures used at college entrance. A primary objective is to find if inferences concerning different populations from high school records and test scores are correct. Includes data concerning Black, Chicano, and White populations.

776. Carnegie Commission on Higher Education. *Continuity and Discontinuity: Higher Education and the Schools*. New York: McGraw-Hill, 1973. 115 pp.

Declining financial support may make it imperative for closer cooperation between high schools and colleges and universities. A flexible curriculum, maximum use of limited resources, and new admissions policies are some topics covered.

777. Carnegie Council on Policy Studies in Higher Education. *Selective Admissions in Higher Education: Public Policy and Academic Policy: The Pursuit of Fairness in Admissions to Higher Education, The Status of Selective Admissions*. Carnegie Council Series. San Francisco, CA: Jossey-Bass, 1977. 256 pp.

Presents 3 discussions: (1) recommendations of the Carnegie Council for public policy and also academic policy; (2) fairness in admissions concerning admissability (dealing with minimal qualifications) and selection of those applicants; and (3) an overview of sample admissions policies. Extensive appendix of admissions statistics.

778. Crossland, Fred E. *Minority Access to College*. New York: Schocken, 1971. 139 pp.

Analysis of present enrollment of minority groups in American colleges and a discussion of the impediments to statistical parity of ethnic groups' access to college. Political and social barriers to minority groups' access to college include testing, poor preparation, money, distance, motivation, and race.

779. Decker, Anne F.; Jody, Ruth; and Brings, Felicia. *Handbook on Open Admissions: Success, Failure, Potential*. Boulder, CO: Westview Press, 1976. 161 pp.

The open admissions experience of the City University of New York in 1973 is the topic. Lack of basic skills is the most pressing problem encountered. Other institutions with similar problems will be interested in the question of lower standards in relation to great accessibility.

780. Doermann, Humphrey. *Toward Equal Access*. New York: College Entrance Examination Board, 1978. 143 pp.

Decline in student enrollment is expected to continue into the 1980s. Discusses the adaptations which will make higher education more relevant to the world of work. Suggests more federal financial aid to students and more efficiency in administering this aid.

781. Etzioni, Amitar. *Postsecondary Education and the Disadvantaged: A Policy Study*. Educational Resources Information Center. New York: Center for Policy Research, 1970. 131 pp.

The concepts and theory promoted by this policy study should be helpful even though the data is out-of-date.

782. Frey, James S. "Admissions of Foreign Students." In *Handbook on Contemporary Education*, edited by S. E. Goodman. New York: Bowker, 1976, pp. 169–72.

Because the number of foreign students who have enrolled in American universities has grown so dramatically since World War II, a new administrative title, foreign student admissions office, and special considerations have been developed for working with this group. Major topics discussed are: enrollment of undergraduate foreign students, availability of financial assistance, and enrollment in "exotic" Ph.D. programs.

783. Gross, Theodore L. *Academic Turmoil*. New York: Anchor Press/Doubleday, 1979. 250 pp.

Experiences of a dean of humanities at City College of New York who was critical of the open admissions at the City College. Discusses the repercussions resulting from the publication of an article in the *Saturday Review* which reported on the extent of remedial teaching, the compromises forced upon the faculty, and other problems.

784. Henderson, Algo D., and Gumas, Natalie B. *Admitting Black Students to Medical and Dental Schools*. Berkeley, CA: Center for Research and Development in Higher Education, 1971. 106 pp.

Changes in admissions to medical and dental schools are needed so that more Black students may be better represented. Admissions tests are not valid and favor White middle-class students.

785. Institute for the Study of Educational Policy. *Equal Educational Opportunity for Blacks in U.S. Higher Education*. Institute for the Study of Educational Policy. Washington, DC: Howard University Press, 1976. 330 pp.

Reports on opportunities for Blacks in higher education. Statistical data are used to consider access, the ability of the student to qualify adequately in academic attainment, and the economic returns to the student.

786. McCormack, Wayne, ed. *The Bakke Decision: Implications for Higher Education Admissions*. Washington, DC: American Council on Education, 1978. 69 pp.

Analyzes and explains the implication of the U.S. Supreme Court's decision concerning *Bakke* vs. *Regents of the University of California*.

787. O'Neil, Robert M. *Discriminating against Discrimination: Preferential Admissions and the DeFunis Case*. Bloomington, IN: Indiana University Press, 1976. 271 pp.

Discusses whether preferential admissions policies are consistent with the letter and spirit of the Constitution. Also examines open admissions, expansion of junior colleges, and Black colleges as alternatives. Believes these alternatives are not adequate to meet the needs or goals for which preferential policies were planned.

788. Shulman, Carol H. *University Admissions: Dilemmas and Potential.* ERIC/Higher Education Research Report No. 5. Washington, DC: American Association for Higher Education, 1977. ED 146 826. 52 pp.

College admissions policies reflect the social and marketing trends in society. Major topics are: admissions policies and goals, the college applicant pools, legal problems, and the student perspective.

789. Simon, Larry G. *Access Policy and Procedures and the Law in U.S. Higher Education.* New York: International Council for Educational Development, 1978. 114 pp.

Written especially for German scholars and officials who are working on a binational study of higher education access policy. Is also an aid for administrators in U.S. higher education. Reviews U.S. admission policies, practices, and testing.

790. Sindler, Allan P. *Bakke, De Funis and Minority Admissions, The Quest for Equal Opportunity.* New York: Longman, 1978. 358 pp.

Examines the issues of minority admissions. Affirmative action goals are to increase Black professionals. In the *Bakke* decision the Supreme Court upheld race as a legal criterion in selective college admissions standards. Equal opportunity under the law is an issue considered.

791. Synnott, Marcia Graham. *The Half-Opened Door: Discrimination and Admissions at Harvard, Yale, and Princeton, 1900–1970.* Contributions in American History, No. 80. Westport, CT: Greenwood Press, 1979. 310 pp.

Social snobbery and elitism among undergraduates were common at Harvard, Yale, and Princeton in the early 1900s. Woodrow Wilson was an early critic of the attitudes of the time. Roman Catholic Irish and European Jews were the objects of discrimination. An historical account of religious and social bigotry at the ''Big Three,'' researched using archives and personal papers at the libraries of those institutions, as well as other sources.

792. Taubman, Paul, and Wales, Terence. *Mental Ability and Higher Educational Attainment in the 20th Century.* Carnegie Commission on Higher Education. New York: National Bureau of Economic Research, 1972. 47 pp.

Discusses the proportion of high-ability students who attended college from 1920 to 1960. Concludes that ''open access'' has not caused a decline in the average mental ability of students.

793. Wechsler, Harold. *The Qualified Student: A History of Selective College Admissions in America.* New York: John Wiley, 1977. 341 pp.

Shows historical development of admissions policies. Traces the development of admissions from faculty examination of the applicant; to certification of high schools by CEEB; to Columbia criteria to ensure cultural, intellectual, cultural, racial and socioeconomic balance; to open admissions. Conflicts of science, humanities, vocational education, academic subjects, testing, high school grades and other problems are discussed. Access to higher education is determined largely by admission policies.

794. Willingham, Warren W. *Free-Access Higher Education.* New York: College Entrance Examination Board, 1970. 240 pp.

Gives information on providing equitable access to higher education. Community colleges, technical institutes and branches of universities have helped to achieve this purpose.

795. Wilson, Logan, and Mills, Olive, eds. *Universal Higher Education.* Washington, DC: American Council on Education, 1972. 342 pp.

Possibilities of wider access to higher education should result in economic and social benefits and costs. Discusses whether all high school graduates should be involved in higher education and the needs of the work force in the United States.

796. Wing, Paul. *Higher Education Enrollment Forecasting: A Manual for State Level Agencies.* Boulder, CO: National Center for Higher Education Management Systems at Western Interstate Commission for Higher Education, 1974. 93 pp.

Provides guidance for enrollment forecasters. Techniques application are illustrated and accuracy, uses, assumptions, and data requirements are discussed.

BUSINESS AFFAIRS

797. Balderston, Frederick E., and Weathersby, George B. *PPBS in Higher Education Planning and Management; From PPBS to Policy Analysis.* Berkeley, CA: University of California, 1972. 106 pp.

The multicampus University of California adapted the use of planing-programming-budgeting systems (PPBS). This was in effect for only a short time and was gradually replaced by other forms of analysis and decision making. A case study of year-round operations at the University of California is described.

798. Bowen, Howard R. *Academic Compensation: Are Faculty and Staff in American Higher Education Adequately Paid?* New York: Teachers Insurance and Annuity Association College Retirement Equities Fund, 1978. 139 pp.

Concludes that the rate of growth in faculty salaries has not equaled that of civilian employees and faculty counterparts in business and industry. This situation is also true of educational administrators and business executives. This report is based upon data gathered from 1903–04 to 1976–77.

799. Carlson, Daryl E. *The Production and Cost Behavior of Higher Education Institutions.* Ford Foundation Program for Research in University Administration. Berkeley, CA: University of California, 1972. 181 pp.

In this study 673 4-year education institutions were put into 7 categories to determine the most efficient institutions and average ones. Results indicate that the most efficient institutions use fewer senior faculty and have more full-time undergraduates.

800. ——— *A Review of Production Function Estimation for Higher Education Institutions.* Cambridge, MA: Graduate School of Education, Harvard University, 1977. 122 pp.

Several factors enter into the decision concerning the type of study to be made about production and cost behavior. The information available and issues raised are 2 considerations. Data, methodology, and results of these studies are reviewed.

801. Caruthers, J. Kent, and Orwig, Melvin. *Budgeting in Higher Education.* AAHE-ERIC/Higher Education Research Report No. 3. Washington, DC: American Association for Higher Education, 1979. 99 pp.

A substantive treatment of the college budget which is not based on profit or income determined from sales of the product. Major topics are: budgeting perspectives, major issues, evaluation of modern budgeting, analysis of current budgeting approaches, responsibilities at different organizational levels, and the years ahead.

802. EDUCOM. *Contracting for Computing.* Vol. 2. Princeton, NJ: EDUCOM, 1975. 148 pp.

Outlines the basic issues which should be covered in contracts for lease or purchase of computer software packages by institutions of higher learning. Terms and clauses represent areas to be covered in any contract and are listed in alphabetical order.

803. Energy Task Force. *Energy Management.* Washington, DC: National Association of College and University Business Officers, 1976. 140 pp.

A handbook for the physical plant director and the chief business officers of an institution of higher education.

804. Farmer, James. *Why Planning, Programming, Budgeting Systems for Higher Education?* Boulder, CO: Western Interstate Commission for Higher Education, 1970. 24 pp.

Effective uses of PPBS and difficulties involved are recognized in this study.

805. Gross, Francis M. *A Comparative Analysis of the Existing Budget Formulas Used for Justifying Budget Request or Allocation Funds for the Operating Expenses of State Supported Colleges and Universities.* Monograph No. 9, Vol. 14. Knoxville, TN: Office of Institutional Research, University of Tennessee, 1973. 114 pp.

In this monograph budget formulas from 25 states are compared and analyzed. Guidelines are offered for developing and applying budget formulas.

806. Linhart, Cynthia A., and Yeager, John L. *A Review of Selected State Budget Formulas for the Support of Postsecondary Educational Institutions.* Pittsburgh, PA: Office of University Planning, University of Pittsburgh, 1978. 114 pp.

This summary of a task force review in Pennsylvania gives an overview of formula budgeting. Three criteria are used to classify: general approach, method of calculation, and major components.

807. Lyden, Fremont J., and Miller, Ernest G., eds. *Planning-Programming-Budgeting: A Systems Approach to Management.* 2d edition. Chicago: Markham Publishing, 1972. 423 pp.

Twenty-one papers are divided into 8 sections, each one informative on that aspect of PPBS. The concluding paper predicts the future trends for management science and operations research.

808. Merewitz, Leonard, and Sosnick, Stephen H. *The Budget's New Clothes: A Critique of Planning-Programming-Budgeting and Benefit-Cost Analysis.* Chicago: Markham Publishing, 1971. 318 pp.

Discuss positive aspects of PPB and also notes the opposite conclusions. The 5 elements of PPB are: program accounting, multiyear costing, description of activities, zero-base budgeting, and cost-benefit analysis.

809. Millett, John D. *Planning, Programming, Budgeting for Ohio's Public Institutions of Higher Education.* Columbus, OH: Ohio Board of Regents, 1970. 216 pp.

Proposes that broad patterns of purpose, organization, and output be determined by individual institutions. The state would propose standard patterns as guidelines.

810. National Association of College and University Business Officers and NCHEMS. *Procedures for Determining Historical Full Costs.* Boulder, CO: National Center for Higher Education Management Systems, 1977. 202 pp.

Presents a method to conduct a study of instructional and institutional costs. Three kinds of costing are discussed: full, variable, and standard. Internal planning and management are considered, as well as interinstitutional.

811. Ohio Board of Regents. *Program Budgeting: Universities.* Management Improvement Program. Columbus, OH: Ohio Board of Regents, 1973. 92 pp.

Good management in universities and colleges is extremely important. Gives guidelines, principles, and recommendations for administrators. The first section gives steps to be used in developing a programing budgeting system and the second section shows the implementation to be used.

812. Robinson, Daniel D., and Turk, Frederick J. *Cost Behavior Analysis for Planning in Higher Education.* Washington, DC: National Association of Colleges and University Business Officers, 1977. 101 pp.

Inadequate methods of projecting costs are frequently in use at institutions of higher learning. Lists various points to be considered in projecting costs and revenues. As an example, one of the appendices records 15 separate decision factors which need to be considered in projecting library costs.

813. Scheps, Clarence, and Davidson, E. E., eds. *Accounting for Colleges and Universities.* Baton Rouge, LA: Louisiana State University Press, 1978. 319 pp.

Outlines general principles of accounting for administrators. Believes that the person who heads the business office should be responsible to the president. This person should be one who prepares and controls budgets and is responsible for the physical plant and all money.

814. Van Alstyne, Carol, and Coldren, Sharon. *The Costs of Implementing Federally Mandated Social Programs at Colleges and Universities.* Washington, DC: American Council on Education, 1976. 62 pp.

Government involvement in higher education is costly to institutions administering federal programs. Compliance with equal opportunity laws and social security taxes are 2 major burdens. Benefits of programs are not considered, only cost.

815. Wildavsky, Aaron. *Budgeting: A Comparative Theory of Budgetary Processes.* Boston: Little, Brown, 1975. 432 pp.

Budgeting, as it exists in several countries of the world, is compared showing differences and similarities. Federal and state budgeting at several levels is examined. Budgeting principles are discussed and some of the political pressures involved.

CAMPUS AND BUILDING PLANNING

816. Athletic Institute. *Planning Facilities for Athletics, Physical Education and Recreation.* Chicago: The Athletic Institute, 1974. 210 pp.

A comprehensive report for campus planners. A glossary and annotated bibliography are helpful but nothing about nondiscrimination by sex is included.

817. Banghart, Frank, and Trull, Albert. *Educational Planning.* New York: MacMillan, 1973. 463 pp.

Deals with the planning process with specific attention given to physical planning. Educational objectives are part of the planning and continuous evaluation is stressed.

818. Biehl, Richard G. *Guide to the Section 504 Self-Evaluation for Colleges and Universities.* Washington, DC: National Association of College and University Business Officers, 1978. 127 pp.

Intended to inform educational institutions about compliance to Section 504 on equal access for the handicapped. Regulations of HEW, provisions contained in the law, and key terms are defined and explained.

819. Boozer, Howard R. *Building Quality Evaluation Procedures Manual.* Columbia, SC: South Carolina Postsecondary Education Commission, 1976. 26 pp.

A method for inspecting buildings and assigning points to them to determine whether to remodel or build new buildings.

820. Brewster, Sam F. *Campus Planning and Construction: Physical Facilities for Universities and Colleges.* Washington, DC: Association of Physical Plant Administrators of University and Colleges, 1976. 396 pp.

A professional physical plant administrator with many years of experience deals with programing, planning, and construction of physical facilities and also with maintenance and operation. The appendix contains a questionnaire and a list of contributing colleges, case studies of several universities, and various forms which may be used in construction or other planning.

821. Carpenter, J. D., ed. *Handbook of Landscape Architectural Construction.* McLean, VA: Landscape Architecture Foundation, 1976. 700 pp.

Teachers and practitioners in the field have contributed to this comprehensive handbook.

822. Coons, Maggie, and Milner, Margaret, eds. *Creating an Accessible Campus.* Washington, DC: Association of Physical Plant Administrators of Universities and Colleges, 1978. 143 pp.

A guide for making colleges and universities accessible to handicapped students in compliance with Rehabilitation Act of 1973. Illustrations included are often helpful.

823. Cotler, Stephen R., and Degraff, Alfred. *Architectural Accessibility for the Disabled of College Campuses.* New York: State University Construction Fund, 1976. 133 pp.

Section 504 of the Rehabilitation Act of 1973 gives regulations for enforcement by HEW of accessibility for the handicapped. Planners can use this as a help in decreasing architectural barriers for the handicapped.

824. Council of Ontario Universities. *Report of the Task Force—Building Costs.* Toronto, Canada: Council of Ontario Universities, 1972. 85 pp.

This task force was established to study building costs, life costs, and comparison of costs of building elements as they are related to design.

825. DeChiara, Joseph, and Callender, John H. *Time Saver Standards for Building Types.* New York: McGraw-Hill, 1973. 1,065 pp.

This book will be helpful to academic administrators who are involved in planning facilities for higher education institutions.

826. Dietz, Albert G. H., and Lam, W. M. C. *An Approach to the Design of the Luminous Environment.* Albany, NY: State University Construction Fund, 1976. 137 pp.

The 2 parts of this book, design principles and design practice, comprise a how-to manual for campus building planning.

827. Educational Facilities Laboratories. *The Economy of Energy Conservation in Educational Facilities.* New York: Educational Facilities Laboratories, 1978. 96 pp.

Electrical and mechanical equipment should be considered in view of long-run operating cost. Information can be used to identify and correct energy waste in buildings.

828. Hopf, Peter S. *Designer's Guide to OSHA.* New York: McGraw-Hill, 1975. 289 pp.

Gives information for managers of the physical plant and planning officers of OSHA standards for specific areas of building design and operation.

829. Illinois State Board of Higher Education. *Statewide Space Survey—A Survey of the Amount and Utlization of the Space Available for Higher Education in Illinois.* Springfield, IL: State Board of Higher Education, 1976. 67 pp.

State level planning must include information concerning physical facilities. The same information is necessary for completing the Higher Education General Information Survey (HEGIS) report.

830. Jones, Michael A. *Accessibility Standards Illustrated.* Springfield, IL: Capital Development Board, 1978. 217 pp.

Gives the revised standards for improving access to public buildings in Illinois for handicapped people.

831. Karwin, Thomas J. *Flying a Learning Center: Design and Costs of an Off Campus Space for Learning.* Carnegie Commission on Higher Education. New York: McGraw-Hill, 1974. 41 pp.

Designing physical facilities to meet the needs of students who want to obtain an academic degree but cannot attend campus classes presents a challenge for traditional institutions. Proposes that a facility should be designed and then analyzed to see the kinds of instruction it could support. Models are identified and described.

832. Lerup, Lars; Cronrath, David; and Liu, J. K. C. *Learning from Fire: A Fire Protection Primer for Architects.* Berkeley, CA: University of California, 1978. 99 pp.

Intends to facilitate communication by architects with fire protection engineers and building officials and to help design buildings which offer better fire protection.

833. Milner, Margaret. *Planning for Accessibility: A Guide to Development and Implementing Campus Transition Plans*. Washington, DC: Association of Physical Plant Administrators of Universities and Colleges, 1977. 86 pp.

A manual for college and university administrators who are engaged in making campus facilities accessible to the physically handicapped.

834. Newman, Oscar. *Defensible Space*. New York: Mac-Millan, 1973. 264 pp.

Uses the term "defensible space" to describe an environment which can be controlled by its residents so that it is a safe, productive, and pleasant space in which to live or work.

835. Peterson, Richard J. *Inventory of Physical Facilities in Institutions of Higher Education, Fall, 1974*. Washington, DC: U.S. Government Printing Office, 1974. 74 pp.

Summary of the HEGIS report which is listed by institutional control, level, and enrollment size.

836. Romney, Leonard C. *Higher Education Facilities Inventory and Classification Manual*. Washington, DC: Government Printing Office, 1974. 152 pp.

This manual can serve as the basis for reporting facilities' inventory data to state and federal agencies. A classification system identifies building area categories and assignable space by room use and program.

837. Stein, Richard G. *Architecture and Energy*. Garden City, NY: Anchor Press/Doubleday, 1977. 322 pp.

Helpful to the nontechnical individual who works with architects and who wishes to look into newer style architecture. New architecture should harmonize with present campus buildings but should be economical and practical.

838. Tolmach, Judy. *Student Housing*. New York: Educational Facilities Laboratories, 1972. 72 pp.

Discusses planning for the handicapped, planning for more economical operating costs, and renovation which includes modernization.

839. UNESCO. *Planning Building Facilities for Higher Education*. Stroundsburg, PA: Dowden, Hutchinson & Ross, 1975. 137 pp.

Intended for administrators, architects, or students in higher education for planning, construction, and operation of facilities. It is intended primarily for developing countries planning higher education institutions.

840. University of Illinois. *Physical, Functional, and Economic Analysis of Harker Hall at the University of Illinois, Urbana, Illinois*. Urbana, IL: University of Illinois, 1977. 20 pp.

Procedures and measures used to evaluate a 1878 building for possibile rehabilitation or for razing are detailed.

841. University of Wisconsin. *Obsolescence Report, Home Economics Building, University of Wisconsin, Madison, Wisconsin*. Madison, Wisconsin: Bureau of Capital Development, 1970. 14 pp.

The decision to remodel a home economics building was made after evaluating the building. Procedures followed are outlined.

842. Washburn, Court, et al. *Inventory and Utilization Study for Public Higher Education Fall 1969*. Sacramento, CA: California Coordination Council for Higher Education, 1971.

Describes availability and efficiency of use of space. Also studies utilization rates as they relate to operation costs and capital outlay.

843. Woolf, James R. *Space Factors and Space Utilization Values for Use in Meeting the Facility Needs of the Texas Colleges and Universities*. Austin, TX: Coordinating Board, Texas College and University System, 1971. 49 pp.

Includes factors, space utilization, and reporting procedures for physical facilities for Texas colleges and universities. Also notes standards which other states use in meeting facility needs.

844. Zachar, Sy. *Space Costing: Who Should Pay for the Use of College Space?* New York: Educational Facilities Laboratories, 1977. 43 pp.

Discusses the relationship between physical plant department and the academic departments regarding space allocation.

COLLECTIVE BARGAINING

845. Abell, Millicent D., ed. *Collective Bargaining in Higher Education: Its Implications for Governance and Faculty Status for Librarians*. Chicago: American Library Association, 1977. 161 pp.

Proceedings of an institute sponsored by the Association of College and Research Libraries in San Francisco in 1975. The majority of the articles are general and not specifically for librarians.

846. Adell, B. I., and Carter, D. D. *Collective Bargaining for University Faculty in Canada*. Ontario: Industrial Relations Centre, 1972. 95 pp.

Describes the reasons why faculty members wish for collective bargaining and the effects on Canadian universities. In 2 parts: "Causal Factors" and "Effect Factors."

847. Angell, George W., et al. *Handbook of Faculty Bargaining*. San Francisco, CA: Jossey-Bass, 1977. 593 pp.

Five sections of this book deal with different aspects of collective bargaining, each written by a person with expertise in that area. The main thesis developed is that collective bargaining can be constructive and useful in higher education.

848. Begin, James P.; Settle, Theodore; and Alexander, Paula. *Academic Bargaining: Origins and Growth*. New Brunswick, NJ: Rutgers University Press, 1977. 232 pp.

Studies the private and public institutions composing the New Jersey System of higher education and the impact of collective bargaining. Description of the study, literature on collective bargaining, and the history of collective bargaining in higher education comprise the first section of the book. In the second part, case studies of bargaining at 30 New Jersey Institutions are enumerated.

849. Bennett, James T., and Johnson, Manuel H. *Demographic Trends in Higher Education: Collective Bargaining and Forced Unionism?* International Institute for Economic Research. Ottawa, IL: Green Hill, 1979. 30 pp.

Evaluates the influence of demographic and economic trends on colleges and universities. Especially interesting are the effect of these trends on future collective bargaining.

850. Carnegie Council on Policy Studies in Higher Education. *Faculty Bargaining in Public Higher Education: A Report and Two Essays*. San Francisco, CA: Jossey-Bass, 1977. 191 pp.

Joseph Garbarino discusses selected state experiences in collective bargaining and David Feller and Matthew Finkin discuss legislative issues. Legislators, public officials, and attorneys would profit from these essays.

851. Carr, Robert K., and Van Eyck, Daniel K. *Collective Bargaining Comes to Campus*. Washington, DC: American Council on Education, 1973. 314 pp.

Issues involved and early experiences in collective bargaining are prime concerns in this book. Evaluates collective bargaining and speculate on the future in academica.

852. Chandler, Margaret K., and Julius, Daniel J. *Faculty vs. Administration: Rights Issues in Academic Collective Bargaining*. New York: National Center for the Study of Collective Bargaining in Higher Education, 1979. 116 pp.

Baruch College, City University of New York, has sponsored a study of the important issues which are often involved in collective bargaining. Some concerns listed are: faculty appointment, promotion, tenure, renewal and nonrenewal of contracts, long-range planning, management rights, and retrenchment.

853. Daniels, Arlene K., et al. *Academics on the Line: The Faculty Strike at San Francisco State*. San Francisco, CA: Jossey-Bass, 1970. 269 pp.

Sixteen authors are sympathetic to the AFT and explain the background, the strike, and the results of the unsuccessful 3-month strike. Some faculty turned left, some right, and some withdrew during this period.

854. Duryea, E. D., and Fisk, Robert S. *Collective Bargaining, the State University and the State Government in New York*. Buffalo, NY: State University of New York, 1975. 51 pp.

A concern of the academic community is the maintenance of institutional autonomy and the influence of collective bargaining. The experience of New York State and the State University of New York in this regard is of great importance.

855. Duryea, E. D., et al. *Faculty Unions and Collective Bargaining*. San Francisco, CA: Jossey-Bass, 1973. 236 pp.

Describes many issues which arise in collective bargaining for faculty. Factors which have encouraged collective bargaining in recent years are a favorable legal climate and tighter labor market. Problems involved concern membership of the bargaining unit, grievance procedures, and persons outside the university making decisions.

856. Garbarino, Joseph William, and Aussieker, Bill. *Faculty Bargaining: Change and Conflict*. New York: McGraw-Hill, 1975. 278 p.

Differentiates between the industrial style of governance and academic issues and professionalism. Discusses different aspects of faculty bargaining and believes the trend is toward faculty unionism.

857. Garfin, Molly, comp. *Collective Bargaining in Higher Education Bibliography No. 7*. National Center for the Study of Collective Bargaining in Higher Education. New York: City University of New York, 1979. 117 pp.

A selective bibliography of literature which concerns collective bargaining. Events of 1978 are included. Includes faculty and nonfaculty members and private and public colleges and universities.

858. Kemerer, Frank R., and Baldridge, J. Victor. *Unions on Campus*. San Francisco, CA: Jossey-Bass, 1975. 248 pp.

Discusses how collective bargaining will intrude upon institutional governance. The consequences of professional unionism for academic senates and institutional administration will be far-reaching and should be of great concern to higher education.

859. Ladd, Everett C., Jr., and Lipset, Seymour M. *Professors, Unions, and American Higher Education*. Berkeley, CA: The Carnegie Commission on Higher Education, 1973. 124 pp.

Analyzes the union movement among faculty members in higher education by inspecting the background, values, and institutional association. Examines the 3 major faculty associations involved in collective bargaining.

860. Lee, Barbara A. *Collective Bargaining in Four-Year Colleges*. AAHE-ERIC/Higher Education Research Report No. 5. Washington, DC: American Association for Higher Education, 1978. ED 162 542. 85 pp.

Concerns the analysis of research and other literature on the implications of faculty bargaining for decision making in 4-year colleges and universities. Major topics are: organizational perspectives, legal structure and development of faculty unionization, impact of unionization upon institutional practice, and recommendations for research and practice.

861. Leslie, David W. *Conflict and Collective Bargaining*. ERIC/Higher Education Research Report No. 9. Washington, DC: American Association for Higher Education, 1975. ED 118 051. 70 pp.

Carefully planned and carefully implemented, this study compares the way conflict is managed in 2 kinds of institutions: those presently involved in collective bargaining relationships and those operating in a more traditional approach with faculty. Major topics discussed are: review of related studies, designs and methods, results, and conclusion.

862. Levenstein, Aaron, ed. *The Uniqueness of Collective Bargaining in Higher Education*. New York: National Center for the Study of Collective Bargaining in Higher Education. Baruch College, CUNY, 1978. 112 pp.

Discusses the impact of collective bargaining on institutional governance, differences in bargaining on public and private campuses, strikes, and finances. Proceedings of the Sixth Annual Conference.

863. Lozier, G. Gregory, and Mortimer, Kenneth P. *Anatomy of a Collective Bargaining Election in Pennsylvania State Owned Colleges*. University Park, PA: Pennsylvania State University Press, 1974. 117 pp.

This research study which concerns the voting behavior of faculty at 13 Pennsylvania State Colleges and Indiana University of Pennsylvania deals with 2 potential sources of variance, namely, faculty characteristics and attitudes and opinions about several key issues of collective negotiations in higher education. Among the results discussed is that of greater homogenization of faculty.

864. Mortimer, Kenneth P., ed. *Faculty Bargaining, State Government and Campus Autonomy: The Experience in Eight States*. Report No. 87. University Park, PA: Pennsylvania State University Press and Denver, CO: Education Commission of the States. 1976. 106 pp.

There are 3 topics considered in this book relative to collective bargaining: bargaining legislation, organization of state government and provision for collective bargaining and systemwide campus authority relations under collective bargaining.

865. Mortimer, Kenneth P., and Lozier, G. Gregory. *Collective Bargaining: Implications for Governance*. University Park, PA: Pennsylvania State University Press, 1972. 69 pp.

Reviews the governance related provisions in 31 collective bargaining contracts. Major changes may result in faculty-administrator relations in the future. Conditions of employment and sharing in institutional decision making are 2 matters of concern.

866. Mortimer, Kenneth P., and Richardson, Richard C. *Governance in Institutions with Faculty Unions: Six Case Studies*. University Park, PA: Pennsylvania State University Press, 1977. 180 pp.

Case studies reveal the impact and origins of collective bargaining at 2 community colleges and 4 4-year institutions. The legal and political conditions in the states and the importance of the bargaining units were significant. Contract negotiation and contract administration phases were next studied in relation to governance. Many variations were found in accommodation during the collective bargaining process.

867. Shark, Alan R., et al. *Students and Collective Bargaining*. Washington, DC: National Student Educational Fund, 1976. 223 pp.

Student participation in collective bargaining between faculty unions and institutions is described. Little evidence is given to show much student impact. Case studies are given of student participation and different perspectives are discussed by a trustee, a professor, and a community college administrator.

868. Shulman, Carol H. *Collective Bargaining on Campus*. ERIC Clearinghouse on Higher Education Report No. 2. Washington, DC: American Association for Higher Education. 1972. ED 058 466. 48 pp.

Among the factors which have caused collective bargaining to become popular with college faculty are: a depressed job market, institutional financial problems, state and federal encroachment, and lack of real faculty governance. Other important topics are: impact on the academic community, professional rights and duties of faculty, and legal problems.

869. Smith, Robert; Axen, Richard; and Pentony, Devere. *By Any Means Necessary: The Revolutionary Struggle at San Francisco State*. San Francisco, CA: Jossey-Bass, 1970. 370 pp.

Written by 3 persons who were prominent in San Francisco State College before Hayakawa became president. The strike by Blacks and Third World students, and faculty supporters of the AFT took place in 1968–69.

870. Tice, Terrence N., ed. *Faculty Bargaining in the Seventies*. Ann Arbor, MI: Continuing Legal Education, 1974. 408 pp.

Describes the bargaining process as it relates to law, employment relations, academic governance, and actual practice. The third section contains information on bargaining arranged by state with specific examples mentioned. An appendix and a bibliography containing additional information concludes the book.

871. ————. *Faculty Power: Collective Bargaining on Campus*. Ann Arbor, MI: Institute for Continuing Legal Education, 1972. 335 pp.

In 1969 the first 4-year institution of higher learning unionized, only a few years after a 2-year institution. It is a comparatively new development. Leaders in labor have some difficulty adjusting from an industrial experience to higher education. This early study in collective bargaining in higher education describes the legal steps and procedure to be followed in collective bargaining by faculty.

872. ————. *Resources on Academic Bargaining and Governance*. AAHE/ERIC Higher Education Report. ED 093 198. Washington, D.C.: American Association for Higher Education, 1974. 49 pp.

This annotated bibliography is divided into 3 categories: agencies, bibliographies, periodicals, and other basic resources; public employment bargaining: labor law and practices; and collective bargaining and governing in higher education.

873. ————. *Student Rights, Decision Making and the Law*. ERIC/Higher Education Research Report No. 10 Washington, DC: American Association for Higher Education, 1976. ED 093 198. 98 pp.

Not only is this report excellent, but it has an unusual arrangement. A bibliography of 327 items with subject, author, and case indexes makes this study very useful. Major topics discussed are: student activism and the courts; law and morality in the open society; the coming new era in student activism; legal, institutional, and moral rights; administration and the law, and guidelines for administrator decisions concerning students.

ECONOMICS

874. Abowd, John M. *An Econometric Model of the U.S. Market for Higher Education*. Working Paper No. 102. Princeton, NJ: Industrial Relations Section, Princeton University, 1977. 134 pp.

Research findings concern the number of enrollment places relative to quality levels of an institution. Uses the theoretical development of a model to obtain empirical results.

875. American Association of University Professors. *Report on the Economic Status of the Profession, 1977–78*. Washington, DC: American Association of University Professors, 1977. 74 pp.

Institutional surveys are made to collect data used in this annual report. Major changes and trends may be predicted from this data concerning such areas as faculty salaries and tenure.

876. American Council on Education. *1972 Faculty Study*. Washington, DC: American Council on Education, 1972.

Professional characteristics of faculty are the main focus of this study. Other topics discussed are research funding, personal and institutional goals, professional activities, productivity, salary, and tenure.

877. Benson, Charles S., and Hodgkinson, Harold L. *Implementing the Learning Society: New Strategies for Financing Social Objectives*. San Francisco, CA: Jossey-Bass, 1974. 147 pp.

Views higher education as an industry. Examines different kinds of "efficiencies" pertaining to education, such as: economic efficiencies, fiscal efficiencies, and social efficiencies. There is a survey of the literature and recommendations for educators. One proposal made is to give each student $2,000 per year for life to finance education. No attempt was made to calculate the cost.

878. Blackburn, Robert T. *Tenure: Aspects of Job Security on the Changing Campus*. Atlanta, GA: Southern Regional Education Board, 1972. 60 pp.

Faculty performance in relation to tenure is examined in this publication. The effects of court decisions and collective bargaining upon tenure and job security is included in the discussion.

879. Bowen, Howard R., et al. *Investment in Learning: The Individual and Social Value of American Education*. San Francisco, CA: Jossey-Bass, 1977. 507 pp.

Focuses on the individual and social value of American higher education. In the background of this documented study was the development of public mistrust of higher education which began in the 1960s and continued in the early 1970s. There are 4 parts to this book: the setting, consequences for individuals, consequences for society, and conclusions.

880. Bowen, Howard. *Socially Imposed Costs of Higher Education*. Urbana, IL: University of Illinois, 1978. 36 pp.

Discusses the rising costs of higher education with emphasis on socially imposed costs. Specific sources of these costs for higher education are: personal security; federal legislation; state and local legislation; institutional practices, such as fringe benefits and tenure; work standards; and collective bargaining.

881. Buchanan, James M., and Devletoglou, Nicos E. *Academica in Anarchy: An Economic Diagnosis*. New York: Basic Books, 1970. 187 pp.

Views the university as belonging to the taxpayers and the general public who do not really control their property. Students are the consumers who do not value their education because of free or low-cost tuition. The faculty are producers who are interested in their own pursuits and not responsive to the students.

882. Caffrey, John, and Isaacs, Herbert H. *Estimating the Impact of a College or University on the Local Economy*. Washington, DC: American Council on Education, 1971. 73 pp.

Explains how to gather, analyze, and present data in a form which can be understood so the local community can see the benefits of having a college or university located in that community. Shows the economic effect of the Claremont colleges on the city of Claremont, California.

883. Carnegie Commission on Higher Education. *College Graduates and Jobs: Adjusting to a New Labor Market Situation*. New York: McGraw-Hill, 1973. 242 pp.

The relationship between higher education and a labor market which cannot absorb all college and university graduates is of great concern. Vocational counseling will be needed to prepare students to adapt to shifts of specialities or even shifts from one occupation to another.

884. ———. *The More Effective Use of Resources: An Imperative for Higher Education*. New York: McGraw-Hill, 1972. 201 pp.

Reducing total institutional expenditures by 10 billion dollars a year is a drastic suggestion. The Commission proposes that savings can be done in 3 ways: reduce the number of students, make more effective use of resources, and take advantage of "windfall" opportunities.

885. Carnegie Council on Policy Studies in Higher Education. *1975 Carnegie Commission National Surveys of Higher Education: Faculty*. Berkeley, CA: University of California, Survey Research Center, 1975.

Assessments of graduate and undergraduate education, affirmative action, academic reward structure, governance, teaching and research, as well as many other subjects, are covered in this survey.

886. Change Panel on Academic Economics. *Colleges and Money: A Faculty Guide to Academic Economics*. New Rochelle, NY: Change Magazine, 1976. 91 pp.

The importance of knowledge of budgetary issues is of great significance to faculty in a time of emphasis on accountability. Large portions of this book concern budgets, management, efficiency, decision making, and educational costs.

887. Davis, J. Ronnie, and Morrall, John F., III. *Evaluating Educational Investment*. Lexington, MA: Lexington Books, 1974. 112 pp.

Explains the concept of investment in education and the factors which enter into this view of education. Tables and diagrams enhance the discussion and several studies are cited. A bibliography encourages further reading.

888. Duncan, Otis Dudley; Featherman, David L.; and Duncan, Beverly. *Socioeconomic Background and Achievement*. New York: Seminar Press, 1972. 284 pp.

Status in America is largely dependent upon education, occupation, and income. Social stratification is examined in relation to equal opportunity.

889. Eckaus, Richard S. *Estimating the Returns to Education: A Disaggregated Approach*. Berkeley, CA: Carnegie Commission on Higher Education, 1973. 95 pp.

Examines the rate of returns to education by treating education as an investment in future income. Concludes that education may not give a high return in a financial way. More research is needed, particularly on demand and supply influences.

890. Fox, Karl A., ed. *Economic Analysis for Educational Planning: Resource Allocations in Nonmarket Systems*. Baltimore, MD: Johns Hopkins Press, 1972. 376 pp.

Concepts from economic theory, mathematical programing, and systems analysis are summarized and applied to systems of higher education.

891. Frances, Carol. *The Short-Run Economic Outlook for Higher Education*. Washington, DC: American Council on Education, 1979. 51 pp.

Predicts the probable effects of recession and inflation on enrollment, tuition, and institutional costs and revenues. Suggests that techniques used by business executives can also be used by administrators in higher education as they plan for the future.

892. Freeman, Richard B. *The Market for College-Trained Manpower: A Study in the Economics of Career Choice.* Cambridge, MA: Harvard University Press, 1971. 264 pp.

Studies the economics of career choice and the adaptability of college-educated persons to respond to changes in the job market. Deals also with faculty hiring, student attitudes, and expectations about careers.

893. ———. *The Over-Educated American.* New York: Academic Press, 1976. 218 pp.

Planners and administrators in higher education should find helpful research on labor markets for college-educated people. Data provided are also forecasts of the job market to 1990.

894. Froomkin, Joseph N., et al., eds. *Education as an Industry.* National Bureau of Economic Research. Cambridge, MA: Ballinger, 1976. 489 pp.

Applies economic analysis to the internal workings of the educational system in the United States educational production, functions, cost functions, productivity, and the demand for output. Issues explored include compensatory education, admissions, computer assisted instruction, costs of higher education, enrollment demand, faculty-student ratios, and learning theory.

895. Gordon, Margaret S., ed. *Higher Education and the Labor Market.* New York: McGraw-Hill, 1974. 630 pp.

Predictions are varied but the outlook is generally pessimistic for demand for college graduates and is especially so for Ph.D.s. One contributor predicts there will be a growing surplus of Ph.Ds in the 1970s with a decline after 1975, and dropping to around zero in the mid-1980s.

896. Harris, Seymour E. *The Economics of Harvard.* New York: McGraw-Hill, 1970. 533 pp.

Describes some aspects of finance at Harvard University as it was handled in the time of President Samuel Eliot Morison. Modern financial practices and current problems are discussed in relation to Harvard as an enterprise. Harvard's productivity and curricular economics are analyzed.

897. Jenney, Hans H. *Higher Education and the Economy.* ERIC/Higher Education Research Report No. 2. Washington, DC: American Association for Higher Education, 1976. ED 124 065. 56 pp.

At the time this report was written, there were some indications that the "depression" in higher education was nearing an end. In addition to discussing sources of higher education revenues and the financial condition of colleges, suggests developing a set of comprehensive indicators of institutional health to be used as a basis for predictions.

898. Juster, F. Thomas, ed. *Education, Income, and Human Behavior.* Report of the Carnegie Commission on Higher Education. New York: McGraw-Hill, 1975. 438 pp.

Six essays concern direct financial returns to individuals; 6 essays explore nonmonetary returns from educational attainment. Higher education influences marriage patterns, family size, savings, political, and social attitudes.

899. Ladd, Everett C. Jr., and Lipset, S. Martin. *Ladd-Lipset 1977 Survey of the American Professoriate.* Storrs, CT: University of Connecticut, Social Science Data Center, 1977. 50 pp.

Many facets relating to professors and their performance, institutions' financial support, research, professional standards, retirement, opinions of professors on national politics, and other subjects are explored.

900. Lumsden, Keith F. *Efficiency in Universities: The Lapaz Papers.* New York: Elsevier Scientific Publishing Company, 1974. 278 pp.

Eleven well-known economists write on various issues in higher education which are related to economic efficiency.

901. McCarthy, Joseph L., and Deener, David R. *The Costs and Benefits of Graduate Education: A Commentary with Recommendations.* Washington, DC: Council of Graduate Schools, 1972. 50 pp.

Collects information on the costs and benefits of graduate education and summarizes and analyzes the information by level, quality of graduate program, and type of institution. More research on this problem is recommended.

902. Machlup, Fritz. *Education and Economic Growth.* Lincoln, NE: University of Nebraska Press, 1970. 106 pp.

Concerns the relation of education to income. Some aspects to consider are the returns on the investment in education, both in monetary and personal satisfaction measurements. As more people have a higher level of education, ability becomes more important.

903. McKenzie, Richard B. *Political Economy of the Educational Process.* Boston: Martinus Nijhoff, 1979. 199 pp.

Economics is a method of studying human behavior. In the learning process there is a relationship between "resources applied and the amount learned by the student." Chapters concern student and professor preferences, grade inflation, evaluation and pay of faculty, committees, intercollegeiate sports, and academic standards.

904. Maynard, James. *Some Microeconomics of Higher Education: Economics of Scale.* Lincoln, NE: University of Nebraska Press, 1971. 186 pp.

Attempts to show a relationship between the size of institutions and the cost per student. Uses 123 4-year state colleges in 13 states as sources of information for the study. The outcome indicates 5,363 FTE students to be the point where "maximum economics of scale are realized."

905. Milner, Murray. *Effects of Federal Aid to Higher Education on Social and Educational Inequality.* New York: Center for Policy Research, 1970. 204 pp.

Discusses types of federal aid to students, and finds that various types of aid do contribute to social and educational equality. Beneficial programs are scholarships based on need, national defense type loans, and work-study. Programs considered more advantageous to upper-income students are guaranteed loan programs, tax relief plans, and low tuition.

906. National Academy of Education. *Economic Dimensions of Education.* Washington, DC: Acroplis Books, 1979. 160 pp.

A collection of essays by economists involved in educational analysis. Highlights include an article by Jacob Mincer which is a survey of research into human capital formation and its effects on earnings; and a chapter by Douglas M. Windham on economic analysis as it applies to higher education. Windham suggests that more rationality and accountability are needed in higher education.

907. ———. *Education for Employment: Knowledge for Action*. Task Force on Education and Employment. Washington, DC: Acroplis Books, 1979. 274 pp.

The report of a task force which studied the relationship between education of young people and the needs of employers. Research is needed so that people can be prepared properly for jobs in new fields and other careers. Career guidance is frequently necessary to encourage students in vocational choice.

908. National Center for Education Statistics. *Salaries and Tenure of Instructional Faculty in Institutions of Higher Education 1974–75*. Washington, DC: U.S. Government Printing Office, 1976. 271 pp.

Statistics gathered from institutions provide information on salary, tenure, and other matters of comparable interest to those in higher education.

909. Powell, John H., and Lamson, Robert D. *Elements Related to the Determination of Costs and Benefits of Graduate Education*. Washington, DC: Council of Graduate Schools in the United States, 1972. 291 pp.

As funding becomes tighter in higher education, more attention will be paid to the costs and outcomes of graduate education. An attempt to look at standardizing allocation procedures and cost information and to identify benefits of graduate education.

910. Radner, Roy, and Miller, Leonard S. *Demand and Supply in U.S. Higher Education*. New York: McGraw-Hill, 1975. 468 pp.

Enrollment demand is the topic of the studies presented here. Enrollment of students and hiring of faculty are 2 issues facing planners that are of current interest.

911. Sewell, William H., and Hauser, Robert M. *Education, Occupation, and Earnings: Achievement in the Early Career*. New York: Academic Press, 1975. 237 pp.

Identifies the major influences affecting socioeconomic achievement in American society through follow-up studies based on research on Wisconsin high school graduates of 1957. Several reports have been done and more are planned. The influences of background, ability, and schooling on occupational status and income are of principal interest.

912. Sewell, William H., et al. *Schooling and Achievement in American Society*. New York: Academic Press, 1976. 535 pp.

The effects of schooling in socioeconomic achievement should be of interest to researchers in economics, sociology, psychology, and education. Many benefits of education are not apparent in the early work experience, but become apparent later.

913. Solomon, Lewis C.; Bisconti, Ann S.; and Ochsner, Nancy L. *College as a Training Ground for Jobs*. New York: Praeger, 1977. 183 pp.

Examines the value of a college education. College graduates who have been in the employment market for almost a decade value their degrees and feel that they have benefited from them.

914. Taubman, Paul, and Wales, Terence. *Higher Education and Earnings*. New York: McGraw-Hill, 1974. 302 pp.

Uses detailed statistics to measure the relationship between earnings, schooling, and ability. Not every aspect has been investigated

but the result seems to indicate some "overinvestment" in education.

915. Thomas, J. Alan. *The Productive School: A Systems Analysis Approach to Educational Administration*. New York: John Wiley, 1971. 160 pp.

Describes procedures to stretch funds, allocation of resources, curriculum change, and evaluation. A textbook on economics with a practical approach.

916. Toombs, William. *Productivity: The Burden of Success*. Research Report No. 2. Washington, DC: American Association for Higher Education, 1973. 60 pp.

Examines productivity both on and off campus and suggests that higher education should be more concerned with management and planning. Input-output relationships are discussed. A small percentage of institutions in 1972 had an institutional research office, computerized management information system, or planning-programing-budgeting system.

917. Verry, Donald, and Davies, Bleddyn. *University Costs and Outputs*. Studies on Education. Vol. 6. New York: Elsevier, 1976. 277 pp.

An economic study of British Universities and an attempt to measure production in higher education.

918. Windham, Douglas M. *Education, Equality, and Income Redistribution*. Lexington, MA: Heath, 1970. 120 pp.

Calculates the cost of education by allotting the taxes collected for higher education among income groups and figures (by income group) whether the benefits exceed the costs. Concludes that the "poor" are sending the "rich" to college.

919. Wirtz, Willard. *The Boundless Resource: A Prospectus for an Education/Work Policy*. National Manpower Institute. Washington, DC: New Republic, 1975. 205 pp.

Concerns the process of bringing school and work closer together. Youth, career years, and plans for change are listed.

920. Withey, Stephen B. *A Degree and What Else? Correlates and Consequences of a College Education*. Carnegie Commission on Higher Education. New York: McGraw-Hill, 1971. 147 pp.

Studies the effects of the college experience on the students' occupation. Benefits to society, as well as individuals, are stressed. Personal benefits to students include becoming generally more liberal and open minded, more appreciative of aesthetic and cultural values, less moralistic and more tolerant, better informed on international events, and gaining more self-confidence and better jobs with more job security.

FINANCE

921. American Council on Education. *Financing Part-Time Students: The New Majority in Postsecondary Education*. Report of the Committee on the Financing of Higher Education for Adult Students. Washington, DC: American Council on Education, 1974. 118 pp.

A majority of postsecondary students attend classes on a part-time basis with little or no financial assistance. Their number is growing and having impact in many ways on various institutions. This group is discriminated against, especially in financial help.

922. Arthur, William J. *A Financial Planning Model for Private Colleges.* Charlottesville, VA: University Press of Virginia, 1973. 118 pp.

Points out the need for long-range planning for private colleges. Develops a model at one private college which can be used by administrators to evaluate plans for the use of financial resources. Tested it at 4 other colleges. The 3 steps of the model are: identification of institutional strategies, classification of expenditures using these strategies, and computation for evaluating the plans.

923. Berke, Joel S., and Kirst, Michael W. *Federal Aid to Education.* Lexington, MA: D.C. Heath, 1973. 384 pp.

Financial problems are becoming more pressing in higher education. These case studies from 6 major states point out the severity of the situation. The location of federal funds is listed in this publication and may indicate one solution.

924. Bowen, Howard R., and Servelle, Paul. *Who Benefits from Higher Education and Who Should Pay?* Research Report No. 5. Washington, DC: American Association for Higher Education, 1972. ED 065 141. 47 pp.

As the title indicates, this topic is controversial. Some people think that state and federal governments should pay most of the cost because of the social value of a college education. Others think that students and their families should bear most of the cost. American higher education seems to be a compromise affair with a mixture of financial support from various sources.

925. Boyd, Joseph D. *National Association of State Scholarships and Grant Programs: 9th Annual Survey, 1977–79.* Deerfield, IL: Illinois State Scholarship Commission, 1978. 54 pp.

This report is the only publication containing information from every state and every program.

926. Brandt, Norman J., and Ni, Anne. *Financial Statistics of Institutions of Higher Education Fiscal Year 1977.* Washington, DC: U.S. Government Printing Office, 1978. 269 pp.

Data listed is from the twelfth annual Higher Education General Information Survey (HEGIS). Some statistics covered are revenue and expenditures, physical facilities, and endowments.

927. Carbone, Robert F. *Alternative Tuition Systems.* Iowa City, IA: American College Testing Program, 1974. 146 pp.

Five models for methods of tuition payment by students to public institutions of higher learning are described. A chapter written by an authority in the field describes each method.

928. Carnegie Commission on Higher Education. *Higher Education: Who Pays? Who Benefits? Who Should Pay?* Report of the Carnegie Commission on Higher Education. New York: McGraw-Hill, 1973. 190 pp.

Discusses tuition costs and recommends that public institutions gradually increase tuition until it equals one-third of actual cost rather than one-sixth. Suggests that the tuition for the first 2 years be lower than following years.

929. Carnegie Council on Policy Studies in Higher Education. *Low or No Tuition: The Feasibility of a National Policy for the First Two Years of College.* San Francisco, CA: Jossey-Bass, 1975. 88 pp.

Explores the issues concerning low or no tuition for the first 2 years of college. Discusses various options but concludes pessimistically. Trustees, administrators, and state and federal agencies and legislators should be interested.

930. Cheit, Earl F. *The New Depression in Higher Education: A Study of Financial Conditions at 41 Colleges and Universities.* General Report for the Carnegie Commission on Higher Education and the Ford Foundation. New York: McGraw-Hill, 1971. 169 pp.

Three questions are answered by this study: What are the characteristics of the financial problems facing higher education? How general are these problems in institutions of various types? What has been the response towards solution of the financial problems? The effects of medical schools on university costs is also discussed, as well as other related topics.

931. ———. *The New Depression in Higher Education—Two Years Later.* Carnegie Commission on Higher Education. New York: McGraw-Hill, 1973. 84 pp.

Reports financial condition of 41 colleges and universities 2 years after they were considered in financial difficulty. Fifteen are worse off, 11 about the same, and 15 are in better shape. Quality and purpose, as well as productivity, may be future concerns for institutions. Public benefits of education should concern the whole nation.

932. Collier, Douglas J. *Higher Education Finance Manual.* Technical Report 69. Boulder, CO: National Center for Higher Education Management Systems, 1975. 159 pp.

This document is intended to standardize financial data to help in communicating and so ease planning and management procedures. This is accomplished by defining terms, accounting procedures, and data categories.

933. Committee for Economic Development. *The Management and Financing of Colleges.* New York: Committee for Economic Development, 1973. 94 pp.

Goals, objectives, accountability, and educational planning are stressed in this report. Tuition costs in both public and private institutions of higher learning should be more realistic.

934. Council for Financial Aid to Education. *Special Programs for Minorities and Women in Higher Education.* New York: Council for Financial Aid to Education, 1978. 48 pp.

Lists programs of help to women and minorities in academic institutions. These programs are supported by corporations who are listed along with grants which they provide. There are chapters on specific help for students in engineering, business, insurance, medicine, dentistry, and law.

935. ———. *Voluntary Support of Education 1975–76.* New York: CFAE, 1976. 70 pp.

An annual report which gives figures on total giving to institutions, sources of support, annual fund support, nonalumni parental support, corporation matching gifts, and current market value of endowment.

936. Cuninggim, Merrimom. *Private Money and Public Service: The Role of Foundations in American Society.* New York: McGraw-Hill, 1972. 260 pp.

The president of the Danforth Foundation from 1961 until 1971 discusses the tax-free money which is dispensed by organized philanthropy in the United States. Many millions are spent for educational purposes.

937. Davis, Jerry S., and Van Dusen, William D. *A Guide to the Literature of Student Financial Aid*. New York: College Entrance Examination Board, 1978. 166 pp.

This annotated bibliography of the literature on student financial aid is arranged into 7 categories. Some of the 7 topics are: history, philosophy, and purpose; administration, management, and problems; federal and state issues and problems; and research.

938. Fein, Rashi, and Weber, Gerald I. *Financing Medical Education: An Analysis of Alternative Policies and Mechanisms*. Report Prepared for the Carnegie Commission on Higher Education and the Commonwealth Fund. New York: McGraw-Hill, 1971. 279 pp.

Gives a detailed look at many aspects of medical schools: functions, finance, medical students and their special problems and needs.

939. Halstead, D. Kent. *Higher Education Prices and Price Indexes*. U.S. Department of Health Education and Welfare. Washington, DC: U.S. Government Printing Office. 114 pp. *Higher Education Prices and Price Indexes: 1978 Supplement*. National Institute of Education. Washington, DC: U.S. Government Printing Office, 1978. 48 pp.

Changes in purchasing power of the dollar caused by inflation are of great concern to administrators in higher education. This contains indexes for higher education calculated from 1961 to the present. Includes current operations index, research and development index, physical plant additional index, and a student charge and tuition index.

940. Halstead, D. K., and Weldon, H. K. *Tax Wealth in Fifty States: 1977 Supplement*. The National Institute of Education. Washington, DC: U.S. Department of Health, Education and Welfare, 1979. 175 pp.

This first supplement to *Tax Wealth in Fifty States, 1978,* presents tax capacity, effort, and calculated revenue data for state and local governments for 1977. Planned for publication every other year, the *Supplement* consists of computer printout tables concerning such areas as: trends in state-level government relative tax capacity, by state (1960–77); trends in state-local government relative tax effort, by state (1960–77); and capacity and effort measures, state rankings, and percent distribution of taxes of state and local governments, by type of tax (1977).

941. Hewitt, Raymond G., ed. *Public Policy for the Financing of Higher Education: Proceedings*. Wellesley, MA: New England Board of Higher Education, 1972. 141 pp.

Gives differing viewpoints on financing higher education in the future at a conference of more than 250 educational and legislative leaders from the northeast. Includes present inefficiencies in financing, the 1971 federal Higher Education Act, state and regional planning, and public responsibility.

942. Hudgins, Garven, and Phillips, Ione. *People's Colleges in Trouble*. Washington, DC: National Association of State Universities and Land Grant Colleges, 1971. 26 pp.

Assesses financial problems of publicly supported institutions. Lists remedies which various institutions have tried in an effort to meet the problem of rising costs and lowered support.

943. Hyde, William D., ed. *Issues in Postsecondary Education Finance*. Denver, CO: Education Commission of the States, 1978. 43 pp.

Describes several current issues involving financial support for higher education. Topics which are discussed include public subsidies for higher education, community college finance, and access and choice of institution as it is related to tuition and financial aid.

944. Jellema, William W. *From Red to Black? The Financial Status of Private Colleges and Universities*. San Francisco, CA: Jossey-Bass, 1973. 174 pp.

Focus is on financial problems of colleges and universities. Some solutions include vigorous fund raising efforts and federal aid.

945. ———, ed. *Institutional Priorities and Management Objectives*. Washington, DC: Association of American Colleges, 1971. 290 pp.

Describes the financial problems faced by many liberal arts colleges and the solutions advanced by several knowledgeable people. Some suggestions include: increasing admissions, curricular reforms, investments which produce more income, and more cooperation between institutions.

946. Jenny, Hans H., and Wynn, G. Richard. *The Turning Point*. Office of Vice President for Finance and Business. Wooster, OH: College of Wooster, 1972. ED 065 019. 102 pp.

Financial conditions in many private 4-year liberal arts colleges have become critical in recent years. Income and income prospects have lessened while costs have escalated. Examines financial records of 48 colleges from 1959–60 through 1969–70. Deficits increased tremendously over that period. An increase in student-faculty ratio is recommended, as well as long-range planning.

947. Keeslar, Oreon. *Financial Aids for Higher Education: 76–77 Catalog*. Dubuque, IA: William C. Brown, 1977. 629 pp.

Contains concise information about financial aid for students. Lists 3,400 programs and the information is useful to students, parents, counselors, and financial aid administrators. Students who are presently enrolled in higher education institutions will also profit from referring to this book. A list of 775 institutions with work/study programs is given.

948. Lanier, Lyle H., and Andersen, Charles J. *A Study of the Financial Condition of Colleges and Universities: 1972–1975*. Washington, DC: American Council on Education, 1975. 102 pp.

Information concerns enrollment trends, operating revenues, student aid, and inflation. The changes in higher education resources are clearly shown.

949. Levi, Julian H., and Steinbach, Sheldon Elliott. *Patterns of Giving to Higher Education*. Vol. 3. Washington, DC: American Council on Education, 1976. 28 pp.

Gives data for 1973–74 donations for current and capital support of American colleges and universities. About half of the voluntary support comes from large gifts from individuals. The support comes in the form of property, real estate, or securities.

950. Leslie, Larry L. *The Role of Public Student Aid in Financing Private Higher Education*. Topical Paper No. 10. Tucson, AZ: University of Arizona, 1978. 29 pp.

Assesses the consequences of public assistance in the form of student aid to private colleges. Demand theory which suggests that enrollment in higher education will increase as the students' net price is reduced is a fundamental assumption.

951. McCoy, Marilyn, and Halstead, D. K. *Higher Education Financing in the Fifty States*. Interstate Comparisons Fiscal Year 1976. Review edition. National Center for Higher Education Management Systems. National Institute of Education. Washington, DC: U.S. Department of Health, Education and Welfare, 1979. 221 pp.

Presents basic data which measure state fiscal effort, financial support levels, and shifts in revenue sources and expenditures. This source of data is very important for state policymakers who are trying to make decisions for the future.

952. MacDonald, Douglas S. *Alternative Tuition Systems*. ERIC/Higher Education Research Report No. 6. Washington, DC: American Association of Higher Education, 1977. ED 146 826. 44 pp.

A review of various alternative tuition systems that have been proposed or are in the developing process by colleges, state governments, and the federal government. Eight state plans and 10 regional plans are examined.

953. McMahon, Walter W. *Investment in Higher Education*. Lexington, MA: Heath, 1974. 200 pp.

Intended for economists and administrators in higher education and members of state governing agencies. The study covers investment behavior by families, state and local interests, and federal government.

954. Mertins, Paul F., and Brandt, Norman J. *Financial Statistics of Institutions of Higher Education, Fiscal Year 1976 State Data*. National Center for Education Statistics. Washington, DC: U.S. Government Printing Office, 1976. 261 pp.

The National Center for Education Statistics (NCES) uses an annual survey (HEGIS) to collect data on institutional finance for U.S. higher education. Data is arranged according to state, type of control, university, 2- or 4-year institutions. Computer tapes may be obtained through NCES with data for individual institutions.

955. Millett, John D. *Mergers in Higher Education: An Analysis of Ten Case Studies*. Washington, DC: American Council on Education, 1976. 105 pp.

Describes the reasons for 10 mergers, the means by which the mergers were accomplished, and the results. Recommendations for those institutions considering mergers are given. Financial problems are generally the reason for mergers.

956. ———. *Personnel Management in Higher Education*. Washington, DC: Academy for Educational Development, Management Division, 1972. 43 pp.

The first paper in this publication describes in general terms the many problems facing personnel management in higher education. The second paper deals specifically with tenure and collective bargaining. The third article lists 163 ways to save money and avoid problems in personnel management.

957. Minter, John W., and Bowen, Howard. *Independent Higher Education*. Fourth Annual Report in Financial and Educational Trends in the Independent Sector of American

Higher Education. Washington, DC: National Association of Independent Colleges and Universities, 1978. 148 pp.

This study includes a sample of all types of private colleges except the autonomous, professional institution. Among the major topics are: enrollment and admissions, faculty and their staff, educational program, operating revenues and expenditures, financial ratios, and retrenchment and quality.

958. National Association of Student Financial Aid Administrators. *Characteristics and Attitudes of the Financial Aid Administrator: A Report on the Survey of the Profession in 1977*. Washington, DC: National Association of Student Financial Aid Administrators, 1978. 189 pp.

Gives tabulations of various aspects of student-financial-aid administrators. Information includes: personal and job characteristics, attitudes, salaries, external contacts, and professional development.

959. National Center for Higher Education Management Systems. *Evaluation of the IEP Costing Procedures: A Pilot Study by Six Major Research Universities*. Boulder, CO: National Center for Higher Education Management Systems, 1979. 54 pp.

Six universities have implemented the N.C.H.E.M.S. information-exchange procedures. The universities are: Colorado, Illinois, Kansas, Washington, Purdue, and State University of New York at Stony Brook. This report is a summary of the technical findings of the study.

960. National Commission on the Financing of Postsecondary Education. *Financing Postsecondary Education in the United States*. Washington, DC: U.S. Government Printing Office, 1973. 442 pp.

The report of the National Commission on the Financing of Postsecondary Education, which was authorized by congress, has been the subject of much controversy and criticism. The debate over tuition began before the commission was appointed and still is the subject of much discussion.

961. National Science Foundation. *Federal Support to Universities, Colleges, and Selected Non-Profit Institutions, Fiscal Year 1976*. Washington, DC: U.S. Government Printing Office, 1976. 150 pp.

This annual guide ranks 100 institutions by dollars received and organizes by state obligations to colleges and universities.

962. Office of Management and Budget. *Special Analyses, Budget of the United States Government, Fiscal Year 1979*. Washington, DC: U.S. Government Printing Office, 1979. 329 pp.

Each January this publication is a companion vol. to the President's budget. The *Special Analyses* contain essential information on higher education, such as medical education and research and development. Of particular interest are Special Analyses J, L, G, and P.

963. O'Neill, June A. *Resource Use in Higher Education: Trends in Output and Inputs, 1930–1967*. Berkeley, CA: Carnegie Commission on Higher Education, 1971. 106 pp.

Shows that the constant dollar cost per credit hour has changed very little over nearly 40 years. Obviously this indicates that the instructional function of higher education has not increased in productivity.

964. O'Neill, June A., and Sullivan, Daniel. *Sources of Funds to Colleges and Universities.* Carnegie Commission on Higher Education, Technical Report. Berkeley, CA: Carnegie Commission on Higher Education, 1973. 45 pp.

Before the HEGIS report was established, this study gave revenue sources of institutions from 1930 to 1968. These statistics can still be used in connection with the HEGIS report for historical data.

965. Orwig, M. D., ed. *Financing Higher Education: Alternatives for the Federal Government.* Iowa City, IA: American College Testing Program, 1971. 383 pp.

Attempts to relate the goals and expectations of higher education to the role of the federal government in financial support. Policymakers will find helpful information concerning financial problems in higher education.

966. Pride, Cletis, ed. *Securing Support for Higher Education: A Bibliographical Handbook.* New York: Praeger, 1972. 403 pp.

Lists books, journal articles, and pamphlets as sources which may be used by fund raisers to attract financial aid for higher education. Compiled in cooperation with American College Public Relations Association.

967. Van Alstyne, Carol, and Coldren, Sharon L. *Financing Higher Education.* Washington, DC: American Council on Education, 1977. 40 pp.

Uses recent data to assess the economic and financial situation of higher education. There is some danger that various segments of education may become real opponents as they compete for funds that are no longer in plentiful supply.

968. Weathersby, George B., and Jacobs, Frederic. *Institutional Goals and Student Costs.* ERIC/Higher Education Research Report No. 2. Washington, DC: American Association for Higher Education, 1977. ED 136 706. 48 pp.

Examines the relationship of institutional goals to student costs and raises the intriguing possibility that students should pay only for costs of services that relate directly to each student—not for the present "bundling" practice. Unless institutions can accommodate, special purpose organizations that focus on only one component, such as counseling centers, may continue to develop.

969. Weld, Edric A., and Burke, John F. *The Financing of Higher Education by the State of Ohio, 1955–1969.* Columbus, OH: Institute of Urban Studies, Cleveland State University, 1971. 115 pp.

The sixth report on the financing of higher education in Ohio outlines the expenditure of state funds in relation to several factors, including students. Measures of quality for faculty, library, undergraduates, and graduates are given. Sources of funds, both private and public, are listed.

GENERAL

970. American Council on Education. *New Academic Institutions.* Washington, DC: American Council on Education, 1972. 128 pp.

Describes the many problems involved in creating a new institution. Some information given includes: beginning steps, purposes and goals definition, designing the curriculum, gaining accreditation, and recruiting faculty and students.

971. Association of American Colleges. *Higher Education, Human Resources, and the National Economy.* Washington, DC: Association of American Colleges, 1974. 200 pp.

The annual meeting of the Association of American Colleges sought the answer to the following questions: What do business and industry expect of higher education? What does higher education expect of business and industry?

972. Corbally, John E., et al. *Conflict, Retrenchment, and Reappraisal: The Administration of Higher Education.* David D. Henry Lectures 1972–78. Urbana, IL: University of Illinois Press, 1979. 166 pp.

Contains the first 5 David D. Henry Lectures and some of the responses. In the 5 lectures, Clark Kerr discusses change and conflict, David Riesman considers quality graduate education and retrenchment, John R. Hogness reappraises the health profession, Harlan Cleveland describes the education of administrators, and Howard R. Bowen looks at the socially imposed costs of higher education.

973. Creager, John A. *Evaluation and Selection of Academic Interns: 1967–1968.* Washington, DC: American Council on Education, 1971. 31 pp.

Evaluates the internship program which uses funds furnished by the Ford Foundation in an attempt to induce capable young people to become administrators in higher education institutions. Those students who are selected are compared with those rejected in an endeavor to assess the predictive success or failure.

974. Dilley, Josiah. *Higher Education: Participants Confronted.* Dubuque, IA: W. C. Brown, 1970. 123 pp.

Intended as a text for students in higher education administration. A brief history brings out many problems which may arise. Students are then expected to discuss the problem and decide upon a solution.

975. Education Commission of the States. *Directory of Professional Personnel.* Denver, CO: Education Commission of the States. 86 pp.

An annual directory which lists names, addresses, and phone numbers of statewide agencies in each state. Other organizations, such as Southern Regional Education Board (SREB) and Western Interstate Commission for Higher Education (WICHE) are included.

976. Fisher, Charles F., and Coll-Pardo, Isabel, eds. *Guide to Leadership Development Opportunities for College and University Administrators September 1979–December 1980.* Washington, DC: American Council on Education, 1979. 197 pp.

An annual guide provides concise descriptions of 392 professional development programs, a convenient calendar of opportunities available from September 1979 through December 1980, and a special section describing inservice training programs at colleges and universities. Can help develop full leadership potential in higher education administration.

977. Glenny, Lyman A., et al. *Presidents Confront Reality: From Office Edifice Complex to University without Walls.* Carnegie Council on Policy Studies in Higher Education. San Francisco, CA: Jossey-Bass, 1976. 261 pp.

Based upon a survey of the nation's colleges and university presidents. However, only about half of those who responded were actually presidents; others were deans, vice-presidents, or other administrators. Perceptions of these executives form the main portions of the book. Some statistics are given to support viewpoints listed.

978. Harris, Seymour E., ed. *A Statistical Portrait of Higher Education.* Carnegie Commission on Higher Education. New York: McGraw-Hill, 1972. 978 pp.

Gives 700 tables from data gathered by government agencies, private surveys, and research projects. Divided into 4 sections: students, enrollment, faculty, and income and expenditures. Some data should be updated in order to be more useful.

979. Heiss, Ann M.; Mixer, Joseph R.; and Paltridge, James G., eds. *Participants and Patterns in Higher Education: Research and Reflections, A Festschrift for T. R. McConnell.* Berkeley, CA: University of California, 1973. 290 pp.

Essays on governance, educational values, beliefs of students, structure of educational process, and student characteristics—subjects that concerned T. R. McConnell.

980. Henderson, Algo D., and Henderson, Jean G. *Higher Education in America: Problems, Priorities and Prospects.* San Francisco, CA: Jossey-Bass, 1974. 282 pp.

Surveys every area of postsecondary education: community colleges, liberal arts schools, universities, and professional schools, both public and private. Includes discussion of objectives, students, curriculum, teaching, research, academic freedom, governance and future problems. Wide in scope but topics are not in-depth.

981. Hook, Sidney, ed. *In Defense of Academic Freedom.* New York: Pegasus, 1971. 266 pp.

Examines the threat posed by militant students and professors to academic freedom. The general tone is to condemn violence and coercive tactics on campus because of the danger to intellectual freedom. Institutions should provide channels for use by students who feel that there is injustice exerted on campus.

982. Hoppe, William A. *Policies and Practices in Evening Colleges, 1971.* Metuchen, NJ: Scarecrow Press, 1972. 587 pp.

This survey will serve as a handbook for institutions who are planning evening classes or continuing education classes. Information is given concerning admissions, fees, faculty and faculty recruitment, scheduling, organization structures, and noncredit programs.

983. Jellema, William W., ed. *Efficient College Management.* San Francisco, CA: Jossey-Bass, 1972. 156 pp.

Outlines ways to cut costs and manage income and expenditures in institutions of higher learning. Fourteen authors contribute their ideas in short essays. Two articles of special interest are Jellema's listing of fiscal problems and one by Douglass and Bowen on instructional costs. More variety in instruction is suggested: lectures, seminars, independent study, and media-based teaching.

984. Jerome, Judson. *Culture out of Anarchy.* New York: Herder and Herder, 1970. 333 pp.

Gives views on the problems of higher education: what is wrong with higher education, what needs to be changed, and the difficulties standing in the way of change.

985. Kerr, Donna H. *Educational Policy: Analysis, Structure, and Justification.* New York: David McKay, 1976. 214 pp.

Analyzes the nature of educational policy, regards decisions as rational choices, and shows justification of educational policies. Makes recommendations for sound educational policymaking.

986. Knowles, Asa S., ed. *Handbook of College and University Administration: General.* New York: McGraw-Hill, 1970. 2 vols.

Intended for use by college administrators as a reference book. Some of the subjects covered are: legal administration, governing boards, personnel, physical plant, finances, planning, public relations, and student aid.

987. Knox, Warren B. *Eye of the Hurricane.* Corvallis, OR: Oregon State University Press, 1973. 147 pp.

Presents a view of the responsibilities and functions of the chief administrator of every educational institution. Dedication is essential to an enlightened administrator, and even though the position is the most powerful in the organization, it entails serving and supporting the institution, the faculty, and students, as well as giving guidance and leadership.

988. Leslie, Larry L., and Miller, Howard T., Jr. *Higher Education and the Steady State.* ERIC/Higher Education Research Report No. 4. Washington, DC: American Association for Higher Education, 1974. ED 091 965. 58 pp.

An era of no growth or steady state in college enrollments is examined within the context of historical perspective and 5 kinds of adjustment efforts: new products, new production methods, new markets, employment of new suppliers of productive factors, and reorganization of higher education.

989. McCoy, Charles S. *The Responsible Campus: Toward a New Identity for the Church Related College.* Nashville, TN: United Methodist Church, 1972. 168 pp.

Calls for the church-related college to become a part of the system of higher education. Believes that the church-related college should concentrate on purposes and functions which make education more responsive to the needs of people. Describes needed changes on campus and declares that trustees should be better informed, as well as more involved.

990. Mayhew, Lewis B. *Surviving the Eighties.* Strategies and Procedures for Solving Fiscal and Enrollment Problems. San Francisco, CA: Jossey-Bass, 1979. 350 pp.

Extends the problems of enrollment and fiscal policy into the 1980s and the 1990s with an emphasis on strategies to alleviate these problems. Some of the chapters deal with improving administrative structures and policies, enhancing administrative leadership, managing crisis and developing management systems, upgrading recruitment and admissions policies, maintaining enrollment, increasing faculty performance, and controlling program and faculty costs. The 319 suggestions in the appendix for increasing income and decreasing expenditures are practical and valuable.

991. Niblett, W. Roy, ed. *Higher Education: Demand and Response.* San Francisco, CA: Jossey-Bass, 1970. 267 pp.

Discusses the pressures upon universities in Great Britain, Canada, and the United States. The new role of students as they seek to change the direction and policies of the universities was debated at the Quail Roost Seminar.

992. Pifer, Alan, et al. *Systems of Higher Education: United States*. International Council for Educational Development. New York: Interbook, 1978. 132 pp.

One vol. of a series of 12 dealing with critical problems in operations and educational planning in higher education. Deals with such problems as: access, elitism, youth problems, institutional autonomy, administration, purposes and goals, and efficiency.

993. Podolsky, Arthur, and Smith, Carolyn R. National Center for Education Statistics. *Education Directory: Colleges and Universities*. Washington, DC: U.S. Government Printing Office, 1979–80. 561 pp.

Basic information concerning institutions of higher learning is listed in alphabetical order by state. In the appendices other information is provided such as: statewide agencies, higher education associations, consortia of institutions of higher education, and various charts and tables.

994. Reck, W. Emerson. *The Changing World of College Relations: History and Philosophy, 1917–1975*. Washington, DC: Council for Advancement and Support of Education, 1976. 473 pp.

Gives the history, development, and organization of the Council for Advancement and Support of Education (CASE). Professionals in public relations, publicity, and news, who are involved in colleges and universities, are the members of this organization. They represent alumni associations, fund raising, public relations, government relations, and various kinds of publications.

995. Southern Regional Education Board. *Higher Education for the Future: Reform or More of the Same?* Atlanta, GA: Southern Regional Education Board, 1971. 40 pp.

Proceedings of a work conference, sponsored by SREB, held at Bay Biscayne, Florida in July 1971. Notes manpower needs, postsecondary educational opportunity, the kinds of students who attend various institutions and why, the reforms needed, educational alternatives, and financing and ways to solve it, as subjects receiving attention.

996. Vaccaro, Louis C., et al. *Reshaping Higher Education*. Irving, TX: A.M. Press, 1975. 143 pp.

Looks at old issues and assesses the quality of education with new approaches in mind. Comments on the many innovations tried in recent years in the new curriculum, calendar changes, nontraditional study, consortia, admissions, and collective bargaining.

997. Woodbury, Marda L. *A Guide to Sources of Educational Information*. Washington, DC: Information Resources Press, 1976. 371 pp.

Includes the following information sources: printed materials which lead to other sources of information, education libraries or information centers, organizations and government agencies in education-related fields, and special search or bibliographic sources.

GOVERNANCE AND COORDINATION

Institutional Role

998. Association of Governing Boards of Colleges and Universities. *Financial Responsibilities of Governing Boards of Colleges and Universities*. Washington, DC: Association of Governing Boards of Colleges and Universities and National Association of College and University Business Officers, 1979. 103 pp.

A handbook useful to members of governing boards of colleges and universities as they are involved in financial operations with pictures, tables, and graphs.

999. Carnegie Commission on Higher Education. *Dissent and Disruption: Proposals for Consideration by the Campus*. New York: McGraw-Hill, 1971. 309 pp.

Attempts to point out difference between dissent and disruption and appropriate ways to deal with both in the light of problems of institutions of higher education. A model bill of rights and responsibilities for campuses is given a foundation upon which further work may be done.

1000. College Center of the Finger Lakes. *Patterns for Voluntary Cooperation*. Corning, NY: College Center of the Finger Lakes, 1971. 126 pp.

Reports a self-study by the College Center of the Finger Lakes consortium which is 10 years old. One conclusion reached by the self-study is that a voluntary cooperative organization could be effective working as a liaison between state agencies and colleges. The planning which will result can preserve the autonomy of each institution but better serve the needs of those people within the region or state.

1001. Corson, John J. *The Governance of Colleges and Universities: Modernizing Structure and Processes*. Revised edition. New York: McGraw-Hill, 1975. 297 pp.

Assesses problem areas in governance of higher education and suggests better management practices. Decision making is discussed from the viewpoint of the student, faculty, and administration. Believes the president should provide strong leadership and that institutional independence is of greatest importance.

1002. Davis, Junius A., and Batchelor, Steve A. *The Effective College and University Board: A Report of a National Survey of Trustees and Presidents*. Research Triangle Institute. Washington, DC: Association of Governing Boards of Universities and Colleges, 1974. 71 pp.

Report of a survey which tried to ascertain the effectiveness of boards of governance in higher education. Questionnaires were sent to trustees and presidents of 7 different types of institutions, community colleges, private junior colleges, public and private 4-year colleges, public and private universities, and private Black institutions.

1003. Dugger, Ronnie. *Our Invaded Universities: Form, Reform and New Starts*. New York: Norton, 1974. 457 pp.

Describes the University of Texas in its corporate role and the political interests which have had a hand in shaping the university. L. B. Johnson, John Connally, and Frank Erwin (chairperson of the Board of Regents of the U.T. System) are involved in a struggle with Harry Ransom (chancellor of the U.T. System), John Silber, and other faculty members over making the university a "first class" university.

1004. Epstein, Leon D. *Governing the University: The Campus and Public Interest*. San Francisco, CA: Jossey-Bass, 1974. 253 pp.

Presents the many facets of the multipurpose university. The roles of state agencies and boards, faculty, and students are also discussed. The power of administrators and their importance in the governing structure is of interest.

1005. Heilbron, Louis H. *The College and University Trustee: A View from the Board Room.* San Francisco, CA: Jossey-Bass, 1973. 239 pp.

Overview of the duties of academic trusteeship. Discusses "Nature of the Trust" and then goes on to policy, academic freedom, tenure, and collective bargaining.

1006. Hodgkinson, Harold L., and Meeth, L. Richard, eds. *Power and Authority: Transformation of Campus Governance.* San Francisco, CA: Jossey-Bass, 1971. 215 pp.

Relays various messages from well-known administrators in higher education concerning their thoughts on the changing role of administrators, faculty, and trustees. Among subjects discussed are: faculty unions, relationships to larger society, constitution of boards of trustees, administrative accountability, and rights of petition.

1007. Ingram, Richard T., et al. *Handbook of College and University Trusteeship.* San Francisco, CA: Jossey-Bass, 1980. 514 pp.

The major emphasis is a synthesis of how governing boards function, how they should function, and how they can be helped to fulfill their obligations. Major parts are: significance of trusteeship, effective board management, effective institutional oversight, resource development and management, performance assessment, and resources.

1008. Johnson, Eldon L. *From Riot to Reason.* Urbana, IL: University of Illinois Press, 1971. 127 pp.

Discusses problems in recent years which affect the prestige and support of the university from the viewpoint of the vice-president of the University of Illinois. Considers the statewide commissions of higher education and the governance of the university, including the president, administrators, faculty and board. Believes that students should participate in academic affairs and both teaching and research are important.

1009. Kaplan, Martin, ed. *The Monday Morning Imagination: Report from the Bayer Workshop on State University Systems.* Palo Alto, CA: Aspen Institute for Humanistic Studies, 1976. 158 pp.

Outlines the current situation in state university systems in the first section; the second section concerns educational goals; and the third section discusses effective means of meeting these goals. Some participants are Ernest Bayer, K. Patricia Cross, George Bonham, and C. Peter Magrath.

1010. Keeton, Morris T. *Shared Authority on Campus.* Washington, DC: American Association for Higher Education, 1971. 166 pp.

Considers governance problems on campus and ways of solving them. Wider sharing of authority and coordination of efforts should bring benefits to all. Special abilities of people could often be used, as well as those of groups of people or departments. Policymaking and management can be divided.

1011. Lee, Eugene C., and Bowen, Frank M. *Multicampus University: A Study of Academic Governance.* Carnegie Commission on Higher Education. New York: McGraw-Hill, 1971. 481 pp.

Surveys 9 large institutions: University of North Carolina, California State University and Colleges, City University of New York, State University of New York, University of California, University of Missouri, University of Texas, and University of Wisconsin. Every aspect of each system is examined and evaluated, including: relationship with legislature, coordinating state agency, governing board, administration, faculty and student organizations, administration and budget, and student personnel problems and transfers.

1012. McConnell, Thomas Raymond. *The Redistribution of Power in Higher Education.* Berkeley, CA: Center for Research and Development in Higher Education, 1971. 73 pp.

Considers the changes in society and education as they affect the governance of the university. Experiences of the University of California are used as illustrations. Lists those to whom faculties and institutions should report.

1013. McConnell, Thomas Raymond, and Mortimer, Kenneth. *Faculty in University Governance.* Center for Research and Development in Higher Education. Berkeley, CA: University of California Press, 1971. 201 pp.

Based on case studies of Fresno State College, the Twin Cities campus of the University of Minnesota, and the University of California at Berkeley. Emphasizes the need for close cooperation between administration and faculty as they fulfill their responsibilities. Other conclusions reached include the need for strong leadership by the central administration and the need for specific goals for the institution.

1014. Mason, Henry L. *College and University Government: A Handbook of Principle and Practice.* Tulane Studies in Practical Science. The Hague: Martinus Nijhoff, 1972. 235 pp.

Describes the principles and procedures of academic governance which apply to decision making by administrators and faculty in higher education.

1015. Mauer, George J., ed. *Crises in Campus Management: Case Studies in the Administration of Colleges and Universities.* New York: Praeger, 1976. 266 pp.

Describes various aspects of college and university administration by using 19 case studies prepared by college or university presidents, chancellors, vice-presidents, provosts, and deans. The case studies are arranged in sections: "Universities in Transition," "Directions of Educational Programs," "Anxieties in Academe," "Challenges of Change," and "Gown Meets Town."

1016. Mayhew, Lewis B. *Arrogance on Campus.* San Francisco, CA: Jossey-Bass, 1970, 155 pp.

Defends the administrators of universities, including presidents. Sees the decline of authority in the administration as working adversely for the students' interests. The faculty are self-centered and guard their power and privileges with zeal.

1017. Millett, John D. *New Structures of Campus Power.* San Francisco, CA: Jossey-Bass, 1978. 294 pp.

Campus governance of individual campuses is examined, using case studies of 30 4-year institutions. Two procedures were used: evaluative criteria to judge experiences in campuswide governance and which one of four models of governance was current on each campus.

1018. Mortimer, Kenneth Paul, and McConnell, T. R. *Sharing Authority Effectively: [Participation, Interaction, and Discretion]*. San Francisco, CA: Jossey-Bass, 1978. 322 pp.

Examines the bases of authority distribution and decision makers both inside and outside the university. Effective planning is possible only if there is mutual trust and cooperation among campus constituencies. Some influences which are discussed include: collective bargaining, increased involvement of trustees, role of the president, and the skills needed by the president in order to ensure effective organization.

1019. Parekh, Satish B. *Long Range Planning*. New Rochelle, NY: Change Magazine Press, 1975. 77 pp.

Contains 10 questionnaires which are designed to aid planning at the divisional level of an institution of higher learning. Planning should consider all levels of administration, faculty, students, board of directors, and the community in which it is located.

1020. Pentony, DeVere; Smith, Robert; and Axen, Richard. *Unfinished Rebellions*. San Francisco, CA: Jossey-Bass, 1971. 315 pp.

Deals with problems of San Francisco State during the 1960s. The urban revolution, Black and ethnic revolution, antiwar feeling, and rapid growth in higher education are all factors. Some solutions suggested are reforms in governance and the curriculum. Sharing of authority and responsibility might also be beneficial.

1021. Ross, Bernard H. *University-City Relations: From Coexistence to Cooperation*. ERIC/Higher Education Research Report No. 3. Washington, DC: American Association for Higher Education, 1973. ED 080 098. 38 pp.

The only report in this series between 1973 and 1979 dealing with this topic. Three major aspects of the problems are considered: impact of the university on local government, growth of the university involvement in urban affairs, and strengths and weaknesses involved in the interaction between universities and local governments.

1022. Rowland, A. Westerly. *Handbook of Institutional Advancement*. San Francisco, CA: Jossey-Bass, 1977. 577 pp.

Describes the field of institutional advancement. There are 6 areas covered: institutional relations, fund raising, alumni, governmental relations, publications, and management.

1023. Shell, Helene I. *A Profile of Upper Level Colleges*. AAHE-ERIC Education Report. Washington, DC: American Association for Higher Education, 1973. ED 071 622. 4 pp.

Upper-level colleges which are colleges and universities offering bachelor's degrees and graduate programs are one solution to articulation for community college transfer students. (At the time of this report, absorbing enrollment pressures was given as another reason.) Among the topics discussed are: a brief history, advantages, innovation opportunities, problems and recommendations.

1024. Wise, W. Max. *The Politics of the Private College*. New Haven, CT: Hazen Foundation (N.D.). 70 pp.

Studies 6 private, liberal arts colleges which have financial problems; they lack endowments and are not tax-supported. Various aspects of the problems are discussed and serious deficiencies are noted.

1025. Zwingle, J. L., and Mayville, William V. *College Trustees: A Question of Legitimacy*. Research Report No. 10. Washington, DC: American Association for Higher Education, 1974. ED 101 619. 60 pp.

Discusses questions of tenure, collective bargaining, accountability, and other issues in institutional governance which interest trustees in higher education.

State Role

1026. Allen, Richard H. *State Level Postsecondary Education Financial Reporting*. Boulder, CO: National Center for Higher Education Management Systems, 1978. 175 pp.

This document should be of assistance to state agencies and their staffs as they collect and compare collected data from the states.

1027. Balutis, Alan P., and Butler, Daron K., eds. *The Political Pursestrings: The Role of the Legislature in the Budgetary Process*. Sage/Halstead Publishers, 1975. 221 pp.

The state legislature of each state is responsible for developing that state's budget. In recent years professional staffs have been used to gather, process, and assess information. The influence of the staff in the legislative process is frequently overlooked.

1028. Barak, Robert J., and Berdahl, Robert O. *State-Level Academic Program Reviews in Higher Education*. Denver, CO: Education Commission of the States, 1977. 123 pp.

Program review is used by state agencies to analyze new programs, as well as existing ones, and make recommendations for the future. Factors which are considered include: quality, output, institutional priority, and cost.

1029. Bassett, Roger, et al. *The State Planning System Documents*. Technical Reports 86–97. Boulder, CO: NCHEMS, 1977.

This is a 12-vol. set which is intended to introduce, describe, and document the state planning system. It is intended for those who use models in planning.

1030. Beals, Ernest. *College Transfer Students in Massachusetts: A Study of 20,000 Transfer Applications to 48 Massachusetts Colleges and Universities for Fall 1973*. Boston: Massachusetts Board of Higher Education, 1974. 103 pp.

A study of transfer students which concerns both public and private institutions of higher learning. A guide which would be useful to those in statewide planning, as well as other administrators.

1031. Berdahl, Robert O. *Evaluating Statewide Boards: New Directions for Educational Research*. San Francisco, CA: Jossey-Bass, 1975. 114 pp.

The present and changing powers of statewide boards are considered by several well-known contributors. Suggestions to improve the performance are made and important questions are raised concerning the future power and political involvement of these boards.

1032. ———. *Statewide Coordination of Higher Education*. Washington, DC: American Council on Education, 1971. 285 pp.

The basis for this study is research done in 19 states. The operations and relationships of state coordinating agencies in higher education are the first emphasis. Next the role of these agencies as intermediaries between the state and higher education institutions is considered.

1033. Berve, Nancy M., ed. *State Postsecondary Education Profiles Handbook*. Denver, CO: Education Commission of the States.

An annual handbook in 4 parts which contains information about postsecondary education in the 50 states. Part 1: narrative description of state coordinating or governing agency and related groups or boards; part 2: statistics on state population, trends, finances, etc.; part 3: annual and biennial reports of state agencies available for distribution; and part 4: special reports and studies.

1034. Budig, Gene A., ed. *Dollars and Sense: Budgeting for Today's Campus*. Chicago: McGraw-Hill, 1972.

The legislative side of budgeting and its relationship to the system of higher education in the state is examined in this volume. A description of the office of the governor and the governor's responsibility, power, and relationship with other governmental affairs is recorded.

1035. Carnegie Commission on Higher Education. *The Capitol and the Campus: State Responsibility for Postsecondary Education*. New York: McGraw-Hill, 1971. 154 pp.

Several recommendations are made in this report. Concern is noted about dominance by state governors and state agencies over higher education in some states. Better accountability by institutions is suggested and also some financial help to private institutions, especially for medical and professional schools.

1036. ———. *Governance of Higher Education: Six Priority Problems*. New York: McGraw-Hill, 1973. 249 pp.

Six major governance problems dealing with institutions of higher education are examined. Recommendations are made in each area.

1037. Carnegie Foundation for the Advancement of Teaching. *The States and Higher Education: A Proud Past and a Vital Future* and *Commentary Supplement*. San Francisco, CA: Jossey-Bass, 1976. 94 p. 66 pp.

The role of the state in American higher education is discussed. The trend towards statewide centralization is noted and careful planning is urged by the states. The *Supplement* contains descriptive information and statistics.

1038. Chambers, M. M. *Higher Education and State Governments, 1970–1975*. Danville, IL: Interstate, 1974. 294 pp.

Begins where the prior volume *Higher Education in the Fifty States* left off and covers fiscal years 1971–74. Data on state support of higher education are linked with evaluative comments.

1039. ———. *Higher Education in the Fifty States*. Danville, IL: Interstate, 1970. 452 pp.

Details progress of each state in the support of higher education. Believes that statewide coordination should be on a voluntary basis. State appropriations for higher education are listed and states are encouraged to press for changes in tax structures which will result in better funding.

1040. ———. *Record of Progress: Three Years of State Tax Support of Higher Education 1969–1970 through 1971–1972*. Danville, IL: Interstate, 1972. 68 pp.

Contains tables showing the amount of state tax funds appropriated for higher education in the 50 states, by state, institution, and fiscal period for 13 years. Also reproduction of the journal *Grapevine* for 1969, 1970, 1971, and part of 1972. This journal provides tax legislation and appropriations information for higher education.

1041. Corson, John J. *Changing Patterns of Governance in Higher Education*. Tucson, AZ: University of Arizona Higher Education Program, 1976. 65 pp.

A collection of papers which identify external pressures which affect higher education. These include state and federal roles, pressures for democratization, demographic changes, and expansion of knowledge.

1042. Education Commission of the States. *Coordination or Chaos?* Report of the Task Force on Coordination, Governance, and Structure of Postsecondary Education. No. 43. Denver, CO: Education Commission of the States, 1973. 110 pp.

There are several recommendations made concerning state coordination and postsecondary education. Planning is urged at every level and the coordination of state agencies with both private and public institutions is stressed.

1043. ———. *Higher Education in the States*. Denver, CO: Education Commission of the States. Paging varies.

A series which is published 3 times a year. Each issue is concerned with one facet of higher education: individual reports on the states, new legislation on a state to state basis, and programs in operation or approved for state support of higher education.

1044. Eulau, Heinz, and Quinley, Harold. *State Officials and Higher Education: A Survey of the Opinions and Expectations of Policy Makers in Nine States*. Carnegie Commission on Higher Education. New York: McGraw-Hill, 1970. 209 pp.

State executives, legislators, and staff members in 9 states were interviewed concerning problems and issues in higher education. The selected states were California, Texas, Illinois, New York, Pennsylvania, Iowa, Kansas, Kentucky, and Louisiana. A lack of information about colleges and universities was mentioned by many who were interviewed.

1045. Glenny, Lyman A. *The Anonymous Leaders of Higher Education*. Berkeley, CA: Center for Research and Development in Higher Education, 1971. 27 pp.

Presents the view that much educational policy does not rest in the hands of presidents, deans, or others in administration. Bureaucrats at local, state, and federal levels are frequently those who usurp authority.

1046. ———. *State Budgeting for Higher Education: Interagency Conflict and Consensus*. Center for Research and Development in Higher Education. Berkeley, CA: University of California, 1976. 170 pp.

An examination of budget professionals and their approach to budgeting is contained in this summary of a study of state agencies. College and university budgets are reviewed by various agencies. Structure, roles, and staff characteristics of the higher education agency, the executive budget office, and legislative budget staffs are examined to determine the amount of competition, cooperation, and overlap involved.

1047. Glenny, Lyman, and Dalglish, Thomas. *Public Universities, State Agencies and the Law: Constitutional Autonomy in Decline*. Berkeley, CA: Center for Research and Development in Higher Education, 1973. 194 pp.

State agencies' powers over higher education have been gradually increasing in recent years. This report surveys the legal relationships between the state and public universities.

1048. Glenny, Lyman A., et al. *Coordinating Higher Education for the 1970's*. Berkeley, CA: Center for Research and Development of Higher Education, 1971. 96 pp.

Reports coordination efforts of political leaders, institutional leaders, statewide governing agencies, and their staffs. Several topics are discussed: membership and organization of the board, planning at various levels, program review, financial arrangements, use of databases and computers. A practical guide for everyone involved in planning in higher education.

1049. ———. *State Budgeting for Higher Education: Data Digest*. Berkeley, CA: Center for Research and Development in Higher Education, 1976. 376 pp.

There is great diversity in the budget process in various states. This study has 3 sections: Part 1, an overview of the higher education budget process by state; part 2, tabular considerations with 84 data tables; part 3, recent or proposed changes. The categories used are: structural classification of staff, staff personnel matters, organizational budget requests, state higher education agency hearings, governor's budget, legislative review, and appropriation and community colleges.

1050. Grant, Arthur T., ed. *The State Legislative Process and Higher Education*. Tucson, AZ: University of Arizona, 1978. 46 pp.

Contains 5 papers presented at a conference cosponsored by the Educational Commission of the States, Center for the Study of Higher Education at the University of Arizona, the ERIC Clearinghouse for Higher Education, and the National Conference of State Legislatures. Emphasizes the importance of developing strong bonds of understanding between college administrators and faculty and state legislators. Among the major topics are: future relationships between state legislators and higher education, the state legislative process and its effect on higher education, quantitative approaches to higher education management, and legislative expectations about the accountability of higher education.

1051. Halstead, D. Kent. *Statewide Planning in Higher Education*. U.S. Department of HEW. Washington, DC: Printing Office, 1974. 812 pp.

A comprehensive study which covers the theories, analyses, and procedures which may be used in statewide planning. Each chapter has an annotated bibliography.

1052. Harcleroad, Fred F. *Institutional Efficiency in State Systems of Public Higher Education*. Washington, DC: American Association of State Colleges and Universities, 1975. 48 pp.

Have state agencies for higher education been responsible for improvements in institutional effectiveness and efficiency? Studies opinions from institutional presidents, data showing savings or added costs because of a coordinating of governing system, and comparisons of business organizations and systems of higher education.

1053. Howard, A. E. Dick. *State Aid to Private Higher Education*. Charlottesville, VA: Michie Company, 1977. 1020 pp.

Contains 50 sections, one for each state, arranged alphabetically by state. Information on each state includes: state constitutional provisions, historical perspectives; and general discussion. Various issues within the state are discussed and include tax-paid aids for private elementary and secondary schools. Among the subjects treated in higher education are: contracts with private institutions, tuition assistance, tax exemptions, formula grants, direct aid to institutions, and aid to students.

1054. Howard, S. Kenneth. *Changing State Budgeting*. Lexington, KY: Council of State Governments, 1973. 372 pp.

The impact of planning-programing-budgeting systems (PPBS) is assessed in this book with emphasis on the state. Planning the budget and allocating the spending are the main aspects.

1055. Howard, S. Kenneth, and Grizzle, Gloria, eds. *Whatever Happened to State Budgeting?* Lexington, KY: Council of State Governments, 1972. 503 pp.

Theory and practice of budgeting at the state level are covered in 51 articles and essays.

1056. Hughes, John F. *Education and the State*. Washington, DC: American Council on Education, 1975. 275 pp.

The 4 general subjects of this collection consist of education goals and financing, equal access, management and governance, and educational innovation and reform.

1057. ———. *Formulating Policy in Postsecondary Education: The Search for Alternatives*. Washington, DC: American Council on Education, 1975. 338 pp.

Decision makers are faced with many critical problems in higher education today. Some areas of concern are: shifts in social conditions and students, more statewide planning and governance, and more federal intervention. Well-known educators propose solutions for major problems. Estelle Feshbein, Joseph W. Garbarino, Ernest L. Bayer, Juanita Kreps, Richard W. Lyman, K. Patricia Cross, and others comment on their areas of expertise.

1058. Johnston, William, ed. *Information and Analysis in the Context of Institutional State Relationships: The Tie That Divides Us*. Proceedings of the 1976 National Assembly. Boulder, CO: NCHEMS, 1976. 133 pp.

A conference on communication between institutions of higher learning and state government. Authorities discuss leadership and creativity, trends, mission, role, increased productivity, and philosophy.

1059. Jones, Dennis, et al. *State Level Information Base*. Technical Report 85. Boulder, CO: National Center for Higher Education Management Systems, 1977. 66 pp.

An account of an effort to improve information bases for state level planning agencies.

1060. Keenan, Boyd R. *Governance of Illinois Higher Education, 1945–74*. Urbana, IL: Institute of Government and Public Affairs, 1975. 108 pp.

Studies the development of governance in Illinois since World War II. The social and political pressures in higher education are discussed and the future role of the state is noted.

1061. McConnell, Thomas Raymond. *Accountability and Autonomy.* Berkeley, CA: University of California, 1971. 25 pp.

In recent years government agencies control over higher education has increased greatly. Several factors have contributed to greater government intervention, such as: irresponsible student and faculty behavior, financial problems and mounting costs, curriculum and degree-granting concerns. As private colleges and universities accept state support, they will also be accountable to state and federal agencies. Both public and private institutions will become increasingly accountable to state and federal governments as financial aid grows.

1062. McFarlane, William, and Wheeler, Charles L. *Legal and Political Issues of State Aid for Private Higher Education.* Atlanta, GA: Southern Regional Education Board, 1971. 78 pp.

States the need for public support of private institutions. Diversity in educational opportunities, interests and needs of students, higher standards of quality, and other benefits would be the result of public support.

1063. Meisinger, Richard J., Jr. *State Budgeting for Higher Education: The Uses of Formulas.* Center for Research and Development in Higher Education. Berkeley, CA: University of California, 1976. 266 pp.

This examination of formula budgets looks at the inter-organizational relationships between executive and legislative budget agencies, higher education coordinating agencies, and institutions of higher learning.

1064. Millard, Richard M. *State Boards of Higher Education.* ERIC/Higher Education Research Report No. 4. Washington, DC: American Association for Higher Education, 1976. ED 129 196. 69 pp.

Due to the rapidly growing influence of state government on higher education, this report about state boards of higher education is very timely. Historical development, types of boards, state postsecondary education commissions, issues, trends and directions are considered.

1065. Millett, John D. *Politics and Higher Education.* Tuscaloosa, AL: University of Alabama Press, 1974. 147 pp.

Discusses the many ways in which higher education should be considered in its relationship to politics and public administration. One conclusion of particular interest is that it is necessary for higher education to have political spokesmen.

1066. Nowlan, James D. *The Politics of Higher Education: Lawmakers and the Academy in Illinois.* Urbana, IL: University of Illinois Press, 1976. 109 pp.

Describes the decision-making role of the Illinois legislature as it enacted legislation which affected the support and structure of higher education. More control by the legislature is the result of legislation passed.

1067. Palola, E. G., et al. *Higher Education by Design: The Sociology of Planning.* Berkeley, CA: Center for Research and Development in Higher Education, 1970. 638 pp.

Presents an overall framework for the study of statewide programs for education, case studies of state planning, cross-comparisons, and model planning in higher education.

1068. Phillips, Ione. *The Added Dimension: State and Land Grant Universities Serving State and Local Government.* Washington, DC: National Association of State Universities and Land Grant Colleges, 1977. 96 pp.

Results of a survey of member institutions of NASULGC suggest additional programs and service operations for members to provide for the states which they serve.

1069. Purves, Ralph A., and Glenny, Lyman A. *State Budgeting for Higher Education: Information Systems and Technical Analyses.* Berkeley, CA: University of California, 1976. 231 pp.

Summarizes the design of information and analysis systems in higher education as institutions submit budget requests to the state. The technical procedures used by the state budget agencies to review these budget requests are listed.

1070. Schick, Allen. *Budget Innovation in the States.* Washington, DC: Brookings, Institution, 1971. 223 pp.

The historical development of 2 innovations in state budgeting is described in this study. They are performance budgeting and planning-programming-budgeting systems (PPBS).

1071. Schmidtlein, Frank, and Glenny, Lyman A. *State Budgeting for Higher Education: The Political Economy of the Process.* Berkeley, CA: Center for Research and Development in Higher Education, University of California, 1977. 275 pp.

Both theory and data are used in this investigation of budgeting processes used by state agencies as they determine college and university budgets. Future trends in the design of budget structures are outlined.

1072. Shulman, Carol H. *State Aid to Private Higher Education.* ERIC Clearinghouse on Higher Education, No. 3. Washington, DC: American Association for Higher Education, 1972. ED 062 962. 38 pp.

Although private colleges need public assistance, there is a reluctance to accept such financial help because of the obligation to accept increased state supervision of their activities. Methods of aid and problems created by state-private college relationships are discussed.

1073. Smelser, Neil J., and Almond, Gabriel, eds. *Public Higher Education in California.* Berkeley, CA: University of California Press, 1974. 312 pp.

Studies a complex, multicampus, stratified state system of higher education. Within the California system of higher education exist 2 incongruous values, populist egalitarianism and competitive excellence.

1074. Southern Regional Education Board. *Higher Education Legislative Issues '79.* Atlanta, GA: Southern Regional Education Board, 1979. 39 pp.

Discusses topics which were of interest at a conference: faculty pay, graduate education, teacher education and certification, vocational and technical education, and statewide coordination.

1075. ———. *Southern Higher Education Legislative Report.* Atlanta, GA: Southern Regional Education Board, 1977. 27 pp.

Southern states which held regular or special legislative sessions in 1977 are listed in this publication. The legislative action which affected higher education in 13 states is summarized in pp. iii through xiii. In the following pp. a more detailed account is given by state.

1076. Williams, Robert L. *Legal Bases of Boards of Higher Education in Fifty States*. Chicago: Council of State Governments, 1971. 185 pp.

Contains descriptions of 50 state boards, as well as their powers and duties.

1077. Wing, Paul, and McLaughlin, James N. *An Overview and Guide to Use of the Statewide Measures Inventory*. Boulder, CO: National Center for Higher Education Management Systems, 1974. 62 pp.

An attempt to standardize terminology and simplify communication in postsecondary planning and management for institutions and state level agencies.

1078. Wing, Paul, and Romney, Leonard. *An Examination of Possible Statewide Applications and Extensions of NCHEMS Program Classification Structures*. Technical Report 50. Boulder, CO: NCHEMS, 1974. 62 pp.

Gives suggestions for statewide planning by using NCHEMS Program Classification Structures.

1079. Wing, Paul; McLaughlin, James; and Allman, Katherine. *Statewide Measures Inventory: An Inventory of Information Relevant to Statewide Postsecondary Education Planning and Management*. Technical Report No. 68. Boulder, CO: National Center for Higher Education Management Systems, 1975. 200 pp.

Definitions and information of various kinds are useful to statewide planners in postsecondary education.

1080. Young, Kenneth E., ed. *Exploring the Case for Low Tuition in Public Higher Education*. American Association of State Colleges and Universities, American Association of Community and Junior Colleges, National Association of State Universities and Land-Grant Colleges. Iowa City, IA: American College Testing Program, 1974. 184 pp.

Six participants in a seminar on low tuition discuss effects of low tuition vs. higher tuition.

1081. Zwingle, J. L., and Rogers, M. E. *State Boards Responsible for Higher Education*. Washington, DC: U.S. Government Printing Office, 1972. 55 pp.

Organizational charts for each state coordinating board are published in this book. There are also descriptions by state, of boards, multicampuses, and individual boards.

Federal Role

1082. American Enterprise Institute for Public Policy Research. *Rising Costs in Education: The Federal Response?* Washington, DC: American Enterprise Institute, 1978. 44 pp.

Discusses proposals on tuition tax credits and federal aid to education. The participants in this forum are: U.S. Commissioner of Education, Ernest L. Boyer, Senator Robert Packwood, National Education Association President John Ryor, and Professor of Economics Thomas Sowell.

1083. Bailey, Stephen K. *Education Interest Groups in the Nation's Capital*. Washington, DC: American Council on Education, 1975. 87 pp.

Pictures the Washington scene where between 250 and 300 education organizations have representatives who attempt to make or influence education policy. These lobbyists make contacts with lower level bureaucrats and members of congress. They keep track of new legislation, rules, or procedures which would be harmful to their constituents.

1084. Bender, Louis W. *Federal Regulation and Higher Education*. ERIC/Higher Education Research Report No. 1. Washington, DC: American Association for Higher Education, 1977. ED 135 323. 79 pp.

Reviews federal influence on higher education. Formerly considered a national resource, now higher education is perceived as a tool or instrument of federal policy. Major topics are: the issue of regulation and overregulation, evolution of the federal presence, the contemporary scene since 1970, federal accountability vs. institutional autonomy, and recommendations.

1085. Carnegie Commission on Higher Education. *Institutional Aid: Federal Support to Colleges and Universities*. New York: McGraw-Hill, 1972. 290 pp.

At the time of this report the federal government was supplying federal funds for student financial aid and grants to institutions and some support for operating expenses. Discusses the amount of aid required and allocations. Appendices with information of various kinds, including statements from associations and commissions in higher education concerning their thoughts on institutional aid.

1086. ———. *Quality and Equality: Revised Recommendations: New Levels of Federal Responsibility for Higher Education*. New York: McGraw-Hill. 37 pp.

Equality of access and quality of educational program are 2 goals proposed by the commission. In order to finance programs to achieve these goals, funding must increase at state, local, and private levels but federal contributions must triple.

1087. Carnegie Council on Policy Studies in Higher Education. *The Federal Role in Postsecondary Education: Unfinished Business, 1975–1980*. San Francisco, CA: Jossey-Bass, 1975. 97 pp.

The Council suggests 3 ways in which the federal government can help finance higher education: establish a national student loan bank, support a matching program with the states to support private institutions, and support major research libraries.

1088. Congressional Budget Office. *Federal Assistance for Postsecondary Education: Options for Fiscal Year 1979*. Washington, DC: U.S. Government Printing Office, 1978. 67 pp.

Discusses how current programs are meeting federal goals in postsecondary education. Tuition tax credit and middle income assistance are also considered.

1089. ———. *Postsecondary Education: The Current Federal Role and Alternative Approaches*. Washington, DC: U.S. Government Printing Office, 1977. 59 pp.

The impact of federal spending in the achievement of higher education goals is of great importance in postsecondary education. Some goals of federal agencies are: providing equal educational opportunity, easing financial burden of students and parents, and continuing and maintaining institutions of higher learning.

1090. ———. *Social Security Benefits for Students.* Washington, DC: U.S. Government Printing Office, 1977. 25 pp.

A description of the origin of Social Security student benefits in 1965 and their subsequent development. Several issues have arisen since that time: method of financing, no test showing need, and no coordination of this program with other federal student aid programs.

1091. Conrad, Clifton, and Cosand, Joseph. *The Implications of Federal Education Policy.* ERIC/Higher Education Research Report No. 1. Washington, DC: American Association for Higher Education, 1976. ED 124 66. 65 pp.

Four stages of federal involvement in higher education are reviewed. Various issues involved in federal policy, such as equality of opportunity, achieving social equality, progress toward institutional health and diversity, and achieving diversity are discussed. New directions for federal policy are recommended.

1092. Consortium on Financing Higher Education: *Federal Student Assistance: A Review of Title IV of the Higher Education Act.* Hanover, NH: University Press of New England, 1975. 82 pp.

Changes in Title IV federal student aid programs are studied by representatives from 23 leading private institutions. Changes in Basic Educational Opportunity Grants (BEOG) are suggested, one of which is the half-cost provision. In the Work/Study program, the National Direct Student Loan and the Guaranteed Student Loan, it is suggested that the Work/Study program be enlarged by increased employer share. The other 2 are to be combined and to include the Health Professions loans.

1093. Department of Health, Education and Welfare. *The Second Newman Report: National Policy and Higher Education.* Special Task Force to the Secretary of Health, Education, and Welfare. Cambridge, MA: MIT Press, 1973. 227 pp.

America's goals for higher education have changed somewhat since the first "Newman Report" of 1971. There is now a more diverse group of citizens who are seeking an education and a broader range of institutions are trying to meet those different needs. Higher education should be concerned that government direction of policy does not lead to government control over operations.

1094. Dershimer, Richard A. *The Federal Government and Educational Research and Development.* Lexington, MA: Lexington Books, 1976. 208 pp.

Reviews the federal role in educational research and development from 1954 to 1972. Educational researchers frequently do not understand the operations at the federal government and bureaucrats find it difficult to comprehend the intricacies of research communities. Written to help both groups understand each other and to encourage further research.

1095. Education Commission of the States. *Postsecondary Education Profiles.* Denver, CO: Education Commission of the States, 1978. 225 pp.

Each annual publication contains data about the 50 states. There are 3 sections: description of state-level organizations, statistics about postsecondary education, and reports and special studies from each state agency.

1096. Finn, Chester E., Jr. *Scholars, Dollars, and Bureaucrats.* Washington, DC: Brookings Institute, 1978. 238 pp.

Discusses 3 major topics: federal aid to students, institutional assistance policy, and regulation of higher education institutions. The role of government has not been clearly defined and there exists much confusion and many contradictions in the relationship of government agencies and higher education.

1097. Froomkin, Joseph. *Aspirations, Enrollments, and Resources.* Washington, DC: U.S. Government Printing Office, 1970. 151 pp.

This study projects for the 1970s the amount of federal money needed to meet the educational desires for higher education, equal access, and quality in higher education. The changing student body will demand curriculum changes. Expanded student assistance by the federal government is suggested to solve problems.

1098. ———. *Needed: A New Federal Policy for Higher Education.* Institute for Educational Leadership, Policy Paper No. 6. Washington, DC: George Washington University, 1978. 82 pp.

Describes the policy issues in higher education: access, choice, innovation, and efficiency. Other problems which have arisen include the drop in enrollment, higher costs, and the question of the value of education. The policy of the federal government toward higher education needs to be evaluated.

1099. Gladieux, Lawrence E., and Wolanin, Thomas R. *Congress and the Colleges.* Lexington, MA: D.C. Heath, 1976. 273 pp.

The story of the participants involved in policymaking during the 1972 reauthorization of the Higher Education Act. Beginning with the 1972 legislation emphasis on federal aid shifted from institutions to aid directly to students.

1100. Glazer, Nathan, et al. *Bureaucrats and Brainpower: Government Regulation of Universities.* San Francisco, CA: Institute for Contemporary Studies, 1979. 171 pp.

The role of state and federal governments in higher education is a matter of concern to colleges and universities. The growth of government interference is a threat to the autonomy and integrity of higher education and may cause many changes. Contributors include 2 university presidents, 3 public policy scholars, a former HEW secretary, and a business man.

1101. Grant, Arthur T., ed. *The Impact of Federal Policies on Higher Education Institutions.* Tucson, AZ: Higher Education Program, College of Education, University of Arizona, 1977. 66 pp.

The encroachment of federal influence and direction upon higher education concerns many educators. Several well-known people in higher education give their views concerning this development and what can be done to change the impact of federal policies.

1102. Halperin, Samuel, and Kaplan, George R., eds. *Federalism at the Crossroads: Improving Educational Policymaking.* Washington, DC: Institute for Educational Leadership, George Washington University, 1976. 108 pp.

The question of federal involvement in education concerns many educators in higher education. Several of them give varying viewpoints about increased federal control, how to stop the present trend, and also how to inform congressional leaders on the needs and policies in institutions of higher education.

1103. Hobbs, Walter C., ed. *Government Regulation of Higher Education.* Cambridge, MA: Ballinger, 1978. 128 pp.

Scrutinizes the incursion of government regulations in colleges and universities from the perspectives of the legal scholar, the university president, the university lawyer, the government lawyer, the university affirmative action officer, the professional association watchdog of government activity, and the statesman-scholar of higher education. The responses are varied and raise some interesting questions.

1104. Hook, Sidney; Kurtz, Paul; and Todorovich, Miro, eds. *The University and the State: What Role for Government in Higher Education.* Buffalo, NY: Prometheus, 1978. 269 pp.

Describes many federal programs which relate to higher education. Educators are divided in their opinions about different programs. More than 2 dozen government officials and educators met together in 1976 to discuss what the relationship between the federal government and campuses ought to be. Opinions vary concerning federal support and there is no attempt to draw conclusions.

1105. King, Lauriston R. *The Washington Lobbyists for Higher Education.* Lexington, MA: D.C. Heath, 1975. 127 pp.

Politics and higher education are discussed in this book. There is a focus on the ''lobby'' for higher education. The Washington-based lobbies for higher education are described. There is a good review of the growth of major education associations and their guiding policies.

1106. Lester, Richard A. *Antibias Regulations of Universities: Faculty Problems and Their Solutions.* New York: McGraw-Hill, 1974. 168 pp.

Discusses the serious faults with present enforcement policies and practices in the affirmative action programs. Identifies and examines these deficiencies.

1107. McGuinness, Aims C.; McKinney, H. T.; et al. *The Changing Map of Postsecondary Education.* Denver, CO: Education Commission of the States, 1975. 268 pp.

Section 1202 of the Higher Education Amendments of 1972 established state comprehensive planning agencies. The origins, development, and state response to this legislation are valuable.

1108. Miles, R. E., Jr. *A Cabinet Department of Education.* Washington, DC: American Council on Education, 1976. 141 pp.

The options, advantages, and disadvantages of the creation of a federal Department of Education are enumerated in this study. Concludes that the need for a Department of Education is justified and recommends an advisory committee, qualifications for the Secretary of Education, and the personnel authority to hire qualified people.

1109. National Board on Graduate Education, Commission on Human Resources. *Federal Policy Alternatives toward Graduate Education.* Washington, DC: National Research Council, 1974. 127 pp.

The federal role in financing graduate education consists of graduate student research, and institutional support. An appendix contains statistical tables on university research and graduate programs.

1110. Seabury, Paul, ed. *Bureaucrats and Brainpower: Government Regulation of Universities.* San Francisco, CA: Institute for Contemporary Studies, 1979. 171 pp.

Examines the growing regulation which is imposed upon universities by various federal agencies. Suggests that business and higher education should combine forces to aid in resistance to government regulation.

1111. Shulman, Carol H. *Compliance With Federal Regulations: At What Cost?* AAHE-ERIC/Higher Education Research Report No. 6. Washington, DC: American Association for Higher Education, 1978. ED 165 552. 52 pp.

Coping with federal laws and regulations that relate to nondiscrimination and equal opportunity seems to be the major problem area for colleges that receive financial assistance. Major topics are: regulatory effects on academic life, college as employer, and cumulative problems with federal regulations.

1112. Student Financial Assistance Study Group, U.S. Department of H.E.W. *Recommendations for Improved Management of Federal Student Aid Programs.* Washington, DC: U.S. Government Printing Office, 1977. 203 pp.

Gives 14 recommendations for reform in the administration of student and programs. Various parts deal with organization and staffing, program management, training, program integrity, student applications, information for parents, and payment processes.

1113. U.S. Department of Health, Education and Welfare. *Lifelong Learning and Public Policy.* Washington, DC: U.S. Department of H.E.W., 1978. 57 pp.

A report of the Lifelong Learning Project authorized by HEW. Discusses the federal role in implementing and supporting services which are now provided locally and statewide to increase learning opportunities for workers, women, older citizens, and urban young people.

1114. Wildavsky, Aaron. *The Politics of the Budgetary Process.* 2d edition. Boston: Little, Brown and Company, 1974. 271 pp.

Budgeting on the federal level is defined and described but much also applies at the state and local level. Reforms are needed to implement and refine the budgetary process in Congress.

INSTITUTIONAL RESEARCH

1115. Adams, Carl R.; Hankins, Russell L.; Schroeder, Roger G. *A Study of Cost Analysis in Higher Education.* 4 vols. Washington, DC: American Council on Education, 1978. Vol. 1, 158 pp.; vol. 2, 180 pp.; vol. 3, 267 pp.; vol. 4, 139 pp.

Four studies conducted at the University of Minnesota, Graduate School of Business Administration. Detailed descriptions of procedures, results, and conclusions of institutional experience. The titles of the four vols. are: 1. *The Literature of Cost and Cost Analysis in Higher Education;* 2. *The Production and Use of Cost Analysis in Institutions of Higher Education;* 3. *Site Visit Descriptions of Costing Systems and Their Use in Higher Education;* 4. *The Future Use of Cost Analysis in Higher Education.*

1116. Allman, Katherine A. *A Reference Guide to Post-secondary Education Data Sources.* Boulder, CO: National Center for Higher Education Management Systems, 1975. 292 pp.

Guide to data sources useful to postsecondary education. Describes publications, articles, and databases.

1117. Andersen, Charles, ed. *A Fact Book on Higher Education.* Washington, DC: American Council on Education. 200 pp.

A publication in loose-leaf form which is published quarterly. Each issue is concerned with statistics in one specific area: demographic and economic data, enrollment data, institutions, faculty, staff, students, and earned degrees.

1118. Churchman, C. West. *ORU'S and Politics: Or, When Is Organizational Murder Justified?* Berkeley, CA: Center for Research in Management Science, University of California, 1976.

Examines moral politics involved in organized research units (ORUs), based on the situation at Berkeley. Three approaches are suggested: the common good approach, political approach, and the spirit of a research organization.

1119. Clark, David L., and Guba, Egon G. *Studies of Productivity in Knowledge Production and Utilization by Schools, Colleges, and Departments of Education.* Bloomington, IN: Rite Occasional Paper Series, Indiana University, 1976. 60 pp.

Conducted by the Research on Institutions of Teacher Education staff at Indiana University. Varied measures of research and development output were used in connection with schools, colleges, and departments of education. Seven separate analyses were accomplished.

1120. Cope, Robert G., ed. *Public Policy: Issues and Analyses.* Seattle, WA: Association for Institutional Research, 1974. 129 pp.

A variety of problems and issues are studied by several contributors. Chapters on national policy issues, policy analyses, and policy for institutional research are included. Statistics, tables, and charts provide supporting evidence.

1121. Dressel, Paul L., et al. *Institutional Research in the University: A Handbook.* San Francisco, CA: Jossey-Bass, 1971. 347 pp.

Blends theory and principles with practical suggestions for organizing and conducting institutional research. Computer data systems are suggested and some problems connected with their use are discussed. Changing goals and objectives, plus lessened financial support are problems in most institutions. Planning and evaluation are 2 important elements in institutional research.

1122. Dressel, Paul L., and Pratt, Sally B. *The World of Higher Education.* San Francisco, CA: Jossey-Bass, 1971. 218 pp.

An annotated guide to the literature of higher education which includes these topics: institutional research as a field of activity; governance, administration, and management; students; faculty and staff; curriculum and instruction; and research methodology. Related bibliographies and other reference materials are also listed.

1123. Drew, David E. *Science Development: An Evaluation Study.* Washington, DC: National Research Council, 1975. 182 pp.

A companion study to the National Research Council's *Science Development, University Development, and the Federal Government.* (See citation 1136.)

1124. Fenske, Robert H., ed. *Conflicting Pressures in Postsecondary Education.* Tallahasse, FL: Association for Institutional Research, 1977. 270 pp.

Authorities in several areas of interest to faculty members discuss such topics as faculty rewards, sex discrimination, collective bargaining, institution accountability, and faculty promotion.

1125. Folger, John K., ed. *Increasing the Public Accountability of Higher Education, New Directions for Institutional Research No. 16.* San Francisco, CA: Jossey-Bass, 1977. 99 pp.

More accountability and more effective performance from public institutions will be required as funding becomes more difficult to acquire. Performance budgeting, performance audits, and program reviews may be helpful in predicting outcomes.

1126. Hall, Norman P. *Identifying Institutional Goals.* Durham, NC: National Laboratory for Higher Education, 1971. 86 pp.

Describes the Delphi technique and the way it is used to identify goals of institutions. Reliable estimates of goals are believed to be obtained by this method.

1127. Hamilton, Malcolm C. *Directory of Educational Statistics: A Guide to Sources.* Ann Arbor, MI: Pierian Press, 1974. 71 pp.

A guidebook to sources of educational statistics on a wide range of topics. Includes current and historical information sources.

1128. Heermann, Emil F., and Braskamp, Larry A., eds. *Readings in Statistics for the Behavioral Sciences.* Englewood Cliffs, NJ: Prentice-Hall, 1970. 419 pp.

Provides an anthology of readings in applied statistics. Organized into 6 sections: history of the application of statistical methods, parametric vs. nonparametric statistics, randomization, testing statistical hypothesis, special topics in the analysis of variance, and correlation and regression.

1129. Heinlein, Albert C., ed. *Decision Models in Academic Administration.* Kent, OH: Kent State University Press, 1974. 135 pp.

Asserts that mathematical and simulation models are beneficial for administration in higher education. Discusses CAMPUS and RRPM and other models. Evaluation of more models and systems would be helpful to academic administrators, especially concerning results to be obtained.

1130. Ikinberry, Stanley, and Friedman, Renee C. *Beyond Academic Departments: The Story of Institutes and Centers.* San Francisco, CA: Jossey-Bass, 1972. 144 pp.

Studies research centers or other organizations connected with universities which sponsor research. New forms of research completed in these centers include interdisciplinary, contract, and applied. There is some conflict between these centers and universities, where research is also done.

1131. Lenning, Oscar T., et al. *A Structure for the Outcomes of Postsecondary Education*. Boulder, CO: National Center for Higher Education Management Systems, 1977. 72 pp.

Presents the development of a system designed to organize information so that it is possible to measure outcomes in institutions of higher learning. The outcome structure has 3 dimensions: audience, type of outcome, and time.

1132. McGee, Reece. *Academic Janus: The Private College and Its Faculty*. San Francisco, CA: Jossey-Bass, 1971. 264 pp.

Attempts to classify reasons why faculty choose to remain at their institutions or try to locate employment at other institutions. Those faculty active in the market are generally younger, have more doctorates from better institutions, and have generally higher salaries and faster promotions.

1133. Micek, Sidney S., and Arney, William R. *The Higher Education Outcome Measures Identification Study: A Descriptive Summary*. Boulder, CO: National Center for Higher Education Management Systems, 1974. 165 pp.

Designed to help practitioners and researchers understand outcome information intended for administrators and state government decisionmakers. Information was gathered from completed questionnaires. Data obtained were analyzed by descriptive statistical techniques.

1134. Miller, Richard I. *The Assessment of College Performance: A Handbook of Techniques and Measures for Institutional Self-Evaluation*. Jossey-Bass Series in Higher Education. San Francisco, CA: Jossey-Bass, 1979. 374 pp.

Identifies aspects of colleges and universities that will become objectives for evaluation in the next decade, and points out techniques for institutional researchers and evaluators. Ten major areas of institutional concern and 45 evaluative criteria are covered.

1135. Morrison, Peter A. *The Demographic Context of Educational Policy Planning*. New York: Aspen Institute for Humanistic Studies, 1976. 32 pp.

A study that reviews trends in birthrate, women in the labor force, migration, and other factors which should influence educational planning.

1136. National Research Council. *Science Development, University Development, and the Federal Government*. Report by the National Board on Graduate Education. Washington, DC: National Research Council, 1975. 48 pp.

Federal Government research programs of the early 1960s concentrated on 2 areas, New England and California. Economic development and quality graduate education in other parts of the United States suffered because of this pattern of research support. The N.S.F. tried to assist other universities to achieve quality research.

1137. Orlans, Harold. *Contracting for Knowledge: Values and Limitations of Social Science Research*. San Francisco, CA: Jossey-Bass, 1973. 286 pp.

Finds that social scientists sometimes make false claims about the validity of their research. Explores the problem in 4 areas: politics of social scientists and professional ethics, responsibility of intellectuals in research and evaluation, location of research and freedom to publish, and uses of social research.

1138. ———. *The Non-Profit Research Institute: Its Origin, Operation, Problems and Prospects*. Carnegie Commission on Higher Education. New York: McGraw-Hill, 1972. 243 pp.

Provides a look at the governance of nonprofit institutes and centers and the relationship of universities to them. Gives the benefits and disadvantages of university management of the research centers and recommends that annual reports be issued.

1139. Reichard, Donald J. "Campus Size: Some Recent Developments." In *Handbook on Contemporary Education*, edited by S. E. Goodman. New York: Bowker, 1976, pp. 184–89.

Due to some recent problems, such as increasing enrollments and maximum size for a compatible social-psychological environment, concern has developed about how large a college should be. Discusses such major topics as scope, size and institutional quality, and current controversies. Also reviews the literature and developments.

1140. Shannon, James A., ed. *Science and the Evolution of Public Policy*. New York: Rockefeller University Press, 1973. 280 pp.

Scientists and research administrators comment on different aspects of federal funding and research policy. Dicusses questions about purpose and utility of science, development and goals, the university, federal support of science, and general support of science.

1141. Sikes, Walter W., et al. *Renewing Higher Education from Within: A Guide for Campus Change Teams*. San Francisco, CA: Jossey-Bass, 1974. 184 pp.

Applies the behavioral science approach to action research teams. Teams may be committees formed by administration, faculty senate, student government, or other campus groups. Committee roles may be traditional, such as defining a problem and suggesting a solution; or they may collect data, obtain feedback, or facilitate change in other ways.

1142. Smith, Bruce L. R., and Karlesky, J. J. *The State of Academic Science*. Vol. 1, *The Universities in the Nation's Research Efforts*. Vol. 2, *Background Papers*. New Rochelle, NY: Change Magazine Press, 1978. 250 pp; 192 pp.

A comprehensive description of the research capability of universities in this country. Vol. 1 examines the trends in financial support and performance of academic research. The relationship of research universities to other research groups (nonprofit or commercial) is discussed. Vol. 2 includes 5 papers discussing issues and problems currently important in academic research.

1143. Sproull, Lee; Weiner, Stephen; and Wolf, David. *Organizing an Anarchy: Belief, Bureaucracy, and Politics in the National Institute of Education*. Chicago: University of Chicago Press, 1978. 282 pp.

Relates the origins of the National Institute of Education in 1972 and the problems which have plagued this governmental organization. Examines organizational theory and government bureaucracy.

1144. Stauffer, Thomas M. *Assessing Sponsored Research Programs*. Washington, DC: American Council on Education, 1977. 26 pp.

Presents information which should stimulate college presidents, academic officers, and other administrators to assess and evaluate possible policy actions which might affect sponsored research programs. Major categories discussed are: determining basic policy, planning the program, organizing the program, coordinating the program, and representing the program externally.

1145. Teich, Albert H. *Trends in the Organization of Academic Research: The Role of Organized Research Units and Full-Time Researchers*. Washington, DC: George Washington University, 1978. 90 pp.

Universities may consider 2 alternatives in the face of declining support for research: Academic activities are sometimes integrated with organized research units (ORUs) and there are also university affiliated laboratories which, though separate, operate under the direction of a university or universities. Some conflicts result from nonfaculty research professionals who have status comparable to regular faculty.

1146. Toombs, William. *Productivity and the Academy: The Current Condition*. University Park, PA: Pennsylvania State University, 1972. 117 pp.

Examines productivity in higher education. Workloads of faculty as related to institutional effectiveness are sometimes used to assess productivity. Improvement in education may result in better educated students rather than more students. Comprehensive planning systems such as PPBS and PERT/CPM are suggested as means to evaluation and increased productivity.

1147. Topping, James, and Myers, Ed. *Information Exchange Procedures for Major Research Universities*. Boulder, CO: National Center for Higher Education Management Systems, 1977.

A handbook developed to facilitate use of information from various major research universities.

1148. U.S. Department of Health Education, and Welfare. *Digest of Education Statistics*. National Center for Education Statistics. Washington, DC: U.S. Government Printing Office. 200 pp.

An annual publication that gives statistics concerning American education from early childhood through graduate school.

1149. Weinschrott, David J. *Demand for Higher Education in the United States: A Critical Review of the Empirical Literature*. Santa Monica, CA: Rand Corporation, 1977. 96 pp.

An evaluation of major empirical studies that examine student demand for higher education in the United States. Five criteria for evaluations are used.

1150. White, Virginia P. *Grants: How to Find Out about Them and What to Do Next*. New York: Plenum Press, 1975. 354 pp.

Devoted to directing the reader to complete grant information and to providing guidance after the information is found. A telephone number which will give latest information on Congressional bills is provided.

LEGAL PROBLEMS

General

1151. Alexander, Kern, and Solomon, Erwin S. *College and University Law*. Charlottesville, VA: Michie, 1972. 776 pp.

Discusses laws governing colleges and universities. Intended for students and practicing administrators. Topics included are: nature of the law, legal structure of higher education, taxes, religion, tuition and student fees, racial problems and segregation, tort liability, and other related legal materials.

1152. Blumer, Dennis H., ed. *Briefing Papers 1: Legal Issues for Postsecondary Education. Briefing Papers 2: Legal Issues for Postsecondary Education*. Washington, DC: American Association of Community and Junior Colleges, 1975. 96 pp.; 88 pp.

The first set of papers in this 2-part publication gives some emphasis to the 2-year institution, but applies to postsecondary education in general. Major topics include legal liabilities of administrators and trustees, legal liability of faculty, developing a faculty and staff personnel records policy, and the First Amendment freedoms of speech, press, and association. Part 2 provides discussion of general application of legal issues to higher education, and especially to teachers and administrators in community and junior colleges. Major topics are: employment, evaluation, and retention or non-retention of faculty and staff; security on the campus; copyright on the campus; disputes settlements; and dealing with federal regulatory agencies.

1153. Brubacher, John S. *The Courts and Higher Education*. San Francisco, CA: Jossey-Bass, 1971. 150 pp.

Summarizes legal questions of interest to college administrators. Advises administrators as the courts begin to intrude into areas which have previously been reserved for college and university resolution.

1154. ———. *The Law and Higher Education: A Casebook*. Vol. 1, *Students, Professors*. Vol. 2, *Administration, Academic Program*. Rutherford, NJ: Fairleigh Dickinson University Press, 1971. 333 pp.; 701 pp.

Administrators in higher education need some knowledge of the legal basis for their operations. These 2 volumes use court cases to illustrate ways of dealing with education-related problems. Vol. 1 includes cases dealing with rights of students and faculty. Vol. 2 contains cases involving administration, academic programs, and torts. An effort has been made to use language which can be easily understood by those without legal education.

1155. Burnett, Collins W., ed. *Legal Problems in Higher Education*. Bureau of School Service Bulletin, Vol. 3. Lexington, KY: College of Education, University of Kentucky, 1974. 117 pp.

Selected papers from students in a graduate seminar taught by professors of higher education and law. Major topics are: student protest, codes of student behavior, due process, academic freedom and tenure, collective bargaining, affirmative action programs, state control, and accreditation.

1156. Chambers, Merritt M. *The Colleges and the Courts*. Danville, IL: Interstate Printers and Publishers, 1972.

Relates both federal and state court decisions concerning students in higher education. Some problems of current interest include admissions, academic exclusion, tuition, out-of-state tuition, student financial aids, confidentiality of records, free speech and assembly, student organizations, freedom of student press, disciplinary due process, and state statutes.

1157. Chronister, Jay L., and Davis, Marlin E. *Nonresident Student Enrollment in the State Institutions of Higher Educa-*

tion: An Overview. Center for Higher Education, School of Education. Charlottesville, VA: University of Virginia, 1975. 56 pp.

Presents an overview of questions and issues. Methodology includes a review of current literature in nonresident enrollment, case law on residency issues, and surveys of state higher education agencies and public institution members of the Association of American Universities. Major topics are: nature of nonresident enrollment constraints and overcoming nonresidency.

1158. Edwards, H. T., and Nordin, V. D. *Higher Education and the Law*. Cambridge, MA: Institute for Educational Management, Harvard University, 1979. 844 pp.

Focuses on the nature of the impact that laws have on higher education. Major areas include the college as a legal entity, faculty rights, student rights, and federal regulation of higher education. Use of case law supports the content.

1159. Hendrickson, Robert M., and Marcum, Ronald S. *Governing Board and Administrator Liability*. ERIC/Higher Education Research Report No. 9. Washington, DC: American Association for Higher Education, 1977. ED 148 256. 63 pp.

Written by a specialist in higher education and an attorney, this report discusses the legal implications of federal and state regulations for colleges and universities. Development of charitable corporations, traditional basis of legal liability, liability for the new torts, and some forms of protection are major topics.

1160. Hollander, Patricia A. *Legal Handbook for Educators*. Boulder, CO: Westview Press, 1978. 287 pp.

Describes various legal issues which may be faced by educators. Some topics discussed are: faculty recruitment, hiring, collective bargaining, student admissions and financial obligations, and legal aspects of funding and facilities. Each chapter concludes with recommendations for educators.

1161. Holloway, Charles M. *The Bakke Decision: Retrospect and Prospect*. New York: College Entrance Examination Board, 1978. 85 pp.

Reports the summaries of a meeting of 500 college and university admissions officials and administrators. Three background papers are included: legal implications of the *Bakke* decision, educational and social implications, and undergraduate admission policies and practices.

1162. Holmes, Grace W., ed. *Law and Discipline on Campus*. Ann Arbor, MI: Institute of Continuing Legal Education, 1971. 381 pp.

Discusses student dissent and related problems such as external law and internal disciplinary system. Campus tension involves the governing board, administrators, faculty, and students in several ways. The appendix cites several documents relating to student rights, legal answers to some questions, and some laws.

1163. Kaplin, William A. *The Law of Higher Education*. San Francisco, CA: Jossey-Bass, 1978. 500 pp.

Written by a professor of law at the Catholic University of America who focuses on the broad reach of postsecondary education and emphasizes the legal implications of administrative decision making. Trustees and administrators, faculty, students, community, state government, and accrediting agencies are among the areas discussed. (Revised edition published in 1980.)

1164. Matheson, Alan A. *Due Process and Non Tenured Teachers: Monographs in Higher Education*. Tempe, AZ: Arizona State University, 1973. 29 pp.

Discusses many legal problems of current interest: tenure, right to teach, rights of nontenure, nonrenewal, termination, and procedural due process. Written by a law school professor who has also been an administrator.

1165. Millington, W. G. *The Law and the College Student*. St. Paul, MN: West Publishing, 1979. 629 pp.

Written by a professor in the Department of Higher and Postsecondary Education, University of Southern California, who uses case law to clarify and document academic discussion. Major topics discussed include higher education and the law, procedural and substantive guarantees, and equal protection of the laws' guarantees.

1166. Mix, Marjorie C. *Tenure and Termination in Financial Exigency*. AAHE-ERIC/Higher Education Research Report No. 3. Washington, DC: American Association of Higher Education, 1978. ED 152 222. 29 pp.

Mix, who holds a Ph.D. in higher education and a law degree, treats this topic well in both its educational and legal aspects. Possible solutions to the negative effect of financial exigency on tenure are faculty-administration consensus and collective bargaining.

1167. O'Hara, William T., and Hill, John G., Jr. *The Student/The College/The Law*. New York: Teachers College Press, 1972. 220 pp.

Summarizes the positions of the student, the college and the law and their relation to one another. Topics are: admissions, confidentiality of records, demonstrations, and due process. A chapter is devoted to each topic, providing the related law and court decisions; specific cases are cited.

1168. Sanders, Jane. *Cold War on the Campus: Academic Freedom at the University of Washington 1949–64*. Seattle, WA: University of Washington Press, 1979. 243 pp.

Recounts the story of a large state university which became involved in a controversy over academic freedom. The reactions of various segments, Board of Regents, public, faculty, administrators, and students are described and the final results are discussed.

1169. Shulman, Carol H. *Employment of Nontenured Faculty: Some Implications of Roth and Sindermann*. Research Report No. 8. Washington, DC: American Association of Higher Education, 1973. 75 pp.

Examines 2 U.S. Supreme Court decisions (Roth and Sindermann) concerning nonrenewal of contracts for nontenured faculty. The First and Fourteenth Amendments are at issue. Reactions by the educational and legal communities are examined. Complete Supreme Court decisions are included in the appendix.

1170. Young, D. Parker. *Proceedings of Conference on Higher Education: The Law and Individual Rights and Responsibilities*. Athens, GA: University of Georgia, 1971. 59 pp.

Discusses several matters of concern on college and university campuses. Some problems are: protection of students' rights, confrontations between groups on campus, court intervention in campus problems, and faculty contract negotiations.

1171. ———. *Higher Education: The Law and Administrative Responsibilities*. Athens, GA: University of Georgia, 1978. 51 pp.

Proceedings of a 1977 conference on the implications of judicial decisions as they affect academic decisions.

1172. Zirkel, Perry A., ed. *A Digest of Supreme Court Decisions Affecting Education*. Bloomington, IN: Phi Delta Kappa, 1978. 132 pp.

Gives brief explanations of 144 cases concerning education which appeared before the Supreme Court from 1859 to 1977. The cases are arranged in categories such as finance, organization, church-state relationships, student rights, employee rights and discrimination.

Women, Blacks, and Other Minorities

1173. Abramson, Joan. *The Invisible Woman*. San Francisco, CA: Jossey-Bass, 1975. 248 pp.

Describes discriminatory conditions in academe by using a personal experience as an example. Several reasons are given to explain the discrimination: male fear of losing preogatives, hatred of women, hatred of a particular woman, jealousy of a competent colleague, candidate judged unqualified, fear of additional loss of bargaining power, and lack of Abramson's bargaining power.

1174. Astin, Helen; Harway, Michele; and McNamara, Patricia. *Sex Discrimination in Education: Access to Postsecondary Education*. Los Angeles: Higher Education Research Institute, 1976. 394 pp.

Examines many facets of discrimination which may influence women's success in higher education. From high school courses all the way through higher education levels, many areas are considered in relation to the aspirations and achievements of women.

1175. Baker, Liva. *I'm Radcliffe! Fly Me! The Seven Sisters and the Failure of Women's Education*. New York: Macmillan, 1972. 246 pp.

The 7 sister colleges were patterned after the Ivy League colleges for men but were not considered equal to the men's colleges. Finds that the 7 sisters must cease to operated in the shadow of the men's colleges and become innovative in curriculum, faculty, financing, and administration.

1176. Benokraites, Nijole, and Feagen, Joe F. *Affirmative Action and Equal Opportunity: Action, Inaction, Reaction*. Boulder, CO: Westview Press, 1978. 255 pp.

Describes affirmative action programs in higher education as they affect women, minority group students, and faculty members. Concludes that affirmative action has been a "compromise."

1177. Berry, Margaret C., ed. *Women in Higher Education Administration: A Book of Readings*. Washington, DC: National Association for Women Deans, Administrators and Counselors, 1979. 184 pp.

A collection of 30 articles concerning the administrative positions of women in higher education. Some areas of interest explored concern training, sex discrimination, roadblocks, performance, and job satisfaction.

1178. Briscoe, Anne M., and Pfafflin, Sheila M., eds. *Expanding the Role of Women in the Sciences*. New York: New York Academy of Sciences, 1979. 344 pp.

Affirmative action has had little impact because it has never been applied in the way in which it should have been. Women should consider long-term career strategies, become more self-disciplined, and acquire new skills in order to advance in business.

1179. Cabrera, Y. Arturo. *Minorities in Higher Education: Chicanos and Others*. Niwot, CO: Sierra Publications, 1978. 205 pp.

Discusses educational opportunities for Chicanos, Blacks, American Indians, Asian Americans, and Puerto Ricans. Statistical tables and bibliographies are included.

1180. Carnegie Commission on Higher Education. *From Isolation to Mainstream: Problems of the Colleges Founded for Negroes*. New York: McGraw-Hill, 1971. 86 pp.

Competition with White institutions for Black students and faculty constitutes a major problem for Black colleges. They should redefine their objectives, understand problems involved, formulate solutions, and supply leaders for Black Americans.

1181. ———. *Opportunities for Women in Higher Education: Their Current Participation, Prospects for the Future, and Recommendations for Actions*. New York: McGraw-Hill, 1973. 282 pp.

Suggests ways to tap the largely underused supply of intellectual abilities of women in the United States. Women are still confined by many barriers in higher education. At each higher level of education the percentage of women declines.

1182. Carnegie Council on Policy Studies in Higher Education. *Making Affirmative Action Work in Higher Education: An Analysis of Institutional and Federal Policies with Recommendations*. San Francisco, CA: Jossey-Bass, 1975. 272 pp.

Deals with a problem in higher education which concerns administrators: what affirmative action should be taken to end discrimination in employment, remuneration, and promotion of women and minority groups. Twenty-seven specific recommendations are made by the council. One of the recommendations indicates the need for the academic community to achieve equal employment, rather than the federal government forcing it upon institutions.

1183. Catlin, Jamie Beth, et al. *Affirmative Action: Its Legal Mandate and Organizational Implications*. Ann Arbor, MI: University of Michigan, 1974. 81 pp.

Explores affirmative action as a law and the influence exerted upon the university. The first 3 chapters contain legal aspects of affirmative action with some historical perspectives, followed by 3 chapters on organizational aspects and a final chapter with a checklist of suggestions and questions.

1184. Change Magazine. *Women on Campus: The Unfinished Liberation*. New Rochelle, New York: Change Magazine, 1975. 256 pp.

Concerns participation of women scholars on campus. Advances have been made, but many frustrations are evident as women strive for intellectual acceptance.

1185. Churgin, Jonah Reuben. *The New Woman and the Old Academe: Sexism and Higher Education*. Roslyn Heights, NY: Libra, 1978. 254 pp.

Views the women's movement and the obstacles women face in their efforts to gain equality. Discusses women's colleges, women's studies, and affirmative action.

1186. Cole, Jonathan R. *Fair Science: Women in the Scientific Community*. New York: Free Press, 1979. 336 pp.

A study of women and men in the physical, biological, and social sciences to determine sex-based discrimination. The number of women scientists has increased sharply since 1970. Investigations in the academic science community are used to provide data. Includes a bibliography.

1187. College Entrance Examination Board. *Barriers to Higher Education: A College Entrance Examination Board Colloquium*. Princeton, NJ: College Board, 1971. 151 pp.

Examines barriers in higher education which are placed in the way of minorities who seek admittance to institutions of higher learning. Adjustments to the curriculum may be necessary for equal access, especially in retaining students.

1188. Conable, Charlotte Williams. *Women at Cornell: The Myth of Equal Education*. Ithaca, NY: Cornell University Press, 1977. 211 pp.

Describes the history of women at Cornell University. The founders planned a coeducational institution, and from 1874 through 1884 women entered the same academic program and had the same personal freedom as men. After that time they were required to live in a special dormitory with supervision and were limited to the School of Home Economics. In the 1960s a movement toward greater equality influenced the university to offer equal opportunity to women.

1189. Deem, Rosemary. *Women and Schooling*. London: Routledge and Kegan, 1978. 170 pp.

Reviews the issue of unequal opportunities and unequal outcomes of women in education and compares them with men. The number of women declines markedly at the postgraduate level. Believes that society and the capitalist state are responsible for some inequality for women.

1190. DuBois, W. E. B., and Aptheker, Herbert, eds. *The Education of Black People: Ten Critiques: 1906–1960*. Amherst, MA: University of Massachusetts Press, 1973. 171 pp.

Ten essays of DuBois which demonstrate the differences concerning education between Booker T. Washington and DuBois. The questions of vocational education vs. more intellectual learning for Blacks cause some controversy.

1191. Feldman, Saul D., ed. *Escape from the Doll's House: Women in Graduate and Professional School Education*. New York: McGraw-Hill, 1974. 208 pp.

Maintains inequality is not the same as discrimination. Women graduate students, generally, do not receive intellectual support from their professors in the same degree as their male counterparts.

1192. Fitzpatrick, Blanche E. *Women's Inferior Education: An Economic Analysis*. New York: Praeger, 1976. 189 pp.

Studies discrimination in the education of women with special reference to the economic aspects. The minority status of women in postsecondary education is explored and suggestions are made concerning equal educational opportunity.

1193. Fleming, John R.; Gill, Gerald R.; and Swinton, David H. *The Case for Affirmative Action for Blacks in Higher Education*. Institute for the Study of Educational Policy, Howard University. Washington, DC: Howard University Press, 1978. 416 pp.

Describes the affirmative action programs and the meaning and significance of these programs for Blacks in higher education. Included are: status of Blacks on campus before affirmative action measures were used, equal opportunity law, and evaluation of affirmative action programs in institutions of higher education. Uses case studies of a state university, a liberal arts college, a major research university, and a community college.

1194. Freeman, Richard B. *Black Elite: The New Market for Highly Educated Black Americans*. Carnegie Commission on Higher Education. New York: McGraw-Hill, 1976. 246 pp.

Describes advances in salary, occupational positions, probability of college attendance and economic status of Black college faculty. The topics covered are varied and the outlook is optimistic. Data was obtained by a survey of Black graduates and Black college placement directors.

1195. Furniss, W. Todd, and Graham, Patricia A., eds. *Women in Higher Education*. Washington, DC: American Council on Education, 1974. 336 pp.

Presents a picture of women in the mid-1970s and examines their roles at American colleges and universities as professors, students, and staff members. Many of the same problems exist at present.

1196. Gallagher, Buell G. *College and the Black Student*. New York: National Association for the Advancement of Colored People, 1971. 56 pp.

Describes problems facing college administrators in relationships with Black students. A checklist is included so that institutions can ascertain their understanding and response to Black students.

1197. Gappa, Judith M., and Uehling, Barbara S. *Women in Academe: Steps to Greater Equality*. AAHE-ERIC/Higher Education Research Report No. 1. Washington, DC: American Association for Higher Education, 1979. ED 169 873. 89 pp.

This comprehensive treatment of research concerning women in higher education discusses relationships between inequities and developments. Major topics are: status of women students, institutional practices and effects on women students, women's studies and women's colleges, women faculty and administrators, academic careers, the law, and recommendations for the future.

1198. Gray, Eileen. *Every Woman's Guide to College*. Millbrae, CA: Les Femmes, 1975. 168 pp.

Intended for the returning woman student. Some topics discussed are: finance, credit by examination, 2- and 4-year institutions, special programs for women, graduate school, and how to get a job. The problems faced by women are also listed: child care, reluctant husbands and children, loans and scholarships, and college red tape. There is a chapter explaining how women are socialized to fail.

1199. Group for the Advancement of Psychiatry. *The Educated Woman: Prospects and Problems*. New York: Scribner, 1975. 160 pp.

Delineates the conflicts faced by women in college. The struggles which occur frequently include: whether to be intellectual or "feminine," how to combine marriage and a career, and the difficulty in finding role models. Living patterns, social values, and changes in roles of men and women are examined.

1200. Haro, M. Carlos, ed. *The Bakke Decision: The Questions of Chicano Access to Higher Education*. Los Angeles: Chicano Studies Center Publication, 1977. 198 pp.

Describes the problems and accomplishments of Chicanos in higher education. A collection of documents, articles, letters, and newspaper clippings concerning the *Bakke* case and how it specifically affects Chicanos.

1201. Hoskins, Robert L. *Black Administrators in Higher Education: Conditions and Perceptions*. New York: Praeger, 1978. 206 pp.

Examines the positions of 457 Black administrators at 66 land-grant institutions. Problems discussed include: tenure, respect by peers and other members of the academic community, and personal problems which are encountered by Black administrators on predominately White campuses.

1202. Howard, Suzanne. *But We Will Persist*. American Association of University Women. Washington, DC: AAUW, 1978. 86 pp.

A survey conducted in 1977 is the basis for this report which outlines AAUW's expectations. Data is compared with a 1970 survey. According to the survey women made small gains but there was still much discrimination.

1203. Howard University. *Equal Educational Opportunity for Blacks in U.S. Higher Education: An Assessment*. Institute for the Study of Educational Policy. Washington, DC: Howard University Press, 1976. 330 pp.

The first annual report of a study of the status and needs of Blacks in higher education describes the years 1973–74. Sketches the economic returns of education, barriers to equal educational opportunity, and persistence of students. Uses tables and charts of data.

1204. Howe, Florence, ed. *Women and the Power to Change*. Carnegie Commission on Higher Education. New York: McGraw-Hill, 1975. 182 pp.

Shows how the present educational system contributes to discrimination against women in higher educaion. There are 4 essays describing personal experiences in the struggle against discrimination.

1205. Institute for the Study of Educational Policy. *Affirmative Action for Blacks in Higher Education: A Report*. Washington, DC: Howard University, 1978. 96 pp.

Examines various aspects of affirmative action and how they have affected employment opportunities for Blacks in higher education.

1206. Jawin, Ann Juliano. *Women's Guide to Career Preparation: Scholarships, Grants, and Loans*. Garden City, NY: Anchor (Doubleday), 1979. 355 pp.

Concerns both vocational guidance for women and a listing of financial aid information. Especially helpful to women who are returning to school and/or looking for jobs and their advisors.

1207. Knoell, Dorothy M. *Black Student Potential*. Washington, DC: American Association of Junior Colleges, 1970. 78 pp.

Studies college attendance of Black and White high school graduates. College attendance depends somewhat on the high school attended, Black, White, or integrated. Black parents encourage their children to attend college.

1208. Lopez, Ronald W.; Madrid-Barela, Arturo; and Macias, Reynaldo Flores. *Chicanos in Higher Education: Status and Issues*. National Chicano Commission on Higher Education, Monograph No. 7. Los Angeles: University of California, 1976. 199 pp.

Discusses problems and issues facing persons of Spanish surnames in higher education. A report of a symposium pertaining to persons in California and Texas primarily but of interest to others. A bibliography on Chicanos in higher education is included.

1209. McGuigan, Dorothy G., ed. *New Research on Women at the University of Michigan*. Ann Arbor, MI: University of Michigan Press, 1974. 289 pp.

Considers past, present, and future information concerning women. Includes completed research and research in progress, elementary and advanced articles. Contributors are at different stages of their careers, including graduate students, faculty, and nonacademics.

1210. Miller, LaMar P., ed. *The Testing of Black Students: A Symposium*. Englewood Cliffs, NJ: Prentice-Hall, Inc., 1974. 113 pp.

Deals with the problems of cultural bias in testing and in the educational and vocational opportunities of Blacks. Some aspects noted are: racial differences of testers, creating variance; heredity vs. environment; development of culture-free tests; general review of current thought, as well as specific issues.

1211. Mohr, Paul, ed. *Equality of Opportunity in Higher Education: Myth or Reality?* Lincoln, NE: Chicago-Southern Network Study Commission on Undergraduate Education and the Education of Teachers, 1976. 101 pp.

Discusses equal educational opportunities from their outlook of 1975. Includes the impact on higher education of the *Brown* vs. *Topeka Board of Education*. A review of state plans, outlook from Black college presidents, and organizational activities comprise the other sections.

1212. Moore, Kathryn M., and Wollitzer, Peter A. *Women in Higher Education: A Contemporary Bibliography*. Washington, DC: National Association of Women Deans, Administrators, and Counselors, 1979. 114 pp.

Annotated bibliography gives an indication of the scope of the field and should be a useful research tool. Concerns undergraduate and graduate students, administrators, and faculty. Books, journal articles, monographs, and some studies are included.

1213. Moore, William Jr., and Wagstaff, Lonnie H. *Black Educators in White Colleges*. San Francisco, CA: Jossey-Bass, 1974. 226 pp.

Reports on recruitment, selection, hiring, professional activities, promotion, and tenure of Black educators in White colleges and universities. The two Black scholars believe the status of Black women is even lower than Black men but are pessimistic about the future for all Black professionals.

1214. National Academy of Sciences. *Climbing the Academic Ladder: Doctoral Women Scientists in Academe.* Committee on the Education and Employment of Women in Science and Engineering of the National Research Council. Washington, DC: National Academy of Sciences, 1979. ED 180 332. 176 pp.

Examines the status of women in academic institutions. Gains are noted in junior positions and in the national science advisory process, but in other areas, such as rank disparities, tenure, and salaries, there is little or no gain. Some myths such as women's mobility and job prospects are examined and found to have little foundation in fact. Statistics are given in many areas and the data regarding employment and training of women scientists should be useful.

1215. National Advisory Committee on Black Higher Education. *Access of Black Americans to Higher Education: How Open Is the Door?* Washington, DC: National Advisory Committee on Black Higher Education and Black Colleges and University, 1979. ED 172 669. 82 pp.

Information from many sources is gathered to review the status, programs, and issues concerning the access of Black Americans to higher education institutions. Some interesting statistical information is given.

1216. Oltman, Ruth M. "Women in Higher Education." In *Handbook on Contemporary Education,* edited by S. E. Goodman. New York: Bowker, 1976. pp. 218–24.

Women as undergraduates, graduate students, and college teachers are discussed in terms of numbers, salaries, legal developments, and current issues.

1217. Panel on Financing Low-Income and Minority Students in Higher Education. *Toward Equal Opportunity for Higher Education.* New York: College Entrance Examination Board, 1973. 71 pp.

The goal of equal opportunity for higher education has not yet been realized in many ways. Two suggestions propose a maximum basic grant of $2,000 and easy access to loans.

1218. Peterson, M. W., et al. *Black Students on White Campuses: The Impact of Increased Black Enrollments.* Ann Arbor, MI: University of Michigan, 1978. 388 pp.

Traces the impact of many Black students upon predominantly White colleges and universities. Includes a literature review and a study of 13 institutions in New York, Pennsylvania, and 12 North Central states. Describes the institutions and their reactions to demands and confrontations by Black students, lists service programs which are intended to assist Black students and administrative reactions, and covers survey data obtained.

1219. Robinson, Lora H. *Institutional Analysis of Sex Discrimination: A Review and Annotated Bibliography.* AAHE-ERIC/Higher Education Report. Washington, DC: American Association for Higher Education, 1973. ED 076 176. 10 pp.

Because colleges and universities are responsible to federal agencies to develop affirmative action programs and comply with requirements to eliminate sex discrimination, this annotated bibliography is timely and helpful. There are 3 major purposes: for cross-comparison with other colleges, to locate useful analytical approaches, and to highlight the variety of concerns that have received attention.

1220. Rossi, Alice S., and Calderwood, Ann, eds. *Academic Women on the Move.* New York: Russell Sage Foundation, 1973. 560 pp.

The status of women in higher education is described in the following areas: goals of women, organizations designed to advance women, and impact to date. Plans for the future include placing women in top administration, women in research, women in academic committees, and changing attitudes of male colleagues.

1221. Sexton, Patricia. *Women in Education.* Bloomington, IN: Phi Delta Kappa, 1976. 189 pp.

Examines sex discrimination in schools and concludes that girls are generally treated equally and sometimes preferentially. Schools fail to encourage qualified women to choose careers in nontraditional areas and women become trapped in low status poorly paid jobs with little chance for advancement.

1222. Shavlik, Donna; Taylor, Emily; and Touchton, Judy. *Putting Principle into Practice: Guidelines for Administrators in Implementing Title IX.* Washington, DC: Resource Center on Sex Roles and Education, 1978. 45 pp.

Deals mainly with equitable policies of hiring women in higher education. Some practical suggestions include: preparing job descriptions, recruiting, interviewing, and screening candidates.

1223. Shulman, Carol H. *Affirmative Action: Women's Rights on Campus.* ERIC Clearinghouse on Higher Education. Washington, DC: American Association for Higher Education, 1972. ED 066 143. 46 pp.

Executive order 11375 issued in 1967 introduced a new element in the academic community and a new source of legal problems. Discusses the legal thrust behind affirmative action and issues raised from Revised Order No. 4.

1224. ———. *Federal Laws: Nondiscrimination and Faculty Employment.* ERIC/Higher Education Research Report No. 4. Washington, DC: American Association for Higher Education, 1975. ED 109 979. 53 pp.

Such laws as Title VII, Executive Order 11246, Post-Civil War Civil Rights Laws, Equal Pay Act, and Title IX are discussed in relationships to application to faculty employment. The appendix listing major federal laws and regulations with their effects on higher education is valuable.

1225. Solmon, Lewis C. *Male and Female Graduate Students: The Question of Equal Opportunity.* New York: Praeger, 1976. 146 pp.

Solmon uses data which is not very conclusive and frequently does not support his major findings. Concludes there is little discrimination, while referring to all graduate students as "he."

1226. Sowell, Thomas. *Black Education: Myths and Tragedies.* New York: David McKay, 1972. 338 pp.

A serious, honest, and informed report on Black education. Criticizes many Black recruitment drives; exposes special courses developed for Blacks; criticizes Black colleges and lack of help for Black middle-class students. Makes some suggestions for improvement.

1227. Steinberg, Stephen, ed. *The Academic Melting Pot: Catholics and Jews in American Higher Education.* Carnegie Commission on Higher Education. New York: McGraw-Hill, 1974. 183 pp.

Surveys the imbalance of Catholics and Jews in higher education and concludes that historic and socioeconomic factors rather than religious ones are responsible for the higher level of Jewish academic achievement and lower level of Catholic achievement. Bigotry does still exist today in higher education.

1228. Stock, Phyllis. *Better than Rubies: A History of Women's Education*. New York: Putnam, 1978. 252 pp.

A historical account of women's education in Western countries from Greek and Roman times. Only a few women were able to break away from the traditional roles of wife and mother for many years. During war times and times when men were occupied with other pursuits, women were able to gain more education and make gains in status.

1229. Vetter, Betty M.; Babco, Eleanor L.; and McIntire, Judith E. *Professional Women and Minorities: A Manpower Data Resource Service*. Washington, DC: Scientific Manpower Commission, 1979. 318 pp.

More and more information is available concerning the status of women and minority groups in the professions. Discusses the participation of women and minority groups in the natural and social sciences, arts, humanities, engineering, education, and other professions.

1230. Walters, Raymond. *The New Negro on Campus: Black College Rebellions of the 1920's*. Princeton University, 1975. 370 pp.

Deals with student strikes and demonstrations at Black colleges and universities in the 1920s. Some institutions discussed are Fisk, Howard, Tuskegee, and Lincoln. Points to the 1920s as a time of rising consciousness among middle-class Blacks who were able to attend college.

1231. Westervelt, Esther M. *Barriers to Woman's Participation in Postsecondary Education: A Review of Research and Commentary as of 1973–74*. Washington, DC: U.S. Department of Health, Education and Welfare, 1975. 76 pp.

Reports the research conducted before 1974 on women's role in higher education. There are 3 sections: institutional barriers, social attitudes, and psychological factors.

1232. Willie, Charles V., and McCord, Arline S. *Black Students at White Colleges*. New York: Praeger, 1972. 110 pp.

Social life, housing, curriculum, and student/teacher relationships of Black students are discussed from their viewpoint. Uses 4 institutions of different types.

1233. Wilson, Thomasyne L. *Toward Viable Directions in Postsecondary Education*. San Francisco, CA: Sapphire, 1976. 78 pp.

Deals primarily with the reentry problems of women but also with other nontraditional students. Appendices contain instruments and charts of various kinds.

1234. Wright, Stephen J., ed. *Beyond Desegregation: Urgent Issues in the Education of Minorities*. New York: College Entrance Examination Board, 1978. 76 pp.

All aspects of desegregation are covered in the 13 essays contained in this book. Issues which are covered include government policies, legal aspects, counseling needs of minorities, and definition of problems.

PLANNING AND MANAGEMENT

Accountability

1235. Coombs, Philip H., and Hallak, Jacques. *Managing Educational Costs*. New York: Oxford University Press, 1972. 304 pp.

Outlines the principles of educational cost analysis, using examples from the files of the International Institute for Educational Planning.

1236. Griffin, Gerald, and Burks, D. R. *Appraising Administrative Operations: A Guide for Universities and Colleges*. Washington, DC: American Council on Education, 1976. 183 pp.

An objective appraisal-review process is described as a method by which colleges and universities may establish and conduct a program to improve administrative operations. Management appraisal principles are cited and a model structure is outlined.

1237. Halstead, D. Kent, ed. *Higher Education Planning: A Bibliographic Handbook*. National Institute of Education, U.S. Department of H.E.W. Washington, DC: U.S. Government Printing Office, 1979. 539 pp.

An annotated bibliography published for higher education literature. Brief descriptions and outlines are given of the different topic areas.

1238. Mortimer, Kenneth P. *Accountability in Higher Education*. ERIC Clearinghouse on Higher Education. Washington, DC: American Association for Higher Education, 1972. ED 058 465. 58 pp.

Accountability which emerged as a major concern in the late 1960s and the 1970s will continue as a concern in the 1980s. The emphasis in this study is on defining the term, external and internal accountability, and consideration for the 1980s.

1239. Patterson, Lewis D. *Survival through Interdependence*. AAHE-ERIC/Higher Education Research Report No. 10. Washington, DC: American Association for Higher Education, 1979. ED 183 116. 53 pp.

In order to survive the serious problems of the 1980s, colleges may need to share and cooperate more than ever before. In doing so, however, the institution may lose its identity and ability to control the future. Among the major topics discussed are: extent of interinstitutional relationships, costs and benefits of cooperation, significant cooperative educational benefits beyond cost advantages, and the future of cooperation.

Management Systems

1240. Alexander, Christopher, et al. *The Oregon Experiment*. New York: Oxford University Press, 1975. 190 pp.

The master plan for the University of Oregon, in operation at that institution, is an adaptable plan which considers users, planning officers and architects, coordinates their needs, and determines best plans for present and future.

1241. American Association of University Professors. *A.A.U.P. Policy Documents and Reports*. Washington, DC: A.A.U.P., 1977. 98 pp.

A compilation of policy statements and guidelines of the A.A.U.P. Also included are statements on topics of interest to faculty, policymakers and planners in institutions of higher education.

1242. Balderston, Frederick E. *Managing Today' Universities*. San Francisco, CA: Jossey-Bass, 1974. 307 pp.

Concerns internal management.

1243. Baldridge, J. Victor, and Tierney, Michael L. *New Approaches to Management: Creating Practical Systems of Management Information and Management by Objectives*. San Francisco, CA: Jossey-Bass, 1979. 220 pp.

Reports the results of a national study of the impact of 2 innovations in college and university administration: MIS computer based management information system) and MBO (management-by-objectives systems). MIS is used to collect and analyze institutional data, such as enrollment trends and financial planning. MBO involves participatory planning and goals which are determined by each unit and evaluated by that unit. The study was based on questionnaires and personal interviews at 48 colleges that received grants under Exxon Education Foundation's Resource Allocation Management Program (RAMP) and published by the Higher Education Research Institute.

1244. Boldman, Carl A. *Help! There's a Computer in the Office*. San Carlos, CA: Rising Star Press, 1979. 248 pp.

A handbook which describes computers and their uses. Hardware, software, system design, and implementation are included in the information given. Case histories are also used.

1245. Bolin, John G., ed. *Management Information for College Administrators*. Athens, GA: Institute of Higher Education, 1971.

Needs for better management and theory are often apparent in higher education. Papers presented at a workshop are critical of present management practices.

1246. Casasco, Juan A. *Planning Techniques for University Management*. Washington, DC: American Council on Education, 1970. 77 pp.

Uses 21 models to show how computer-aided university planning can be used as a management tool by administrators in higher education.

1247. Doenges, Byron F., ed. *Accountability*. Corvallis, OR: Oregon State University Press, 1972. 196 pp.

The report of the thirty-third Pacific Northwest Conference on Higher Education focuses on accountability. Considers all aspects of accountability: expectations, aspirations, evaluation, and accountability through management systems.

1248. EDUCOM. *North American Perspective*. Proceedings of the Educom Fall Conference. Princeton, NJ: EDUCOM, 1975. 222 pp.

Compares various aspects of computer use and networking in higher education in Canada and the United States. Discusses use of computers in instruction and in management of institutions.

1249. Emery, James C., ed. *The Reality of National Computer Networking for Higher Education*. EDUCOM Series in Computing and Telecommunications in Higher Education, Vol. 3. Boulder, CO: Westview, 1979. 91 pp.

Describes the current status of computer networks in institutions of higher learning. The prospects, problems, and financial needs are analyzed.

1250. Frankel, Martin M., and Harrison, Forrest W. *Projections of Education Statistics*. National Center for Education Statistics, U.S. Department of H.E.W. Washington, DC: U.S. Government Printing Office. Paging varies.

This annual publication projects enrollments, graduates, faculty, expenditures, and student charges for institutions of higher education.

1251. Gambino, Anthony J. *Planning and Control in Higher Education*. New York: National Association of Accountants, 1979. 115 pp.

Studies the present and future application of management accounting in higher education. Interviews, mail questionnaires, and a literature search were used to gather data. The final chapter discusses accountability and the use of outcome measures and evaluation.

1252. Gamso, Gary S., and Service, Allan L. *Introduction to Information Exchange Procedures: A Guide for the Project Manager*. Technical Report 76. Boulder, CO: National Center for Higher Education Management Systems, 1976. 115 pp.

Compatible information is necessary to compare internal activities and also for exchange with other institutions. The NCHEMS Information Exchange Procedures (IEP) are described in this report.

1253. Genova, William J., et al. *Mutual Benefit Evaluation of Faculty and Administrators in Higher Education*. Cambridge, MA: Ballinger, 1976. 222 pp.

A valuable new approach to both faculty and administrator evaluation, which provides participants with incentives generally absent from such programs.

1254. Goddard, Suzette, et al. *Data Element Dictionary: Second Edition*. Technical Report No. 51. Boulder, CO: National Center for Higher Education Management Systems, 1973. Paging varies.

This manual is looseleaf and designed to be updated regularly by inserting new information. It contains postsecondary education data definitions and codes.

1255. Hamelman, Paul W., ed. *Managing the University: A Systems Approach*. New York: Praeger, 1972. 139 pp.

Discusses methodologies for management that may help educational institutions to determine goals and ways in which to meet those goals.

1256. Hartley, H. J. ''Program-Planning-Budgeting Systems.'' In *Handbook on Contemporary Education,* edited by S. E. Goodman. New York: Bowker, 1976, pp. 117–22.

Although this concept is applied to public schools, the discussion is also valid for application to colleges and universities. Advantages, implementation of PPBS, constraints, and potential abuses are considered.

1257. Heaton, C. P., ed. *Management by Objectives in Higher Education: Theory, Cases & Implementation*. Durham, NC: National Laboratory for Higher Education, 1975. 110 pp.

The case studies are the most valuable part of this book and range from a small community college to a multiversity. Problems that educational administrators may encounter if they wish to manage by objectives are pointed out. Faculty members frequently resist MBO and dislike the evaluation of the program.

1258. Heimstra, Roger. "Program Planning and Evaluation." In *Handbook on Contemporary Education,* edited by S. E. Goodman. New York: Bowker, 1976, pp. 113–17.

This reference concerns a management system that can be applied to an educational program when the intention is to bring about a change. Major topics are: needs assessment, development of objectives, planning the activities, evaluation, feedback and modification, and controversies.

1259. Herbert, Theodore T., and Yost, Edward B. *Management Education and Development: An Annotated Resource Book.* Westport, CT: Greenwood, 1978. 211 pp.

Presents an annotated bibliography on 9 management topics. Includes publications from 1948 to the present. There is a special section devoted to audiovisual resources.

1260. Higher Education Management Institute. *Management Development and Training Program for Colleges and Universities.* Coconut Grove, FL: Higher Education Management Institute, 1978. 93 pp.

Describes ways of training and developing employees using campus-based personnel and campus facilities. A comprehensive handbook which outlines programs for academic administrators.

1261. Hostrop, Richard W. *Managing Education for Results.* Palm Springs, CA: ETC Publications, 1975. 248 pp.

Describes the management implementation process by applying management principles and theories. Administrators, teachers, trustees, and others in education should find this book of interest. Includes charts, glossary, and bibliography.

1262. Hussain, Khateeb M. *Development of Information Systems for Education.* Englewood Cliffs, NJ: Prentice Hall, 1973. 419 pp.

Defines the terminology, knowledge, and procedures which administrators need to know in order to communicate with experts in systems design. The needs of the institution should be the focus of the system's design. Data processing methodology, management, and information systems potential for decision making are the principal topics of the book.

1263. Jones, Dennis P., and Drews, Theodore H. *A Manual for Budgeting and Accounting for Manpower Resources in Postsecondary Education.* Washington, DC: U.S. Government Printing Office, 1977. 66 pp.

The management of manpower resources in institutions of postsecondary education will be more effective if data can be collected and used. This manual will be of assistance in this context.

1264. Kaufman, Roger. *Educational System Planning.* Englewood Cliffs, NJ: Prentice-Hall, 1972. 165 pp.

Presents the systems approach as logical problem solving which will insure valid and human change. There are 6 stages involved and the first 2 are discussed in detail. The 6 stages are: problem identification, solution requirements and alternatives, solution strategies, implementation of selected strategies, determination of performance effectiveness and revision.

1265. ———. "System Approaches to Education." In *Handbook on Contemporary Education,* edited by S. E. Goodman. New York: Bowker, 1976, pp. 107–13.

Increased use of system approaches is due in part to the emphasis in accountability. Management by objectives (MBO) and planning, programing, budgeting system (PPBS) are 2 of the most commonly used systems. Figure 1 shows a possible integration of the various tools and modes used in system approaches.

1266. Kieft, Raymond N. *Academic Planning: Four Institutional Case Studies.* Boulder, CO: National Center for Higher Education Management Systems, 1978. 143 pp.

Four case studies are used to identify and understand the processes of planning and resource allocation which bring about institutional change and also to develop guidelines for institutions that wish to establish their own procedures and planning processes. The 4 case studies are of West Virginia University, Western Washington University, Villa Maria College, and the Kansas City Metropolitan Community Colleges.

1267. Lawrence, G. Ben, and Service, Allan L. *Quantitative Approaches to Higher Education Management.* ERIC/ Higher Education Research Report No. 4. Washington, DC: American Association for Higher Education, 1977. ED 144 439. 91 pp.

During the present era of accountability colleges have begun to use management systems to provide, for example, measurement of outcomes and benefits, analysis of productivity, and deployment of resource allocations. Warns that administrators must keep in mind human values, attitudes, and perceptions as a balance with dollars, costs, and restraints.

1268. Lee, Eugene C., and Bowen, Frank M. *Managing Multicampus Systems: Effective Administration in an Unsteady State.* Carnegie Council on Policy Studies in Higher Education. San Francisco, CA: Jossey-Bass, 1975. 174 pp.

Studies 9 multicampus systems: California, Illinois, Missouri, North Carolina, Texas, City and State Universities of New York, and California State Universities and Colleges. Data was gathered by using questionnaires and interviews. Flexibility is important in large systems. Chapters concern: academic planning, budgeting, faculty retrenchment, renewal, and mutlicampus systems in the eighties.

1269. Lenning, Oscar T. *The Outcomes Structure: An Overview and Procedures for Applying It in Postsecondary Education Institutions.* Boulder, CO: National Center for Higher Education Management Systems, 1977. 79 pp.

A review of the outcomes structure and how it may be implemented in higher education institutions.

1270. Lessinger, Leon, and Sabine, Certa D., eds. *Accountability: Systems Planning in Education.* Homewood, IL: ETC Publications, 1973. 242 pp.

Attempts to show how to use systems planning techniques in relation to different levels of educational agencies: classroom, school, district office, state office, community college, and university. Includes study of instructional cost in higher education.

1271. McCoy, Marilyn, and Orwig, Melvin. *A Federal Postsecondary Education Data Core: An Executive Summary.* Technical Report 85. (Included is *Toward a Post-*

secondary Education Data Core.) Boulder, CO: National Center for Higher Education Management Systems, 1978. 230 pp.

A manual helpful for planning in federal postsecondary data collection.

1272. McManis, Gerald L., and Harvey L. James. *Planning, Management, and Evaluation Systems in Higher Education*. Littleton, CO: Ireland Educational Corp., 1978. 97 pp.

Explains several methods of planning and managing in higher education: planning, management and evaluation (PME); management by objectives (MBO); planning, programing, and budgeting (PPB); and zero-base budgeting (ZBB).

1273. McManis, Gerald L., and Parker, William C. *Implementing Management Information Systems in Colleges and Universities*. Littleton, CO: Ireland Educational Corp., 1978. 116 pp.

A handbook for administrators which describes some of the newer management concepts. Information contained in this book includes: definition of a management information system (MIS): how to implement an MIS in relation to a planning, management, and evaluation system (PME).

1274. Meeth, L. Richard. *Quality Education for Less Money*. San Francisco, CA: Jossey-Bass, 1974. 206 pp.

Shows administrators a planning strategy, a technique for cost analysis, and good management practices. Trustees, presidents, deans, faculty, as well as administrators, could profit from reading this book. Changes in the curricula, trimmed down programs and a faculty with diverse skills in teaching may be necessary in the future.

1275. Merson, John C., and Qualls, Robert L. *Strategic Planning for Colleges and Universities: A Systems Approach to Planning and Resource Allocation*. San Antonio, TX: Trinity University Press, 1979. 79 pp.

Colleges and universities should plan to use more effectively available resources and decide upon priorities which will benefit the institution. Describes 4 stages to be followed in higher education: identify actual and potential problems; decide upon mission, goals, and choices to be made; determine allocation of resources for programs by assessing objectives for these programs; and evaluate progress towards these objectives.

1276. Miyataki, Glenn K., and Byers, Maureen L. *Academic Unit Planning and Management*. Boulder, CO: National Center for Higher Education Management Systems, 1976. 170 pp.

Intends to assist administrators to plan and manage academic units. Organized into modules, each concerned with a particular aspect of planning and management of an academic unit. Academic unit may be the academic department, division, school, or college.

1277. Mood, Alexander, et al. *Papers on Efficiency in the Management of Higher Education*. Berkeley, CA: Carnegie Commission on Higher Education, 1972. 90 pp.

Four studies which deal with the resources of a university and how they are allocated. UCLA spends more on administration than on research and teaching combined. One chapter is devoted to innovative practices in California colleges and the other 2 chapters are concerned with management practices such as PPBS and computerized management information systems.

1278. Mosmann, Charles. *Academic Computers in Service*. San Francisco, CA: Jossey-Bass, 1973. 186 pp.

The computer has become a permanent fixture on campus and an important tool for research. Administrators and faculty need to plan for future use in administration and in instruction. Recommends that computer science departments be kept separate from the computer services center.

1279. Organization for Economic Cooperation and Development. *Institutional Management in Higher Education*. Paris: Organization for Economic Cooperation and Development, 1972. 70 pp.

Discusses 3 important basic issues: management in higher education, including objectives, research reports, and evaluation of the conference with proposals for continued cooperation. Concludes that there should be more international collaboration and sharing of experiences, including exchange of students, staff, and research.

1280. Parekh, Satish B. *Long-Range Planning: An Institution Wide Approach to Increasing Academic Vitality*. New Rochelle, NY: Change Magazine Press, 1977. 77 pp.

Successful planning is dependent upon the identification of the missions of the institution. Feedback is important as the institution proceeds towards implementation of the plan. Survival and growth depend upon planning and implementation.

1281. Pfnister, Allan O. *Planning for Higher Education: Background and Application*. Boulder, CO: Westview Press, 1976. 354 pp.

Using information collected from the sixties and early seventies the author examines 5 problem areas: enrollment, students, governance, curriculum, and financing.

1282. Powell, Ray M. *Management Procedures for Institutions*. Notre Dame, IN: University of Notre Dame Press, 1979. 401 pp.

Describes planning procedures for non profit institutions including 2-year and 4-year colleges and universities. Some topics discussed are: resource allocation, investment, budgeting, and personnel relations.

1283. Richman, Barry M., and Farmer, Richard N. *Leadership, Goals, and Power in Higher Education*. San Francisco, CA: Jossey-Bass, 1974. 364 pp.

Advocates the need for a managerial approach to change in higher education. The open systems model and contingency approach to management is intended for presidents, chancellors, and other high ranking administrators.

1284. Robbins, Martin D., et al. *Who Runs the Computer? Strategies for the Management of Computers in Higher Education*. Boulder, CO: Westview, 1975. 102 pp.

Gives an evaluation framework for computer installation. Other topics discussed are: computer services, computer installations, costs, institutional policies, and human factors.

1285. Sanders, Susan, et al. *The Computer in Educational Decision Making: An Introduction and Guide for School Administrators*. Hanover, NH: Time Share, 1978. 189 pp.

Provides a practical, nontechnical manual for students, professors, and administrators to assist in operations research techniques. The use of computer programs and their applications are described.

1286. Sargent, Cy, and Dober, Richard. *Campus in Transition*. New York: Educational Facilities Laboratories, 1975. 74 pp.

Administrators and planners in higher education will find this study helpful as they plan for the best use of physical facilities with new programs and services in mind.

1287. Smith, G. Kerry, ed. *Twenty-Five Years: 1945 to 1970*. San Francisco, CA: Jossey-Bass, 1970. 330 pp.

The 29 essays comprising this book were selected because the editors believed they had many of the answers to questions which now concern higher education. The majority of the questions are ones which still are largely unanswered. For example, how can equality of education be achieved, and what should be taught and learned?

1288. Tierney, Michael Lloyd. *The Impact of Management Information Systems on Resource Allocation Decisions of Selected Private Liberal Arts Colleges*. Los Angeles: University of California, 1977. 251 pp.

A study (Ph.D. dissertation) which looks at the computer based management information systems and their effect on direct costs of academic departments.

1289. Topping, James R., and Miyataki, Glenn K. *Program Measures*. Technical Report 35. Boulder, CO: National Center for Higher Education Management Systems, 1973. 245 pp.

A manual which is a companion volume to NCHEMS *Program Classification Structure*. Will be helpful to administrators in higher education.

RETIREMENT

1290. Ingraham, Mark H. *My Purpose Holds: Reactions and Experiences in Retirement of TIAA-CREF Annuitants*. New York: Educational Research Division, Teachers Insurance and Annuity Association, College Retirement Equities Fund, 1974. 163 pp.

Responses to a survey conducted by TIAA to find reactions of retirees to their retirement. Two kinds of data are solicited: first, age, health, housing, finance, and activities; and second, comments on problems faced in retirement, evaluation of retirement, and advice for those expecting to retire soon.

1291. Jenny, Hans H. *Early Retirement: A New Issue in Higher Education*. New York: Teachers Insurance and Annuity Association, 1974. 50 pp.

Gives a definition of early retirement and reasons both for and against it. The financial aspects of early retirement for the individual and the institution are discussed. A bibliography is included.

1292. Seltzer, Mildred M.; Sterns, Harvey; and Hickey, Tom, eds. *Gerontology in Higher Education: Perspectives and Issues*. Belmont, CA: Wadsworth Publishing Company, 1978. 261 pp.

Details of discussions and papers on teaching, program administration, research, and community relationships are of interest to administrators and faculty.

STUDENT AFFAIRS

1293. Adams, Frank C., and Stephens, Clarence W. *College and University Student Work Problems: Implications and Implementations*. Carbondale, IL: Southern Illinois University Press, 1970. 272 pp.

Describes work-study and co-op programs in 18 colleges and universities. The philosophy of Berea College is used as a theme: "to learn to live and work at a higher level." Colleges and universities will continue to be involved in student work programs because of the heavier financial problems of students. Research is needed showing effects of these programs on students.

1294. Bayer, Alan E.; Royer, Jeannie T.; and Webb, Richard M. *Four Years after College Entry*. Washington, DC: American Council on Education, 1973. 45 pp.

A survey of 1967 freshman students in an endeavor to study attrition rates in American colleges and universities. Findings show that in 4 years 51 percent of the women and 41 percent of the men had completed the work for the bachelor's degree.

1295. Berg, Ivar. *Education and Jobs: The Great Training Robbery*. Boston: Beacon Press, 1971. 200 pp.

The increasing tendency for workers to be in jobs where they are overqualified causes job dissatisfaction and increased mobility. From new data review of studies in the area, gives recommendations that may solve the problem.

1296. Bisconti, Ann Stouffer. *College Graduates and their Employers: A National Study of Career Plans and Their Outcomes*. Bethlehem, PA: College Placement Council, 1975. 35 pp.

College professors, instructors, and faculty advisors have active roles in the influence of choice of careers for students. College placement officers and others who work with graduates will find this study of interest. Planning and preparation, as well as work experience, are examined in the light of early years of employment.

1297. Bowman, James L. *Educational Assistance to Veterans: A Comparative Study of Three GI Bills*. Princeton, NJ: Educational Testing Service, 1973. 443 pp.

A historical and statistical account of a study which compared veterans' educational assistance programs. The veterans' programs of World War II, the Korean War, and Vietnam were compared, according to participation rates, benefits, kinds of training obtained, amount of counseling provided, frauds and abuses, and other items.

1298. Brothers, Joan, and Gatch, Stephen. *Residence and Student Life: A Sociological Inquiry into Residence in Higher Education*. London: Tavistock Publications (distributed by Harper and Row), 1971. 419 pp.

Reports research done in England by the Department of Higher Education of the University of London to determine the purposes, problems, and effects of residence on campus, at home, or off campus. Describes the historical background; details case studies of 8 colleges; and lists student survey.

1299. Brown, Robert D. *Student Development in Tomorrow's Higher Education—A Return to the Academy.* Washington, DC: American Personnel and Guidance Association, 1972. 55 pp.

Summarizes new roles, functions, and methods which are associated with administrators and educators in student personnel. Student personnel people must become more involved in the teaching/learning process and be willing to work with the teaching faculty. Total student development should be considered.

1300. Brown, William F. *Student to Student Counseling: An Approach to Motivation Academic Achievement.* Austin, TX: University of Texas Press, 1977. 356 pp.

Outlines a program developed in the late 1950s to help beginning freshman to adjust academically and to motivate them. Upperclassmen are used as paraprofessionals to aid freshman. The program has proven to be effective and acceptable, as well as adaptable.

1301. Budig, Gene A., and Stanley G. Rivers. *Academic Quicksand: Some Trends and Issues in Higher Education.* Professional Education Series. Lincoln, NE: Professional Educators Publication, 1973. 74 pp.

Deals with the expectations of students, faculty, trustees, government, and the public regarding higher education. Some real dangers are involved for professionals and some problems are created for administrators and the institutions involved.

1302. Chickering, Arthur W. *Commuting versus Resident Students.* San Francisco, CA: Jossey-Bass, 1974. 150 pp.

Provides needed information on collegiate experiences of three groups of students: those who attend college while living at home, those who live in campus housing, and students who commute to campus but live independently from their families. The data is interesting when viewed in the light of the type of institution attended: public urban 4-year, private liberal arts colleges and universities, or community and junior colleges.

1303. College Entrance Examination Board. *New Approaches to Student Financial Aid.* Report of the Panel on Student Financial Need Analysis. New York: College Entrance Examination Board, 1971. 133 pp.

A recurring debate in institutions of higher learning is how to compute the need of a student. Three groups are responsible for payment of costs, parents, students, and society. Federal funds are used by most institutions to assist students. This study found a trend in institutions which indicates more students are receiving aid without referring to need.

1304. ———. *Perspectives on Financial Aid.* New York: College Entrance Examination Board, 1975. 179 pp.

A guide for new student aid administrators in higher education. The first part gives organizational structure of financial aid offices, budget requirements, and relationship to other parts of the institution. The second part lists sources of aid.

1305. College Scholarship Service, College Entrance Examination Board. *Making It Count: A Report on a Project to Provide Better Financial Aid Information to Students.* Princeton, NJ: College Board, 1977. ED 139 307. 85 pp.

Shows that there is a need to develop communication techniques so that prospective students may find information concerning financial aid in higher education. Institutions should provide resources concerning costs and financial aid for students. Sample forms are included.

1306. College Scholarship Service. *Student Expenses at Postsecondary Institutions, 1979–80.* Princeton, NJ: College Board, 1979. ED 172 163. 95 pp.

An annual report which shows an analysis of student costs at 2,700 institutions. Describes costs for 4 different types of students: dependent resident students living on or off campus, dependent commuting students, and independent students. Average costs of reporting institutions are listed.

1307. ———. *CSS Need Analysis: Theory and Computation Procedures for the 1979–80 FAF.* Princeton, NJ: College Board, 1979. ED 172 646. 133 pp.

The annual College Scholarship Service's (CSS) system for determining financial need of students gives case samples, tables, and methods of dealing with special cases to help campus financial aid administrators.

1308. ———. *Who Pays? Who Benefits?* A National Invitational Conference on the Independent Student. Princeton, NJ: College Board, 1979. ED 096 924. 109 pp.

Many young people now claim status as independent adults. This affects the role of the institution as regulator of student behavior, financial information, and responsibility of parents, and the need to determine the status of students as independent or dependent.

1309. DeCoster, David A., and Mable, Phyllis, eds. *Student Development and Education in College Residence Halls.* Washington, DC: American College Personnel Association, 1974. 278 pp.

Considers the attempts which are currently in use in residence halls to provide for student development, humanizing the environment, providing learning opportunities, role of residence educators, and inservice education of student staff. Justification for the residence program and coeducation living are included. There are separate chapters for minority student concerns and psychology of women.

1310. Eddy, John. *College Student Personnel Development, Administration, and Counseling.* Washington, DC: University Press of America, 1977. 480 pp.

An experienced counselor administrator, and professor discusses many problems facing students, faculty, and counselors in higher education.

1311. Eisendrath, Craig R., and Cottle, Thomas J. *Out of Discontent: Visions of the Contemporary University.* Cambridge, MA: Schenkman, 1972. 181 pp.

Discusses changes in families and child rearing which affect the transition of young people into the traditional university setting. Tenured faculty are described as a hindrance to student development. Student discontent is fostered by tenured faculty and elitest educational philosophy.

1312. Feldman, Kenneth A., ed. *College and Student Selected Readings in the Social Psychology of Higher Education.* New York: Pergamon, 1972. 492 pp.

Describes the problems of higher education in the United States and some techniques which may help to solve these problems. The book discusses the student as an individual and the college as an institution. Stress is placed upon the interaction and interrelationship of the student and the institution.

1313. Fife, Jonathan D. *Applying the Goals of Student Financial Aid.* ERIC/Higher Education Research Report No. 10. Washington, DC: American Association for Higher Education, 1975. ED 118 052. 67 pp.

Analyzes how a changing social philosophy has affected financial aid for college students. Major topics are: goals of student financial aid, growth of student aid programs, access to colleges, choice of college, and implementing access and choice through need analysis.

1314. Gallagher, Buell G. *Campus in Crisis.* New York: Harper and Row, 1974. 288 pp.

Recounts the problems of the sixties; gives a general history of higher education from the Middle Ages to the present; and then gives specific problems from some campuses. Gives some suggestions for improving the university in the future.

1315. Ginzberg, Eli. *The Manpower Connection: Education and Work.* Cambridge, MA: Harvard University Press, 1975. 258 pp.

Developing human resources through education is of great importance in higher education. Education is an aid to acquiring basic skills which are necessary for a successful and satisfying life.

1316. Gottlieb, David, et al. *Study Report: Youth and the Meaning of Work.* University Park, PA: College of Human Development, Pennsylvania State University, 1973. 317 pp.

Gives data about work attitudes, job expectations, and career expectations of college seniors.

1317. Grasso, J. T., and Shea, J. R. *Vocational Education and Training: Impact on Youth.* Technical Report, Carnegie Council on Policy Studies in Higher Education. San Francisco, CA: Jossey-Bass, 1979. 243 pp.

Outlines a study of access to and impact of vocational training beginning in 1966 with 5,000 men and in 1968 with 5,000 women. Studies responses of students from general, occupational, and college preparatory high school programs through 1972 and 1973.

1318. Haagen, C. Hess. *Venturing beyond the Campus: Students Who Leave College.* Middletown, CT: Wesleyan University Press, 1977. 272 pp.

Attempts to deal with problems and possibilities of students who go on leave during their undergraduate years. Some topics discussed are the reasons students leave, activities during leave, and reasons for return to college. Survey questionnaires were sent to students from 6 private colleges and universities in New England.

1319. Hammond, Edward H., and Shaffer, Robert H., eds. *The Legal Foundations of Student Personnel Services in Higher Education.* Washington, DC: American Personnel and Guidance Association, 1978. 174 pp.

Cites growth of numbers of legal cases in student development work in recent years. Administrators who are not lawyers need to be aware of educational issues or administrative acts which may have legal implications. A chapter by T. Richard Mager supplies a list of citations and quotations which every administrator ought to keep for quick reference.

1320. Hanfmann, Eugenia. *Effective Therapy for College Students: Alternatives to Traditional Counseling.* San Francisco, CA: Jossey-Bass, 1978. 347 pp.

Outlines the work of therapeutic counselors with college students. On the basis of 25 years of experience working with students, believes it is possible to facilitate and advocate change and aid the student to become a healthy adult.

1321. Harkness, Charles A. *Career Counseling: Dreams and Reality.* Springfield, IL: Charles C Thomas, 1976. 311 pp.

Personal experiences form the basis for this book. Theory and practice of career counseling, decision making, and placement are considered. References at the end of each chapter guide the reader to further information on each subject.

1322. Hartman, Robert W. *Credit for College: Public Policy for Student Loans.* Carnegie Commission on Higher Education. New York: McGraw-Hill, 1971. 152 pp.

Discusses philosophical basis for analysis of student loan programs and the question of how large student subsidies should be. Ends with a look at NDSL teacher loan cancellations as an example of student subsidies.

1323. Hecht, Miriam, and Traub, Lillian. *Alternatives to College.* New York: Macmillan, 1974. 227 pp.

Since 80 percent of the jobs in the United States do not require a college degree, it is surprising that so little attention is given to alternatives in education. Vocational and career guidance suggestions are given.

1324. Henderson, Jean G., and Henderson, Algo D. *Ms. Goes to College.* Carbondale, IL: Southern Illinois University Press, 1975. 180 pp.

Answers many questions which might be asked by students who are considering college. Students, parents, and counselors would find useful information concerning differences in colleges and curricula. Problems which concern depression, drug abuse, pregnancy, and sexual behavior are described objectively; career courses and maturity are also discussed.

1325. Hoppock, Robert. *Occupational Information: Where to Get It and How to Use It in Career Education, Career Counseling, and Career Development.* 4th edition. New York: McGraw-Hill, 1976. 383 pp.

Educators who counsel students concerning occupational choice, distribution mobility, and adjustment will find helpful information.

1326. Hull, Frank M. *Foreign Students in the United States of America: Coping Behavior within the Educational Environment.* New York: Praeger, 1978. 224 pp.

Reported on 952 foreign students at 3 American universities. Students were questioned on many subjects from friendship to academic programs. Also discussed were coping mechanisms, adjustments, educational and social environment, as well as other topics of interest.

1327. Johnstone, D. Bruce. *New Patterns for College Lending: Income Contingent Loans.* New York: Columbia University Press, 1972. 209 pp.

This lending program provided loans to students with the stipulation that repayments could take place over a 25-year period. Other income lending plans with variations have been proposed and implemented since that time.

1328. Keene, Roland, et al. *Money, Marbles, or Chalk; Student Financial Support in Higher Education.* Carbondale, IL: Southern Illinois University Press, 1975. 343 pp.

Depicts all aspects of student financial aid in American higher education: history and philosophy, programs and problems, organization and administration, professional careers, and recommendations for the future.

1329. ——. *Work and the College Student.* Carbondale, IL: Southern Illinois University Press, 1975. 466 pp.

Describes student work programs of various kinds at many institutions. Administrators, former students, and businessmen express their thoughts. Problems, issues, and possibilities are explored by several authors. The government's involvement in financial assistance for students and future prospects is discussed.

1330. Kellams, Samuel E. *Emerging Sources of Student Influences.* ERIC/Higher Education Research Report No. 5. Washington, DC: American Association for Higher Education, 1975. ED 114 027. 55 pp.

Explores the new and more sophisticated strategies of students for influence in the academic community due to their concern about costs, freedom, and participation in decision making. Major topics are: students as a separate political force and participation in established political structures and processes.

1331. Kemerer, Frank R., and Deutsch, Kenneth L. *Constitutional Rights and Student Life: Value Conflict in Law and Education, Cases and Materials.* St. Paul, MN: West Publishing, 1979. 735 pp.

Major court decisions related to students are used to help students understand legal principles and the process courts use to resolve legal disputes. There are chapters on student suspensions, freedom of speech, freedom of religion, due process, and equal protection.

1332. Keniston, Kenneth; Duffield, Mary-Kay; and Martinek, Sharon. *Radicals and Militants: An Annotated Bibliography of Empirical Research on Campus Unrest.* Lexington, MA: Lexington Books, 1973. 256 pp.

Each abstract contains information under the following headings: setting, subjects or institutions, methods, results, and comments.

1333. McGrath, Earl J. *Should Students Share the Power? A Study of Their Role in College and University Governance.* Philadelphia, PA: Temple University Press, 1970. 124 pp.

Discusses student participation in governance in higher education institutions. Believes increased student power will result in fewer disorders. Boards of trustees are of special interest and student participation is examined carefully.

1334. Malnig, Lawrence R., and Morrow, Sandra L. *What Can I Do with A Major in . . . ?* Jersey City, NJ: Saint Peter's College Press, 1975. 101 pp.

The 19 most popular majors of more than 10,000 graduates have led to more than 190 careers from 1950 to 1975. Information about these careers has been compiled briefly and should be helpful in counseling college and university students.

1335. Maw, Ian L.; Richards, Nancy A.; and Crosby, Howard J. *Formula Budgeting: An Application to Student Affairs.*

Washington, DC: American College Personnel Association, 1976. 130 pp.

Few formulas have been developed for student affairs which permit resources to be allocated rationally. Career development and placement, counseling, financial aid, health, and student development are 5 areas in which data were collected and a formula budget was developed.

1336. Meabon, D. L.; Alexander, R. E.; and Hunter, K. E. *Student Activity Fees: A Legal and National Perspective.* Columbia, SC: National Entertainment and Campus Activities Association, 1979. 70 pp.

Collection of student fees and allocation systems are 2 main topics of this survey. There are also chapters on the history of student activities, legal issues, and recommendations for student activity fees guidelines.

1337. Miller, Theodore K., and Prince, Judith S. *The Future of Student Affairs.* San Francisco, CA: Jossey-Bass, 1976. 220 pp.

Reviews examples of successful programs in student affairs work in the United States. Ideas for use of those involved in student personnel development in higher education are suggested.

1338. Moos, Rudolf H. *Evaluating Educational Environments.* San Francisco, CA: Jossey-Bass, 1979. 334 pp.

Student attitudes and behavior are affected by their living groups and classrooms. Uses the University Residence Environmental Scale and the Classroom Environmental Scale with 10,000 college students in 225 living groups and more than 10,000 junior and high school seniors in more than 500 classrooms to gather data for a conceptual model of person-environment interaction.

1339. Morison, Robert S. *Students and Decision Making.* Washington, DC: Public Affairs Press, 1970. 136 pp.

Describes the current ideas of students on decision making by the chairman of the Cornell University Commission on Student Involvement in Decision Making. In the context of university goals, society and university relationship, and role of administrators, analyzes student unrest.

1340. National Task Force on Student Aid Programs. *National Task Force on Student Aid Problems, Final Report.* Washington, DC: National Association of Student Financial Aid Administrators, 1975. 92 pp.

This task force was charged with the goal of the administration and operation of federal, state, and institutional aid programs. The major recommendations included a common data form for applicants, a uniform method for determining need, and a uniform schedule for aid applications and awards.

1341. Osipow, Samuel H. *Theories of Career Development.* 2d edition. New York: Appleton-Century-Crofts, 1973. 328 pp.

Discusses theoretical and practical aspects of career development as they may be of value to counselors. Research which may be used to consider personality traits of people in specific occupations is of interest.

1342. O'Toole, James. *Work, Learning, and the American Future.* San Francisco, CA: Jossey-Bass, 1977. 238 pp.

Shows that work is not a demeaning experience and that learning is more than a necessary route to a good job. Long-range planning presented is practical.

1343. Packwood, William T., ed. *College Student Personnel Services*. Springfield, IL: Charles C Thomas, 1977. 53 pp.

Summarizes college student personnel services with one chapter on each of 16 services. Each chapter includes history, definition, administration, programs, personnel, and a bibliography. The chapters include admissions, financial aid, orientation, housing, religion, discipline, security, health, counseling, placement, graduation, and alumni and junior college seminars.

1344. Parker, Clyde A., ed. *Encouraging Development in College Students*. Minneapolis, MN: University of Minnesota Press, 1978. 295 pp.

Explores the development of college students from a scholarly viewpoint using both theory and practical suggestions. Believes the purpose of student development is to provide an environment which challenges and supports students and which encompasses all sectors of campus life. Five theories are noted as important in development of students.

1345. Patrick, Cathleen; Myers, Edward; and Van Dusen, William. *A Manual for Conducting Student Attrition Studies*. Revised edition. Boulder, CO: National Center for Higher Education Management Systems. New York: College Board, 1979. 93 pp.

Intended to assist planners and administrators of colleges and universities who wish to study dropouts in higher education. Directors of institutional research will find this publication of assistance. It is a step-by-step guide to planning procedures for attrition studies instruction, with samples of instruments to use, processing data, data analysis, and samples of other needed forms.

1346. Penney, James F. *Perspective and Challenge in College Personnel Work*. Springfield, IL: Charles C Thomas, 1972. 93 pp.

Traces the development of college personnel work from the 1930s to the present. Discusses the role and background of campus ombudsman and the attempt by institutions to be more responsive to the needs and rights of students.

1347. Quinn, Robert P., and de Mandilovitch, Martha S. Baldi. *Education and Job Satisfaction: A Questionnaire Payoff*. Ann Arbor, MI: Survey Research Center, University of Michigan, 1975. 83 pp.

Examines the relationship between education and job satisfaction. The conclusions show that education helps in social advancement but the evidence in job satisfaction is inconclusive.

1348. Rice, Lois D., ed. *Student Loans: Problems and Policy Alternatives*. New York: College Entrance Examination Board, 1977. 169 pp.

Gives a thoughtful presentation of the entire spectrum of federal student loan programs and a realistic look at possible solutions.

1349. Riesman, David, and Stadtman, Verne, eds. *Academic Transformation: Seventeen Institutions under Pressure*. New York: McGraw-Hill, 1973. 489 pp.

Relates how 17 institutions of higher learning were able to cope with academic crises in the late sixties and early seventies. Some changes which took place as a result of the disruptions have been drastic but some institutions changed very little. The major issues in each case are: political and individual rights of students, equal access to education, Vietnam war, and decision making on campus which involved students.

1350. Schoenberg, B. Mark, ed. *A Handbook and Guide for the College and University Counseling Center*. Westport, CT: Greenwood, 1978. 305 pp.

Covers the history and development of the academic counseling center, structure and organization, and programs. Each chapter is written on one aspect of counseling by an authority in the field and contains a bibliography for further consideration.

1351. Solmon, Lewis C. *Reassessing the Link between Work and Education*. San Francisco, CA: Jossey-Bass, 1978. 112 pp.

The link between education and work is discussed. Issues are considered and recommendations are made. Evaluation of the total impact of education is needed to solve problems.

1352. Spaeth, Joe L., and Greeley, Andrew M. *Recent Alumni and Higher Education: A Survey of College Graduates*. New York: McGraw-Hill, 1970. 199 pp.

Reports information from a national survey of 4,868 alumni who graduated from college in 1961. These alumni were asked questions concerning their concepts of goals of higher education and reforms which are needed, their attitudes toward their colleges, their political and social attitudes, and their ideas regarding student influence and power in universities. Many had unrealistic ideas about college responsibilities toward students, such as teaching students to be independent but at the same time acting in loco parentis.

1353. Stark, Joan, et al. *The Many Faces of Educational Consumerism*. Lexington, MA: Lexington Books, 1977. 224 pp.

Describes the student as the educational consumer and notes a concern for protecting the student in dealings with government agencies and institutions.

1354. Stern, George G. *People in Context: Measuring Person-Environment Congruence in Education and Industry*. New York: Wiley, 1970. 402 pp.

Reviews 20 years of study and research on need-press theory and its procedural concepts. Uses several indexes to assess individual needs and environmental press. Applies to the college student and his/her environment.

1355. Stickney, Patricia J., ed. *Student Participation in Decision Making in Graduate Schools of Social Work and in Higher Education*. New York: Council on Social Work Education, 1972. 181 pp.

Divided into 3 parts. One part deals with student rights and responsibilities in policy development, procedures concerning students performance, information release, and grievances. Student participation in decisions in schools of social work is discussed, pro and con. Various viewpoints are given concerning decision making in several situations involving higher education.

1356. Tilley, David C., et al. *The Student Affairs Dean and the President: Trends in Higher Education*. Washington, DC: ERIC Counseling and Personnel Services Clearinghouse and National Association of Student Personnel Administrators, 1979. ED 169 459. 84 pp.

Viewpoints of the college president, faculty, deans, and the influence of socioeconomic trends are examined in relation to the topics of accountability, teaching and learning environment, and current trends.

1357. Tollefson, Arthur L. *New Approaches to College Student Development*. New York: Behavioral Publications, 1975. 150 pp.

Describes programs for the educationally disadvantaged, curricular innovations related to student development, and concepts which enable students to develop a sense of community. Background material for those interested in the past, present, and future development of college students.

1358. Toole, K. Ross. *The Time Has Come*. New York: William Morrow, 1971. 178 pp.

Criticizes student protestors and points out the irrationality of many arguments by students. Lists many accomplishments of American society but also admits errors made. Believes that violations of the law should merit punishment and that society does change and adjust to conditions.

1359. Wallerstein, Immanuel, and Starr, Paul, eds. *The University Crisis Reader*. Vol. 1: *The Liberal University under Attack*. Vol. 2: *Confrontation and Counterattack*. New York: Random House, 1971. 592 pp; 512 pp.

Concerns student insurrection and all its implications on campus. Vol. 1 deals with the university position, the relation of higher education to society, politics, business, the immediate community, racism, and other issues. Vol. 2 lists dynamics, anatomy, development, and moral position of confrontation politics as they related to the liberal approach and the political system.

1360. Warnath, Charles F. *New Myths and Old Realities: College Counseling in Transition*. San Francisco, CA: Jossey-Bass, 1971. 172 pp.

Discusses counseling issues, counseling procedures, and counselor education programs. Believes that counselors should be more assertive and use professional talents for a more positive role in college counseling.

1361. Williamson, Edmund G., and Biggs, Donald A. *Student Personnel Work; A Program of Developmental Relationships*. New York: Wiley, 1975. 390 pp.

Proposes strategies for all interested administrators, student personnel workers, and faculty. More research needs to be done in this field; current programs and studies are cited.

1362. Willingham, Warren W. *College Placement and Exemption*. New York: College Entrance Examination Board, 1974. 272 pp.

Summarizes developments in the area of college placement and exemptions over the years. Twelve models are used and applications are made in the light of research and current practices. An annotated bibliography of 82 studies in the area is included.

1363. Wolfbein, Seymour L. *Labor Market Information for Youths*. Philadelphia, PA: Temple University School of Business Administration, 1975. 262 pp.

Case histories describe new programs for school-work connections. Evaluation and recommendations are also included.

Community and Junior Colleges

ADMINISTRATION

1364. American Association of Community and Junior Colleges. *The Presidents*. Washington, DC: American Association of Community and Junior Colleges, 1978. 128 pp.

A biographical listing of presidents of community, junior, and technical colleges. Each listing has a brief sketch of the professional background of the person and pictures are included in most listings.

1365. Graham, R. William. *Instant College*. Boston: Brandon Press, 1971. 255 pp.

The first part describes the making of a junior college president. The second part discusses a president who is instrumental in founding and developing a junior college.

1366. Lahti, Robert E. *Innovative College Management: Implementing Proven Organizational Practice*. San Francisco, CA: Jossey-Bass, 1973. 182 pp.

Reviews basic principles and concepts in college management and applies them to administration of the 2-year college. Management by objectives (MBO) is stressed. Innovation and faculty evaluation are 2 other areas which need attention.

1367. Moore, William Jr. *Blind Man on a Freeway: The Community College Administrator*. San Francisco, CA: Jossey-Bass, 1971. 173 pp.

Based on one man's experiences as an administrator in a community college during the sixties, describes the administrative requirements of the job, the problems that occur, and the people who are involved. More practical training for administrators is recommended.

1368. Pray, Francis C. *A New Look at Community College Board of Trustees and Presidents and Their Relationships*. Washington, DC: American Association of Community Junior Colleges, 1975. 41 pp.

Criticizes the politics involved in boards of trustees. Many of these boards do not feel the responsibility of governance. State boards do not solve the problems and may increase them. Qualified persons are discouraged from service because of politics, sunshine laws, disclosure, and financial liability.

1369. Rushing, Joe B. *Changing Role of the Community College President in the Face of New Administration Pressures*. Washington, DC: American Association of Community Junior Colleges, 1976. 59 pp.

Examines the job of the community college president with its demands and pressures. Trends and developments affecting administrators are noted and suggestions are made which may be helpful.

1370. Woodress, Fred A. *Public Relations for Community/Junior Colleges*. Danville, IL: Interstate, 1976. 62 pp.

Based on 35 years of experience, outlines ways to improve public relations. Pressure on community and junior colleges necessitates good public relations.

COLLECTIVE BARGAINING

1370a. Hankin, Joseph N. *Negotiating a Better Future*. Washington, DC: American Association of Community Junior College, 1977. 34 pp.

Concerns planning and organizing for collective bargaining at the community college. About half of the states have collective bargaining in the community colleges and the number is growing. The appendices contains legal reference to individual states and various statistics. A bibliography is included.

1371. Moore, John W., and Patterson, Robert A. *Pennsylvania Community College Faculty*. University Park, PA: Pennsylvania State University, 1971. 135 pp.

Outlines the attitudes of junior-college faculty members toward collective bargaining. Generally, faculty are very favorable toward collective negotiations.

ARTICULATION

1372. Altman, Robert A. *The Upper Division College*. San Francisco, CA: Jossey-Bass, 1970. 202 pp.

Upper division colleges or universities have been established in some states to supplement and extend the community college system. Florida, Illinois, and Texas have most of these institutions.

1373. California Postsecondary Education Commission. *California Community College Students Who Transfer: A Continuation of Through the Open Door: A Study of Patterns of Enrollment and Performance in California's Community Colleges*. Research Report. Sacramento, CA: California Postsecondary Education Commission, 1979. 47 pp.

A follow-up study of 35,000 students enrolled in 32 California community colleges in 1972. California State University and University of California searched their records to check transfer rates which were less than 15 percent. Other information concerning these transfer students was discussed.

1374. Chambers, M. M. *Above High School*. Danville, IL: Interstate, 1970. 61 pp.

Discusses the relationship between high school and college and makes a case for the modern community college. Administrative, legal, and fiscal aspects of public community colleges are discussed.

1375. Ferrin, Richard I. *A Decade of Change in Free Access Higher Education*. New York: College Entrance Examination Board, 1971. 75 pp.

A study of the accessibility of higher education from 1958 through 1968. The study points out that accessibility depends in large part on 3 characteristics: An institution should not be expensive, should admit most high school graduates, and should be within a reasonable distance. Community colleges fulfill these needs and have made higher education more accessible to more people than ever before.

1376. Kintzer, Frederick. *Middleman in Higher Education*. San Francisco, CA: Jossey-Bass, 1973. 188 pp.

Concerns transfer of students from the community college to a baccalaureate-degree granting institution. Sample articulation programs which states have studied and implemented are presented, which will help state planners evaluate their effectiveness.

1377. Menacker, Julius. *From School to College: Articulation and Transfer*. Washington, DC: American Council on Education, 1975. 229 pp.

The facilitation of student movement from one educational level to another is referred to as "articulation." Concerns the ease of the process of admitting students from one level to another. Students need guidance to make these transitions. Administrators should improve communication with other institutions and cooperate in sharing information, resources, and policy changes in order to benefit students and the public.

1378. Palola, Ernest G., and Oswald, Arthur R. *Urban Multi-Unit Community Colleges: Adaptation for the '70's*. Berkeley, CA: University of California, 1972. 128 pp.

Many large cities have developed urban multiunit colleges in recent years. These 2-year community colleges are more responsive to the needs of urban areas. Low-income disadvantaged students present special educational problems.

1379. Sandeen, Arthur, and Goodale, Thomas. *The Transfer Student*. Gainesville, FL: University of Florida, 1976. 95 pp.

Brings up-to-date the research on the problems and needs of transfer students. Incoming freshmen are generally given much attention in institutions of higher learning. Transfer students are growing in numbers, sometimes exceeding numbers of freshmen, but receive little notice from administrators and faculty. Discusses the problems and makes recommendations for institutional action.

EVALUATION

1380. Armijo, Frank, ed. *Assessing Community-College Impacts: Three Case Studies*. Boulder, CO: National Center for Higher Education Management Systems, 1979. 58 pp.

This study, financed by NIE, describes the experiences of 3 institutions in conducting their impact studies. These institutions are: Kalamazoo Valley Community College, Kalamazoo, Michigan; Eastfield College, Mesquite, Texas (a Dalla suburb); and Valencia Community College, Orlando, Florida.

1381. Commonwealth of Kentucky, Council on Higher Education. *A Study of Community College Education in Kentucky*. Frankfort, KY: Council on Higher Education, 1977. 56 pp.

A thorough study and evaluation with recommendations for the community colleges in Kentucky which are under the aegis of the University of Kentucky.

1382. Howard, B. London. *The Culture of a Community College*. New York: Praeger, 1978. 181 pp.

Describes an urban community college which offers career programs and liberal arts transfer programs and is the fastest growing type of community college. Howard, who attended a college in the northeast for a year, interviewed faculty and students, and visited homes of students, reports that students were resistant, cheated, frequently absent, and had very low levels of achievement in studies, and he does not believe that working-class students move upward because of their experiences with the community college.

1383. Priest, Bill J., and Pickelman, John E. *Increasing Productivity in the Community College*. Washington, DC: American Association of Community and Junior Colleges, 1976. 36 pp.

Describes productivity approaches often used in industry. Work measurement, time and motion studies, and process flow charting are used. One multicollege community college tries to increase efficiency by improving each operation.

FACULTY

1384. Bloom, Karen L., et al. *Goals and Ambivalence: Faulty Values and the Community College Philosophy.* Center for the Study of Higher Education. Report No. 13. University Park, PA: Pennsylvania State University, 1971. 57 pp.

A study of 250 2-year college faculty covers the extent to which the faculty support the missions of their institutions. Sources of ambivalence are in the following areas: institutional goals, daily associations, reference groups, and previous experiences.

1385. Cohen, Arthur, and Brawer, Florence B. *Confronting Identity: The Community College Instructor.* Englewood Cliffs, NJ: Prentice-Hall, 1972. 257 pp.

Describes the major issues which face the faculty of the 2-year college and the meaning of the forces relating to the institution and to the students. Presents an interesting and perceptive view of faculty in various roles. The teacher/manager is able to select from all methods and technologies the most effective way to teach using behavioral objectives.

1386. ———. *The Two-Year College Instructor Today.* New York: Praeger, 1977. 174 pp.

Details changes in community colleges in the 1970s because of student growth, restricted funds, and changes in mission, goals, and objectives of 2-year institutions. These changes affect the faculty of the institutions and will continue to do so in the future. Teaching effectiveness is the major emphasis of the faculty. Quality and professionalism varies greatly among 2-year faculty.

1387. Kelly, Win. *Teaching in the Community-Junior College.* New York: Appleton-Century-Crofts, 1970. 295 pp.

The development, scope, and environment of the community-junior college are described. The outline of faculty and administrators' duties and philosophy of the 2-year institution are reviewed. Attitudes and opinions of the faculty and various issues and problems comprise the final chapters.

1388. King, Francis P. *Benefit Plans in Junior Colleges.* Washington, DC: American Association of Community Junior Colleges, 1971. 643 pp.

Discusses various benefit plans currently in use in nearly 200 2-year colleges. Some topics of interest are retirement, life insurance, health plans, and disability plans.

1389. Lombardi, John. *The Department/Division Chairman: Characteristics and Role in the Community College.* Topical Paper No. 40. Los Angeles: ERIC Clearinghouse for Junior Colleges, 1974. ED 091 035. 22 pp.

Describes characteristics and relationships of department/division chairpersons with faculty, administrators, and students. Also on the same subject: *Department/Division Chairman Structure in the Community College* (ED 085 051) and *Duties and Responsibilities of the Department/Division Chairman in Community Colleges* (ED 089 811). Chairpersons have many characteristics of other administrators; role and power vary in institutions; and it is still a desirable position for most faculty.

1390. O'Banion, Terry. *Organizing Staff Development Programs That Work.* Washington, DC: American Association of Community and Junior Colleges, 1978. 32 pp.

A step-by-step plan for administrators who are interested in improving the staff and contributing to the effectiveness of the teaching/learning programs of 2-year institutions. The process is described all the way from assessing the needs to the evaluation.

1391. ———. *Teachers for Tomorrow: Staff Development in the Community-Junior College.* Tucson, AZ: University of Arizona Press, 1972. 185 pp.

Describes the special characteristics of the community/junior college, students, and staff. Believes that there should be more attention given to developing and enhancing the skills of the teaching faculty. Suggests preservice and inservice programs.

1392. Park, Young. *Junior College Faculty: Their Values and Perceptions.* Monograph Series No. 12. ERIC Clearinghouse for Junior Colleges. Washington, DC: American Association for Junior Colleges, 1971. ED 050 725. 68 pp.

Concerns survey responses from faculty and staff at 3 diverse community colleges in Southern California, with emphasis on perceptions of the institution and values held by faculty and staff.

1393. Poort, Stephen M. *Guidelines for the Recruitment and Selection of Community College Faculty.* Institute of Higher Education. Gainesville, FL: University of Florida, 1971. 35 pp.

Emphasizes the importance of selecting faculty who meet the criteria to teach in a community college. Major topics are: considerations confronting the dean, new institutions vs. older institutions, the effective faculty member, role of the interview, and guidelines.

FINANCE

1394. Arney, Lawrence H. *State Patterns of Financial Support for Community Colleges*. Gainesville, FL: University of Florida, 1970. 53 pp.

Compiles information on community college finance in 42 states. Many differences are evident in finance, control, coordination, and sources of funds. Suggests that financing should come from all levels of government, local, state, and federal.

1395. Augenblick, John. *Issues in Financing Community Colleges*. Denver, CO: Education Commission of the States, 1978. 66 pp.

Financial studies of 2-year college systems in California, Illinois, Mississippi, and New Jersey. Community colleges are supported at different levels according to the wealth in their districts. State support does not always result in equalizing support.

1396. Lombardi, John. *Managing Finances in Community Colleges*. San Francisco, CA: Jossey-Bass, 1973. 145 pp.

Pictures sources of revenue and patterns of use by 2-year colleges. Advocates better managerial efficiency, better utilization of existing physical facilities, and increased faculty performance.

1397. Martorana, S. V., et al. *Dollars and Directives: Issues and Problems Related to Financial Support and Legal Authorizations of Community Colleges*. Washington, DC: American Association of Community and Junior Colleges, 1978. 55 pp.

Describes issues and problems which affect financial support in community colleges. The first part discusses legislation which affects community colleges and the second part discusses policy frameworks and decision-making environment.

1398. Wattenbarger, James L., and Starnes, Paul M. *Financial Support Problems for Community Colleges 1976*. Gainesville, FL: Institute of Higher Education, University of Florida, 1976. 118 pp.

Describes existing formulas used by each state to support community colleges. Discusses philosophy and purpose of community college.

GENERAL

1399. Burnett, Collins W. "Community and Junior Colleges." In *Handbook on Contemporary Education*, edited by S. E. Goodman. New York: Bowker, 1976, pp. 49–53.

An overview of the development of the community college and the private junior college, with discussion of such topics as enrollment, research, major publications such as those by the Carnegie Commission on Higher Education, characteristics of the comprehensive community college, and current issues.

1400. ———. *The Two-Year Institution in American Higher Education*. Lexington, KY: Bureau of School Service Bulletin, College of Education, University of Kentucky, 1971. 177 pp.

Topics concern Ph.D.s as faculty, planning necessary change by qualitative disruption, articulation between junior college and senior college, the state of the community college system in Kentucky, faculty morale, the academic deanship in the private junior college, and problems and proposals.

1401. Cohen, Arthur M., et al. *A Constant Variable*. San Francisco, CA: Jossey-Bass, 1971. 238 pp.

A critical assessment and an analytical review by specialists of the institution, the people, and the processes which are a part of the community college. There are 25 pages of selected bibliography, with author and subject indexes.

1402. Gleazer, Edmund J. *Project Focus: A Forecast Study of Community Colleges*. New York: McGraw-Hill, 1973. 239 pp.

Reports on the critical issues facing the community college in the early seventies. Discusses student population, curriculum and instruction, organization and governance, financial support, and community relations. Uses information gathered from 25 community colleges throughout the country.

1403. Gleazer, E. J., Jr., and Houts, P. L., eds. *American Junior Colleges*. 8th edition. Washington, DC: American Council on Education, 1971. 850 pp.

Describes more than 800 U.S. junior and community colleges. Facts are given concerning staff, fees, student aid, history, enrollments, academic calendar, buildings and grounds, finance, administration, admission and graduation requirements. Other information includes state systems of junior colleges, programs offered, faculty, and special training facilities.

1404. Johnson, Bryon Lamar, ed. *Toward Educational Development in the Community Junior College*. Los Angeles: University of California, 1972. 90 pp.

Educational development in the community junior college was the focus of participants attention at this conference. Emphasis on several areas was of special interest: improved teaching, needed research, state agencies and foundations, budgeting, and organization.

1405. Ogilvie, William K., and Raines, Max R., eds. *Perspectives on the Community-Junior College: Selected Readings*. New York: Appleton-Century-Crofts, 1971. 635 pp.

Nearly 100 readings give a diverse view and description of the community-junior college. Arranged by topical headings, including the history, role and mission, students, programs, community services, faculty, structure and control, and evaluation.

1406. Schenkman, Carolyn R., ed. *A Policy Primer for Community Based Community Colleges*. Washington, DC: American Association of Community Junior Colleges, 1975. 42 pp.

The basic mission of the community college involves meeting the educational needs, interests, and requirements of its community.

Designed to recommend policy stands for leaders in federal and state governments, boards of control, chief administrators, department heads, and faculty senates who have the authority to establish policy for community colleges.

1407. Thornton, James W. *The Community Junior College*. 3rd edition. New York: John Wiley & Sons, 1972. 304 pp.

Intends to introduce the principles and practices of the community college to graduate students who plan to teach in the 2-year institution. Chapters are devoted to historical development, organization, curriculum, and future development.

1408. Yarrington, Roger, ed. *International Development of the Junior College Idea*. Washington, DC: American Association of Junior Colleges, 1970. 288 pp.

Outlines the development of the community college in several countries and areas in the world: Japan, Canada, Taiwan, Jordan, Iran, Ceylon, India, and South America. Some articles are more general in nature and discuss other aspects of international education.

GOALS AND PURPOSES

1409. Armijo, J. Frank; Micek, Sidney S.; and Cooper, Edward M. *Conducting Community-Impact Studies: A Handbook for Community Colleges*. Boulder, CO: National Center for Higher Education Management Systems, 1978. 250 pp.

The objectives of a community college are generally considered to be "community-based" and "performance-oriented." This handbook was developed in order to determine the impact of the community college and to decide how to meet the educational needs in a more effective way. The data-collection tools and study procedures were field tested in three communities.

1410. Bushnell, David S. *Organizing for Change: New Priorities for Community Colleges*. New York: McGraw-Hill, 1973. 237 pp.

A study intended to establish the future direction of the community and junior college and the students who will be served. Uses surveys of students and faculty of 956 community and junior colleges and offers conclusions on the needs to define the roles of administrators on campus and of local and state authorities, to establish more budgeting and accountability, to set goals, to recognize that the student population will be older, and to adjust programs to meet requirements of students.

1411. Cosand, Joseph P. *Perspective: Community Colleges in the 1980's*. Washington, DC: American Association of Community and Junior Colleges, 1979. 59 pp.

A professor and administrator for 35 years views the future of the community college. Discussion is centered around prospective developments which concern students, operation, resources, and accountability.

1412. Furth, Dorotas, ed. *Short Cycle Higher Education: A Search for Identity*. Organization for Economic Cooperation, 1973. 414 pp.

Postsecondary education which usually takes place in an institution other than a university, requires less than 4 years, and does not lead to a university degree is short-cycle higher education. In the United States this takes place in a junior or community college; in Norway, the Regional College; and in Yugoslavia, the Vise Skole. There is no clear identity. Political decisions and other considerations are responsible for creation of these colleges and sometimes there is conflict between participants and those who control the institutions.

1413. Garms, Walter J. *Financing Community Colleges, 1976*. New York: Teachers College Press, Columbia University, 1977. 120 pp.

Garms says that community colleges perform 3 functions: provide access to 4-year institutions for many students, provide courses and programs not available in other institutions, and serve educational needs of the local community. Lists 9 criteria for finance plans to meet needs of the three functions.

1414. Gleazer, Edmund J., Jr. *Responding to the New Spirit of Learning*. Washington, DC: American Association of Community and Junior Colleges, 1976. 20 pp.

Cites the tremendous increase in adults who are attending community and junior colleges. Community college administrators need to evaluate their programs and financial resources in relation to goals and purposes. Diversity in institutions is important in assessing future needs.

1415. Gollattscheck, James F., et al. *College Leadership for Community Renewal*. San Francisco, CA: Jossey-Bass, 1976. 160 pp.

Discusses the educational role in community renewal and advocates a community renewal college which would combine all functions presently shared by community colleges, land-grant universities, urban multiversities, Black colleges, and private universities and colleges. Several chapters describe programs and cooperative arrangements of specific community/junior colleges.

1416. Harper, William A. *Community, Junior, and Technical Colleges*. Washington, DC: Hemisphere, 1977. 212 pp.

Discusses aspects of public relations in community, junior, and technical colleges. Cooperation and support of the community is vital to the effectiveness of the community college. The mission of this institution should be clearly stated and advantages to the community need to be made known.

1417. Lombardi, John. *Community Education: Threat to College Status?* Topical Paper, No. 68. Los Angeles: ERIC Clearinghouse for Junior Colleges, 1978. ED 156 296. 41 pp.

The educational programs of traditional full-time student of college age who intends to transfer to a 4-year institution and the student in vocational or technical education seeking a career have taken second place to adult and continuing education in many 2-year colleges. Views this change as a threat which may change 2-year colleges into noncollegiate institutions.

1418. McFadden, Dennis N., ed. *USHER Redesign Model*. Columbus, OH: Battelle Center for Improved Education, 1975. 402 pp.

Directed to community college organizations USHER (Uniting Science and Humanness for Educational Redesign) is a model intended to change the management system of a college by involving the whole educational community in order to attain certain goals and objectives. Top administrators are first to reorganize into teams for participative management skills.

1419. Medsker, Leland L., and Tillery, Dale. *Breaking the Access Barriers*. Carnegie Commission on Higher Education. New York: McGraw-Hill, 1971. 183 pp.

The strength of the community college is described as its diversity and flexibility in adapting its programs and instructional services to a varied student body. Seven recommendations include clarifying goals, increased financial support, strengthening support of independent junior colleges, and better prepared faculty and administrators.

1420. Monroe, Charles R. *Profile of the Community College: A Handbook*. San Francisco, CA: Jossey-Bass, 1972. 435 pp.

Begins with the historical development of the community-junior college and gives a general survey of the present status, objectives, curriculum, students, faculty, governance, organization, and finance. A review of the literature is included.

1421. Moore, William, Jr. *Against the Odds: The High Risk Student in the Community College*. San Francisco, CA: Jossey-Bass, 1970. 244 pp.

Written by a Black community college administrator who was himself a "high risk" student at one time but now is president of Seattle Central Community College. Urges those who are involved to look again at the community college to see if it is fulfilling the purposes for which it is organized. Believes the least effective area is in teaching and counseling the "high risk" students. Suggestions are made to improve programs.

1422. Roueche, John E., et al. *Accountability and the Community College: Directions for the 70's*. Washington, DC: American Association of Community Junior Colleges, 1971. 46 pp.

Suggests that the community college is accountable for the success or failure of students. The president and staff should identify goals and be able to translate these goals into action.

1423. Zwerling, Steven L. *Second Best. The Crisis of the Community College*. New York: McGraw-Hill, 1976. 382 pp.

Believes that community colleges keep the lower classes in their place and restrict upward mobility. Contends that the purpose of schooling is socialization and reproduction of the social order.

HISTORY

1424. Brossman, Sidney W., and Roberts, Myron. *The California Community Colleges*. Palo Alto, CA: Field Educational Publications, 1973. 116 pp.

Describes the California community college system which began in 1910 in Fresno, California. The other 49 states have followed the example of California and have developed state systems of various kinds of community colleges. Emphasizes the wide range of subjects offered and the opportunities for many people.

1425. Campbell, Gordon. *Community Colleges in Canada*. Toronto: Ryerson Press, 1971. 346 pp.

Gives a history of the community college movement in Canada, administrative structure, and current developments and issues in the provinces. Each institution is described and the arrangement is by province.

1426. Palinchak, Robert S. *The Evolution of the Community College*. Metuchen, NJ: Scarecrow Press, 1973. 373 pp.

Covers historical state development of some state community colleges. Shows that the community colleges have evolved from the land-grant college. Suggests colleges band together for research purposes.

ORGANIZATION

1427. American Association of Community and Junior Colleges. *Research Report: A Study of Community and Junior College Boards of Trustees*. Washington, DC: American Association of Community and Junior Colleges, 1977. 59 pp.

Describes the functions, characteristics, attitudes, and opinions of 2-year college boards, private and public. Differences between chairpersons of boards and presidents are also assessed.

1428. Evans, N. Dean, and Neagley, Ross L. *Planning and Developing Innovative Community Colleges*. Englewood Cliffs, NJ: Prentice-Hall, 1973. 372 pp.

A handbook which presents comprehensive information on all aspects of planning, design, and development of community colleges. Following the main body of the publication are 11 appendices with useful information.

1429. Landrith, Harold F. *Introduction to the Community Junior College*. Danville, IL: Interstate Printers and Publishers, 1971. 321 pp.

Discusses a wide range of topics concerning the community college. Begins with a brief historical background and continues to describe other matters of interest, such as objectives, curricula, administration, faculty characteristics and attitudes, teaching load formulas, and student personnel services.

1430. Morsch, William. *State Community College Systems*. New York: Praeger, 1971. 166 pp.

Views junior-college systems generally and then devotes special emphasis to 7 states. The states in which research is reported are: California, Florida, New York, Michigan, Illinois, Washington, and Texas.

1431. Richardson, Richard C.; Blocker, Clyde E.; and Bender, Louis W. *Governance for the Two-Year College*. Englewood Cliffs, NJ: Prentice-Hall, 1972. 295 pp.

Deals with the organization and administration of the community college. Suggests the participative model as an alternative to traditional administration. Numerous charts illustrate in detail organizational design for administrative services, business services, instructional services, and student personnel.

1432. Zoglin, Mary Lou. *Power and Politics in the Community College*. Palm Springs, CA: ETC Publications, 1976. 166 pp.

Governance in the community college is in a period of change and institutional autonomy at the local level is in danger. Federal and state money and power bring control and regulations. A former community college board member and state board member discusses the role of each participant involved.

PHILOSOPHY

1433. Carnegie Commission on Higher Education. *The Open Door Colleges: Policies for Community Colleges*. Special Report and Recommendations by the Carnegie Commission on Higher Education. New York: McGraw-Hill, 1970. 74 pp.

Provides data for future growth of community colleges and suggests that these colleges should be within commuting distance of all persons. Other topics of discussion include mission and program of the community college, open access, 2-year institutions remaining 2-year institutions, transfer rights to 4-year colleges and universities, tuition and enrollment size, and governance and financial support.

1434. Hunter, John O. *Values and the Future: Models of Community College Development*. Sherman Oaks, CA: Banner Books International, 1978. 166 pp.

With many excellent ideas this study is suited primarily for graduate students or faculty or perhaps discussion in a graduate seminar.

1435. Knoell, Dorothy, and McIntyre, Charles. *Planning Colleges for the Community*. San Francisco, CA: Jossey-Bass, 1974. 149 pp.

Reviews philosophy of community college and describes how important it is to plan to carry out the mission of the community college. Planning for future needs include curriculum offered, means for instruction, student access, and nontraditional forms of education

PROGRAMS

1436. A.E.C.T., A.L.A. College and Research Libraries, A.A.C.J.C. *Guidelines for Two Year College Learning Resource Programs.* Washington, DC: Association for Educational Communications and Technology; American Library Association, College and Research Libraries; American Association of Community and Junior Colleges, 1972. 12 pp.

Lists guidelines for 2-year college learning with resources and services.

1437. American Association of Community and Junior Colleges. *Career Education in Community Colleges: A Sourcebook.* Washington, DC: American Association of Community and Junior Colleges, 1978. 95 pp.

Outlines the career education programs which are offered at 66 community, junior and technical colleges in the United States.

1438. Barbee, David E. *A Systems Approach to Community College Education.* Princeton, NJ: Auerbach Publishers, 1972. 184 pp.

A philosophy of education emerges from a discussion of a theory of instruction based on behavioral science and a theory of curriculum. Discusses the systems approach and its application to community colleges.

1439. Bilovsky, D., and Matson, J. *Community Colleges and the Developmentally Disabled.* Washington, DC: American Association of Community and Junior Colleges, 1977. 92 pp.

A guide to help community colleges develop programs to train direct-care workers who will work with developmentally disabled people in residential facilities.

1440. Brightman, Richard W. *The Computer and the Junior College: Curriculum.* Washington, DC: American Association of Junior Colleges, 1970. 42 pp.

Discusses principles and programs needed to develop computer curricula. The junior and community colleges are taking the lead in preparing students to work with computer programing and also data processing.

1441. Burnett, Collins W., ed. *The Community and Junior College.* Lexington, KY: College of Education, University of Kentucky, 1977. 147 pp.

Nine papers, each with a bibliography, cover such topics as articulation, faculty, the transfer problem, student personnel, private junior college, and background and present status.

1442. Cass, James, and Birnbaum, May. *Comparative Guide to Two Year Colleges and Career Programs.* New York: Harper and Row, 1976. 549 pp.

This companion to *Comparative Guide to American Colleges* describes 1,740 2-year (and some 4-year) institutions which offer 2-year terminal programs. Included are enrollment, founding date, and affiliation, admission requirements, degrees offered, pro-

grams, tuition and fees. Accredited programs, as well as the 1973–74 graduates, are listed.

1443. Cohen, Arthur M., et al. *College Responses to Community Demands: The Community College in Challenging Times.* San Francisco, CA: Jossey-Bass, 1975. 190 pp.

Proposes a few ideas concerning new community college responses to community demands. This review of the literature and survey of practices is divided into 3 parts: social pressures, institution adjustment, and faculty.

1444. Fuller, Jack W. *Continuing Education and the Community College.* Chicago: Nelson-Hall, 1979. 127 pp.

Describes various forms of continuing education which exist today and suggests ways to streamline and consolidate efforts. Promotes the management by objectives approach to planning and teaching. Believes that universal education will be achieved by self-study and that there will be knowledge-module-satellite feeding knowledge into regional learning centers which will serve students with "home-learning subsystems."

1445. Hawthorne, Mary E., and Perry, J. Warren. *Community Colleges and Primary Health Care: A Study of Allied Health Education Report.* Washington, DC: American Association of Community and Junior Colleges, 1974. 293 pp.

A report of the Study of Allied Health Education (SAHE) emphasizes the role and potential of community and junior colleges in primary and ambulatory care. A variety of information is offered: survey instrument, recommendations, tables of statistics, and a long annotated bibliography.

1446. Heermann, Barry. *Cooperative Education in Community Colleges: A Sourcebook for Occupational and General Educators.* San Francisco, CA: Jossey-Bass, 1973. 219 pp.

Describes innovations in cooperative education provided by the community college. Cooperative education combines learning in the classroom and related job experience. The study is divided into 4 parts: history and philosophy, with a model program; planning and organization; operations and expected outcomes; sample forms, letters, and questionnaires.

1447. Korim, Andrew S. *Government Careers and the Community College.* Washington, DC: American Association of Community Junior Colleges, 1971. 73 pp.

Outlines requirements and needs for programs on public service career education in 2-year colleges. Korim is an occupational education specialist.

1448. ———. *Older Americans and Community Colleges: A Guide for Program Implementation.* Washington, DC: American Association of Community and Junior Colleges, 1974. 123 pp.

Suggests ways in which community colleges may contribute to improving the quality of life for older Americans. New programs and trained personnel may be needed to meet challenges posed by the educational needs of older citizens.

1449. Lombardi, John. *The Decline of Transfer Education*. ERIC Clearninghouse for Junior Colleges. Los Angeles: University of California, 1979. ED 179 273. 37 pp.

Decrease of courses leading to a baccalaureate degree is the trend in many 2-year colleges.

1450. Mezirow, Jack, and Marsick, Victoria. *Education for Perspective Transformation: Women's Re-entry Programs in Community Colleges*. Center for Adult Education, Teachers College. New York: Columbia University, 1978. 59 pp.

Outlines programs for women who are returning to college by the way of 2-year institutions. Quality of the programs needs to be improved and made more responsive to the needs of these women.

1451. Miller, Bob W. *Higher Education and the Community College*. Washington, DC: University Press of America, 1977. 218 pp.

Quality control in community colleges results from using a systems approach combined with short- and long-range planning. Offers suggestions to administrators and faculty concerned with many aspects of the teaching/learning process, public relations, student personnel problems, and community relations.

1452. Morrison, James L., and Terronte, Reynolds. *Compensating Education in Two-year Colleges*. Report No. 21. Center for the Study of Higher Education. University Park, PA: Pennsylvania State University, 1973. 51 pp.

Data are presented and discussed from a sample of approximately 50 institutions across the nation. Major topics are: social mobility, current compensatory practices and programs in higher education as described in the literature, and survey results.

1453. Pratt, Arden L. *Environmental Education in the Community College*. Washington, DC: American Association of Junior Colleges, 1971. 117 pp.

Reports on programs in environmental education which are offered in community colleges. Cautions that better planning is desirable in this area.

1454. Raines, Max R., and Myran, Gunder. *Developing Constituency Programs in Community Colleges*. Washington, DC: American Association of Community and Junior Colleges, 1977. 64 pp.

Needs assessment and program planning are essential to the success of the community college. Various suggestions are made in order to make community assessments and translate community needs into programs to meet those needs.

1455. Roueche, John E., and Kirk, R. Wade. *Catching Up: Remedial Education*. San Francisco, CA: Jossey-Bass, 1973. 106 pp.

Describes remedial programs in community colleges. Five colleges are used as examples, 3 in Texas, one each in North Carolina and New Jersey. Each program is described as to student performance and attitudes evaluated, analysis of problems, and recommendations.

1456. Roueche, John E., et al. *Time as the Variable, Achievement as the Constant: Competency-Based Instruction in the Community Collge*. Washington, DC: American Association of Community and Junior Colleges, 1976. 46 pp.

Innovations in institutional management, curriculum, and instruction have resulted because of increased accountability. Competency-based instruction is designed to provide learning experiences and skills so that the student can demonstrate agreed-upon specific competences.

1457. Southern Regional Education Board. *The Black Community and the Community College: Action Programs for Expanding Opportunity*. Atlanta, GA: Southern Regional Education Board, 1970. 61 pp.

Reports the 2-year results of a study of community college programs as the colleges try to respond to the needs of Black students. Five junior colleges in Florida, North Carolina, and Texas have pilot programs. Innovative programs in 12 other community colleges in Alabama, Florida, Maryland, North Carolina, South Carolina, and Texas are also included.

1458. Swift, Joan W. *Human Service Career Programs and the Community College*. Washington, DC: American Association of Junior Colleges, 1971. 79 pp.

Comments on changes in the role of the community college, especially in human services career programs. Human services careers include the fields of social services, and health and education. A curriculum model, faculty assignments, and field experiences are subjects for discussion.

1459. Van Voorhees, Curtis, et al. *Four Case Studies: Working Partnerships between Community Colleges and Community Schools*. Office of Community Education Research. Washington, DC: American Association of Community and Junior College, 1977. 63 pp.

Cooperation is a necessity between community colleges and community schools in order to achieve better service for the community. Research is needed concerning joint activities and also needs assessments, goals, and programs. Local and state planners should become aware of the potential in cooperative ventures.

1460. Yarrington, Roger. *Using Mass Media for Learning*. Washington, DC: American Association of Community and Junior Colleges, 1979. 89 pp.

Reports the use of television by the telecourse and the experiences of community colleges with this medium. The development of educational television is traced and the involvement of faculty, financing patterns, college consortia, telecourse design, and community promotion of telecourses are emphasized.

1461. ———. *Educational Opportunity for All: An Agenda for National Action*. Washington, DC: American Association of Community and Junior Colleges, 1973. 159 pp.

Those administrators, boards, faculty, and others involved in planning for community colleges should develop programs that are student-centered. Evaluations of community colleges should also be different from those of 4-year institutions. Access for students means access to programs which meet the needs of students.

1462. ———. *Internationalizing Community Colleges*. Washington, DC: American Association of Community and Junior Colleges, 1978. 103 pp.

International education is becoming more important among community and junior college leaders. Papers given at a conference in 1978 include information on internationalizing the curriculum, student and faculty exchanges, technical assistance programs, and a model agreement with a foreign junior college. Authors include Edmund J. Gleazer, jr.; Moses S. Koch; Seymour Eskow; Fred H. Harrington; and Daniel R. McLaughlin.

STATE COORDINATION

1463. Bender, Louis W. *The States, Communities, and Control of the Community College: Issues and Recommendations*. Washington, DC: American Association of Community and Junior Colleges, 1975. 60 pp.

Considers the change in control of community colleges. The governance of these colleges is gradually shifting from local to state control. The causes behind this trend, the issues involved, and the effects upon institutional development comprise the main part of the publication. Recommendations and suggestions concerning control of these institutions are presented.

1464. Martorana, S. V., and Nespoli, Lawrence A. *State Legislation Relating to Community and Junior Colleges, 1976*. Report No. 27. Center for the Study of Higher Education. University Park, PA: Pennsylvania State University, 1977. 79 pp.

Presents the second annual survey and analysis of state legislation relating to community and junior colleges. Two types of data serve as the basis for this study: the legislative situation in each state as reported by state directors and actual legislative documents are analyzed.

1465. Wattenbarger, James L., and Cage, Bob N. *More Money for More Opportunity: Financial Support of Community College Systems*. San Francisco, CA: Jossey-Bass, 1974. 109 pp.

Surveys the theory, history, and resources of financing the public community college. An important resource for this study is a researched summary of state formulas used to fund community colleges. Mention is made of the trend toward increased state financing and control, as opposed to the capacity for responsiveness to community service.

1466. Wattenbarger, James L., and Christofoli, Luther B. *State Level Coordination of Community Colleges: Academic Affairs*. Institute of Higher Education. Gainesville, FL: University of Florida, 1971. 26 pp.

Presents analaysis of a survey response from 44 state agencies responsible for community college education. Major topics are: methods of academic cooperation, the statewide council to coordinate community college academic affairs, occupational or vocational education, and relationships with 4-year colleges and universities.

1467. Wattenbarger, James L., and Sakaguchi, Melvyn. *State Level Boards for Community Junior Colleges: Patterns of Control and Coordination*. Institute of Higher Education. Gainesville, FL: University of Florida, 1971. 71 pp.

Surveys state level boards which are responsible for community colleges. This study indicates the trend towards more planning and financial support from state sources and also an increase in state control. Characteristics and activities of boards are noted and tables of statistics are included.

STUDENTS

1468. Brawer, Florence B. *New Perspectives on Personality Development in College Students*. San Francisco, CA: Jossey-Bass, 1973. 232 pp.

Reviews personality theory in relation to college student development and learning. The author attempts to show methods that will allow better ways to assess a student and to prepare that student to live and work effectively. She does not believe in a teaching/ learning situation which is rigid.

1469. ————. *Values and the Generation Gap: Junior College Freshman and Faculty*. Washington, DC: American Association of Junior Colleges, 1971. 66 pp.

Discusses the values of teachers and freshman students in 3 junior colleges in the Los Angeles area. The differing values among the groups are examined very specifically.

1470. Eliason, Carol. *Women in Community and Junior Colleges: Report of a Study on Access to Occupational*

Education. Washington, DC: Association of Community and Junior Colleges, 1977. 64 pp.

Summarizes a project in which data were collected and students were interviewed on 10 campuses. Asks for better counseling and direction by faculty and administrators to meet the needs of women students. More women should be directed into nontraditional courses in 2-year institutions.

1471. Gibson, Walker, ed. *New Students in Two Year Colleges: Twelve Essays*. Urbana, IL: National Council of Teachers of English, 1979. 130 pp.

Twelve essays written by teachers of English in 2-year colleges focus on teaching the "new" student. Rather than to lower standards for the benefit of these students who are from the lower one-third of their high school classes and who score low on tests, the objective is to try to rearrange elements in the environment to fit the needs of students. Major topics include ways of looking at the open door, scientism and the teaching of English, traditional literature for nontraditional students, popular fiction as remedial literature, folklore and the new student, and composition and moral education.

1472. Gladieux, Lawrence E. *Distribution of Federal Student Assistance: The Enigma of the Two-Year Colleges*. New York: College Entrance Examination Board, 1975. 30 pp.

Examines the low percentage of students in 2-year institutions who receive federal financial assistance. Outlines the distribution of funds under the Basic Educational Opportunity Grant Program (BEOG) which gives direct aid to students and also the Supplemental Educational Opportunity Grants (SEOG), Work/Study Program, and National Direct Student Loans.

1473. Healy, Charles. *Career Counseling in the Community College*. Springfield, IL: Charles C Thomas, 1974. 140 pp.

Describes 13 counseling approaches which may be used by counselors in community colleges. The criterion of replicability is used to select the counseling approaches.

1474. Kerr, Lornie. *Foreign Students in Community and Junior Colleges*. Washington, DC: American Association for Community Junior Colleges, 1973. 30 pp.

Discusses the role of the community college and its relationship to foreign students. Specific topics addressed are admissions, advising, orientation, housing, community volunteers, and programs offered.

1475. Koos, Leonard V. *The Community College Student*. Gainesville, FL: University of Florida Press, 1970. 580 pp.

Uses more than 300 research reports on late adolescence and the community college student as a basis. Includes material on physical and mental development and occupational and recreational in-

terests. Describes the characteristics of students; their attitudes, interests, social status, and aptitudes; and adult students. Reviews the curriculum and discusses student personnel practices.

1476. Laking, Joyce J., et al. *The Impact of Community Colleges. Health Survey: Students Entering Postsecondary Education in British Columbia in Fall, 1971*. Washington, DC: American Association for Higher Education, 1972. 59 pp.

Outlines results of health survey of 11,000 students in British Columbia. Few serious physical health problems are noted but psychological and emotional or situational problems are common and are concerned with lack of money, academic and career problems, and family problems.

1477. Moore, William, Jr. *Community College Response to the High Risk Student: A Critical Reappraisal*. Washington, DC: American Association of Community and Junior Colleges, 1976. 53 pp.

Points out the need for research in many facets of the community college but especially in the claims made concerning the "high-risk" student. Some aspects of the "culturally disadvantaged" students which are discussed are: self-concept, motivation, remedies, teaching/learning process, and institutional response.

1478. Olivas, Michael A., and Alimba, Nan. *The Dilemma of Access: Minorities in Two Year Colleges*. Institute for the Study of Educational Policy. Washington, DC: Howard University Press, 1979. 259 pp.

Studies the issues which affect equal opportunity for Blacks in 2-year colleges. Points out that opportunities for Blacks and other minorities do exist but inequities also continue. Includes a bibliography, appendix, charts, and other useful data.

Comparative Systems of Higher Education

AFRICA

1479. Beckett, Paul, and O'Connell, James. *Education and Power in Nigeria: A Study of University Students*. London: Hodder & Stoughton, 1977. 224 pp.

This study of students in Nigeria, based on questionnaires, teacher observations, and analysis of essays and discussions from 1970 through 1975, attempts to measure values and attitudes of students who will become leaders in government and administrators in educational institutions. The majority of the students recognize that many changes are needed in their country but do not wish for radical change and chaos.

1480. Fafunwa, A. Babs. *History of Nigerian Higher Education*. Lagos, Nigeria: Macmillan, 1971. 363 pp.

An historical account of the origins and development of the Nigerian universities. The appendix lists documents used and other data.

1481. Ike, Vincent Chukwuemeka: *University Development in Africa: The Nigerian Experience*. Ibadan, Nigeria: Oxford University Press, 1976. 232 pp.

Describes historical development of Nigerian universities, including the curricula and objectives of higher education. Lists recommendations for improvement. Academic freedom is also mentioned.

1482. Okafor, Nduka. *The Development of Universities in Nigeria*. New York: Humanities Press, 1971. 214 pp.

Examines academic freedom, autonomy, and the university in relation to their social settings. Some topics are: courses and degrees, politics and education, and the relation of the universities to the government.

1483. Sanyal, Bikas C., et al. *Higher Education and the Labour Market in Zambia: Expectations and Performance*. Paris: UNESCO Press and the University of Zambia, 1976. 371 pp.

Explores the relationship between admission policies of institutions of higher learning and the employment of graduates. The researchers also delve into the attitudes and aspirations of students, employed graduates, and employers.

1484. Van den Berghe, Pierre L. *Power and Privilege at an African University*. Cambridge, MA: Schenkman, 1973. 273 pp.

A study which concentrates on the oldest and most influential university in Nigeria. The historical background is given and the importance of the university in the country. Concludes that the university has not adapted to the country but that the country has adapted to a social system which the university has helped to create.

1485. Van Der Merwe, Hendrick W., and Welsh, David, eds. *The Future of the University in South Africa*. New York: St. Martins, 1977. 302 pp.

Analyzes higher education in South Africa. Some topics covered are: the expatriate in African universities, Afrikaner universities, Rhodesian higher education, and Black and Indian education.

1486. Wagaw, Teshome G. *Education in Ethiopia: Prospect and Retrospect*. Ann Arbor, MI: University of Michigan Press, 1979. 256 pp.

A native educator and scholar examines educational change in Ethiopia. Shows the development of education from the church-controlled system to a modern public school system to a modern public school system. Includes higher education and its predictions for the future.

AUSTRALIA

1487. Anderson, S., et al., eds. *Regional Colleges*. Canberra, Australia: Australian National University Press, 1975. 3 vols: 646 pp., 580 pp., 396 pp.

The Regional Colleges project, a multidisciplinary team, is responsible for the research in this description of the large, growing program of nonmetropolitan colleges of higher education in Australia.

1488. Burn, Barbara B., and Karmal, Peter. *Federal/State Responsibilities for Postsecondary Education: Australia and the United States*. New York: Interbook, 1977. 69 pp.

Report of a seminar in Australia in which representatives from Australia, Canada, and the United States discuss developments in higher education related to their federal and state governments. Some topics are: diversity; range of higher education; federal-state structures; institutional governance, finance, and access.

1489. Harman, G. S., and Smith, C. Shelby, eds. *Australian Higher Education: Problems of a Developing System*. Sydney, Australia: Angus and Robertson, 1972. 196 pp.

Gives a good description of higher education in Australia. Chapters are written by authorities who discuss problems and accomplishments in their area of expertise. The book includes the history of higher education, role and purpose of a university, demography and financing higher education, access, research, professional education, and the future of higher education.

1490. McCaig, Robert, ed. *Policy and Planning in Higher Education*. Brisbane, Australia: University of Queensland Press, 1973. 183 pp.

Reports conclusions of a conference of educators, political leaders, officers of the government, researchers, and administrators. Clark Kerr and J. E. Vaizey are included in the conference. Clark Kerr offers two papers; one on evaluation and the other entitled "The Speed of Change: Towards 2000 A.D." Higher education has grown rapidly in Australia since 1963 and planning is needed.

1491. Musgrave, Peter William. *Society and the Curriculum in Australia*. Winchester, MA: Allen and Unwin, 1979. 160 pp.

Describes the development of Australian curriculum, identifies problems in planning a comprehensive curriculum, and discusses academic issues and needs.

1492. Williams, Bruce. *Systems of Higher Education: Australia*. International Council for Educational Development. New York: Interbook, 1978. 93 pp.

In 1977 a new Tertiary Education Commission at the national level was formed to provide better coordination in higher education. Committee planning is an important aspect of Australian higher education. This report is based on a study in 1975–77. Topics discussed include the system design, objectives, influence of federal and state governments, management, and effectiveness of the system.

CANADA

1493. Campbell, Gordon. *The Community College in Canada: An Annotated Bibliography*. Calgary, Alberta: The University of Calgary, 1971. 82 pp.

Major topics range from historical development through administration and finance to continuing education and research.

1494. Harris, Robin S. *A History of Higher Education in Canada: 1663–1960*. Toronto: University of Toronto Press, 1976. 715 pp.

Describes the founding of each college and university in Canada, curricula and research programs of these institutions, and the organization of learned societies and scholarly journals connected with them.

1495. Houwing, J. F. and Kristjanson, A. M., eds. *Inventory of Research into Higher Education in Canada 1979*. Ottawa: Association of Universities and Colleges of Canada, 1979. 59 pp.

Describes projects in postsecondary education in Canada.

1496. ———. *Inventory of Research into Higher Education in Canada*. Ottawa: Association of Universities and Colleges of Canada, 1976. 53 pp.

Outlines about 250 research projects which are underway or completed in 1975. The inventory also includes statistics and reports on new and innovative studies. The 6 sections are: general, administration, finance and personnel, curriculum, academic and non-academic staff, students, and extension and continuing education.

1497. Pike, Robert S., et al. *Innovation in Access to Higher Education: Ontario, England, Wales and Sweden*. New York: Interbook, 1978. 332 pp.

Compares access and admissions policies in Ontario, England, Wales, and Sweden. Reports on current practices and some case studies.

1498. Royce, Gloria, ed. *Directory of Canadian Universities 1978*. Ottawa: Association of Universities and Colleges of Canada, 1978. Vol. 1, 345 pp; vol. 2, 134 pp.

Covers higher education in Canada. Vol. 1 discusses the history of Canadian universities.

1499. Sheffield, Edward, et al. *Systems of Higher Education: Canada*. International Council for Educational Development. New York: Interbook, 1978. 219 pp.

The Canadian system of higher education is based on the 10 provincial systems supported by federal aid. Planning is done at provincial and regional levels. This study is based on the 1975–77 study.

1500. Vickers, Jill McCalla, and Adam, June. *But Can You Type?: Canadian Universities and the Status of Women*. Toronto: Clark Irwin, 1977. 142 pp.

Tables in this book show that only 36 percent of undergraduates at Canadian universities are women and only 23 percent are full-time masters level students. In architecture and medicine the numbers of female graduate students are higher than at the undergraduate level. This proportion reflects the status of women in society and in higher education and should be corrected.

CHINA

1501. Price, R. F. *Education in Modern China*. Boston: Routledge and Kegan Paul, 1979. 345 pp.
Although this book deals with the entire educational system in China, there is an important section dealing with third level schools (higher education). The educational system is put within the context of history, culture, and political system.

EASTERN EUROPE

1502. Szczepanski, Jan. *Higher Education in Eastern Europe*. New York: Interbook, Inc., 1974. 241 pp.
Discusses the characteristics of higher education in Poland and Eastern Europe. Outlines elements of higher education such as goals, functions, tasks, access, adult education, faculty, management, and administration.

1503. ———. *Systems of Higher Education: Poland*. International Council for Educational Development. New York: Interbook, 1978. 76 pp.

Higher education should provide graduates whose scientific knowledge, motivation to acquire professional skills, and attitudes are needed to safeguard the future growth of individuals, communities, the economy, and the cultural heritage. Institutions of higher learning are also expected to provide trained staff for research and development. In a Marxist political economy, education is important because of the relationship between education and employment. The government is committed to providing employment for the graduates, so admissions are set according to estimated demand.

GENERAL

1504. Altbach, Phillip G. *Comparative Higher Education*. ERIC/Higher Education Research Report No. 5. Washington, DC: American Association for Higher Education, 1973. ED 082 623. 81 pp.

American higher education which reflects the old of Oxford and Cambridge, the borrowed of the German universities, and the new of the land-grant colleges and community colleges in this country is a model for many nations. Major areas of concern in comparative higher education are: planning, student activism, faculty, governance, research, and general policy.

1505. ———. *Comparative Higher Education Abroad: Bibliography and Analysis*. New York: Praeger, 1976. 274 pp.

A bibliography of interest to scholars, planners, governmental agencies and officials who are concerned with higher education. Also contains an article on the "Economics of Higher Education" by Douglas M. Windham and an article on "Japanese Higher Education" by William K. Cummings and Ikuo Amano.

1506. ———. *Comparative Perspectives on the Academic Profession*. New York: Praeger, 1978. 214 pp.
Faculty influence is not the same in every country of the world but there is a growing consciousness of faculty as a profession. There is also more interest in the study of comparative education. Areas investigated in this report are: Great Britain, Italy, Japan, Australia, Canada, India, Latin America, and the United States.

1507. ———. *University Reform: Comparative Perspectives for the Seventies*. Cambridge, MA: Schenkman, 1974. 211 pp.
Discusses and compares educational problems in several cultures: India, Germany, France, Nigeria, Columbia, Great Britain, Japan, Yugoslavia, and the United States. Little progress in reform is apparent in issues, such as equal access, financial and public support, and relations between community and university.

1508. Altbach, Philip G., and Kelley, David H. *Higher Education in Developing Nations: A Selected Bibliography 1969–1974*. New York: Praeger, 1975. 230 pp.

An unannotated bibliography of 2500 articles, theses, books, and monographs. Entries are arranged by country in the geographic areas of Africa, Asia, Latin America, Middle East–North Africa, and Japan.

1509. Altbach, Philip G., and Nystrom, Bradley. *Higher Education in Developing Countries: A Select Bibliography.* Cambridge, MA: Harvard, 1970. 118 pp.

Helpful information on aspects of higher education in developing countries.

1510. Archer, Margaret Scotford. *Students, University, and Society.* London: Heinemann Educational Books, 1972. 280 pp.

Uses a sociological perspective to compare higher education in 10 countries. Discusses connections between politics and universities: governance, transfer of political beliefs, and recruitment into politics. Mentions concerns for the increasing control of society over universities.

1511. Bailey, Stephen K., ed. *Higher Education in the World Community.* Washington, DC: American Council on Education, 1977. 219 pp.

Recounts the national goals of better understanding and fuller cooperation among nations. Among the common problems which may be discussed and solved by educational institutions are: accountability, equality, vocational education, public expectations, financial problems, and research.

1512. Ben-David, Joseph. *Centers of Learning: Britain, France, Germany, United States.* Carnegie Commission on Higher Education. New York: McGraw-Hill, 1977. 208 pp.

Surveys present higher education practices and tries to prescribe remedies for the ills which are common today. Believes that higher education is able to give specialized education for the professions but is failing to provide general education for those who wish enlightenment and wish to live a useful and satisfying life.

1513. Berdahl, Robert O., and Altomare, George. *Comparative Higher Education: Sources of Information.* Occasional Paper No. 4. New York: International Council for Educational Development, 1972. 115 pp.

Reviews and analyzes the leading journals with respect to policy, format, and coverage of comparative and noncomparative studies. Also included are other journals, bibliographies, abstracts, associations, and centers in comparative higher education.

1514. Bereday, George Z. F. *Universities for All.* San Francisco, CA: Jossey-Bass, 1973. 158 pp.

Focuses on mass education in North America, Russia, Japan, and Canada, the most industrialized areas with the exception of Europe. Consideration is given to enrollment, barriers to enrollment, curriculum reform, off-campus study for credit, and academic freedom.

1515. Berstecher, Dieter, et al. *A University of the Future.* The Hague: Martinus Nijhoff, 1974. 195 pp.

Vol. 6 of the European Cultural Foundation's study of education for the twenty-first century, Plan Europe 2000. Considers the problems facing European higher education in the coming years. Some topics include aims and purposes of the university, teaching methods, financial problems, governance, and relationship to society.

1516. Bowman, Mary Jean, and Anderson, C. Arnold. *Mass Higher Education: Some Perspectives from Experience in the United States.* Paris: Organization for Economic Cooperation and Development, 1974. 145 pp.

Concerns the economic aspects of the growth of higher education in the United States. The expansion of higher education is related to the transformation of the American labor force. The example of adjustments made in higher education expansion in the United States should be helpful to other countries. French and English are used in the text.

1517. Burn, Barbara B. *Expanding the International Dimension of Higher Education.* Carnegie Council on Policy Studies in Higher Education. San Francisco, CA: Jossey-Bass, 1979. 176 pp.

Urges a curriculum with international implications in order to give students a better understanding of international issues and knowledge of the international community. Suggestions which may be helpful include course offerings, faculty exchanges, student travel, special programs for foreign students, and more foreign language study.

1518. Burn, Barbara B., et al. *Higher Education in Nine Countries: A Comparative Study of Colleges and Universities Abroad.* Carnegie Commission on Higher Education. New York: McGraw-Hill, 1971. 387 pp.

Adaptation to national conditions is widespread in the 9 countries surveyed but some trends are common to all universities. Rapid enrollment growth and a demand for equal access, as well as financial problems, are important in each country.

1519. ———. *Higher Education Reform: Implications for Foreign Students.* New York: Institute of International Education, 1978. 172 pp.

Concerns student exchange programs in France, West Germany, Britain, Italy, Scandinavia, Spain, and the United States. Current reforms in higher education are connected to prospects for student exchanges.

1520. Clark, Burton R., and Youn, Ted I. K. *Academic Power in the United States.* ERIC/Higher Education Research Report No. 3. Washington, DC: American Association for Higher Education, 1976. ED 127 853. 53 pp.

Compares the nature and structure of academic power in American higher education with that of the British and Continental forms of academic organization. Generally, the structure in American higher education has served well in meeting needs and in adapting to changes in society.

1521. Fogel, Barbara R. *Design for Change: Higher Education in the Service of Developing Countries.* New York: International Council for Educational Development, 1977. 82 pp.

Explains the results of a 2-year study of ways in which higher education institutions can assist in social and economic development in developing nations. Trained evaluators who can set goals and design methods to measure goal attainment are needed in projects.

1522. Glenny, Lyman A., ed. *Funding Higher Education: A Six Nation Analysis.* New York: Praeger, 1979. 235 pp.

The factors that influence the success or failure of financing higher education can sometimes be established by comparing one system to another system. In this study the higher education systems of the United States, Greece, France, Italy, Spain, and Sweden are compared. Faculty, students, and budget are treated at some length.

1523. Griffin, Willis H., et al., eds. *The Role of Higher Education in the Lifelong Learning Process of the Third World and Appalachia*. Washington, DC: American Association of Colleges for Teacher Education, 1977. 128 pp.

Explores nonformal education as an alternative approach in preparing children and adults to meet the demands of our changing world. Appalachia in eastern Kentucky is regarded as a developing area. Case studies are cited from Africa, Asia, Latin America, and the United States.

1524. Halls, W. D. *International Equivalances in Access to Higher Education*. New York: UNESCO, 1971. 137 pp.

Describes the procedures of access in Argentina, Cameroon, Czechoslovakia, France, the Phillipines, Russia, Great Britain, and the United States. Examines aims, objectives, and content of curricula.

1525. ———. *World Guide to Higher Education: A Comparative Study of Systems, Degrees, and Qualifications*. New York: UNESCO, 1976. 302 pp.

Briefly summarizes 135 systems of education. Each entry gives a general description of the system of higher education, number of universities and programs, access information, levels of higher education, description of levels, and a glossary.

1526. Holmberg, Borje. *Distance Education: A Survey and Bibliography*. London: Kogan Page, 1977. 167 pp.

Innovations in education, such as University without Walls, Keller Plan, behavioral objectives, motivation, and good learning materials are discussed in relation to distance education.

1527. Kerr, Clark, et al. *12 Systems of Higher Education: 6 Decisive Issues*. New York: International Council for Educational Development, 1978. 181 pp.

A study by the International Council for Educational Development, 1975–77, is the basis for the book. Five general areas (planning and administration, coordination, effectiveness in meeting social purposes, flexibility, and efficiency) are discussed in 12 selected countries, including Australia, Canada, France, Federal Republic of Germany, Japan, Mexico, Poland, Sweden, Thailand, United Kingdom, and the United States.

1528. Kertesz, Stephen D., ed. *Task of Universities in a Changing World*. Notre Dame, IN: University of Notre Dame Press, 1971. 503 pp.

Covers many subjects concerning higher education in the United States and several other countries. Topics include traditional organizations and contemporary realities, goals, financial needs, continuing education, role of the Peace Corps, educational exchange, and relations among developed and developing countries.

1529. McIntosh, Naomi E., et al. *A Degree of Difference: The Open University of the United Kingdom*. New York: Praeger, 1977. 326 pp.

Gives the historical development of the open university and a description of the teaching system; discusses admissions and access, methodology, students, occupation, mobility, and leisure time activities; and offers recommendations for the future.

1530. MacKenzie, Norman Archibald McRae. *Open Learning: Systems and Problems in Post-Secondary Education*. Paris: UNESCO Press, 1975. 497 pp.

Describes systems that teach at a distance when teacher and learner are physically separated. Seventeen case studies cover a wide variety of innovations.

1531. Medsker, Leland L. *The Global Quest for Educational Opportunity*. Berkeley, CA: Center for Research and Development in Higher Education, 1972. 99 pp.

Summarizes postsecondary education which has been organized to provide more educational opportunities in countries other than the United States. Career programs of 2 years of less are discussed because they are decentralized and the curricula is relevant to the needs of the students.

1532. National Congress on Church Related Colleges and Universities. *Accountability: Keeping Faith with One Another*. Center for Program and Institutional Renewal. Sherman, TX: Austin College, 1979. 182 pp.

Delineates the legal issues, public policy, and financial problems which face religiously affiliated colleges and supporting churches.

1533. Niblett, W. Roy, and Butts, R. Freeman, eds. *Universities Facing the Future: An International Perspective*. San Francisco, CA: Jossey-Bass, 1972. 400 pp.

Presents an overview of world educational trends. Internal innovations are frequently changed or cancelled by external constraints, and these constraints are often the result of political pressure. Gives observations on universities in China, Russia, Southeast Asia, and developing countries.

1534. Perkins, James A., and Israel, Barbara Baird. *Higher Education: From Autonomy to Systems*. New York: Manhattan, 1972. 286 pp.

Describes university systems in the United States and 11 foreign systems. Discusses the coordination of institutions with state, regional, and national groups. Some countries mentioned are Great Britain, Germany, Ghana, Caribbean, Japan, and India.

1535. Ross, Murray G. *The University: The Anatomy of Academe*. New York: McGraw-Hill, 1976. 310 pp.

Discusses the universities of Canada, Great Britain, and the United States. Comparisons are made about the background, people, issues, and the future. Believes that the university must work to restore the faith of society in that institution, and the trust of colleagues must be renewed.

1536. Sanders, Irwin, and Ward, Jennifer C. *Bridges to Understanding: International Programs of American Colleges and Universities*. Carnegie Commission on Higher Education. New York: McGraw-Hill, 1970. 285 pp.

Discusses international studies programs and points out the weaknesses of most of them. Financial and organizational problems plague these programs. Improvements are recommended and steps to be used are suggested.

1537. Schuller, Tom, and Megarry, Jacquetta. *World Yearbook of Education 1979: Recurrent Education and Lifelong Learning*. London: Kogan Page, 1979. 335 pp.

Contains more than 20 articles on continuing education by educators from around the world. The educational-leave program of

France makes possible special training for workers. China's policy of lifelong education for the whole population has been quite successful in helping solve problems with drought, starvation, and homelessness. Germany has difficulty integrating adult education into the traditional system of higher education.

1538. Scott, Peter. *Strategies for Postsecondary Education.* New York: Halsted Press, 1975. 161 pp.

Describes various kinds of postsecondary education in the United States, the United Kingdom, and France. Believes that the community colleges are a unique contribution of the United States to higher education.

1539. Seabury, Paul, ed. *Universities in the Western World.* Riverside, NJ: Free Press, 1975. 303 pp.

This study is divided into 2 sections. The first concerns issues which affect all universities: governance, equality, and standards. The second is a series of essays on specific countries and their institutions: West Germany, Italy, the United States, Japan, and France.

1540. Sprinkle, Robert M., ed. *Administration of International Cooperative Education Exchanges.* Columbia, MD: International Association for the Exchange of Students for Technical Experience/US, 1978. 57 pp.

Describes cooperative education and the placements for cooperative education students in 31 countries. Surveys the role of the United Nations and evaluation of administrative and support services.

1541. Taylor, Harold. *A University for the World: The United Nations Plan.* Bloomington, IN: Phi Delta Kappa, 1975. 51 pp.

Describes the United Nations University which was established in December 1973 by the General Assembly with the purpose of aiding in building a world community. Suggests areas where young people may work effectively together.

1542. Teather, David C. B. *Staff Development in Higher Education: An International Review and Bibliography.* London: Kogan Page, 1979. 336 pp.

Describes practices of staff development in several countries. Pressures on teachers to improve the teaching/learning process and on administrators for more accountability have resulted in more self-appraisal in recent years. More efficient operations and better teaching may be the outcome of financial problems.

1543. Thomas, Jean. *World Problems in Education: A Brief Analytical Survey.* Paris: UNESCO Press, 1975. 166 pp.

A review of major issues in education in many countries of the world. Many problems in education found around the world are quite similar, including the relation of education to work-force needs, inequality of opportunity, access to higher education, and

the need to adapt new methods and technologies even though the costs have increased.

1544. Thompson, Kenneth W. *Higher Education for National Development: One Model For Technical Assistance.* New York: Interbook, 1972. 27 pp.

Describes a design for university development overseas. Several universities are discussed: Universidad del Valle in Cali, Columbia, 3 colleges in East Africa, and the University of the Philippines.

1545. Thompson, Kenneth W.; Fogel, Barbara R.; and Danner, Helen E. *Higher Education and Social Change: Promising Experiments in Developing Countries.* Vols 1 and 2. New York: Praeger, 1976, 1977. 224 pp; 564 pp.

Vol. 1 contains reports of current efforts in higher education to meet the educational needs of developing countries. Problems are enumerated and solutions suggested. Case studies describe programs in Africa, Asia, and Latin America. Vol. 2 gives accounts of case studies in Africa, Asia, and Latin America and their approaches to problems of development. These case studies outline the response of higher education to rural problems, health care, manpower training, and other community needs.

1546. University of Minnesota, Office of International Programs. *Directory of Financial Aids for International Activities.* 2d ed. Minneapolis, MN: Office of International Programs, University of Minnesota, 1978. 345 pp.

Individuals who are interested in international projects and the grants which make them possible will find helpful information concerning 231 sources of grants.

1547. Van de Graaff, John H., et al. *Academic Power: Patterns of Authority in Seven National Systems of Higher Education.* New York: Praeger, 1978. 217 pp.

This study which developed from a seminar held at Yale deals with organization and control in 7 countries: Federal Republic of Germany, Italy, France, Sweden, Great Britain, the United States, and Japan. Two sets of conclusions deal with systems of higher education and academic power.

1548. Von Moltke, Konrad, and Schneevoigt, Norbert. *Educational Leaves for Employees: European Experience for American Consideration.* San Francisco, CA: Jossey-Bass, 1977. 269 pp.

Workers' conception of work and nonwork as hostile elements combine to motivate or discourage them in regard to educational leave. Educational leaves are regarded as employment rather than education. Generally, workers at higher levels take advantage of educational leaves but those at lower levels seldom do. This type of education/work experience is common practice in Europe.

GREAT BRITAIN

1549. Ashby, Eric, and Anderson, Mary. *Rise of the Student Estate in Britain*. Cambridge, MA: Harvard University Press, 1970. 186 pp.

Covers the student movement in Great Britain. Some aspects considered are: student opinion at present, rise of the student estate, and the development of student influence on universities.

1550. Becher, Tony, et al. *Systems of Higher Education: United Kingdom*. International Council for Educational Development. New York: Interbook, 1977. 158 pp.

The University Grants Committee which formerly stood between the central government and the universities has been placed under the Department of Education and Science. The Department of Education and Science gives national objectives and funding to UGC and the UGC allocates funds. Based on a 12-country study in 1975–77.

1551. Bell, Robert; Fowler, Gerald; and Little, Ken, eds. *Education in Great Britain and Ireland*. Boston: Routledge & Kegan Paul, 1973. 290 pp.

Gives information concerning the background of British education and the forces which created and shaped the system. Of special interest is the first essay, ''Education in England,'' by Ann Corbett, which describes clearly the various educational institutions in Great Britain, a source of confusion to most people. Also discussed are the educational systems of Scotland, Wales, Northern Ireland, and various islands.

1552. Boehm, Klaus, and Wellings, Nick, eds. *The Student Book 1979–80: The Discriminating Students' Guide to U.K. Colleges, Polytechnics and Universities*. Totowa, NJ: Littlefield, Adams, 1979. 424 pp.

Lists higher education institutions in Great Britain for students who are considering study there. Arranged alphabetically by subject and institution.

1553. British Council and the Association of Commonwealth Universities. *Higher Education in the United Kingdom 1978–80: A Handbook for Students from Overseas and Their Advisers*. London: Longman, 1978. 308 pp.

Directs students from other countries to colleges, polytechnics, and universities in Great Britain. Information on accreditation, admission procedures, money, and student life are of particular interest. Courses offered are described. The first edition of this book appeared in 1936 and it is now in the seventeenth edition.

1554. Brosan, George; et al. *Patterns and Policies in Higher Education*. New York: Penguin Books, 1971. 186 pp.

Considers enrollment projections and alternatives for expansion. The Open University is mentioned as an alternative for college-age students.

1555. Butcher, H. J., and Rudd, Ernest, eds. *Contemporary Problems in Higher Education: An Account of Research*. New York: Crane-Russak Co., 1972. 401 pp.

Description of research carried out in Great Britain. Depicts the rapid changes in higher education, shows the influence of research on these changes, and projects future needs and problems.

1556. Craig, T., ed. *Commonwealth Universities and Society*. London: Association of Commonwealth Universities, 1974. 442 pp.

Proceedings of the eleventh Congress of the Association of Commonwealth Universities, 1973, held in Edinburgh. Topics of papers concern the universities' relationship to the environment, contemporary culture, resources, cooperation with other universities, and university government.

1557. Dent, Harold C. *Education in England and Wales*. Hamden, CT: Shoe String Press, 1977. 171 pp.

Examines the educational systems of England and Wales. Every level is described from the primary through the university.

1558. Fielden, John, and Lockwood, Geoffrey. *Planning and Management in Universities: A Study of British Universities*. London: Sussex University Press, 1973. 352 pp.

Defines the best methods of day-to-day university administration. The concept of the changing university and the role of management are emphasized. Points out the need for universities to adapt to external change through planning and management techniques of financial control.

1559. Halsey, A. H., and Trow, M. A. *British Academics*. Cambridge, MA: Harvard University Press, 1971. 560 pp.

Traces historical and sociological development of academic professions and British universities through the past century. Discusses society and the university tradition as exemplified by Oxford and faculty.

1560. Heim, Alice. *Teaching and Learning in Higher Education*. Atlantic Highlands, NJ: Humanities, 1976. 134 pp.

Expanded interest in the problems of teaching and learning has occurred as growth rate has become slower in higher education. Analyzes the lecture method and points out defects. Other items of interest mentioned are booklists and handouts, graduate teaching, seminars, student assessment, and undergraduate projects.

1561. King, Ronald. *School and College: Studies of Post-sixteen Education*. Boston: Routledge & Kegan Paul, 1976. 222 pp.

In Britain today, more young people between the ages of 16 to 19 are receiving full-time education than ever before. Courses and institutions are tailored to service their needs. Reported research compares different organizational forms and students perceptions of them.

1562. Lawlon, John, ed. *Higher Education: Patterns of Change in the 1970's*. London: Routledge and Kegan Paul, 1972. 155 pp.

British higher education consists of colleges of education, polytechnics, universities, and adult education centers. Some contributors feel that the universities should be more concerned with teacher education and adult education.

1563. Litt, Edgar, and Parkinson, Michael. *U.S. and U.K. Educational Policy: A Decade of Reform.* New York: Praeger, 1979. 161 pp.

Describes educational policymaking in Britain and the United States. Both countries face similar problems, financial situations, and a demand for equal educational opportunities. In both cases there is more control by the government. The British have preferred lower-cost mass colleges with government aid. In the United States student aid is more popular than institutional aid programs.

1564. Moodie, Graeme C., and Eustace, Rowland. *Power and Authority in British Universities.* London: Allen & Unwin, 1974. 254 pp.

Describes how British universities operate. Some problems which may become greater in the future are: less money, nonprofessorial academic staff, and trade unions.

1565. Morris, Jan, ed. *The Oxford Book of Oxford.* New York: Oxford, 1978. 402 pp.

Describes Oxford from the Middle Ages to the end of World War II. Gives accounts of daily life and descriptions of famous students and the colleges. An Oxford glossary is included.

1566. Newman, Michael. *The Poor Cousin: A Study of Adult Education.* Winchester, MA: Allen & Unwin, 1979. 249 pp.

Discusses adult education in Great Britain today. Between 2 and one-half million and 3 million adults enroll each year in classes taught by part-time teachers. These teachers are professionals and amateurs in special fields and they teach in make-shift classrooms.

1567. Rudd, Ernest. *The Highest Education: A Study of Graduate Education in Britain.* London: Routledge & Kegan Paul, 1975. 198 pp.

Begins with a history of graduate education in Great Britain and then describes the characteristics of graduate students in the 1960s and early 1970s. Economic conditions may show a need for loans for postgraduate work.

1568. Sanderson, Michael. *The Universities and British Industry, 1850–1970.* London: Routledge & Kegan Paul, 1972. 436 pp.

Traces the origins and development of civic university colleges in cities like Birmingham, Bristol, and Manchester. They were founded to educate the children of the middle classes and to produce workers for local industry and commerce. Discusses content of curricula, social status of students, careers of graduates, industrial research, and the endowment of the universities.

1569. Smith, Eric H. F. *St. Peter's, The Founding of an Oxford College.* Atlantic Highlands, NJ: Colin Smythe, 1979. 301 pp.

A history of the first 50 years of the intellectual and institutional development of St. Peter's College, Oxford. The college was started to provide an education for "men of moderate means" by the evangelical movement of the Church of England.

1570. Watts, Anthony Gordon. *Diversity and Choice in Higher Education.* Boston: Routledge & Kegan Paul, 1972. 268 pp.

The choice of college is an important decision for Britons. Transfer is nearly impossible with the exception of the Open University. Suggests that young people have little choice because of social-class distinctions and the esteem in which Oxford and Cambridge Universities are held.

INDIA

1571. Altbach, Philip G. *The University in Transition: An Indian Case Study.* Cambridge, MA: Schenkman, 1973. 136 pp.

Describes the structure of Bombay University and its relationship to society. Academic quality has been poor; planning for future growth has not been satisfactory; and participation in national development has not been as great as expected. Specific colleges are cited and their development academically is discussed.

1572. Dickinson, Richard D. N. *The Christian College in Developing India: A Sociological Inquiry.* New York: Oxford, 1971. 370 pp.

Christian colleges have been very important in higher education in India and are still considered among the best. Provides historical background, sociological analysis, information on teachers and students, and recent developments.

1573. Kaul, J. N. *Higher Education in India: 1951–1971; Two Decades of Planned Drift.* Simla, India: Indian Institute of Advanced Study, 1974. 203 pp.

A good analysis of Indian higher education which is documented and supported by statistics. Believes that Indian universities have grown but without the necessary planning, and that the curriculum should be related to national needs. Other topics discussed include the brain drain and declining standards.

IRAN

1574. Samii, Abdol Hossein, et al. *Systems of Higher Education: Iran*. New York: Interbook, Inc., 1978. 43 pp.

Jondishapur University in Ahwaz was established 1,700 years ago, making Iran's system of higher education the predecessor to Salerno and Bologna Universities or Oxford. It was a center for higher education from the third century until the sixth when it went out of existence. Iran's historical development in higher education is described as erratic until the year 1925 when Reza Shah gave tremendous support to education.

ISRAEL

1575. Globerson, Ayre. *Higher Education and Employment: A Case Study of Israel*. New York: Praeger, 1978. 171 pp.
This study of college graduates in Israel and other countries was motivated, in part, by the needs of some professional groups. Retraining effectiveness was investigated. Other areas studied included humanities and social science graduates, mobility, employment, work satisfaction, occupational training, and counseling.

JAPAN

1576. Cummings, William K.,; Amano, Ikuo; Kitamura, Kazuyuki. *Changes in the Japanese University: A Comparative Perspective*. New York: Praeger, 1979. 261 pp.

Describes the Japanese system of higher education with special emphasis on the great expansion which took place in the 1960s. During this time the students in 4-year universities doubled and in junior colleges increased 3.5 times. Educators and institutions find great difficulty adjusting to mass education. Discusses political pressures, education as a tool for economic advancement, education directed to examination goals, and a comprehensive educational plan.

1577. Narita, Katsuya. *Systems of Higher Education: Japan*. International Council for Educational Development. New York: Interbook, 1978. 142 pp.
The Japanese system of higher education is comprised of 75 percent private institutions. These private institutions have changed curricula with changing times whereas the public institutions are more selective and rigid. Based on a 12-country study, 1975–77.

1578. Pempel, T. J. *Patterns of Japanese Policymaking: Experiences from Higher Education*. Boulder, CO: Westview Press, 1978. 248 pp.
Three approaches to policymaking in Japan are applied in university administration. Shows the relationship between universities, the government, and external events.

LATIN AMERICA

1579. Benveniste, Guy. *Bureaucracy and National Planning: A Sociological Case Study in Mexico*. New York: Praeger, 1970. 141 pp.

In Mexico, those people involved in national planning in education do not involve those who will implement their plans. The beneficiaries who are frequently left out of the planning process react negatively.

1580. da Silva, J. V. *Higher Education and University Reform in Brazil*. Monograph Series No. 15. Latin American Sudies Center. East Lansing, MI: Michigan State University, 1977. 78 pp.

Describes higher education in Brazil, beginning with a brief history. Major changes began in 1968 with an attempt to restructure the system. Discusses changes in the structure, and components of the structure, such as curriculum, faculty, student body, and finance and expansion.

1581. Guerra, Alfonso Rangel. *Systems of Higher Education: Mexico*. International Council for Educational Development. New York: Interbook, 1978. 84 pp.

Part of a 12-country study of higher education which examines governing bodies of higher education. This study describes the system, discusses objectives and management, and comments on the effectiveness of higher education in Mexico.

1582. Harr, Jerry. *The Politics of Higher Education in Brazil*. New York: Praeger, 1977. 222 pp.

Brazil has made efforts in recent years toward modernization of higher education, particularly regarding admissions into institutions and graduates who are needed in the job market. A centralized military government does not tend to encourage innovations, experimental programs, planning, or evaluation.

1583. Haussman, Fay, and Harr, Jerry. *Education in Brazil*. Hamden, CT: Shoe String, 1978. 169 pp.

The past 50-year period has been one of tremendous growth in higher education in Brazil. The number of institutions of higher education has grown from almost none to a total of 57 universities, 5 college ''federations'' and 786 single-purpose colleges. New programs have been developed, including the Amazonian studies on the economy, ecology, and resources of this large area.

1584. King, Richard G., et al. *The Provincial Universities of Mexico: An Analysis of Growth and Development*. New York: Praeger, 1971. 234 pp.

Nine provincial universities are studied. The responsiveness to regional needs is examined in relation to aims, program changes, faculty interchange, and local research projects. Assessment of instruction includes ability and education of professors, library, instructional methods, and work load. Also considered are administrative affairs such as budget, planning, financing, and student affairs.

1585. Liebman, Arthur, et al. *Latin American University Students: A Six Nation Study*. Cambridge, MA: Harvard University Press, 1972. 296 pp.

Gives the attitudes and opinions of Latin American students on many issues. Family background and the historical development of student activism in Latin America are discussed. Case studies from Mexico and Puerto Rico are included.

1586. Maier, Joseph, and Weatherhead, Richard W., eds. *The Latin American University*. Albuquerque, NM: University of New Mexico Press, 1979. 237 pp.

Describes contemporary higher education in relation to politics and social change in Latin American countries. Historical background is reviewed, as well as current conditions.

1587. Osborn, Thomas Noel, II. *Higher Education in Mexico: History Growth, and Problems in a Dichotomized Industry*. Center for InterAmerican Studies. University of Texas at El Paso. El Paso, TX: Texas Western Press, 1976. 150 pp.

Reviews the history of Mexican higher education and describes the characteristics of the institutions and the typical university student. Public and private sectors are discussed and income sources are noted. Projections and future planning comprise the final chapter.

1588. Parker, Franklin, and Parker, Betty, eds. *Education in Puerto Rico and of Puerto Ricans in the U.S.A.: Abstracts of American Doctoral Dissertations*. Puerto Rico: Inter American University Press, 1978. 601 pp.

Contains abstracts of doctoral dissertations all concerning education of Puerto Ricans. Arranged in alphabetical order by author, with an author and a subject index.

1589. Renner, Richard E., ed. *Universities in Transition: The U.S. Presence in Latin American Higher Education*. Gainesville, FL: University of Florida, 1973. 147 pp.

Six position papers presented at the Center for Latin American Studies at the University of Florida in 1970, followed by a discussion. Representatives of Chile, Columbia, and Peru and other authorities speak of various aspects of higher education. One basic difference in Latin American and U.S. institutions is the difference in cultures. Latin American Universities are agents of change and creators of values.

RUSSIA

1590. Grant, Nigel. *Soviet Education*. New York: Penguin Books, 4th edition, 1979. 223 pp.

Within this complete description of education in the Soviet Union, the section on higher education (pp. 123–50) is very helpful. Major topics within this section include growth, aims, kinds of postsecondary education, admissions, courses, degrees, organization, and future developments.

1591. McClelland, James C. *Autocrats and Academics: Education, Culture and Society in Tsarist Russia*. Chicago: University of Chicago Press, 1979. 150 pp.

An original study of education in imperial Russia which shows that the autocrats and academics assisted in the growth of national culture. The emphasis on an elite educated group made an even larger gap until 1917 between the illiterate masses and the educated.

1592. Onushkin, Victor G., ed. *Planning the Development of Universities.* UNESCO. 4 vols. New York: Unipub, 1975

The 4 vols. comprise a 5-year research project concerning 2 case studies of Leningrad State University and the University of Sussex. Students of higher education will be interested in the many facets of educational planning presented. Of special interest is much information about higher education in USSR and the German Democratic Republic.

SOUTHEAST ASIA

1593. Aaneson, Charles R. *Republic of Indonesia.* International Education Activities. Washington, DC: American Association of Collegiate Registrars and Admissions Officers, 1979. 118 pp.

Describes the educational system of Indonesia with the majority of the study devoted to all aspects of higher education. "A Study of the Educational System of the Republic of Indonesia and a Guide to the Academic Placement of Students from the Republic of Indonesia in Educational Institutions of the United States" is the subtitle. Appendix A contains a list of institutions of higher learning.

1594. Johnson, Johnny K. *Thailand: A Study of the Educational System of Thailand and a Guide to the Academic Placement of Students from Thailand in Educational Institutions of the United States.* Washington, DC: American Association of Collegiate Registrars and Admissions Officers, 1978. 118 pp.

Describes the educational institutions in Thailand from elementary through higher education, including vocational education. The purpose of the book is to assist admissions officers with knowledge

which will enable them to place Thai students in the United States. A large part of the volume is devoted to postsecondary education.

1595. Ketudat, Sippanondha, et al. *Systems of Higher Education: Thailand.* International Council for Educational Development. New York: Interbook, Inc., 1978. 138 pp.

Higher education is a relatively new development in Thailand. Buddhist monasteries, the royal court, and small private schools offered education until about 1917. Government universities and private colleges are supervised and coordinated by the office of University Affairs.

1596. Sudarmo, Muhammdi Siswo, ed. *Alternatives for Optimization of Teaching-Learning Processes in Southeast Asian Universities.* Singapore: Regional Institute of Higher Education and Development, 1977. 106 pp.

Summarizes information concerning higher education in Indonesia, Malaysia, the Philippines, Singapore, and Thailand. Before 1960 technicians were needed and trained, since that time expansion has provided more opportunities in these countries. Quality of education should be improved and more effort to meet local needs is necessary.

WEST INDIES

1597. Hunte, Christopher Norman. *The Development of Higher Education in the West Indies.* Sherman Oaks, CA: Banner Books, 1978. 131 pp.

British academic traditions have remained virtually intact in the West Indies, resulting in a system of higher education which is competitive, selective, and unresponsive to student needs. There has been an increase in vocational-technical training in order to meet the needs of students.

WESTERN EUROPE

1598. Berg, Barbro, and Ostergren, Bertil. *Innovations and Innovation Processes in Higher Education.* Stockholm, Sweden: National Board of Universities and Colleges, 1977. 157 pp.

Presents 2 special studies, educational changes, and 7 case studies of processes of innovation. The present trend in Sweden is toward decentralization of planning in higher education.

1599. Bienayme, Alain. *Systems of Higher Education: France.* International Council for Educational Development. New York: Interbook, 1978. 144 pp.

Describes the educational situation in France which operates the universities under the Minister of Higher Education. This Minister is also responsible for primary and secondary schools and this causes many problems. Planning is based on 1975–77 study.

1600. Bourdieu, Pierre, and Passeron, Jean-Claude. *The Inheritors: French Students and Their Relation to Culture.* Chicago: University of Chicago Press, 1979. 158 pp.

Describes studies undertaken by sociology students in Lille and Paris working under the Center for European Sociology. These studies concern various aspects of student life, such as mutual acquaintance, examination anxiety, integration, students' leisure, students' image of the student, and the Sorbonne Greek Drama Society and its audience.

1601. Clark, Burton R. *Academic Power in Italy: Bureaucracy and Oligarchy in a National University System.* Chicago: University of Chicago Press, 1977. 205 pp.

Reports the historical development of the Italian University from the twelfth century. Very few changes have taken place since that time even though the enrollment has grown tremendously. Teaching and research activities have declined both in quantity and quality. Senior professors have great power and resist reform but the labor market does not need better prepared employees and cannot absorb larger numbers.

1602. Cohen, Habiba S. *Elusive Reform: The French Universities, 1968–1978.* Boulder, CO: Westview, 1979. 280 pp.

The progress of university reform in France in the past 10 years may be attributed to political forces both inside and outside the university. The Ministry of Education has limited more than it has encouraged autonomy and flexibility among the new universities. Some statistics are included.

1603. Council of Europe's Council for Cultural Cooperation. *Reform and Development of Higher Education: A European Symposium.* Atlantic Highlands, NJ: Humanities Press, 1978. 176 pp.

Summarizes a conference on higher education reform in Europe using 7 papers from the conference. The countries the book covers are: Britain, Germany, Spain, France, and Western Europe. Increased enrollment in recent years has caused many changes.

1604. Embling, Jack. *A Fresh Look at Higher Education: European Implications of the Carnegie Commission Reports.* Amsterdam: Elsevier, 1974. 263 pp.

Uses some of the important issues brought to the surface by the Carnegie Commission to look at similar issues in Britain and Europe. In Britain higher education is referred to as "further education." The British universities have more autonomy than those in Western Europe, and there is very little cooperation among them. There is no separate body called "administration," but the university is run by academics.

1605. International Council for Educational Development. *Access to Higher Education: Two Perspectives.* New York: Interbook, 1978. 79 pp.

Report of the German-U.S. Study Group which compares problems in access and admission in the Federal Republic of Germany and the United States. Some related topics discussed in connection with access are: educational articulation, employment, and the role of government.

1606. Neave, Guy. *Patterns of Equality.* Windsor, England: NFER, 1976. 150 pp.

Describes changes in the structure of European higher education and the effects upon the equality of educational opportunity. Covers 1945 through 1974. Manpower planning is a related educational development which is the subject of current debate.

1607. Peisert, Hansgert, and Framkein, Gerhild. *Systems of Higher Education: Federal Republic of Germany.* New York: Interbook, 1978. 206 pp.

Studies the organization of the German university which is committed to uniform educational opportunity for the whole country. Some reforms have been made in recent years. Discusses management and effectiveness of the universities and inflexibility of West German institutions.

1608. Premfors, Rune, and Ostergen, Bertil. *Systems of Higher Education: Sweden.* International Council for Educational Development. New York: Interbook, 1978. 208 pp.

The National Board of University and Colleges is responsible for higher education in Sweden. Much democratic planning with resulting changes has occurred since 1968. There is a tendency, however, toward more control by bureaucrats and politicians.

1609. Ringer, Fritz K. *Education and Society in Modern Europe.* Bloomington, IN: Indiana University Press, 1978. 370 pp.

Gives the history of French and German secondary and higher education systems from the eighteenth century to 1960. The relationship of these systems to society is probed.

1610. Sauvy, Alfred. *Access to Education: New Possibilities.* The Hague: Martinus Nijhoff, 1973. 157 pp.

Vol. 3 of the series, *Plan Europe 2000,* comments on research findings and social trends. The series, sponsored by the European Cultural Foundation, is part of a project designed to predict future possibilities in education, industry, urbanization, and rural life. Nine volumes have been published in the education series.

Higher Education as a Specialized Field of Study

EDUCATION AS A FIELD OF STUDY

1611. Altbach, Philip G. *Comparative Higher Education: Research Trends and Bibliography*. London: Mansell, 1979. 206 pp.

Discusses comparative higher education as a field of study and gives the history of the area. Specific areas of the field are noted and the issues interpreted: planning in higher education, the professoriate, governance, university-society relations, and student activism. A selective bibliography for further research is included.

1612. Association of Professors of Higher Education. *Higher Education as a Field of Study*. Proceedings of the First Annual Meeting. Chicago: Association of Professors of Higher Education, 1972. 488 pp.

Consists of 4 papers which deal with some aspects of higher education, such as the specialized field, programs, reactions to programs, and departmental development.

1613. Dressel, Paul L., and Mayhew, Lewis B. *Higher Education as a Field of Study*. San Francisco, CA: Jossey-Bass, 1974. 214 pp.

In the only book-length treatment of this topic, such areas are considered as emergence of higher education as a field of study, current scene, research and scholarships, problems and issues, new models, and prospects and needs. List of 6 universities with doctoral programs in the appendix indicates where the major programs and research centers are located.

1614. Harcleroad, Fred F., ed. *Higher Education: A Developing Field of Study*. Iowa City, IA: American College Testing Program, 1974. 97 pp.

Intended to present the current status of the study of higher education, this report which was published for the Association of Professors of Higher Education includes 3 major sections: the knowledge base of higher education, graduate programs on higher education, and functions of professors of higher education within or outside of the institution.

1615. ———. *The Study of Higher Education: Some Papers on Administrative Theory and Practice*. Tucson, AZ: Association of Professors of Higher Education, 1976. 57 pp.

Covers administrative theory, planning and management systems, collective bargaining, individualized education, leadership and values, and law and higher education.

1616. *Higher Education as a Field of Study*. Proceedings of the First Annual Meeting of the Association of Professors of Higher Education. Chicago, March 5, 1972. 49 pp.

Discusses higher education as a field of study, including a comprehensive review of the literature, services for Black students, programs, reactions to these programs, and departmental development.

1617. *Journal of Research and Development in Education*. Vol. 6, no. 2, Winter, 1973. 130 pp.

Entire issue emphasizes higher education as an emerging discipline and the need for reform.

1618. Smith, Barbara G. ''Toward a Theory Base for the Study of Higher Education: A Methodology Using Citation Patterns and Content Analysis to Identify a Community of Higher Education Specialists and a Vocabulary in Which They Communicate.'' Unpublished dissertation, University of Kentucky, 1975. 133 pp.

With 7 original citing sources (6 journal articles and one book), uses content and citation analysis via a computer program to determine that a community of higher education specialists exists but only in a beginning form.

Appendices

APPENDIX 1
SELECTED REFERENCE SOURCES

R1. American Association of Community and Junior Colleges. *1980 Community, Junior, and Technical College Directory*. Washington, DC: American Association of Community and Junior Colleges, 1980. 84 pp.

An annual publication which lists community colleges, junior colleges, and technical colleges by states. State administrators, summaries of statistics, associations, and organizations are also listed.

R2. *Barron's Compact Guide to College Transfer*. Woodbury, NY: Barron's, 1979. 315 pp.

Lists more than 300 colleges and universities. Information is brief since only transfer-admission procedures are included. Published annually.

R3. Beach, Mark. *Words for the Wise: A Field Guide to Academic Terms*. Portland, OR: Coast to Coast, 1979. 124 pp.

Defines terms in higher education and sometimes gives information on their origin.

R4. Bina, James V., et al. *Databases and Clearinghouses: Information Resources for Education*. Columbus, OH: National Center for Research in Vocational Education, 1978. 132 pp.

Fifty-five databases of interest to people in education are listed in the first section of this book. A one-page summary of each database lists pertinent information on each. Sample search sheets are included for several databases. The second section of the book consists of one-page summaries of 12 clearinghouses with appropriate information.

R5. Buros, Oscar Krisen. *The Eighth Mental Measurements Yearbook*. Highland Park, NJ: Gryphon, 1978. 2 vols., 2182 pp.

The most complete, authoritative source of information concerning standardized tests. A new edition is periodically published. Ordering information, reviews and descriptions of tests are included. Readers are referred to the original review unless a test has been revised. Several indexes assist the location of a test, title, author, subject, and publisher.

R6. California Postsecondary Education Commission. *Postsecondary Education in California: Information Digest*. Sacramento, CA: California Postsecondary Education Commission, 1979. 260 pp.

Gives statistics on enrollment, degrees conferred, faculties, staffs, students, financing, student test scores, and programs in California's public and private colleges and universities.

R7. Cass, James, and Birnbaum, Max. *Comparative Guide to American Colleges for Students, Parents, and Counselors*. New York: Harper and Row, 1978. 741 pp.

This guide is published frequently and is now in the ninth edition. It contains information on admission requirements, academic pro-

grams, campus environments and other matters of interest. Material included has been gathered from student leaders, administrators, and deans of students.

R8. Chronicle Guidance Research Department: *Student Aid Annual, 1978–79*. Moravia, NY: Chronicle Guidance, 1978.

An annual publication which lists financial aids for graduates and undergraduates. Scholarships and loans are also given. The 3 indexes are: undergraduate programs subject; graduate programs subject; and source index for graduate, undergraduate, and state programs.

R9. Consortium of Associatons for Educational Dissemination. *Private Organizations and Associations: Information Resources for Education*. Arlington, VA: The Consortium, 1978. 186 pp.

More than 60 professional education associations are listed in this book with the hope that they will share ideas, policies, strategies, and programs. Also listed are educational laboratories and centers, education-related organizations, multimedia organizations, foundations, and activities of various groups.

R10. Gollay, Elinor, and Bennett, Alwina. *The College Guide for Students with Disabilities*. Cambridge, MA: Abt Publications, 1976. 545 pp.

Outlines higher education services, programs, and facilities accessible to handicapped students in the United States. Information is provided about existing resources in higher education, state, and federal agencies.

R11. Gourman, Jack. *The Gourman Report: A Rating of American and International Universities*. 2d edition. Los Angeles: National Education Standards, 1977. 135 pp.

Endeavors to evaluate the quality of institutions of higher learning. The total structure, direction, and performance of colleges and universities are appraised; and the policies, method of evaluation, and criteria are listed in the introduction. Undergraduate programs, administrative areas, law school, medical schools, and dental schools are rated. American institutions compose most of the ratings, but some international schools are included.

R12. Hawes, Gene R. *Careers Tomorrow: Leading Growth Fields for College Graduates*. New York: New American Library, 1979. 305 pp.

Identifies more than 100 career possibilities in growing fields which may be of interest to undergraduates as they plan their college programs. Some recommended programs are in medicine and allied health fields, business, science, and industrial positions.

R13. Hegener, Karen C., ed. *National College Databank*. Peterson's Guides. Princeton, NJ: Peterson's Guides, 1979. 876 pp.

Contains glossary of terms used in the book. Sections cover: institutions offering undergraduate work, college characteristics, undergraduate enrollment characteristics, colleges reporting special programs, campus life characteristics, admissions facts, entrance difficulty data, financial aids, and colleges reporting unusual majors. Over 2,400 colleges are indexed.

R14. Kay, Ernest, ed. *The World Who's Who of Women in Education*. New York: International Biographical Centre, 1978. 559 pp.

Short biographies of women in education. Entries are arranged alphabetically by name of person.

R15. Kelsay, Roger R. *AAHE Bibliography on Higher Education*. Washington, DC: American Association for Higher Education, 1972. 60 pp.

Bibliography on higher education arranged in subject categories and alphabetically in the category by name of author. A directory of publishers is included.

R16. Knowles, Asa S., ed. *The International Encyclopedia of Higher Education*. San Francisco, CA: Jossey-Bass, 1977. 10 vols.

Intended as a guide and basic source of information on all topics related to higher education. It is international in scope and covers postsecondary education including 2-year and 4-year colleges and universities, and technical institutes. Vol. 10 is an index volume with cross references.

R17. Livesey, Herbert B., and Doughty, Harold. *Guide to American Graduate Schools*. 3d edition. New York: Viking Press, 1975. 437 pp.

Gives basic information students need concerning graduate programs. Colleges and universities are listed in alphabetical order with general information followed by lists of graduate programs offered.

R18. Mayhew, Lewis B. *The Literature of Higher Education 1972*. San Francisco, CA: Jossey-Bass, 1972. 184 pp.

The beginning chapter discusses trends in higher education during 1965–70 as shown in the literature. Analytical and critical annotations.

R19. Middle States Association of Colleges and Secondary Schools. *Basic Information about Higher Education Institutions in the Middle States Region—1973*. Newark, NJ: Commission on Higher Education, M.S.A., 1973. 603 pp.

Reports information about institutions of higher learning. Information includes sponsorship and control, faculty, students, programs, library, finances, plant, and recent changes. A supplement was issued in 1974.

R20. Mitchell, Janet, ed. *Higher Education Exchange: 78/79*. Philadelpha, PA: J. B. Lippincott, 1979. 766 pp.

Directory to 5,700 private, public, and proprietary postsecondary education institutions. Includes 200,000 administrators and academic personnel, 1,300 associations, publishers, an almanac with financial data, and faculty and student profiles.

R21. Mullins, Carolyn J. *A Guide to Writing and Publishing in the Social and Behavioral Sciences*. New York: John Wiley & Sons, 1977. 430 pp.

Intended for authors, typists, and publishers, this excellent guide will be helpful for any type of writing. Practical information is given about preparing journal articles and writing books.

R22. *National Faculty Directory 1978 (and 1979): An Alphabetical List with Addresses, of about 449,000 Members of Teaching Faculties at Junior Colleges, Colleges, and Universities in the United States and Selected Canadian Institutions*. 2 vols. Detroit, MI: Gale, 1978. 2,668 pp.

Arranged alphabetically with departmental or administrative positions and college or university address. The best resource available for this information.

R23. Nelson, A. Gordon. *Colleges Classified: A Guide for Counselors, Parents and Students*. Moravia, NY: Chronicle Guidance Pub., 1975. 56 pp.

Information is of value to students, parents and counselors as they plan. Four-year colleges are listed by student body, size of enrollment, and annual tuition and fees. Two-year colleges listings contain the same information. A combined index is also available, listing names and location in the publication.

R24. Pell, Arthur R., and Furbay, Albert L. *College Student Guide to Career Planning*. New York: Simon and Schuster, 1975. 133 pp.

Intended to help undecided students plan for a career. The Self-Evaluation Inventory is intended to reveal strengths, aptitudes, interests, and accomplishments. Resume writing and job interviews are discussed.

R25. Priestley, Barbara, comp. *British Qualifications*. 4th edition. London: Kogan Page, 1973. 923 pp.

Describes various types of educational institutions in England, Wales, Scotland, and Northern Ireland. Examinations which are required for entrance to higher education are discussed. Qualifications gained after completing classes or degrees are outlined. Professional bodies, such as study associations and learned societies, are included along with individual trade qualifications.

R26. Quay, Richard H. *Research in Higher Education: A Guide to Source Bibliographies*. New York: College Entrance Examination Board, 1976. 54 pp.

Contains lists of bibliographies, reviews of literature, and research related to higher education. Arrangement is alphabetical by author and there is a subject index.

R27. Schlachter, Gail Ann. *Directory of Financial Aids for Women*. Los Angeles: Reference Service Press, 1979. 200 pp.

Encourages women to continue their education by listing 670 references for scholarships, loans, grants, and awards. Administrators in higher education, state agencies, credit unions, and financial aid should find this book of interest.

R28. Society for Research in Higher Education. *Register of Research into Higher Education 1974–5*. London: Society of Research into Higher Education, 1974. 152 pp.

A bibliography of research in higher education, published biannually. Information given for each entry is: abstract, researcher, institution, dates of beginning, and final report. There are indexes of authors and institutions and the book is divided into sections by subjects.

R29. Teachers Insurance and Annuity Association. *Digest of Statistics on Higher Education in the United States, 1973/74–77/78*. New York: T.I.A.A., Educational Research Division, 1979. 23 p.

Gives statistics and summaries on higher education. Information is gathered from U.S. Office of Education and other public and private educational organizations.

R30. United States Office of Education. *Dissemination Networks: Information Resources for Education.* San Francisco, CA: Far West Laboratory for Educational Research and Development, 1978. 87 pp.

This resource catalog is part of an effort to encourage the exchange of information in education. Each network title is listed in alphabetical order and the following information is given: major functions, network members, audience, description, and other available information. In the appendices information is included, such as ERIC Clearinghouses with addresses of each, similar information for other networks, publications, and contents of databases and clearinghouses.

R31. Wilkins, Kay S. *Women's Education in the United States: A Guide to Information Sources.* Detroit, MI: Gale Research, 1979. 217 pp.

Contains over 1,100 sources of information in an annotated bibliography. There are sections on educational levels, women's colleges, government legislation, counseling, continuing education, and other topics.

R32. Willingham, Warren W. *The Sourcebook for Higher Education.* New York: College Entrance Examination Board, 1973. 478 pp.

This annotated bibliography has more then 1,500 references concerning access literature which was published in 1960s through spring of 1971.

R33. *World of Learning 1978–79.* 29th edition, 2 vols. Detroit, MI: Gale Research Company, 1978. 2,038 pp.

Includes names, addresses, and other information concerning 24,000 academies, universities, colleges, libraries, archives, museums, art galleries, learned societies, research institutes, and 150,000 people involved in them. Professors at major universities and subjects they teach are listed. Important libraries, number of volumes, and outstanding collections are included.

R34. *Yearbook of Higher Education, 1979–0.* 11th edition. Chicago, IL: Marquis Academic Media, 1979. 844 pp.

An annual publication which contains a directory of institutions of higher education, statistics of higher education, and resource information. The resource section consists of lists of ERIC clearinghouses, education associations, institutional consortia, and Canadian associations of higher learning.

R35. Young, D. Parker, ed. *Yearbook of Higher Education Law, 1978.* Topeka, KS: National Organization in Legal Problems of Education, 1979. 226 pp.

Summarizes and analyzes federal and state court cases in higher education. Topics include governance, finance, property, employees, and students.

APPENDIX 2
AN ANNOTATED BIBLIOGRAPHY OF SELECTED PROFESSIONAL JOURNALS RELATED TO THE STUDY OF HIGHER EDUCATION

AAHE Bulletin
American Association for Higher Education
One Dupont Circle, NW, Suite 780
Washington, DC 20036

Recent issues feature a special report, e.g., the shakeups in California higher education; trends and findings; and Association plans and developments. Published monthly except in July and August.

Academe: Bulletin of A.A.U.P. (formerly *A.A.U.P. Bulletin*)
American Association of University Professors
One Dupont Circle, NW, Suite 500
Washington, DC 20036

A quarterly that deals with accreditation, salaries, ethics, morality, legal aspects, role examination, retirement policies, role of administrators, and case studies of universities.

Administrative Science Quarterly
Cornell University
American Science Quarterly
Malott Hall
Ithaca, NY 14853

A highly theoretical journal which emphasizes organizational theory and administrative behavior.

American Educational Research Journal
American Educational Research Association
1230 17th St., NW
Washington, DC 20036

A quarterly that presents experimental and theoretical studies in education, focusing on educational psychology-learning theory, applications of statistical data, and motivation.

Black Scholar
Black World Foundation
Box 908
Sausalito, CA 94965

The intent of this journal is to educate and expose social change ideologies for debate and analysis. The articles are critical and scholarly. Ten issues per year.

Change
Helen Dwight Reid Educational Foundation
4000 Albemarle St., NW
Washington, DC 20016

Presents commentary on fundamental issues, reports constructive educational reforms, and cites new models in academic experimentation in the form of opinion articles and viewpoints by leaders in education. Reports and interprets changes in higher education. Nine issues each year.

Chronicle of Higher Education
1333 New Hampshire Ave., NW
Washington, DC 20036

Provides a news synopsis of current events in higher education. Regular features include a bibliography of recent publications, information on new college presidents, and changes in faculty and administrative positions. Published weekly during the school year, with a format similar to that of a newspaper.

College and University
American Association of Collegiate Registrars and Admissions Officers
One Dupont Circle, NW, Suite 330
Washington, DC 20036

A quarterly that covers foreign students, enrollment figures, federal legislation, academic freedom, faculty attitudes, and accreditation.

College and University Bulletin
American Association for Higher Education
One Dupont Circle, NW, Suite 780
Washington, DC 20036

Presents new developments on federal and state legislation, major research projects at selected colleges, and book reviews.

College Board Review
College Board Publication Orders
Box 2815
Princeton, NJ 08540

A quarterly published by the College Entrance Examination Board that serves as a forum for exchange of ideas in education for secondary and postsecondary institutions. Special attention is given to the transitional period between secondary school and higher education.

College Student Journal
Box 566
Chula Vista, CA 92010

A quarterly published by Project Innovation that contains research and theoretical papers dealing with student values, attitudes, opinions, and learning.

College Student Personnel Abstracts
Claremont Graduate School
1019 Dartmouth Ave.
Claremont, CA 91711

Contains abstracts from journals, conference proceedings, and research reports concerning students and student services.

Community and Junior College Journal
American Association of Community and Junior Colleges
One Dupont Circle, NW
Washington, DC 20036

Formerly *Junior College Journal*, this contains case studies of the development of junior and community colleges, some research on students, faculties, administrators, and many opinion essays.

Community College Frontiers
Sangamon State University
Springfield, IL 62708

Emphasis is on analysis, interpretation, and research with a special interest in ideas and practices which provide new insight into old and new phenomena related to the 2-year institution. Published quarterly under the joint sponsorship of Governors State University and Sangamon State University.

Community College Review
North Carolina State University
310 Poe Hall
Raleigh, NC 27650

A quarterly that deals with a variety of broad topics related to the community college, such as collective bargaining, faculty morale, and performance appraisal of college administrators.

Community/Junior College Research Quarterly
Hemisphere Publishing Company
1025 Vermont Ave., NW
Washington, DC 20005

A quarterly published by Virginia Commonwealth University includes original research and papers which concern developments in study and practice at community and junior colleges.

Educational Record
American Council on Education
One Dupont Circle, NW, Suite 800
Washington, DC 20036

Contains research- and nonresearch-based articles dealing with current important topics in higher education, such as financial health of colleges, trustee/president relations, governmental relations, community college, and academic decision making.

Educational Researcher
American Educational Research Association
1230 17th St., NW
Washington, DC 20036

Scholarly articles are published in this journal but they are generally in nontechnical language. Research and development articles are included. Eleven issues a year.

Graduate Woman
American Association of University Women
2401 Virginia Ave., NW
Washington, DC 20037

Formerly *A.A.U.W. Journal*, this intends to further the educational development of women and to support education for women, especially continuing or reentry education. This journal also attempts to encourage women with degrees to attain greater self-development and to be involved in community affairs.

Higher Education (The International Journal of Higher Education and Planning)
Elsevier Scientific Publishing Company

P.O. Box 211
1000 AE
Amsterdam, The Netherlands

A bimonthly, this contains articles of international interest in higher education. Recent issues have had articles on student activism in Greece, Japan, and West Germany; assessment of medical students; race and sex in relation to college entry; and problems in the Arab University of Kuwait.

Higher Educational and National Affairs
American Council on Education
One Dupont Circle, NW, Suite 800
Washington, DC 20036

A weekly that gives research notes, grant and financial aid information, government proposals, policies, benefits, and legal aspects related to the national scene.

Improving College and University Teaching
Heldref Publications
4000 Albemarle St., NW
Washington, DC 20016

Contains articles by college and university teachers in the form of personal opinions, research studies, and case study examples. Serves as an international colloquium for university teachers.

JGE: Journal of General Education
Pennsylvania State University Press
215 Wagner Building
University Park, PA 16802

A quarterly that promotes liberal education and tries to counteract overspecialization. Scholarly articles on a variety of subjects are written by specialists for education nonspecialists.

Journal of College Student Personnel
American College Personnel Association
Two Skyline Place, Suite 400
5203 Leesburg Pike
Falls Church, VA 22041

Covers many student personnel topics such as the older college student, rights of campus groups, the community college transfer student, advising undergraduate women, community college counseling, and role of the college counselor.

Journal of Counseling Psychology
American Psychological Association
1200 17th St., NW
Washington, DC 20036

Contains studies of individuals and groups relating to counseling theory and practice. Subjects covered of use to the university administrator include graduate student problems, vocational choice, personality factors, curriculum planning, religious factors, and psychological problems affecting the college student.

Journal of Developmental and Remedial Education
Center for Developmental Education
Appalachian State University
Boone, NC 28608

Emphasis on programs, techniques, and instructional technology for the disadvantaged student. Three issues a year.

Journal of Educational Psychology
American Psychological Association

1200 17th St., NW
Washington, DC 20036

A bimonthly that contains ''original investigations and theoretical papers dealing with the problems of learning, teaching, and psychological development, with special emphasis to the individual and his adjustment.'' All levels of education and all age groups are included.

Journal of Higher Eduation
Ohio State University Press
2070 Neil Ave.
Columbus, OH 43210

A bimonthly published by the American Association of Higher Education that is concerned with philosophical issues, educational problems, and viewpoints of leading educators. It contains many essays, opinion articles, reproduction of speeches, and book reviews.

Journal of Negro Education
Howard University
Bureau of Educational Research
School of Education
Washington, DC 20059

A quarterly that serves as a forum for dissemination of general information and research on the education of Black people.

Journal of Research and Development in Education
University of Georgia
G-3 Aderhold Building
Athens, GA 30602

A quarterly that translates research into educational application. A substantial part of each issue is devoted to a central theme, such as the study of higher education, and an assessment of research and development centers.

Journal of Teacher Education
American Association of Colleges for Teacher Education
One Dupont Circle, NW, Suite 610
Washington, DC 20036

A quarterly that deals with all phases of the teacher-learner situation.

Journal of the National Association for Women Deans, Administrators and Counselors
National Association for Women Deans, Administrators and Counselors
1625 I St., NW, Suite 624-A
Washington, DC 20006

A quarterly that contains articles on personnel counseling, residence halls, role of women, legal considerations, and matriculation problems.

Liberal Education
Association of American Colleges
1818 R St., NW
Washington, DC 20009

A quarterly that contains cultural and philosophical essays, historical views, case studies of academic programs, liberal arts issues, and organizational convention reports.

Negro Educational Review
P.O. Box 2895

General Mail Center
Jacksonville, FL 32202

A quarterly that provides a forum for discussion of Afro-American ideas. Presents scholarly articles, research reports, and description and analysis of current problems.

Peabody Journal of Education
Peabody College of Vanderbilt University
Nashville, TN 37203

An interdisciplinary quarterly that intends to foster the professional development and enrichment of teachers, administrators, and other educational leaders. Contains articles, book reviews, editorial comments, and occasional special features.

Phi Delta Kappan
Phi Delta Kappa
Eighth and Union, Box 789
Bloomington, IN 47402

Contains opinion articles, essays, some research and philosophical issues. Promotes educational leadership, research and service. Ten issues a year.

Research in Higher Education
Fulfillment Department
49 Sheridan Ave.
Albany, NY 12210

A quarterly that includes only empirical research studies dealing with higher education. Among those primarily interested in this journal are institutional researchers, faculty, administrators, student personnel specialists, and behavioral scientists.

Review of Higher Education
Association for the Study of Higher Education
One Dupont Circle, NW, Suite 630
Washington, DC 20036

Includes both research-oriented articles, as well as those of a scholarly nature dealing with major concerns in the study of higher education. Three issues a year.

Studies in Higher Education
Carfax Publishing Company
Haddon House
Dorchester-on-Thames
Oxford OX9 8JZ, England

Central aim of journal is to bring together subject specialists from a wide variety of fields in the discussion of teaching issues in an interchange into which all participants bring individual perspectives in order to throw light on the day-to-day processes of teaching and learning and the social and institutional contexts in which they take place. Two issues a year are published by the University of Aberdeen, Aberdeen, Scotland.

U.S.A. Today
Society for the Advancement of Education
1860 Broadway
New York, NY 10023

Formerly *Intellect, School and Society*, this offers commentary on all levels of education, including college admissions and trends, enrollment, politics, and previews of forthcoming books. Nine issues a year.

APPENDIX 3
DEFINITIONS OF SOME TERMS IN HIGHER EDUCATION

Adult Education—part-time and full-time programs at the postsecondary level offered usually late afternoon or evening for adult learners (older than 22).

Community College—may have most of the characteristics of the comprehensive community college. For example, the University of Kentucky Community College System has 12 community colleges and one technical institute, but some cannot be designated as comprehensive.

Community Education—a term sometimes used to replace an older term, adult education, to indicate that the institution offers educational programs to meet the needs of all learners in the immediate community.

Comprehensive Community College—a community college which has the 5 characteristics as described by Ralph Fields (*The Community College Movement*, 1962):

a. Comprehensive program
b. Democratic
c. Community-centered
d. Lifelong education
e. Adaptable

Higher education—organized learning programs leading to recognized degrees in accredited 2-year and 4-year colleges and universities in about 2,600 institutions.

Higher Education—the professional study in master's and doctoral programs which deal with the study of such phenomena as faculty, student, and administrators' behavior; historical backgrounds; admissions; professional and graduate schools; alumni; and comparative systems.

Multiversity—a term used by Clark Kerr (*The Uses of the University*, 1963) to indicate the scope of the modern American university, with the influence and impact of a graduate school, the various professional schools, the undergraduate body, research activity, experiment stations, projects abroad, and with outreach to business and industry and to local, state, and federal government.

Open university—a confederation of several regional universities which offer a variety of educational resources (correspondence packages, television and radio programs, other media, tutorials, and counseling) in a system where there may be no formal academic qualifications for registration as a student.

Postsecondary education—formal programs in accredited 2-year and 4-year colleges and universities leading to recognized degrees, as well as all informal learning programs, such as business colleges, seminars sponsored in business and industry, educational TV, and adult education programs sponsored by various community agencies.

Public junior college—usually financed mostly by the state with little or no funding from the local community.

Private junior college—financed entirely by private sources and student tuition. Such a college may be independent or church-related.

Technical institute—a 2-year institution leading to associate degrees in technical and occupational areas, but without a liberal arts emphasis leading to transfer to a 4-year college or university.

University branch center—not a junior college but rather the first 2 years of the baccalaureate program of the university, located at various points in the state away from the main campus.

University without walls—both a concept and a program which focuses on research and innovation in higher education and offers a broad mix of learning resources for individual learners.

APPENDIX 4
WORKING OUTLINE TO STUDY THE DEVELOPMENT OF AMERICAN HIGHER EDUCATION

I. Founding of Colonial Colleges (1636–1776)
    A. Colleges:

Harvard	1636
William and Mary	1693
Yale	1701
Princeton	1746
Columbia	1754
University of Pennsylvania	1755
Brown	1764
Rutgers	1766
Dartmouth	1769

    B. Curriculum
    C. Students
    D. Faculty
    E. Administration

II. Experiment and Diversity (1776–1862)
    A. Pressure for professional training
    B. Transylvania University (1780)
    C. University of Virginia (1825), first state university to reflect the new democracy
    D. Normal schools
    E. Dartmouth College Case (1819)
    F. Monticello Junior College, first private junior college founded at Godfrey, Illinois, 1835.

III. Rise of the University (1862–1900)
    A. Land-Grant College Acts (Morrill, 1862); Morrill-McComas Act, 1890)
       1. Provisions
       2. Importance
    B. Johns Hopkins University (1876), first research university patterned after German model
    C. Other major public and private universities

IV. Period of Expansion (1900–1970)
    A. Further expansion of private and state colleges
    B. Four major functions
    C. 1902, Joliet, Illinois, beginning of community college movement
    D. Present characteristics reflect historical roots
       1. Old—the medieval universities, particularly Oxford and Cambridge, served as models for colonial colleges
       2. Borrowed—the concept of the German university, including the lecture, seminar, laboratory, and large library
       3. New—the land-grant concept in the 1862 and 1890 legislation and the concept of the community college.
    E. Impact of World War I

F. Impact of World War II
  1. Enrollment
  2. Curriculum
G. Golden age of development (1957–1967)
H. Berkeley revolution, 1964, and other student unrest
I. Growth and impact of community colleges

V. Period of Adjustment (1970–1980)
  A. Student unrest (Early 1970s)

  1. Changes in formal curriculum
  2. Impact on state legislatures and general public
B. Increasing control by state and federal governments which has been strongly noticeable since late 1950s
C. Decline in enrollments
D. Increasing problems in finance
E. State patterns of support and control
F. Emphasis on management and accountability
G. Development of a legalistic culture

APPENDIX 5
SELECTED HIGHER EDUCATION PROGRAMS, DEPARTMENTS, AND CENTERS IN THE UNITED STATES

ARIZONA STATE UNIVERSITY
Richard Richardson, Jr.
Higher and Adult Education
Arizona State University
Tempe, AZ 85281
(602) 965-6248

ARIZONA, UNIVERSITY OF
Fred F. Harcleroad
Center for the Study of Higher Education
University of Arizona
1415 Fremont St.
Tucson, AZ 85719
(602) 626-2283

CALIFORNIA, UNIVERSITY OF (BERKELEY)
Dale Tillery
Higher Education
Division of Higher Education, Administration and Policy
  Analysis
University of California, Berkeley
4607 Tolman Hall
Berkeley, CA 94720
(415) 642-0709

CALIFORNIA, UNIVERSITY OF (LOS ANGELES)
Helen S. Austin
Higher Education Specialization
Graduate School of Education
University of California, Los Angeles
405 Hilgard Ave.
Los Angeles, CA 90024
(213) 825-8331

FLORIDA STATE UNIVERSITY
M. L. Litton
Higher Education
Educational Leadership
Florida State University
107 Stone Building
Tallahassee, FL 32306
(904) 644-4706

FLORIDA, UNIVERSITY OF
James L. Wattenbarger
Institute for Higher Education
Educational Administration
University of Florida
Gainesville, FL 32611
(904) 392-0745

GEORGE WASHINGTON UNIVERSITY
(No Program Director)
Higher Education Program
Department of Education
The George Washington University
2201 G. St., NW
Washington, DC 20036

GEORGIA, UNIVERSITY OF
Cameron Fincher
Institute of Higher Education
University of Georgia
Room 312, Candler Hall
Athens, GA 30602
(404) 542-3464

MICHIGAN STATE UNIVERSITY
Vandel C. Johnson
Administration and Higher Education
Michigan State University
419 Erickson Hall
East Lansing, MI 48824
(517) 353-2972

MICHIGAN, UNIVERSITY OF
Marvin W. Peterson
Center for the Study of Higher Education
School of Education
University of Michigan
Ann Arbor, MI 48109
(313) 764-9472

NEW YORK, STATE UNIVERSITY OF (BUFFALO)
Robert Berdahl
Department of Higher Education
State University of New York at Buffalo
Buffalo, NY 14260
(716) 636-2481

NORTH CAROLINA, UNIVERSITY OF (CHAPEL HILL)
James L. Morrison
Eugene R. Watson
Graduate Program in Higher and Adult Education
School of Education
University of North Carolina at Chapel Hill
Peabody Hall
Chapel Hill, NC 27514
(919) 966-1354

PENNSYLVANIA STATE UNIVERSITY
William Toombs
Higher Education Program
Division of Education Policy Studies
Pennsylvania State University
319 Rackley Building
University Park, PA 16802
(814) 865-1487, 865-6347

STANFORD UNIVERSITY
Lewis B. Mayhew
Administration and Policy Analysis
School of Education
Stanford University
Stanford, CA 94305
(415) 497-4051

TEXAS, UNIVERSITY OF (AUSTIN)
John E. Roueche
Program in Community College Education
Educational Administration and Curriculum Instruction
University of Texas, Austin
EDB 348
Austin, TX 78712
(512) 471-7545

VIRGINIA, UNIVERSITY OF
Jennings L. Wagoner, Jr.
Center for the Study of Higher Education
School of Education
University of Virginia
405 Emmet St.
Charlottesville, VA 22903
(804) 924-3880

APPENDIX 6
FEDERAL LEGISLATION AFFECTING HIGHER EDUCATION

1787—The Northwest Ordinance authorized land grants for the establishment of educational institutions.

1802—An act (21 Stat. 34) established the U.S. Military Academy.

1862—The First Morrill Act (12 Stat. 503) donated public lands to the states and territories to establish institutions, which came to be called "land-grant colleges," for students to study agriculture and the mechanical arts.

1867—The Department of Education Act (14 Stat. 434) established an agency to collect and disseminate information on education in the states and territories. The following year the agency's name was changed to the Office of Education.

1876—An appropriations act established the U.S. Coast Guard Academy.

1890—The Second Morrill Act (26 Stat. 417) provided federal funds for instruction in the land-grant institutions.

1911—The State Marine School Act authorized federal funds for any nautical school in 11 specified seaport cities.

1917—The Smith-Hughes Act (P.L. 64-347), also called the Vocational Education Act of 1917, provided grants to states for agricultural, industrial, and trade-related education below the college level.

1918—The Vocational Rehabilitation Act provided grants for job training for World War I veterans.

1920—The Smith-Bankhead Act authorized grants to states for vocational-rehabilitation programs.

1936—An act (P.L. 84-415) established the U.S. Merchant Marine Academy.

1944—The Servicemen's Readjustment Act (P.L. 78-346), also called the GI Bill, provided federal aid for World War II veterans to continue their education.

1945—The Fulbright Act (P.L. 79-584) established the Board of Foreign Scholarships to finance exchanges of school teachers, graduate students, and faculty members between the United States and other countries.

1946—The George-Barden Act (P.L. 79-586), also called the Vocational Education Act, expanded federal support for vocational education.

1948—The United States Information and Educational Exchange Act (P.L. 80-402) established the exchange of persons, knowledge, and skills between the United States and other countries.

1950—The School Construction in Areas Affected by Federal Activities Act (P.L. 81-815) provided assistance for school construction in locales where enrollments were increased as a result of federal activities.

1954—An act (P.L. 83-325) established the U.S. Air Force Academy.

The Cooperative Research Act (P.L. 83-531) authorized cooperative arrangements between the Office of Education and colleges, universities, and state education agencies for educational research.

An act (P.L. 83-532) established the National Advisory Committee on Education to recommend to the Secretary of Health, Education, and Welfare national studies needed in education.

1957—The Practical Nurse Training Act (P.L. 85-865) provided grants to states for training practical nurses.

1958—The National Defense Education Act (P.L. 85-865) provided funds for programs in science, mathematics, foreign languages, and other subjects to ensure that the United States would have enough people trained in critical areas to meet national defense needs.

The Education of Mentally Retarded Children Act (P.L. 85-926) authorized federal funds to train teachers for handicapped persons.

1961—The Area Redevelopment Act (P.L. 87-27) provided assistance to state vocational-education agencies.

1962—The Manpower Development and Training Act (P.L. 87-415) supported training for unemployed and underemployed persons.

1963—The Health Professions Educational Assistance Act (P.L. 88-129) provided funds to expand teaching facilities and loans for students in the health professions.

The Higher Education Facilities Act (P.L. 88-204) authorized financial assistance for classrooms, libraries, and laboratories in 2- and 4-year colleges and universities and technical institutes.

The Vocational Education Act (P.L. 88-210) increased federal support for residential vocational schools, work-study programs, and research and training in vocational education.

1964—The Civil Rights Act (P.L. 88-352), under Title IV, mandated the desegregation of public educational institutions and, under Title VI, made racial and ethnic discrimination illegal in programs that receive federal financial assistance.

The Economic Opportunity Act (P.L. 88-452) authorized grants for college work-study programs, support for vocational training for unemployed youths, and a number of other educational and training programs.

1965—The Elementary and Secondary Education Act (P.L. 89-10) provided financial assistance to local educational agencies to educate the children of low-income families and provided grants for testing, guidance and counseling. Title VII, called the Bilingual Education Act, provided funds for bilingual programs at the preschool, elementary, and secondary levels.

The Health Professions Educational Assistance Amendments (P.L. 89-290) authorized scholarships for needy students in the health professions and grants to improve the quality of instruction in professional schools.

The Higher Education Act (P.L. 89-329) provided funds to colleges and universities for community service, continuing education, cooperative education, and libraries. It also established the Teacher Corps and offered support for graduate education. Title III provided funds for "developing institutions," while Title IV authorized the Basic and Supplemental Educational Opportunity Grants programs and other student financial aid and established the Student Loan Marketing Association. Title XII includes Section 1202, which required state postsecondary-education commissions.

The National Foundation on the Arts and the Humanities Act (P.L. 89-209) authorized grants and loans for projects in the creative and performing arts and research, training, and scholarly publications in the humanities.

The National Vocational Student Loan Insurance Act (P.L. 89-287) encouraged state and nonprofit private institutions to establish loan insurance programs to assist students.

1966—The Adult Education Act (P.L. 89-750) authorized grants to states for programs to help adults continue their education at least through high school and obtain training for jobs.

The Elementary and Secondary Education Amendments (P.L. 89-750) authorized additional funds for programs for handicapped children.

The International Education Act (P.L. 89-698) authorized grants to higher-education instititions for graduate and undergraduate international-studies centers.

The National Sea Grant College and Program Act (P.L. 89-688) authorized sea-grant colleges and programs of education and research in marine resources.

1968—The Elementary and Secondary Education Amendments (P.L. 90-247) authorized support for regional centers for education of handicapped children and programs in bilingual education.

The Higher Education Amendments (P.L. 90-575) authorized new programs for disadvantaged college students and clinical experience for law students.

The Vocational Education Amendments (P.L. 90-576) provided federal grants to states for vocational education and part-time employment for persons of all ages and all educational levels.

1970—The Alcohol and Drug Abuse Education Act (P.L. 91-527) provided grants for educational programs and teacher training to combat drug abuse.

The Environmental Education Act (P.L. 91-516) established the Office of Environmental Education to develop elementary, secondary, and community programs in ecology.

1971—The Comprehensive Health Manpower Training Act of 1971 (P.L. 92-257), amended Title VII of the Public Health Service Act, increased and expanded provisions for health manpower training and training facilities.

The Nurse Training Act of 1971 (P.L. 92-158), amended Title VIII, Nurse Training, of the Public Health Service Act, increased and expanded provisions for nurse training facilities.

1972—The Education Amendments of 1972 (P.L. 92-318) established a National Institute of Education; general aid for institutions of higher education; federal matching grants for state student incentive grants; a National Commission on Financing Postsecondary Education; State Advisory Councils on Community Colleges; a Bureau of Occupational and Adult Education and State grants for the design, establishment, and conduct of postsecondary occupational education; and a bureau-level Office of Indian Education. Amended current Office of Education programs to increase their effectiveness and better meet special needs. Prohibited sex bias in admissions to institutions of vocational, professional, graduate higher, and public institutions of undergraduate higher education, including athletics (Title IX).

The Equal Pay Act of 1963 was amended. To date, these amendments as used involve mostly women, especially faculty women.

The Higher Education Amendments called for establishment of state commissions on higher education for planning and to receive federal funds and modified and broadened the supplemental grants program which aids students.

1973—The Comprehensive Employment and Training Act (P.L. 93-203) established a system of federal, state, and local programs to train economically disadvantaged and unemployed persons and provide job opportunities.

The Rehabilitation Act of 1973 was passed to protect handicapped individuals and provides that no person shall be kept from participating in any federally assisted program solely on the basis of the fact that she/he is handicapped.

1974—The Education Amendments (P.L. 93-380) consolidated several programs and established the National Center for Education Statistics.

The Privacy Act or the Buckley Amendment of 1974 authorized student access to educational record and provided authority to withhold federal financial assistance to institutions for noncompliance.

1975—The Indian Self-Determination and Education Assistance Act (P.L. 93-683) provided for more participation by Indians in their educational programs.

1976—The Education Amendments (P.L. 94-482) provided federal assistance to the states for career development and educational programs and for guidance and counseling activities.

The Health Professions Educational Assistance Act of 1976 stipulated support for the education and training of people involved in health professions.

1978—The Career Education Incentive Act (P.L. 95-207) authorized career-education programs for the elementary and secondary schools.

The Education Amendments (P.L. 95-561) established a comprehensive basic skills program for reading, writing, and mathematics in public schools.

The Middle Income Students Act (P.L. 95-566) extended the Basic Educational Opportunity Grants program to students from families earning up to $25,000 a year and made it easier for independent students to receive financial aid.

The Tribally Controlled Community College Assistant Act (P.L. 95-471) provided federal funds to improve tribally controlled community colleges for Indian students.

1979—The Department of Education Organization Act (Section 210) created a Cabinet-level Department of Education, consolidating under a Secretary of Education 152 programs from the Education Division of the Department of Health, Education, and Welfare, and other agencies.

---

† Material in Appendix 6 reprinted by permission from *The Chronicle of Higher Education*, October 19, 1979, p. 13.

APPENDIX 7
LAND-GRANT COLLEGES AND UNIVERSITIES

Alabama
    Alabama A & M University
    Auburn University

Alaska
    University of Alaska

Arizona
    University of Arizona

Arkansas
    University of Arkansas,
        Fayetteville
    University of Arkansas, Pine
        Bluff

California
    University of California at Davis

Colorado
    Colorado State University

Connecticut
    Connecticut Agriculture
        Experiment Station,
        University of Connecticut

Delaware
    Delaware State College
    University of Delaware

District of Columbia
    University of the District of
        Columbia

Florida
    Florida A & M University
    University of Florida

Georgia
    Fort Valley State College
    University of Georgia

Guam
    University of Guam

Hawaii
    University of Hawaii

Idaho
    University of Idaho

Illinois
    University of Illinois

Indiana
    Purdue University

Iowa
    Iowa State University

Kansas
    Kansas State University

Kentucky
    Kentucky State University
    University of Kentucky

Louisiana
    Louisiana State University
    Southern University

Maine
    University of Maine

Maryland
    University of Maryland

Massachusetts
    Massachusetts Institute of
        Technology
    University of Massachusetts

Michigan
    Michigan State University

Minnesota
    University of Minnesota

Mississippi
    Alcorn A & M College
    Mississippi State University

Missouri
    Lincoln University
    University of Missouri

Montana
    Montana State University

Nebraska
    University of Nebraska

Nevada
    University of Nevada, Reno

New Hampshire
    University of New Hampshire

New Jersey
    Rutgers, The State University of
        New Jersey

New Mexico
    New Mexico State University

New York
    Cornell University

North Carolina
    North Carolina A & T State
        University
    North Carolina State University

North Dakota
    North Dakota State University

Ohio
    Ohio State University

Oklahoma
    Langston University
    Oklahoma State University

Oregon
    Oregon State University

Pennsylvania
    Pennsylvania State University

Puerto Rico
    University of Puerto Rico

Rhode Island
    University of Rhode Island

South Carolina
    Clemson University
    South Carolina State College

South Dakota
    South Dakota State University

Tennessee
    Tennessee State University
    University of Tennessee,
        Knoxville

Texas
    Prairie View A & M University
    Texas A & M University System

Utah
    Utah State University

Vermont
  University of Vermont

Virgin Islands
  College of the Virgin Islands

Virginia
  Virginia Polytechnic Institute and
    State University
  Virginia State College

Washington
  Washington State University

West Virginia
  West Virginia University

Wisconsin
  University of Wisconsin

Wyoming
  University of Wyoming

APPENDIX 8
MAJOR NATIONAL ASSOCIATIONS IN AMERICAN HIGHER EDUCATION

THE AMERICAN COUNCIL ON EDUCATION (ACE), the most prestigious of this group, consists of individual institutions and organizations of institutions, with a membership of approximately 1,505.

THE NATIONAL ASSOCIATION OF STATE UNIVERSITIES AND LAND-GRANT COLLEGES (NASULGC), which consists of 133 institutions, represents primarily large, public, research-oriented universities (land-grant colleges and major public universities).

THE AMERICAN ASSOCIATION OF STATE COLLEGES AND UNIVERSITIES (AASCU) includes about

321 public colleges which primarily emphasize undergraduate education.

THE AMERICAN ASSOCIATION OF COMMUNITY AND JUNIOR COLLEGES (AACJC) represents about 1,000 2-year institutions, most of which are community colleges.

THE ASSOCIATION OF AMERICAN UNIVERSITIES (AAU) is composed of 50 of the most prestigious public and private research universities.

THE ASSOCIATION OF AMERICAN COLLEGES (AAC) represents about 800 liberal arts colleges, most private and some church-related.

APPENDIX 9
ACCREDITING ASSOCIATIONS

REGIONAL

Middle States Association of Colleges and Schools

New England Association of Schools and Colleges

North Central Association of Colleges and Schools

Northwest Association of Schools and Colleges

Southern Association of Colleges and Schools

Western Association of Schools and Colleges

SPECIALIZED AND PROFESSIONAL

ALLIED HEALTH EDUCATION—American Medical Association and Committee on Allied Health Education and Accreditation

ARCHITECTURE—National Architectural Accrediting Board

ART—National Association of Schools of Art

BIBLE COLLEGE EDUCATION—American Association of Bible Colleges

BUSINESS—American Association of Collegiate Schools of Business

CHEMISTRY—American Chemical Society

COMMUNITY HEALTH EDUCATION—American Public Health Association

DENTAL HYGIENE—American Dental Association

DENTISTRY—American Dental Association

ENGINEERING—Accreditation Board for Engineering and Technology

ENGINEERING TECHNOLOGY—Accreditation Board for Engineering and Technology

FAMILY COUNSELING—American Association of Marriage and Family Therapy

FORESTRY—Society of American Foresters

HOME ECONOMICS—American Home Economics Association

HOSPITAL ADMINISTRATION—Accrediting Commission on Graduate Education

INDUSTRIAL TECHNOLOGY—National Association for Industrial Technology

JOURNALISM—American Council on Education for Journalism

LANDSCAPE ARCHITECTURE—American Society of Landscape Architects

LAW—American Bar Association; Association of American Law Schools

LIBRARIANSHIP—American Library Association

MEDICAL RECORD ADMINISTRATION—American Medical Association in collaboration with the American Medical Record Association

MEDICAL TECHNOLOGY—American Medical Association, in collaboration with the Board of Schools of Medical Technology

MEDICINE—Liaison committee on Medical Education, American Medical Association and Association of American Medical Colleges.

MICROBIOLOGY—American Academy of Microbiology

MUSIC—National Association of Schools of Music

NURSING—National League for Nursing

OCCUPATIONAL THERAPY—American Medical Association, in collaboration with the American Occupational Therapy Association

OPTOMETRY—American Optometric Association

OSTEOPATHIC MEDICINE—American Osteopathic Association

PHARMACY—American Council on Pharmaceutical Education

PHYSICAL THERAPY—American Medical Association, in collaboration with the American Physical Therapy Association

PODIATRY—American Podiatry Association

PSYCHOLOGY—American Psychological Association

PUBLIC HEALTH—Council on Education for Public Health

REHABILITATION COUNSELING—Council on Rehabilitation Education

SOCIAL WORK—Council on Social Work Education

SPEECH PATHOLOGY AND AUDIOLOGY—American Speech, Language, Hearing Association

TEACHER EDUCATION—National Council for Accreditation of Teacher Education

THEOLOGY—American Association of Theological Schools in the United States and Canada

VETERINARY MEDICINE—American Veterinary Medical Association

ASSOCIATE DEGREES

DENTAL ASSISTING—American Dental Association
DENTAL HYGIENE—American Dental Association
DENTAL TECHNOLOGY—American Dental Association
ENGINEERING TECHNOLOGY—Engineers' Council for Professional Development
NURSING—National League for Nursing

COMMISSIONS

COMMISSION ON HIGHER EDUCATION
COMMISSION ON INSTITUTIONS OF HIGHER EDUCATION
COMMISSION ON VOCATIONAL-TECHNICAL INSTITUTIONS
COMMISSION ON INSTITUTIONS OF HIGHER EDUCATION
COMMISSION ON HIGHER SCHOOLS
COMMISSION ON COLLEGES
COMMISSION ON OCCUPATIONAL EDUCATION INSTITUTIONS
ACCREDITING COMMISSION FOR SENIOR COLLEGES AND UNIVERSITIES
ACCREDITING COMMISSION FOR JUNIOR COLLEGES

PROPRIETARY INSTITUTIONS

ACCREDITING COMISSION, Association of Independent Colleges and Schools
ACCREDITING COMMISSION, National Association of Trade and Technical Schools

APPENDIX 10
ABBREVIATIONS OF SELECTED NATIONAL AGENCIES AND ORGANIZATIONS RELATED TO HIGHER EDUCATION

AACRAO—American Association of Collegiate Registrars and Admissions Office

AAMC—Association of American Medical Colleges

AASCU—American Association of State Colleges and Universities

AAUP—American Association of University Professors

ACE—American Council on Education

AFT—American Federation of Teachers (AFL-CIO)

AIAW—Association for Intercollegiate Athletics for Women

CCAIT—The Community College Association for Instruction and Technology, an Affiliate of the Association for Educational Communication and Technology and an Institutional Supporter of Community College Frontiers

CETA—Comprehensive Employment and Training Act

CFAE—Council for Financial Aid to Education

CREF—College Retirement Equities Fund

DE—Department of Education (formerly HEW—Health, Education, and Welfare)

ECS—Education Commission of the States

EEOC—Equal Employment Opportunities Commission

EPA—Environmental Protection Agency

ETS—Educational Testing Service

FIPSE—Fund for the Improvement of Postsecondary Education

FRACHE—Federation of Regional Accrediting Commissions of Higher Education

HEGIS—Higher Education General Information Survey

HHR—Department of Health and Human Resources (formerly HEW)

NACAC—National Association of College Admissions Counselors

NAICU—National Association of Independent Colleges and Universities

NASA—National Aeronautics & Space Administration

NASULGC—National Association of State Universities and Land-Grant Colleges

NCAA—National Collegiate Athletic Association

NCES—National Center for Education Statistics

NCHEMS—National Center for Higher Education Management Systems

NEA—National Education Association

NIE—National Institute for Education

NIICU—National Institute of Independent Colleges and Universities

NLRB—National Labor Relations Board

NSF—National Science Foundation

OCR—Office for Civil Rights, HEW

OSHA—Occupational Safety and Health Administration

ROTC—Reserve Officers Training Corps

SAT—Scholastic Aptitude Test

TIAA—Teachers Insurance and Annuity Association

APPENDIX 11
ADDRESSES OF SELECTED PUBLISHERS

Academic Press, 111 5th Ave., New York, NY 10003

AHM Publishing Corporation, 3110 N. Arlington Heights Rd., Arlington Heights, IL 60004

Allyn and Bacon, Rockleigh, NJ 07647

American Law Institute, 4025 Chestnut St., Philadelphia, PA 19104

American Library Association, 50 E. Huron St., Chicago, IL 60611

American Psychological Association, 1200 17th St., N.W., Washington, DC 20036

Arco Publishing, Inc., 219 Park Ave. S., New York, NY 10003

Aspen Systems Corporation, 20010 Century Blvd., Germantown, MD 20767

Avery Publishing Group, 89 Baldwin Terrace, Wayne, NJ 07470

AVI Publishing Co., PO Box 831, Westport, CT 06880

Ballinger Publishing Company, 17 Dunster St., Harvard Sq., Cambridge, MA 02138

Barron's Educational Series, 113 Crossways Park Dr., Woodbury, NY 11797

Basic Books, 10 E. 53rd St., New York, NY 10022

Bobbs-Merrill Company, 4300 W. 62nd St., Indianapolis, IN 46268

R. R. Bowker Company, 1180 Ave. of the Americas, New York, NY 10036

Cambridge University Press, 32 E. 57th St., New York, NY 10022

Caratzas Brothers, Publishers, 481 Main St., Box 210, New Rochelle, NY 10802

CBI Publishing Company, 51 Sleeper St., Boston MA 02210

Change Magazine Press, NBW Tower, New Rochelle, NY 10801

Collegium Book Publishers, 525 Executive Blvd., Elmsford, NY 10523

Cornell University Press, Box 250, 124 Roberts Pl., Ithaca, NY 14850

Thomas Y. Crowell Company, 10 E. 53 St., New York, NY 10022 (Harper & Row)

Brian C. Decker, Publisher, 381 Park Avenue South, New York, NY 10016 (Thieme-Stratton)

Duke University Press, College Station, Box 6697, Durham, NC 27708

Dushkin Publishing Group, Sluice Dock, Guilford, CT 06437

Educational Technology Publications, Englewood Cliffs, NJ 07632

Elsevier North-Holland, Inc., 52 Vanderbilt Ave., New York, NY 10017

ETC Publications, Drawer 1627-A, Palm Springs, CA 92262

Fearon-Pitman Publishers, Inc., 6 Davis Dr., Belmont, CA 94002

Forum Press, Inc., 2640 Pine St., St. Louis, MO 63166

Franklin Institute Press, Box 2266, Philadelphia, PA 19103

Free Press, 866 Third Ave., New York, NY 10022 (MacMillan, Inc.)

W. H. Freeman & Company, 660 Market St., San Francisco, CA 94104

Gale Research Company, Book Tower, Detroit, MI 48226

Goodyear Publishing Company, Inc., 1640 Fifth St., Santa Monica, CA 90401

Greenwood Press, 51 Riverside Ave., Westport, CT 06880

Harcourt Brace Jovanovich, Inc., 757 Third Ave., New York, NY 10017

Harper & Row Publishers, Inc., 10 E. 53rd St., New York, NY 10022

Harvard University Press, 79 Garden St., Cambridge, MA 02138

D. C. Heath and Company, 125 Spring St., Lexington, MA 02173

Holt, Rinehart, & Winston, 383 Madison Ave., New York, NY 10017

Humanities Press, 171 First Ave., Atlantic Highlands, NJ 07716

Johns Hopkins Press, Baltimore, MD 21218

Jossey-Bass, Inc., Publishers, 433 California St., San Francisco, CA 94101

J. B. Lippincott Company, E. Washington Sq., Philadelphia, PA 19105

Macmillan, Inc., 866 Third Ave., New York, NY 10022

Mayfield Publishing Company, 285 Hamilton Ave., Palo Alto, CA 94301

McGraw-Hill Book Company, 221 Ave. of the Americas, New York, NY 10020

Charles E. Merrill Publishing Company, 1300 Alum Creek Dr., Columbus, OH 43216

M. I. T. Press, 28 Carleton St., Cambridge, MA 02142

National Textbook Company, 8259 Niles Center Rd., Skokie, IL 60077

Nelson-Hall Publishers, 111 N. Canal St., Chicago, IL 60606

New York University Press, Washington Sq., New York, NY 10003

Open Court Publishing Company, 1058 Eighth St., LaSalle, IL 61301

Oryx Press, 2214 North Central at Encanto, Phoenix, AZ 85004

Oxford University Press, 1600 Pollitt Dr., Fair Lawn, NJ 07410

Praeger Publishers, 521 Fifth Ave., New York, NY 10017

Prentice-Hall, Englewood Cliffs, NJ 07632

Princeton University Press, Princeton, NJ 08540

Prometheus Books, 1203 Kensington Ave., Buffalo, NY 14215

Random House, 201 E. 50th St., New York, NY 10022

Regents Publishing Company, 2 Park Ave., New York, NY 10016

Russell Sage Foundation, 230 Park Ave., New York, NY 10017

Rutgers University Press, 30 College Ave., New Brunswick, NJ 08903

Scarecrow Press, Inc., 52 Liberty St., Metuchen, NJ 08840

Schenkman Publishing Company, 3 Mt. Auburn Pl., Cambridge, MA 02138

Schirmer Books, 866 Third Ave., New York, NY 10022 (MacMillan, Inc.)

Schocken Books, Inc. 200 Madison Ave., New York, NY 10016

Science Research Associates, Inc., 155 N. Wacker Dr., Chicago, IL 60606

Scott, Foresman & Company, 1900 E. Lake Ave., Glenview, Il 60025

Slavica Publishers, Box 14388, Columbus, OH 43214

Southern Illinois University Press, P.O. Box 3697, Carbondale, IL 62901

Springer-Verlag New York, Inc., 175 Fifth Ave., New York, NY 10010

State University of New York Press, State University Plaza, Albany, NY 12246

Superintendent of Documents, U.S. Government Printing Office, Washington, DC 20402

Syracuse University Press, 1011 E. Water St., Syracuse, NY 13210

Teachers College Press, 1234 Amsterdam Ave., New York, NY 10027

Thieme-Stratton Inc., 381 Park Ave. S., New York, NY 10016

Charles C Thomas, Publisher, 30127 E. Lawrence Ave., Springfield, IL 62717

Transaction Books, Rutgers, The State University, New Brunswick, NJ 08903

University of Arizona Press, Box 3398, Tucson, AZ 85722

University of California Press, 2223 Fulton St., Berkeley, CA 94720

University of Chicago Press, 5801 Ellis Ave., Chicago, IL 60637

University of Georgia Press, Athens, GA 30602

University of Illinois Press, 54 E. Gregory Dr., Box 5081, Station A, Champaign, IL 61820

University of Iowa Press, Graphic Services Bldg., Iowa City, IA 52242

University of Massachusetts Press, Box 429, Amherst, MA 01002

University of Michigan Press, 839 Greene St., Box 1104, Ann Arbor, MI 48106

University of Minnesota Press, 2037 University Ave., S.E., Minneapolis, MN 55455

University of North Carolina Press, Box 2288, Chapel Hill, NC 27514

University of Texas Press, P.O. Box 7819, University Station, Austin, TX 78712

University Press of Kentucky, Lexington, KY 40506

University Press of Mississippi, 3825 Ridgewood Rd., Jackson, MS 39211

University Presses of Florida, 15 N.W. 15th St., Gainesville, FL 32603

D. Van Nostrand Company, 135 W. 50th St., New York, NY 10020

Vantage Press, 516 W. 34th St., New York, NY 10001

Viking Press, 625 Madison Ave., New York, NY 10022

Warren, Gorham & Lamont, Inc., 210 South St., Boston, MA 02111

West Publishing Company, 50 W. Kellogg Blvd., St. Paul, MN 55102

John Wiley & Sons, Inc., 605 Third Ave., New York, NY 10016

Winthrop Publishers, 17 Dunster St., Cambridge, MA 02138

Yale University Press, 92 A Yale Station, New Haven, CT 06520

AUTHOR INDEX

In the list below, the numbers after each name refer to item number in the *Bibliography*. All numbers which are preceded by R refer to Appendix 1, the reference section.

A

A.E.C.T., 1436
Aanenson, C. R., 1593
Abell, M. D., 845
Abercrombie, N., 392
Abowd, J. M., 874
Abramson, J., 1173
Academy for Educational
    Development, 747, 770
Adams, C. R., 1115
Adams, F. C., 1293
Adams, H., 329
Adams, W., 709
Adell, B. I., 846
Adkins, D. L., 217
Advisory Panel on Research Needs in
    Lifelong Learning During
    Adulthood, 237
Aiken, H. D., 330
Aleamoni, L. M., 771
Alexander, C., 1240
Alexander, K., 1151
Allen, E. L., 267
Allen, G. R., 403
Allen, K. W., 527
Allen, R. H., 1026
Allman, K. A., 1116
Altbach, P. G., 65, 623, 1504, 1505,
    1506, 1507, 1508, 1509, 1571,
    1611.
Altman, R. A., 1372
American Assembly of Columbia
    University, 106
American Association for Higher
    Education, 382
American Association of Community
    and Junior Colleges, 1364, 1427,
    1437, R1
American Association of Presidents of
    Independent Colleges and
    Universities, 33
American Association of University
    Professors, 875, 1241
American Council on Education, 876,
    921, 970
American Enterprise Institute for
    Public Policy Research, 1082
Anders, M. E., 528
Anderson, C., 1117
Anderson, C. A., 772

Anderson, D. S., 1487
Anderson, G. L., 162, 577
Anderson, R. E., 680
Anderson, S. B., 393, 594
Angell, G., 847
Apps, J. W., 238, 239
Archer, M. S., 1510
Argyris, C., 578
Armijo, J. F., 1380, 1409
Armstrong, R. H. R., 473
Arney, L. H., 1394
Arthur, W. J., 922
Ary, D., 595
Ashby, E., 163, 218, 1549
Ashworth, K. H., 88, 164
Askew, T. A., 34
Association for Educational
    Communications and Technology,
    440, 474, 1436
Association of American Colleges, 971
Association of Governing Boards of
    Colleges and Universities, 998
Association of Professors of Higher
    Education, 1612
Astin, A. W., 35, 331, 616, 624, 625,
    626, 748
Astin, H. S., 627, 773, 1174
Atelsek, F. J., 107
Athletic Institute, 816
Augenblick, J., 1395
Averill, L. J., 394
Avram, H. D., 529
Axelrod, J., 268

B

Bailey, F. G., 219
Bailey, R., 774
Bailey, S. K., 1083, 1511
Baird, L. L., 628
Baker, L., 1175
Balderston, F. E., 797, 1242
Baldridge, J. V., 689, 698, 711, 1243
Ballotti, G. A., 75
Balutis, A. P., 1027
Banghart, F., 817
Barak, R. J., 1028
Barbee, D. E., 1438
Barley, S. K., 269
Barron's, R2
Bass, R. K., 441

Bassett, R., 1029
Baumol, W. J., 530
Bayer, A. E., 332, 629, 1294
Beach, M., 5, R3
Beals, E., 1030
Beann, J., 710
Beard, R. M., 270, 475
Becher, R., 1550
Beck, R. H., 1
Beckett, P., 1479
Begin, J. P., 848
Belknap, R. L., 572
Bell, R. E., 76, 1551
Ben-David, J., 89, 220, 1512
Bender, L. W., 1084, 1463
Bender, R. N., 36
Benezet, L. T., 37
Bengelsdorf, W., 271
Bennett, J. T., 849
Bennis, W. G., 165, 681
Benokraitis, N., 1176
Benson, C. S., 877
Benveniste, G., 1579
Berdahl, R. O., 1031, 1032, 1513
Bereday, G. Z. F., 1514
Berg, B., 1598
Berg, I., 1295
Bergman, B. A., 630
Bergquist, W. H., 333
Berke, J. S., 923
Berry, M. C., 1177
Berstecher, D., 1515
Berte, N. R., 476
Berube, M. R., 166
Berve, N. M., 1033
Biehl, R. G., 818
Bienayme, A., 1599
Bilovsky, C., 1439
Bina, J. V., R4
Bird, C., 631
Birenbaum, W. M., 749
Bisconti, A. S., 1296
Blackburn, R. T., 878
Blau, P. M., 690
Blaze, W., 477
Bledstein, B. J., 167
Blocker, C. E., 168
Bloland, H. G., 77
Bloom, K. L., 1384
Bloustein, E. J., 712
Blumer, D. H., 1152

SUBJECT INDEX

The basis for this subject index is the *Thesaurus of ERIC Descriptors,* Revised Edition, 1980. Phoenix, AZ: Oryx Press. All numbers which are preceded by R refer to titles in the reference section, Appendix 1.